TALKING TO THE
SHAMAN
WITHIN

MUSINGS ON HUNTING

MANFRED F. R. KETS DE VRIES

TALKING TO THE SHAMAN WITHIN
MUSINGS ON HUNTING

iUniverse books may be ordered through booksellers or by contacting:

iUniverse LLC
1663 Liberty Drive
Bloomington, IN 47403
www.iuniverse.com
1-800-Authors (1-800-288-4677)

Because of the dynamic nature of the Internet, any web addresses or links contained in this book may have changed since publication and may no longer be valid. The views expressed in this work are solely those of the author and do not necessarily reflect the views of the publisher, and the publisher hereby disclaims any responsibility for them.

Any people depicted in stock imagery provided by Thinkstock are models, and such images are being used for illustrative purposes only.
Certain stock imagery © Thinkstock.

ISBN: 978-1-4917-3034-8 (sc)
ISBN: 978-1-4917-3035-5 (hc)
ISBN: 978-1-4917-3151-2 (e)

Library of Congress Control Number: 2014906587

Printed in the United States of America.

iUniverse rev. date: 06/16/2014

To my uncle Jaap, who introduced me to the "koãn" of hunting. For as long as I can remember, nature has always been a source of comfort, inspiration, adventure, and delight to both of us. Our shared memories of these days past in the great outdoors—our journeys toward the "happy hunting grounds"—will always keep their special place in my inner theater.

CONTENTS

Deer tracks make mighty thin soup.
    —Proverb

City Folk got therapy, and we
got hunting and fishing.
    —Proverb

I ask people why they have deer heads
on their walls. They always say because
it's such a beautiful animal. There you
go. I think my mother is attractive,
but I have photographs of her.
    —Ellen DeGeneres

For us hunting wasn't a sport. It was a way
to be intimate with nature, that intimacy
providing us with wild unprocessed food free
from pesticides and hormones and with the
bonus of having been produced without the
addition of great quantities of fossil fuel. In
addition, hunting provided us with an ever-
scarcer relationship in a world of cities, factory
farms, and agribusiness, direct responsibility
for taking the lives that sustained us. Lives
that even vegans indirectly take as the growing
and harvesting of organic produce kills deer,
birds, snakes, rodents, and insects. We lived
close to the animals we ate. We knew their
habits and that knowledge deepened our
thanks to them and the land that made them.
    —Ted Kerasote

PREFACE

The poet Guillaume Apollinaire once said, "Memories are the hunting horns whose sounds die in the wind." The catalyst for these meditations on hunting was an accident I had while hunting for brown bear on top of a mountain plateau on the Kamchatka peninsula in Siberia in May 2008. I had been sitting on the back of a snowmobile driven by a "Kamchatka cowboy" who, in his impatience to reach the next mountain range where he had spotted a bear, drove his machine, at far too high a speed, into a deep hole. As the "cowboy" had a very firm hold on the snowmobile, he escaped unscathed. For me, however, the outcome was very different. At the point of impact, I blacked out, saw a scattering of lights interwoven with images of my life flashing by. I thought I had died. As I returned to consciousness, I could hear the cowboy saying, "No problem, antibiotics." I truly wish the remedy had been that simple. It was the beginning of a long *via dolorosa*. Although I am now one of the "twice-born," to quote the American psychologist and philosopher William James—having come back from the dead more than once—I had also smashed two vertebrae in my spine.

The sleigh ride down the mountain was an experience that later returned in nightmares. Amazingly, I had drifted into a half-dazed state beyond pain but I was very glad that my daughter, Oriane, was with me. The snowmobile continually got stuck in patches of melting snow as we returned downhill and had to be rocked backwards and forwards to free it, not an activity to be recommended with crushed vertebrae. To put a positive spin on things, the accident was a learning opportunity for me. Apart from my insight into existential matters—the "tragic transience of things" and our insignificance in the march of time—I also got a deeper understanding of pain management.

Kamchatka is one of these special locations where bad weather seems to originate, so I was lucky that the next day, the guilt-stricken "cowboy" decided to climb the mountain next to the camp. With some kind of radio arrangement, he managed to get in touch with people at the village of Esso to report the accident. Esso is described in Russian travel brochures as one of Kamchatka's Swiss-type settlements—having visited the place, I can say that this is a bit of an over-statement. The local authorities put a helicopter rescue plan into motion. This was not entirely encouraging news. I had memories of the many times I had been in Kamchatka waiting for helicopters that never arrived due to bad weather. While these attempts were being made to get me out of there, I was bent over, crippled, in my sleeping bag and doing the essentials of pain management on my own, with a few paltry aspirins as painkillers. But then a miracle happened. At noon the next day, I heard the glorious whirring of helicopter blades. After a very tough ride, lying flat on the metal floor of the gigantic, ex-military machine, I arrived in Petropavlovsk, the capital of Kamchatka, whose spectacular ugliness is offset by the spectacularly beautiful snowy mountain range that frames it. I was immediately taken to the local hospital for x-rays to be taken. That hospital could have been featured in a Dostoyevsky novel. It had traces of blood on the floor in the hallway. I decided not to take advantage of their services, and my daughter agreed. I was moved into a small hotel close by, to await repatriation to Thailand, Japan, or preferably France.

Between my various spine operations, I had to stay horizontal for a very long time but I was lucky not to have been paralyzed, and not to have ended up in a wheelchair. As I am not very good at lying still and doing nothing, and to amuse myself, I did a lot of writing. Most of it was done in my field of expertise, which is the interface of psychoanalysis, clinical psychology, leadership, the study of organizations, and change management. But my prolific output left my long-suffering editor, Sally Simmons, aghast. The large doses of morphine I was taking had affected my perception of what I was writing, and the amount. She has told me since that the material I sent her became known as "The Morphine Papers"—certainly they never saw the light of day in their original versions. Sally suggested I calm down, and do something different, and passed on a suggestion from her colleague—"Tell him to take up knitting." This fell well outside my area of expertise but her comments resonated with me and I decided to do something very different: to get out of my comfort zone and write about my experiences in the outdoors.

At the time, it seemed like a great idea; I have a large collection of books about hunting and fishing adventures that I enjoy reading. Without wishing to denigrate these books that have given me a lot of pleasure, after a time, many of them just seem more of the same. Usually, one animal after another bites the dust, while the hunter is portrayed as the heroic survivor of a variety of dangerous exploits. The question was, how to be different?

I thought a book of hunting memories would be more interesting if I combined it with philosophical reflections on hunting. After all, we owe much of our biology, psychology, and cultural history to hunters. Through hunting, we have become the most ingenious, creative, but also most dangerous creature in the world. Hunting is the matrix on which much of human behavior is based.

Over the years, I have kept a series of diaries of my hunting explorations. These rather illegible scribbles helped me put my various outdoor activities in perspective. Although I had assembled lots of notes, for some psychological reason or another, I had never really looked back at them. Perhaps I was afraid of doing so, at the risk of shattering my illusions of *"la vie en rose"* in the oudoors. Now, however, I *did* look at those notes and discovered that my diaries were powerful treasure troves, containing descriptions that brought back all the immediacy of things that I had done over many years. They helped me with the "knitting."

Re-reading my hunting diaries, I realize that my hunting (and fishing) career has gone through three phases (with—who knows—perhaps more to come). The first was the hunting I did in my country of birth, Holland. Although I made a few excursions to other countries during that period, these hunting trips remained limited in scope. The second phase started when I moved to Cambridge, Massachusetts. In the "New World" I graduated from being primarily a small game hunter to larger game. Big game hunting became even more of a preoccupation when I moved to Montreal in Canada. This was also where I learned the pleasures of fly-fishing for trout, and later for salmon.

The third phase in my hunting activities coincided with moving to France. Although I did (and still do) some hunting in France, for small and big game, I became an accidental hunting "tourist." I finally had the opportunity to act out many of my childhood fantasies about being an explorer, which led to hunting trips throughout the world. Africa and Asia beckoned, although I also hunted in places like Australia, Argentina and New Zealand.

I gave this book the title *Talking to the Shaman Within*. Shamanism is the origin of all the psychotherapies in our world. Shamans—those masters of ecstasy and mystery—can be compared to more intuitive psychoanalysts. I am no stranger to this world because in my "other life" I happen to be a psychoanalyst (with a great interest in biology, evolutionary psychology, and social anthropology). Indeed, some people have suggested (not necessarily as a complement) that I may be the world's only hunting psychoanalyst. Although psychoanalysts play an important role in shedding light on salient themes in society, hunting has never been a prime interest for most of them.

I find this intriguing because the hunt played such an important role in the development of humankind's inner and outer worlds. Our ancient ancestors needed to acquire a great deal of accuracy in order to distinguish dinner from danger. In that respect, shamans played a crucial role. They ensured that the proper steps were taken for the sustainability of the hunt and that everything was done to make sure that game remained plentiful. Shamans had the

responsibility of deciphering what had gone wrong when game was scarce; they needed to understand both the hunters and the game—in this, they were the mediators between people and the spiritual world of nature.

Just as shamans mediate between the hunter, prey, and spiritual world (organizing relationships and harmonizing conflicts), psychoanalysts mediate between their patients' conscious and unconscious worlds. The famous anthropologist Claude Lévi-Strauss once said, "the psychoanalyst listens, whereas the shaman speaks."[1] In shamanistic activities, mythical realities come to the fore in the healing process; compare this to the implied historical (or autobiographical) metaphors unwittingly deployed in psychoanalytic attempts at psychological cures. In both cases, the purpose is to bring to consciousness conflicts and resistances that have remained unconscious.

Both shamans and psychoanalysts can help their clients understand the symbolic meaning of the hunt by explaining the underlying reality of what they are experiencing. They may use different words, but they mean the same things. Both believe in the healing power of dialogue. A predetermined role—listener for the psychoanalyst, speaker for the shaman—establishes a direct relationship with their clients' conscious, and an indirect relationship with their unconscious. Shamans, like psychoanalysts, deal with the conflicts we experience on the border between the physical and the psychic world. I believe that as a psychoanalyst (and perhaps a modern-day shaman) and hunter, I may

have a small advantage. The collective unconscious contains many of the configurations of our evolutionary past, often related to the hunt. In this context, I would like to thank my two psychoanalysts who helped me to take a path rarely taken, Joyce McDougall and Maurice Dongier; both always encouraged my strange explorations. As guides in my magic mystery tours, they couldn't have been more supportive.

I have written many books in my life, but this one is different. Here, I am not writing, as I usually do, about the world of work. I am writing far beyond it, about a world in which magic and illusion play major roles. I wrote it quickly but I found this particular book difficult to let go, not least because many of the things I describe in it are very personal. Its disclosure is more problematic, in the light of the psychoanalytic mystique.

As well as presenting my personal reflections about the reasons why people (especially I) hunt (and fish), I hope this book will make a contribution to reopening the dialogue between people who recognize the importance of hunting, and anti-hunting advocates. Although both parties want the same thing—sustainability of natural resources—the dialogue, such as it is, has increasingly turned into a dialogue of the deaf. Most city dwellers do not realize that there is a difference between loving animals and saving wildlife. In the latter case, hard choices have to be made. It is important not to get stuck in ideologies but make realistic choices about sustainability. And whatever choices are made, these need to fit reality. Paradoxical as it may seem, as an intense lover of nature and wildlife, I have never seen hunting and wildlife conservation as a contradiction in terms. If game doesn't have economic value—an equation particularly valid for emerging economies like Africa—it will be replaced with livestock and crops. Unfortunately, when hunting is demonized, catastrophe usually follows, as I illustrate with many examples in this book.

I have always liked the expression *"chacun à son gout,"* (to each his or her own taste). For me, nature is my sanctum sanctorum, my reserved, private, sacred place, where, to quote the emperor Marcus Aurelius, "Each thing is of like form from everlasting and comes round again in its cycle." Having said as much, I will simply add that whatever I have written, warts and all, mistakes and prejudices, belongs to me, and nobody else.

1 — Lévi-Strauss, Claude. *Structural Anthropology*. New
York: Basic Books, 1962, p. 199.

ACKNOWLEDGEMENTS

I would like to thank Sally for encouraging me to write a more personal book. I have kept her knitting metaphor in mind throughout.

I knew I wanted to illustrate my book and initially I rummaged through many old photographs and made a selection. But on further reflection I decided I would prefer drawings, many based on these photographs, and others derived from outdoor scenes that touched me, and seemed relevant. I would like to thank Lorraine Duval, who did all the drawings in this book, for her contribution.

This book is dedicated to my uncle Jaap, who left for the happy hunting grounds many years ago. He really earned this dedication, as he was the inspiration for many of my early hunting endeavors. As a passionate outdoorsman and a champion shot, he was my role model during the first period of my hunting career. The mystique that surrounded him, having been part of the Dutch Resistance Movement against the Germans during World War II, probably added to my hero warship. Much whispering—whether *"Dichtung"* or *"Wahrheit"*—went on about his deadly marksmanship with the pistol during the war years. I remember with deep feelings of nostalgia the many times I hunted with my uncle, the days when we walked together in the fields—the old man and the boy—and he gave me his wisdom about hunting. These journeys became an intricate element of what makes me who I am today. He was also responsible for my passion for wildlife, nature, and hunting, interests that have stayed with me throughout my life.

It was Jaap who introduced my father, Jo, to hunting. My father was not really a hard-core hunter; hunting provided my father with a form of recreation, a break from his busy business life. My father became famous in Dutch hunting circles less for his hunting prowess than for the "hunting restaurant" he ran in his cabin in the woods of Dronte, a small village in the center of Holland. It was hard not to be impressed by his dramatic culinary productions. The "hut," where we gathered after the hunt, was a place of revelry, where many tall tales were told. These memories of my father will always stay with me.

Many other exemplary hunting role models remain in the part of my inner theater that concerns hunting, most of them now also departed to the happy hunting grounds. A great example of a *"wijdelijke"* (fair chase) hunter was Kees Blauwboer—a giant of a man, a farmer, and a true gentleman in the hunting field. I always admired his self-restraint, his wise council, and his very accurate character assessment of the various hunters that were invited to my father's hunting area. Unfortunately, he died far too young.

Another frequent guest at my father's hunting territory was Mr. Bloemers (I never knew his first name), the "man of the dogs"—in this instance pudelpointers—another true fair chase hunter. There was also the game warden, Mr. Spaans, who was always very encouraging despite his semi-tragic way of looking at life. I also very much enjoyed the company of Henk Oldenburg, who was extremely knowledgeable about guns (a no-brainer, as he owned a hunting shop in the heart of Amsterdam) and who was also my landlord during my student days at the university. Among other regular visitors to the hunting cabin was Gerrit ten Broeke, a businessman who was unstoppable when faced with an audience that appreciated his jokes—and other tall tales. He was always a major source of entertainment. Another person who helped me in maintaining the dialogue about hunting was Mient Faber, a true Frisian and a fellow student at the university. Mient was passionate about hunting, but even more passionate about an archaic Frisian activity: the "hunt" (or rather, the very complex search) for lapwing eggs. I very much appreciated him taking me on a number of these very special explorations.

In North America, the person who, beyond doubt, had the most influence on my hunting career was Jack Ondrack, truly a man for all seasons—a real outdoorsman, a very good sportsman, a self-made philosopher, and a good friend. In some ways, Jack played the role of the older brother I never had. I have many memories of driving together through the province of Alberta, Canada, philosophizing about life, and learning about the outdoors. Jack also had a great sense of humor. I always appreciated his and his wife Esther's hospitality. I am extremely grateful for all the great experiences I had due to them, and can only hope that they enjoyed my company as much as I enjoyed theirs.

Another person who greatly contributed to my North American hunting and fishing experiences was Murray Palevsky, a man who is passionate about whatever he undertakes, and extremely competent. It was Murray who introduced me to fly-fishing for trout and salmon. Of course, his greatest passion has always been enticing an Atlantic *salmo salar* with a fly, and as a fly fisherman he is unsurpassable and unstoppable. While we were both living in Montreal, we had many adventures together, searching for elusive, mysterious rivers and lakes where fish would be plentiful, and grow to monstrous sizes. Murray helped me understand what makes a river so restful to people: it doesn't have any doubts—it

is sure to get where it's going, and it doesn't want to go anywhere else. Another plus is that Murray has a great sense of humor. Although a very ethical hunter and fisherman, catch and release hasn't always been his cup of tea. As a great lover of smoked, wild salmon, "catch and freeze" has always been more to his liking.

Back in Europe, two people took me into the "Wild East"—from the Volga delta, to Siberia, Tajikistan, and Kamchatka—and extended my hunting experiences: Shahin Aghayan and Stanislav Shekshnia. Shahin is someone for whom *"Dichtung und Wahrheit"* have always been somewhat intermingled. While he was living in

Moscow, he was an enthusiastic organizer of various hunting adventures. Stanislav, whom I first came to know professionally, turned out to be a passionate hunter, and our shared interest marked the beginning of a long friendship.

Finally, in these acknowledgements, I cannot forget Elisabet and Katharina who have accompanied me on many of my hunting exploits. I am proud to say that I have turned them into passionate hunters and it goes without saying that hunting has always been enriched by their presence. I would also like to acknowledge my children, who have often been with me on hunting trips. Thank you, Eva, Fredrik, Oriane, and Alicia. All of you have given me much joy and I have learned a lot from you. I would just like to add that I hope Eva will eventually get her moose.

I think over again my small adventures, my
fears. These small ones that seemed so big.
For all the vital things I had to get and to
reach. And yet there is only one great thing;
the only thing. To live to see the great day that
dawns. And the light that fills the world.
　　—Inuit song

Nature creates while destroying, and
doesn't care whether it creates or destroys
as long as life isn't extinguished, as
long as death doesn't lose its rights.
　　—Ivan Turgenev

A true conservationist is a man who
knows that the world is not given by his
fathers but borrowed from his children.
　　—Audubon

I have killed you because I need your
skin for my coat and your flesh for my
food. I have nothing else to live on.
　　—Abnaki hunter

We cannot but pity the boy who has never
fired a gun; he is no more humane, while
his education has been sadly neglected.
　　—Henry David Thoreau

INTRODUCTION

I was breathless. I could hear my heart pounding in my chest like the hoof beats of a horse. My lungs were almost bursting. Another hundred meters to go, or was it more? With the exhaustion I had lost my bearings. Would I be able to get closer without being seen? My hunting guide and I were trying to accomplish mission impossible, and the weather wasn't helping. It was raining hard and relentlessly, not the kind of weather you want for hunting, particularly if you wear glasses, as I do. At least we had waterproof clothing, so I was relatively dry. I stopped to make a half-hearted attempt to clean my glasses and while I was at it, used my binoculars once more. They were just as fogged up and I had to wipe the water off before I could see anything. But when I did, the moose were still there, two of them. They were not yet spooked—but for how long? I had good reason to be nervous as on many occasions I had seen these huge beasts seem to evaporate into the thick willow brush, like steam in a breeze. One of the moose, although it was not a monster, had quite an acceptable rack. After ten days of trying, I would be more than satisfied to get this one.

Not only would I be happy, but also so would everyone in the camp. It had been a while since we last had fresh meat. The daily regime of freeze-dried and canned food was getting to us. To supplement our food supply, we had even lowered ourselves to eat a hapless porcupine that had bumbled by our camp. In that respect, we were not much different from the hungry Indians, trappers, and miners who had worked this area in times past. I hadn't minded eating porcupine, although I wasn't in a hurry to do it again. The only other game close to hand was spruce grouse, or "fool's hens" as the locals called them, for good reason. These birds are not the smartest kids on the block. If disturbed, they fly up, then sit and look at you from the nearest bush.

For more than a week now, Heather, our camp manager, had been hinting, not too subtly, that something needed to be done about our food supply. She reminded us that her Indian neighbors had another name for vegetarians: poor shots. But I had discovered that the northern part of British Columbia doesn't give up its bounty so easily. Moose are hard to get if the weather is too warm and the rut too late.

The two moose were close to the edge of the lake, nibbling on willow twigs. We had first seen them from high up on the mountain. When we spotted them, they were only two vague, hardly distinguishable, shadowy forms, like featureless puppets in a wajang play. After glassing carefully, we managed to identify them. But identifying them was one thing; getting closer to them was another matter altogether. Coming down the muddy, slippery slopes of the mountain on horseback had been nightmarish. The lake where we had seen the two dots was much further away than we had imagined and the descent, which had looked straightforward at first sight, turned out to be long and very hazardous. At one point, my horse lost its footing on a stretch of shale, but by some miracle, recovered. At the last moment, just as I thought the unthinkable was about to happen and that horse and I would go rolling down the mountainside, another leg kicked in like magic. I tried to feel philosophical about the fortunate fact that horses have four legs but it wasn't something I wanted to dwell on. Eventually we got down, more or less in one piece—a few scrapes excepted.

When we reached the bottom of the valley, and got closer to the river, we hobbled the horses and continued on foot, running part of the way. We needed to close the gap, fast. According to my calculations, we should have been very close to the moose but it took us a while to pinpoint where they were standing. It had been much easier to identify the moose from the top of the mountain. Spotting them at the edge of the river, camouflaged by thick cover, was a real challenge.

Out of the corner of my eye I saw one of the willow branches shake violently. Only a moose could make such a racket. They had to be there. Then I saw the flash of a shiny object and through my binoculars I recognized the tine of an antler. But then nothing. Once again, the animals were nowhere to be seen. I was getting increasingly agitated. I needed to find a clearing in the bush to be able to make the shot. We needed to get closer, and quickly, because the wind was shifting. If the moose got our scent, all our efforts would be in vain. There was one thing in our favor, however, to counterbalance the misery: the rain masked the noise we were making as we struggled to make our way through the willow bushes.

Was that movement in the opening in the bush? There had to be one there. I moved forward, trying to control my breathing. If I didn't, I wouldn't be able to keep my rifle steady for a shot. Listening to my shaky breath, I realized how tense I had become. How long had we now been at it, trying to get closer? I couldn't remember; I'd lost all track of time. But did I really care? Did it really matter? Every nerve in my body was concentrated on finding a window in the bushes to identify the moose. At that moment, it seemed there was nothing more important in life than getting closer to one of these giants. It was excitement as well as exhaustion that was making my heart beat almost out of my chest. There was too much adrenalin pumping through my veins. There was little of the civilized man left in me. I had entered another space and time. I was a predator. I was Paleolithic man. I was the provider for my clan. I would bring meat. Just a little distance to go, and then... Suddenly, I realized that we were not alone. There were others interested in the moose. Isn't there an Indian saying that the moose feeds the wolf, but it's the wolf that keeps the moose strong?

The desire to hunt

What makes me want to hunt (or fish)? Where does the desire to hunt come from? Why are so many people so passionate about this activity? What are some of the psychological dynamics that make us do it? And why has it become also such a controversial activity, at least in post-industrial society? How can we reconcile the uncomfortable contradictions of killing beautiful creatures while professing a deep reverence for nature and wildlife? There are no easy answers to these questions. Hunting is like a kōan, a paradoxical riddle, and it can't be understood only by rational thinking, because it is full of contradictions. Like a kōan, hunting's purpose is to open the mind that has been closed due to our habitual responses to the world around us.

Predators hunt in order to survive. They need food for subsistence. The equation is quite simple. Contemporary hunters are less transparent, which makes hunting much more of a conundrum. When I ask hunters (or fishermen for that matter) what this activity means to them, they respond with suggestions like freedom from the hassles of modern society, communion with nature, an instinctual tie to our ancestral past, a search for peace, contentment, happiness, and joy. Although all these responses touch upon certain truths, are they good enough explanations? A much more reflective response comes from the psychoanalyst Erich Fromm:

> "In the act of hunting, man becomes, however briefly, part of nature again. He returns to the natural state, becomes one with the animal, and is freed from the burden of the existential split: to be part of nature and to transcend it by virtue of his consciousness. In stalking the animal he *and* the animal become equals, even though man eventually shows his superiority by the use of his weapons. In primitive man this experience is quite conscious. Through disguising himself as an animal, and considering an animal as his ancestor, he makes this identification explicit. For modern man, with his cerebral orientation, this experience of oneness with nature is difficult to verbalize and to be aware of, but it is still alive in many human beings."[2]

Fromm added, "The psychology of hunting, including that of the contemporary hunter, is a very complex phenomenon which would require an extensive study."[3] Unfortunately, very few of these "extensive studies" on the psychology of hunting exist. Most hunting reports are phenomenological; in them, hunters describe a number of subjective experiences and elaborate on what those experiences mean to them. Interesting as these might be, they will only bring us a short way toward understanding what hunting is all about.

Some hunters take a short cut in lifting the veil of what hunting is all about by describing it as a purely instinctual process. According to them, *Homo sapiens*, the ultimate predator, inherited the "hunting instinct" from its Paleolithic ancestors. In an unambiguous and simplified way they argue that hunting is our "natural state" of being, and that the desire to hunt is one of the most fundamental aspects of human nature. *Homo sapiens* is first and foremost a hunter-gatherer, and many of our many other characteristics derive from this predisposition. Hunting is the behavioral template of the human species. We are hardwired to be hunters. In short, it's part of our heritage.

Another, more ecologically-oriented school of thought sees hunting as a very intense personal relationship between our "prey," the environment, and ourselves. The killing of individual members of a healthy and reproductively sound species is merely the continuance of ancient human predatory patterns that are part of the cycle of life. As we are at the top of the food chain, it is our role as predators to assume this responsibility. Hunting is ecologically necessary, particularly in areas that have suffered from the removal of other large predators—apart from man, the most dangerous one of them all.

Yet again, for others, hunting offers the opportunity to get back to basics; the journey into nature and towards the hunt is experienced as a reprieve from the stresses and strains of modern living. It contributes to ones physiological and psychological well-being. Among those who subscribe to this point of view, there are some who see hunting as the royal road to spirituality, a form of "ecological worship." It provides them with a coveted opportunity for complete immersion in nature.

I feel more comfortable with some of these points of view than others—but whatever my personal and philosophical inclinations are, hunting remains a common and ancient legacy. As the outdoor writer, Ted Kerasote, noted in his insightful book, *Bloodties*: "Hunting, along with procreation, is the oldest expression of our genetic nature, and ... those who hunt, rather than being bloodthirsty killers, are actually more concerned with preserving healthy, sustainable wildlife populations than those animal rightists who would sever all connections between humans and animals. Hunting is a legacy that should be passed along."[4]

The description of hunting as vestiges from our prehistoric past made a lot of sense to the influential Spanish philosopher José Ortega y Gasset, who went to great lengths to arrive at an understanding of the various socio-psychological forces that drive us to hunt. In his famous essay, *Meditations on Hunting*—probably, the most renowned book in the hunting literature—he notes that life is a dynamic interchange between man and his surroundings. And although Ortega considered human beings fugitives from nature, they are also very much linked to their Paleolithic ancestry.

> "...hunting is a universal and impassioned sport...it is the purest form of human happiness. The essence of hunting or fishing involves a complete code of ethics of the most distinguished design. The sportsman who accepts the sporting code of ethics keeps his commandments in the greatest solitude with no witnesses or audience other than the sharp peaks of the mountain, the stern oak, and the passing animal."[5]

In addition, Ortega made the interesting observation that, "One does not hunt in order to kill; on the contrary, one kills in order to have hunted."[6] The virtue of the hunt is not the possession of game, but the pursuit of it. Killing animals—in spite of what anti-hunting groups may want us to believe—is not what hunting is all about. The death of the quarry is only a part of the complex exchange that makes up the hunt. Fair chase hunters are those who have reverence for the animals they hunt. For the true hunter, possession is

meaningless if the animal has no chance to escape. The hunt should be fair chase. Animals need to be able to get away.

⌐┤

The Kill

The kill is one of the ways to complete the hunt. It is the symbol of the success of the quest. It is a way of taking possession. The kill symbolizes the need to obtain the tragic knowledge of death first hand. Without the possibility of death, the hunt would have a less emotional impact. The kill is the acknowledgement of the reality of life.

What makes the hunt truly real is the kill, a differentiator that gives the hunt an almost religious quality. In doing so, the hunter rolls the dice of life and death. But, playing God or not, taking any life is always a momentous act and should be done while giving proper respect to the animal. In true hunting, the kill always remains a solemn act, something that shouldn't be done frivolously. Just as hunters did in prehistoric times, hunters today realize that taking a life is anything but "sport." They will have weighed the pros and cons of making the "kill", and must be prepared to take the consequences. Every serious hunter needs to be prepared to engage deeply with this ethical struggle when making the final decision to end a life. The kill, itself, takes a microsecond. Most of the time in hunting is spent on the physical and psychological prelude to that act, which Ted Kerasoke portrays so perfectly in his description of an elk hunt:

> "Still she stands, strangely immobile. I raise the rifle, and still she stands, and still I wait, for there have been times that I have come to this final moment, and through the air the animal's spirit has flown into my heart, sending me its pride and defiance, or its beseeching, frightened voice, saying, 'I am not for you.' And I have watched them walk away. She sweeps her eyes across the forest and begins to graze down the north slope, exposing her flank for one more instant, and allowing me to decide. I listen, hearing the air thrum with the ambivalence of our joining, about which I can only say, once again, 'I am sorry.' As she disappears from sight, I fire behind her left shoulder, the sound of the shot muffled by the forest....
>
> ... I climb over several fallen trees and find her lying not thirty feet away, her head turned over her left shoulder, great brown eyes utterly calm. My heart tears apart."[7]

Nature worship

Paradoxical as it may sound to people who know nothing about hunting, fair chase hunters are profound nature lovers. Nature is the shrine at which they worship. The human need to be immersed in nature is described very well in the work of Peter Mathiessen, the noted naturalist and explorer, known for his passionate advocacy of the natural world. He writes about the aesthetic pleasure of being in nature and how nature can be a source of psychological renewal:

> "Lying back against one tree, staring up into another, I could watch the olive pigeon and the olive thrush share the black fruit for which neither bird is named; to a forest stream nearby came the paradise fly-catcher, perhaps the most striking of all birds in East Africa. Few forests are so beautiful, so silent, and here the silence is intensified by the apprehended presence of wild beasts—buffalo and elephant, rhino, lion, leopard. Because these creatures are so scarce and shy, the forest paths can be walked in peace; the only fierce animal I saw was a small squirrel pinned to a dead log by a shaft of sun, feet wide, defiant, twitching its tail in time to thin pure squeaking."[8]

Any cultural anthropologist or prehistoric archaeologist would confirm that hunting is not just about killing, important as it may be for putting food on the table. It has also been a major catalyst for our personal and cultural development. Hence, another major function of hunting is to connect to our ancient past and arrive at a deep understanding of the natural world, of survival skills, the development and application of woodcraft.

Although hunting is no longer essential for our survival, the desire to hunt hasn't disappeared; the hunting "instinct," a drive tied to our most basic motivational need systems, has remained. It is highly questionable, given the deeply ingrained effects of our evolutionary past, whether modern man has experienced such a transformation that the fundamental urge to hunt has completely vanished. *Homo sapiens'* most recent stage of development represents only an infinitely small segment of the trajectory of time.

Like other basic drives, such as sex, we cannot simply deny our origins and dismiss the hunting instinct from our evolutionary past. In a subliminal or non-subliminal way, they continue to influence us. Even though few of us have to go out with a gun to put food on the table, the hunting drive is still there, in the same way that the fact that we can now make babies in laboratories has had no effect on our sex drive.

Although most of us get our meat from a supermarket, does this mean it is necessary to ban hunting altogether? And to take this line of reasoning to its ultimate conclusion, should we give up eating meat and stop outsourcing killing to slaughterhouses? Should we regress to our prehistoric vegetarian diet? Is the biblical image of the Garden of Eden, with Adam and Eve living in harmony with nature, a realistic portrayal of what life on earth once was, and should be like? Hardly, knowing what we do about the evolution of our species. If we scratch modern man, we will find many of the characteristics of our Paleolithic ancestors. Most of us have discovered for ourselves how quickly our primitive fight/flight mechanisms kick in when we find ourselves in stressful situations. Paleolithic man is never far away, however much we try. And Earth has never been a perfect Paradise where every animal created lived peacefully together. They mostly want to eat each other.

Nature intelligence

While acknowledging the practical and moral aspects of hunting, its mystical and emotional aspects also loom large. In contrast to anti-hunting advocates, hunters are not detached observers. We participate actively in the cycle of life. We are both spectators *and* participants in a dramatic "dance" with the forces of nature. We, like our "cousins" the carnivores, play an essential role in the intense relationship of predator and prey. But as hunters, we also are acutely aware that we—like everything in the animal and plant kingdoms—will eventually end up as the prey of recyclers, tiny though the microorganisms that clear up after us may be. (Although there is always the chance that we will fall prey to bigger recyclers and end up as bear food on top of a mountain in Kamchatka, as almost happened to me.) As the Pulitzer Prize-winning writer, John McPhee, noted:

> "...life and death are not a duality. They're just simply here—life, death—in the all-pervading mesh that holds things together. Less than five minutes after a wolf stops chasing a moose, the moose is browsing. The wolf chases the moose again. Stops. Five minutes later, the moose is browsing. The moose does not go on thinking—worrying—about the wolf. Death is as much a part of life as breathing. People in cities seem to want life and death to remain at a standstill. Perhaps, people who are against killing are horribly afraid to die. They seem to think that you can have life without death, and if so they have withdrawn from life. They seem to think that animals up there smell flowers. They use the word 'ecology' for everything but what it means. It means who is eating whom, and when."[9]

I remember once hunting for kudu in Southern Africa. I was crouching not far from a watering hole, on the basis that "where there is water, there is life." Life in this case consisted mainly of a large flock of guinea fowl, busily foraging for seeds and insects. All of a sudden, and very unexpectedly, the whole flock seemed to explode and took to the air—highly unusual in the middle of the day. Usually, when disturbed, guinea fowl do a very subtle disappearing act into the brush. These birds had panicked. It wasn't long before I discovered the reason for their agitation. A hawk eagle had struck one of them, and it was now pinned to the ground in its talons. The guinea hen was flapping desperately but that didn't go on for long. The eagle moved its victim into the shade and started to pluck and tear at its flesh. Very soon afterwards, the flock of guinea fowl returned to their original spot and, circling round the eagle, continued their foraging. It was as though they were participating in a macabre dance. Life goes on….

I pondered the significance of this particular "dance." Why were the guinea fowl behaving like this? Why were they anywhere near the eagle? Did they know that the bird had had its fill? Did they feel safe? Were they trying to drive the eagle away from its victim? I would never know; I could only speculate.

This memory will stay with me for a long time. It was yet another mysterious encounter with the natural world. Would our ancestors have made sense out of what was happening? Who knows? Would they know why the guinea fowl returned, and moved so close to the eagle? Perhaps. How much woodcraft, how much knowledge, has been lost in our post-industrial world?

This question preoccupied the Russian army officer and explorer Vladimir Klavdievich Arseniev, who in the early decades of the last century undertook a number of journeys into the Siberian Far East, in an area that has always been of great interest to me. Arseniev's writings describe expeditions undertaken to map the cold, uncharted, and (still today) little-known region where Manchuria and Korea meet southeastern Siberia. In these explorations Arseniev was befriended and accompanied by an aboriginal hunter named Dersu, a Naina hunter from the Amur region. Dersu's was an animist world where trees, winds, and animals were labeled as "people." The urban, rationalist cartographer tries to make sense of Dersu. What's this pure man of nature all about? How does he look at the world?

From Dersu's behavior and observations, Arseniev obtained a good idea of how our ancestors must have lived for tens of thousands of generations as subsistence hunters, how their nature intelligence was developed. Dersu felt sorry for the "nature illiterate" European explorer, and undertook to teach him how to survive in such harsh places. Dersu could read tracks like a book, a talent only a few people, like the bushmen or pygmies of Central Africa, still possess today. During their travels together, he instructed Arseniev in the ways of tigers, bears, wild boar, deer, mountains, and weather. Water was an elder cousin to humans ("Him can cry, him can sing, him can play"); in wild places, follow the lead of animals ("Captain, look-see road well; horses go, you go; horses no go, you no go"); the natural world was being despoiled by the greed of miners and commercial hunters.

For Arseniev, Dersu was an animist archetype:

"Dersu was really astonishingly adapted to life in the *taiga*. As a couch for the night he would choose a spot under a big tree between two big roots, so that they would protect him from the wind; as a mattress he would put down a strip of bark off a cork tree, and hang his moccasins on a branch so that they dried over the fire without being burnt. He would keep his rifle by his side, not on the ground itself, but supported on a couple of forked sticks stuck in the ground. His firewood always burned better than ours, never scattering sparks, and the smoke always blew to one side. If the wind changed, he fired up a screen on the weather side. With him everything he wanted was on the spot and at hand.

Nature is merciless to man. She will flatter and caress him one moment, and then suddenly fall upon him, as though driving home his helplessness. The wayfarer has constantly to brave the elements, rain, wind, flood, flies, bogs, cold, snow, and ice. The very forest itself is an element. Dersu did not feel himself under the influence of nature, but rather in intimacy with his surroundings, a part and parcel of them. (p. 116)…

For [Dersu] every [animal in the taiga] has its soul, just like man. He had even his own system of classification of them. He arranged the big animals in one class, for instance, the little ones in another, and the clever ones he separated from the foolish. The sable he included among the clever ones…." (p. 148)."[10]

Arseniev's accounts—portraits of cultures in collision—resonate with my memories of the many primitive true hunters I have been with, and who have helped me, myself something of a latter-day city dweller, and left me with unforgettable impressions of the beauty of the wilderness and how to survive in it.

We invent tools to make our lives easier, and once we have them, they change who we are; they change our beliefs and values. Innovative technologies contribute to a highly complex society but eventually muddle our way of living. Life has a much greater degree of stability for the contemporary Dersus I have met in the Arctic, in Central and Southern Africa, in South America, in the jungles of Asia, or the mountains of the high Altai or Pamir. They have taught me unforgettable lessons about the intricacies of woodcraft and intensified my deep appreciation for nature. They have contributed significantly to my ability to "read" nature.

Opponents of the hunt

Most people who are against hunting cannot reconcile the reverence hunters have for nature, and the rich emotional, psychological and ancestral link they have to the hunting experience. Perhaps it is too much to ask those who do not hunt to understand the complexities of the hunt. They are unlikely to want to make the effort at sense-making, and are often more inclined toward binary thinking—things are either "good" or "bad." In today's popular press, hunting falls into the latter category. Some may reserve a salon-anthropologist attraction to primitive tribes that hunt—their art, habits, and rituals—but are horrified when it comes to contemporary hunters. To quote the prominent animal rights spokesman, Cleveland Armory, "Hunting is an antiquated expression of macho self-aggrandizement, with no place in civilized society."[11]

However, the typical anti-hunter is far more familiar with asphalt jungles than real ones. Most of them have never bothered to study nature and wildlife seriously and have no idea what living in the wilderness means. They have not built up the store of memories that Theodore Roosevelt described so well:

"No one, but he who has partaken thereof, can understand the keen delight of hunting in lonely lands. For him is the joy of the horse well-ridden and the rifle well-held; for him the long days of toil and hardship, resolutely endured, and crowned at the end with triumph. In after years there shall come forever to his mind the memory of endless prairies shimmering in the bright sun, of vast snow-clad wastes lying desolate under gray skies; of the melancholy marshes; of the rush of mighty rivers; of the breath of evergreen forest in the summer; of the crooning of ice-armored pines at the touch of the winds of winter; of cataracts roaring between hoary mountain masses; of all the innumerable sights and sounds of the wilderness; of its immensity and mystery; and of the silences that brood in its still depths."[12]

I strongly believe that hunting should only be undertaken by people who understand our hunting heritage, our wildlife, and its habitat; people who truly care about our planet; people who believe in sustainability. This includes involvement and commitment to wildlife, habitat, and environmental issues. Interestingly, hunters are some of the most engaged individuals in the conservation movement, who contribute significant resources (in contrast to the mere rhetoric of anti-hunters) to the preservation of wildlife.

Nature lovers come in many different forms and, given the fragility of our environment, they should pursue togetherness, not conflict, the anti-hunting lobby included. Haven't both parties, deep down, a great concern for our natural environment?

The Royal Road forward

The study of hunting practices is the royal road to understanding nature and wildlife, and cultural sense making. In addition, given our common ancestry, the historical role of hunting provides a revealing window through which to examine society. Although Paleolithic man now sits in the past, his legacy—in the form of hunting—is still with us. Through this legacy, we have the responsibility to maintain a mutually enhancing relationship with the Earth and all the communities the Earth supports. As temporary stewards of these communities, we must change our individual and collective actions to protect the fragile environment we love and share. This is the only way to preserve and restore the bioregion we call home for future generations and all life on Earth. Hunting is a window into the understanding of nature, the understanding of our wild heritage, the reaffirmation of a core element of our social identity, and our sense of self. In the act of hunting, contemporary human beings reconfirm their compact with nature, transcend death, and create meaning.

2 — Fromm, Erich. *The Anatomy of Human Destructiveness*. New York: Holt, Rinehart and Winston, 1973, p. 132.

3 — Fromm, Erich. "Man would as soon Flee as Fight." *Psychology Today*, August, 1973, p. 42.

4 — Kerasote, Ted. *Bloodties: Nature, Culture, and the Hunt*. New York: Kodanska International, 1993, p. xvii.

5 — Ortega y Gasset, José. *Meditations on Hunting*, H. B. Wescott (trans.). Belgrade, MT: Wilderness Adventures Press, 1995, p. 42.

6 — *Ibid*, p. 105.

7 — Kerasote, Ted. *Bloodties: Nature, Culture, and the Hunt*. New York: Kodansha International, 1993, pp. 245-246.

8 — Mathiessen, Peter. *The Tree where Man was Born*. London: Harville Press, 1998, pp. 79-80.

9 — McPhee, John. *Coming into the Country*. New York: Bantam Books, 1977, p. 397.

10 — Arseniev, Vladimir Klavdiyevich. *Dersu the Trapper*. (transl. Malcolm Burr). Kingston, NY: McPherson & Co., 1996.

11 — Armory, Cleveland. *U.S. News & World Report*, February 5, 1990.

12 — Roosevelt, Theodore. *The Wilderness Hunter*. New York: Elibron Classics, 2004, p. xiv.

What an ugly beast the ape, and how like us.
　—Marcus Tullius Cicero

There is a passion for hunting something
deeply implanted in the human breast.
　—Charles Dickens

It is even harder for the average ape to
believe that he has descended from man.
　—Henry Louis Mencken

I have found the missing link between the
higher ape and civilized man; it is we.
　—Konrad Lorenz

I viewed my fellow man not as a
fallen angel, but as a risen ape.
　—Desmond Morris

Look deep into nature, and then you
will understand everything better.
　—Albert Einstein

CHAPTER 1

VENATO ERGO SUM

For many people the notion that we humans are descended from primitive ape-like creatures is still very hard to accept. Some don't like to acknowledge that a conclusive body of data supports the theory of evolution and that all life came from the same common ancestor; these people won't accept that fossil evidence has shown that life has existed for billions of years and has changed over time through evolutionary processes. For many, their views of scientific evolution are clearly influenced by their religious outlooks. The idea of being descended from the apes is both repellent and sacrilegious.

But it's not only religious fundamentalists who recoil from such ideas. As a species, we are convinced of our uniqueness—we are seemingly the only thinking creatures, the only animals with the gift of self-awareness, the only organisms that can reason and extrapolate. We like to think of ourselves as special beings. But could it be that we have too high an opinion of ourselves, preferring to align ourselves with the gods rather than the higher primates? Primatologists have done a good job in dispelling this illusion and the more we know about our closest relatives, the apes, the less different we seem to be.

It seems to me self-evident that humankind is directly descended from apes or monkeys. But it is often more convenient and more comforting to join the creationists in their assumption that *Homo sapiens* enjoys a unique status in the natural world. Those of us who are religious transform this idea by talking about "intelligent design," the ambiguous theory that the exquisitely intricate

1

mechanisms of our universe are best explained by the intervention of an intelligent deity and are not the result of any undirected process, such as natural selection. Intelligent design is merely a more modern form of the traditional argument in favor of the existence of God, albeit one that purposefully avoids specifying the nature or identity of the designer. Intelligent design looks clever, modern, and sophisticated, but in reality it is only a subversive way of dealing with evolutionary realities. It doesn't much help us make sense of what we are all about, where we come from, what drives us, why we do what we do.

One of the reasons for this denial of reality is that we may not always like what we see when we take a closer look at where we came from. The anthropologist, Robert Ardrey, in his book *African Genesis*, noted:

"Our ancestry is firmly rooted in the animal world, and to its subtle, antique ways our hearts are yet pledged. Children of all animal kind, we inherited many a social nicety as well as the predator's way. But most significant of all our gifts, as things turned out, was the legacy bequeathed to us by those killer apes, our immediate forebears. Even in the first long days of our beginnings we held in our hand the weapon, an instrument somewhat older than ourselves."[13]

"Killer apes"? What can he mean? Our closest living relatives—the great apes—are for most part peaceful vegetarians, quite different from the rapacious and aggressive creature that *Homo sapiens* has become. Except, of course for some—we now know that certain chimpanzee communities have adopted hunting as a way of supplementing their vegetable diet. Primatologists Robert Ardrey and Jane Goodall (who first observed chimpanzees hunting red colobus monkeys in Tanzania's Gombe National Park over 40 years ago) have taught us that we are indeed descended from omnivorous hominids—"killer apes"—and that, by implication, hunting is one of our oldest activities.

The fossil record clearly shows that hunting was an essential activity for our ancestors. And our contemporary behavior reveals that the ghosts of our ancestors continue to haunt us. Hunting has always meant more to humankind than merely a means of obtaining food. No sooner did humans start hunting other creatures that the activity became imbued with deep ritual significance. It became a spiritual act, part of our religious worship, and contributed to our evolutionary and socio-cultural development. Hunting was a key factor in the development of many of the tools and skills that make us human: language, reasoning, the ability to objectify, the ability to co-operate and work in teams, tool-making and artistic expression. The co-operation needed for the hunt became the catalyst that spurred human development.[14]

As they ventured out of the dense rain forests where they originated, our earliest ancestors needed to develop more creative hunting kills. Without them, they would not have been able to survive the harsh climates that they encountered during their migrations, or provide themselves and their families with food, clothing, or shelter. Without their ability to hunt, early humans would not have been able to obtain the bones, antlers, teeth, and feathers that they subsequently transformed into tools and weapons.

The film *Ao, le dernier Neanderthal* (the last Neanderthal), adapted from the novel by Marc Klapczynski, tells the story of a Neanderthal man who travels across Europe in search of the last survivors of his clan. It portrays encounters between Neanderthal and Cro-Magnon people, the first early modern humans—and recent archaeological evidence has confirmed that these hominids co-existed for a short period before the Neanderthals became extinct 30,000 years ago, having been the Earth's dominant hominid for some 300,000 years. (Hominids are included in the super-family of all apes, the *Hominidae*, which today is commonly considered to include living and extinct humans, chimpanzees, gorillas, and orangutans.) Ao—who is depicted as a peaceful, intelligent creature living in harmony with the natural world—is also an exceptional hunter and a determined survivor who battles with terrifying animals in a lost world of savage landscapes.

Today, it is hard to say anything conclusive about the Neanderthals other than that they were an extinct species of humanoid appearance. It has been said that the psychology and sociology of Neanderthals belong in the private junkyard of evolutionary theory—in other words, with the limited evidence currently available, any effort to draw inferences about Neanderthal psychology is pretty worthless. My enjoyment of the film came from its convincing portrayal of the terrible, destructive, unpredictable forces with which these early people had to contend on a daily basis. The film evokes brilliantly the brutal, hostile environment the Neanderthals inhabited. Clearly, they must have possessed great stamina and ingenuity simply to stay alive; although they were not as advanced in their development as *Homo sapiens*, they were immensely resourceful and had sufficient intelligence to conceive and manufacture weapons, clothing, and tools.

Although the Neanderthals and our human forebears started as equals, the fact is that hundreds of thousands of years ago the two species took different evolutionary pathways that determined their eventual survival. It is often assumed (possibly rightly), that competition with *Homo sapiens* was one of the reasons for the extinction of the Neanderthals. As more advanced developmental patterns started to emerge among *Homo sapiens*, the Neanderthals were at a disadvantage. One of the reasons for this may have been that Neanderthals did not have *Homo sapiens'* symbolic, cognitive capabilities, in particular our more effective use of language. They may have lacked the creative spark that comes with symbolic reasoning. Eventually, such differences came to their ultimate conclusion and one species rose to global dominance while the other disappeared.

¬

An evolutionary march

At various times, on hunting trips in Namibia, I have come across a number of very large constructions hanging from trees. They are the nests of the sparrow weaver—an extremely social bird. The gigantic nests these birds construct can weigh up to 300 kilograms, and can hold more than 500 birds. Bushmen—Stone Age survivors who, as one of the longest-living traditional hunter-gatherer groups, have occupied Southern Africa for over 50,000 years—exploit these nests, opening the tops of them and collecting the eggs that they know the birds will continue to lay. This harvesting technique must have been going on for tens of thousands of years. Our prehistoric ancestors almost certainly did the same thing, passing this knowledge on to their offspring. The bushmen's contemporary foraging gives us a glimpse of our own origins; these people are directly in touch with the long line of human evolution which links modern humans to their ape-like ancestors.

Lucy and the missing link

In a specially designed container at the National Museum of Ethiopia in Addis Ababa lies a priceless 3.2-million-year-old fossil: the remains of the world's most famous early human ancestor. This is Lucy. Lucy's skeleton was found in 1974 by paleontologist Don Johanson and his team in the Afar Depression of Ethiopia. The fossil was named Lucy in honor of the Beatles' song "Lucy in the Sky with Diamonds," which was playing as the triumphant paleontologists celebrated their find. Lucy, an extinct hominid, is a representative of *Australopithecus afarensis,* a group of ape-like creatures that inhabited Africa three to four million years ago.

As the fossil was subjected to extensive examination, it soon became clear that Lucy's skeleton was quite different from those of other primates, while at the same time, it could be seen that *Australopithecus afarensis* was far more primitive than other known hominid-like creatures. Lucy had an ape-like appearance above the neck and a strongly human-like form below it. Comparison with other fossils from the site appeared to show extreme sexual dimorphism in body size with males being larger than females. The creature's dentition and brain size, however, brought *Australopithecus afarensis* closer to the modern human form. Lucy, although she had a mixture of ape and human features, was small and slender (107 cm tall) and was able to walk upright.[15]

In 1924, one of Johanson's predecessors, Robert Dart, an Australian physical anthropologist and paleontologist, had revolutionized the study of human origins by presenting *Australopithecus africanus,* the "southern ape of Africa," having discovered fossil remains at Taung, in northwest South Africa. This other human predecessor, who lived between two and three million years ago, was similar to *afarensis*, being bipedal, but had a slightly larger body size. Although the teeth and jaws of *Australopithecus africanus* are much larger than those of humans, they resemble human much more than ape teeth. Also, skeletally, this intermediate species appeared less ape-like than earlier specimens of the australopithecines. Not only did *Australopithecus africanus* have more humanoid facial features, it also had a more human-like cranium, indicating a larger brain. At the time of his discovery, Dart postulated that this new find was the "missing link" between apes and humans.[16] These two fossil finds firmly established Africa as the cradle of mankind and these australopithecines came to be regarded as our earliest ancestors. Although the intelligence of these early hominids was no more sophisticated than that of modern apes, their bipedal stature was the key signifier that distinguished this group of ape-like creatures from previous quadruped primates.

Since Lucy, an even older representative has emerged. For example, Ardi (short for *Ardipithecus ramidus*, from the word for "root" in the local Afar language) is one of the latest fossils to come out of Africa, pushing the origin of hominids even further back in time. Ardi lived well before Lucy and had an even more primitive build. She (the fossil is of a female) lived about 4.4 million years ago and probably looked something halfway between a chimpanzee and a human. But in differentiating Ardi from the apes, paleo-anthropologists have speculated that this creature must have been a more generalized feeder than today's chimpanzee. Ardi is currently the oldest known predecessor of man. She was taller than Lucy, almost twice her weight, but her brain capacity was similar to that of a chimpanzee. She could climb trees but also walk upright. Her teeth suggest that Ardi was probably an omnivore, eating any fruit, plants, and meat she could find. She did not have the chimpanzee's pointed teeth, characteristic of animals adapted to eating fruit.[17]

In 2010 yet another transitional species joined the stream of discoveries emanating from Africa. *Australopithecus sediba* had a human-like face and could walk well upright, but was very apelike in other ways.[18] Indeed, this new discovery is thought to fit somewhere between *Austrolopithecus* and *Homo habilis* and has been hailed by some as the "missing link" between the two. It illustrates once more the great diversity of hominid species in bygone times. More, similar finds are likely to come to light.

The making of the hunter

How did these predecessors of humankind live? What turned them into meat eaters? What made them become hunters? Like Marc Klapczynski in his depiction of the life of Ao, I can only offer speculation: our answers to questions about the dawn of humankind must remain extremely tentative.

Over the past 12 million years, sub-Saharan Africa has been subjected to dramatic climatic and geological changes induced by continental drift, such as formed the great Rift Valley, a 6,000-mile fissure in the Earth's crust that runs right across the African continent. One consequence of these changes was that the region where humankind originated became increasingly dry. Gradually, much of what once had been rain forest began to turn into dry scrub and savannah. Many paleontologists reason that these climatic changes had an evolutionary effect on the ape-like creatures that lived in this changing environment. Thus Africa became the place where the world's greatest human evolutionary experiments took place.

As climate change created openings in the forests, and travel through the tree canopy became increasingly difficult, the ape-like creatures that lived there needed to adapt to life at ground level. The apes came down from the trees and started to spend more time foraging on the ground. This led to changes in food gathering techniques and eventually to changes in the types of food that could be gathered. Over many millennia, these tree-dwelling ape-creatures adopted an erect posture, more suited to their life in the open, and with erect posture came bipedal walking and a higher brain quotient. Gradually, these apes left their closest ancestors behind: the now-extinct herbivorous hominids, and the great ape species that are represented today by the gorilla, bonobo, chimpanzee, and orangutan. Eventually, these evolving hominids left the rain forest for the open plains and savannahs, where they needed to develop different strategies for foraging, hunting, and defense against predators. The changes forced upon them created a set of social behavior patterns that differentiated them even more from their predecessors—and thus the likes of Lucy, Ardi, *Australopithecus africanus*, and *Australopithecus sediba* evolved.

One of the changes forced by this transition to a mixed forest-savannah habitat seems to have been a diversification away from the almost exclusively vegetarian diet of the early tree-dwellers. They became omnivores, collecting eggs, shellfish, nuts, and roots, as well as fruit. Over time, however, we can speculate that meat became an increasingly important part of their diet. Initially, at least, these early hominids would have been scavengers rather than hunters. They may have eaten the carcasses of large animals killed by other predators or animals that died of natural causes. As time passed, however, this food pattern would change. From having an essentially passive approach to obtaining meat, their evolving intelligence and ingenuity would have led them to take matters into their own hands rather than rely on chance to provide meat. They turned into true hunters. Again—and I can only make inferences about these developments— a major contributing factor to this change was probably bipedalism, which truly differentiated these ape-like creatures from their rainforest ancestors.

The development of bipedalism was a momentous evolutionary step forward. Walking upright was a logical adaptation to living in a mixed scrub and grassland habitat. Being able to stand upright makes it easier to look further ahead when moving through areas covered with tall grasses and the ability to scan the horizon while scavenging for food has obvious advantages (one only has to watch the behavior of meerkat colonies to see that standing on their hind legs improves their chances of spotting predators). There is also evidence to suggest that bipedal animals can walk and run greater distances because they expend less energy with their longer strides. But perhaps one of the most important evolutionary benefits of bipedalism was that it left the hands free for grasping objects, carrying food or the young, and handling tools—like weapons.

Before the discovery of hunting per se, it is almost certain that groups of hominids obtained meat by driving large carnivores away from their kill. Then they would strip the remaining flesh from the carcasses and use primitive tools to break the long bones and skulls to get at the bone marrow and brain tissue inside. Fossil records, such as the cut- and bite-marks on bone fragments, show that early humans scavenged in this way. But although they appear to have been quite adept at scavenging, early hominids seem to have been driven by their desire for meat to take the next logical next step and kill their own prey, transitioning from scavenging to hunting. The earliest weapons would have been found objects— rocks, or sticks, which hunting chimpanzees use today. Dating such evolutionary speculations is extremely difficult. Evidence has been found, however, that Lucy's fellow *Australopithecenes* were using stone tools to butcher meat 3.4 million years ago—about 800,000 years earlier than has been previously estimated.[19] The evolution from scavenging to hunting is tremendously significant: it contributed to activities like food sharing, cooperative group behavior, language development, and a sexual division of labor.

But even with the various fossil records, it is still difficult to determine with any accuracy how early hominids really lived. We can only speculate and draw inferences from observing the behavior of the great apes.[20] However, it is dangerous to draw conclusions about our ancestors from observing the behavior of our contemporary relatives; we need to distinguish between what is transmitted through cultural practices and what is the result of change through natural selection.

For example, in the case of primates, a considerable amount of observed behavior seems to be the result of learning rather than genetic evolution. Certain behavior patterns are passed from generation to generation as part of a cultural process, even contributing to the existence of sub-cultures among primates: chimpanzee groups behave differently in different habitats. Tool use is generally an acquired cultural phenomenon, observed in the habit of some chimpanzees that use sticks to extract termites or honey, or other groups that use sticks to dig for roots.

As evolution continued its steady march forward, our ancient ancestors bequeathed to us both physical and cultural characteristics that established *Homo sapiens* as a hunting species. For example our opposable thumbs, upright posture, and increasing brain capacity all resulted from evolutionary processes and would have contributed to the development of new skills. The bigger brains of early hominids made up for having a body that was poorly adapted for hunting, when compared to other talented predators, such as the big cats. A larger brain also improved the ability of these hominids to adapt to their environment and modify it to suit them. It gave them the intellectual capacity to experiment with and develop tools and weapons. Weapons and specialized hunting techniques gave these hominids a great competitive advantage over other animals, including other apes; it also gave them the means to defend themselves against the many dangerous animals that prowled the land. Thus, over time, humans became the most adaptable and most effective hunters the world has ever known.

With their superior intelligence and their enhanced ability to kill, these early humans soon started to explore their surroundings and migrate to new territories. One popular hypothesis is that they left Africa during two distinct periods of migration. One genetic line, believed to have emerged from Africa around 700,000 years ago, led to the Neanderthals who colonized the temperate zone of Europe and the Middle East. Another line evolved into modern humans, who first appeared about 195,000 years ago. As I mentioned before, the earliest modern human was Cro-Magnon man—*Homo sapiens sapiens*—who lived from about 10,000–45,000 years ago during the Upper Paleolithic period of the Pleistocene. Cro-Magnon culture took tool-making to a high level of sophistication and new technical and cultural activities began to emerge with the first recorded appearance of clothing, engraving, sculpting, and painting.

The significance of meat eating

Precisely when meat first became part of the diet of these early humans nobody knows. But once a taste for meat had been acquired, hunting was just one step away; a step that would alter the course of human history. There is no reason to believe that, without the desire to eat meat, our early ancestors would ever have left the rain forests. The ability to acquire food through hunting, I believe, has been chiefly responsible for the existence of our species in its present form. The desire to eat meat, and the need to hunt for meat, became the catalyst for crucial socio-cultural developments, the most important of which was language. Hunting large mammals, especially, was a major driving force in human evolution because it necessitated the division of labor, sophisticated patterns of communication, group organization, and a social structure based on cooperation and interdependence. As well as requiring sophisticated tool-making skills, hunting as a group demonstrated early humans' ability to understand and manipulate the environment in which they lived.

But why should the desire to eat the flesh of other animals be such a powerful driving force in human development? Fruit, nuts, and leaves also taste good and procuring them is far easier and less risky than hunting. The answer is that meat eating has many benefits. Meat is an excellent source of high-quality protein and contains fats and other compounds, such as amino acids, not found in vegetables. Adding meat to their diet improved nutrition amongst our ancestors, strengthened their immune system, promoted better physiological growth and development, and generally enhanced health, energy, and well being. No wonder meat became such an exciting, even precious, commodity to early hunter-gatherers.

There is a great difference, however, between being an accidental (or scavenging) meat-eater and turning the quest for meat into a primary task. It was the latter that stimulated new developmental processes. The males, being generally larger and more physically suited to the activity than the females, were the primary hunters, as they still are today. Bringing a carcass back from the hunt provided the male of the species not only with precious nutrients but also with a special kind of currency that could be exchanged for sexual favors—an activity that continues today among some tribal groups.[21]

John Vaillant, in his thoughtful book *The Tiger: A True Story of Vengeance and Survival*, includes this vignette:

"Describing the return of a successful hunting party in the Kalahari Desert, the ethnographer Lorna Marshall summed up the gatherer's age-old dilemma: 'We heard the sound of voices in the encampment, rising in volume and pitch like the hum of excited bees. Some people run toward the hunters…some danced up and down, children squealed and run about…I venture to say that no women have been greeted this way when they returned with vegetables.'"[22]

On many occasions I have had a similar experience when returning to camp in Africa or Asia. When they saw us arriving with the dead animal, people would dance, shout, sing, and bang drums. They would cry out their longing for meat, overjoyed that the successful hunt would break the monotony of their diet. Several times, in Africa, I was raised aloft by the rejoicing villagers and paraded around, creating the illusion that I was the great provider. It was easy to see how such enthusiastic rejoicing might be a powerful stimulus to continue to hunt.

Hunting made early humans more successful as a species compared to the great apes, as the anthropologist John Pfeiffer observes:

"[Hunting] increased cooperation among all members of the group, not only among certain males. Man became the only primate to kill regularly for his living, and the only primate to share regularly on a day-to-day basis involving the entire group. All other primates are supremely self-centred when it comes to feeding; they forage strictly for themselves. Even more important ... another unique development came with hunting—a division of labor between the sexes, with the males concentrating on obtaining animal foods and females concentrating on plant foods."[23]

There is an interesting mutual iterative process here. From an evolutionary biological point of view, not only does hunting—aided by greater brain capacity— yield high-value nutrition in the form of meat, but having greater brain capacity also necessitates the intake of more concentrated nutrients. *Homo sapiens'* search for meat would tend to accelerate their intellectual development and a more complex brain would stimulate their ability to innovate. An omnivore, with a diet that incorporates a large proportion of meat, needs less time to consume and digest food compared to, say, the large ruminants that must devote most of their waking life to grazing, chewing, and digesting their food. With more time between meals, early humans could experiment, explore, discover, and invent new ideas.

Although hunting today is often a very solitary activity, our early ancestors discovered that hunting in groups would have a much higher rate of success—particularly when hunting large and dangerous animals. Just as modern social animals like wolves, lions, wild dogs, and hyenas hunt in packs, humans too discovered that group efforts led to a much higher probability of success. And the cooperative and reciprocal behavior that evolved through hunting turned out to have major developmental consequences. Not only did hunting play a significant role in the development of language but it also laid the foundations for moral and ethical cultural systems.

In short, humankind's desire for meat became the catalyst for increasingly sophisticated socio-cultural behavior patterns and hunting was crucial in advancing our early hominid ancestors along the path of evolution. Early tools for foraging would lead to the development of tools for scavenging meat from abandoned carcasses and ultimately to the sophisticated implements required for killing prey. Hunting was the engine of technological change. And even when humans started to abandon their hunter-gatherer lifestyle in favor of the more efficient and complex practices of animal husbandry and agriculture some 12,000 years ago, hunting would continue to play a pivotal role in socio-cultural developmental.

ᛁ

Of apes and men

Primatologists have gone to great lengths to demonstrate that meat eating and hunting predates the rise of *Homo sapiens*. When Jane Goodall first observed wild chimpanzees hunting and eating meat, skeptics at the time suggested that this behavior was aberrant and that the amount of meat eaten was trivial. But today, even though we know that chimpanzees are mainly fruit eaters, we also know that they can turn into predators in their forest ecosystems.[24] To them, however, unlike *Homo sapiens*, the acquisition of meat is not a systemic, strategic process but more an opportunistic activity. Similarly, although we can find many examples of chimpanzees modifying sticks in order to probe for termites or dig for roots, or using rocks to crack nuts, primates have rather limited hunting and tool-making abilities.[25] And in spite of the impressive social achievements of chimpanzees, bonobos, orangutans, and gorillas (such as the use of elementary sign language and the ability to establish long-term bonds), none of these great apes seems capable of taking the dramatic evolutionary journey undertaken by early humans.

Indeed, what truly differentiates *Homo sapiens* from the great apes is the capacity to develop a culture. At some point in the history of the human species, our ancestors moved from being elementary tool-using and meat-eating animals into social beings who communicated and cooperated to accomplish tasks that they would never have been able to accomplish on their own. Hominids mastered fire, developed sophisticated hunting techniques, and developed weapons that enabled them not only to kill prey but also to defend themselves against the large carnivores that preyed upon them (including cannibalistic neighbouring tribes). To quote the philosopher David Livingston Smith:

"There is little doubt that our ancestors were hunted by larger, stronger, more ferocious predators, and that their long experience of being hunted, generation after generation, for millions of years played an important role in configuring the human mind. They survived by foraging for plants and small animals and scavenging what meat they could get from the partially eaten carcasses left by large carnivores. But it is equally true that they eventually managed to turn the tables on the monsters that stalked them and became the most masterful predators that the world has ever known (today, the lions and tigers need more protection from *us* than we need from them)."[26]

The mastery of fire and the ability to cook food was another turning point in the history of human evolution, contributing to *Homo sapiens'* spectacular success by separating these evolving hominids from their more primitive brethren and providing our early ancestors with much greater control over their natural environment.

Cooking rendered starchy plant matter and meat protein more digestible and permitted early humans to extract nutrients from many new types of food. Cooked food was also easier on the teeth, the jaws, and the gut—an important consideration for creatures that, like modern humans, had relatively small teeth and weak jaws ill-suited to ripping into raw meat. As I have already noted, meat is a highly concentrated food and quicker to digest than tough fibrous vegetation; cooked meat is even quicker. In the wild, chimpanzees spend up to five hours a day gathering food and chewing it and early humans would have had to do much the same; but once they had invented cooking, our ancestors were spared these marathons of mastication.

I hypothesized earlier that females would be sexually more available to hunting males willing to exchange high protein food for sexual favors. Such incentives would have served to encourage the specialized psychological behavior patterns that led to cooperative behavior and a degree of division of labor among the sexes. Men would naturally be the most likely to engage in hunting, not only because of their superior size and strength but also because the demands of pregnancy and child-bearing meant that women would be unable to hunt for months at a time. Furthermore, those women with the physical strength to hunt large dangerous prey would also be at the peak of their reproductive ability; their loss would be a severe blow to the whole community. So from an evolutionary biological point of view, it is reasonable to assume that human males have evolved in such a way to make hunting even more satisfying and rewarding psychologically, in spite of its many risks. For our prehistoric ancestors the task of getting food would have been divided along gender lines with men mostly being the meat providers and women and children hunting for smaller game, and foraging for roots, vegetables, and fruits. But this division of labor according to gender was far from rigid. If the situation warranted it, women would also hunt.

Nature intelligence: a digression

In trying to explain the evolution of our carnivorous habits, I have suggested that the need to obtain meat stimulated cognitive development. It is fair to assume that, in order to become effective as hunters, our early hominid ancestors would have required a deep understanding of natural phenomena and the behavior of animals. They will have acquired what can be termed "nature intelligence"—an almost instinctive knowledge of nature and the ability to use its resources to their advantage. Today's primitive tribes still possess and use this nature intelligence—for example, to track and spot animals and to predict weather patterns. It is an ability retained by those who still live as part of the natural environment and lost to those of us who have concreted over our environment and lost touch with it. Nature intelligence seems to incorporate a kind of topographical memory, which enables hunters to locate themselves accurately in a landscape and find their way in wild places without getting lost—a skill critical for survival.

In the Arctic, hunting for caribou, musk oxen and barren ground grizzlies, it was sufficient for my Inuit guide to be in a place just once in order to build a perfectly accurate mental picture of the area. His memory was critical as we tracked musk oxen—those shaggy, hump-backed survivors of the Pleistocene era—through a barren, featureless landscape. I acquired a musk ox pelt and marvelled at it: musk oxen must survive temperatures as low as minus 40° Celsius, arctic storms, and blowing snow. I have been told that the wool, or *"qiviut,"* is stronger than sheep's wool, eight times warmer, yet finer than cashmere. The Inuit name for the musk ox is *"oomingmak,"* meaning "bearded one," while its Latin name derives from the words *"ovis"* (sheep) *"bos"* (ox) and *"moschatus"* (musky).

The Inuit and oomingmak have a long tradition of coexistence. From prehistoric times to the present, this shaggy mammal has provided the Inuit with meat, warm sleeping robes, and horns used in the manufacture of weapons and implements. Apart from man, wolves (and occasionally polar bears) are the only natural enemies of the musk ox. However, the musk ox does not often run away from predators. When threatened, the herd forms a protective circle, horns facing outward, with their young hidden in the centre of the ring—this habit, useful as it may be against wolves, is pretty useless when facing the human hunter.

My hunt for the musk ox took place high above the Arctic Circle. To survive in this harsh land without the high-tech navigational equipment available to modern hunters, you really need nature intelligence. I initially flew in to the outpost of Cambridge Bay in the Northwest Territories, then flew even further north in a floatplane to connect and hunt with two Inuit guides, a father and son (plus the latter's wife and children) who had set up a base camp in what looked to me like Central Nowhere. Before leaving, I had been told by the outfitter that the weather would be "like Paris in November"—words that returned to me when I found myself in the center of a mosquito universe. It was unnaturally mild. But two days later, the weather changed dramatically: a storm came our way, winter arrived—and far too soon. The arctic grizzlies denned, and we denned too; it was too miserable to be out in the open. I made one brief excursion with the younger Inuit to get meat for the camp. Walking back through the whiteout of an intensifying storm that evening with one of the two caribou that I had killed, I was keenly aware that, without my young guide's extraordinary special memory, I would never have would been able to find my way back to camp. What could he find to guide him through such a blank, white terrain?

After a week under canvas—the only highlight being the night storm that blew my tent away—the elder Inuit decided we had better go by boat to the nearest village. Staying at the camp any longer would put us at too great a risk. Crossing the bay, watching the salty water blowing over the edge of the boat and freezing instantly in my clothing, is something I will not quickly forget.

Landing at the Inuit village, we were welcomed extremely hospitably. I was invited into one of the cabins where my glasses instantly fogged up due to the difference in temperature. When I finally managed to see properly, I made out a big bubbling pot of caribou stew and bloody caribou hides laid out all over the floor to dry. Immediately, a bowl of hot meat was put in my hands.

The next day, the storm abated and we went hunting for musk ox. Close to dusk, we saw a large herd in the distance. I climbed a hill with the younger Inuit, glassing to spot a male with a good boss—not an easy task, as their long coats make it difficult to distinguish the sexes. As it would soon be dark, the herd was milling around, trying to find a good bedding place for the night. The young Inuit took his time to identify a big male. The light was disappearing fast, and I was getting increasingly worried whether I would still be able to make the shot. Finally, he pointed out what he thought was an old male in the herd and I shot. At the sound of the rifle, the herd, which had been ready to bed down for the night, went into overdrive, and galloped away. They made a turn past the hill and disappeared, my bull included.

We ran down the hill to intercept them, not easy given the extreme sogginess and strange bounciness of the tundra. It was like walking on a trampoline. As we rounded the hill, we saw all the musk oxen disappearing into the distance, with the exception of one that stayed immobile and glared at us. Assuming this must be the animal I had wounded, the Inuit told me to shoot. I shot once more, and the musk ox fell.

When we got closer to the body, we discovered that I had shot a female that was not on license—I did not have a good night's sleep. Again, finding the route back, in the dark, on a sled, necessitated a solid dose of nature intelligence. The next day, the Inuit found the animal I had originally shot

at, a male, lying dead just behind the hill. Why the female behaved as it did—giving the impression of being wounded—remained a mystery. In hunting, despite the best of intentions, mistakes are made. The musk ox meat, I remember, was delicious.

I witnessed the same kind of nature intelligence in a very different context when I hunted with the pygmies in the vast, dense rainforest of Cameroon. The pygmies' understanding of the ways of the forest was so complete that in comparison I was as helpless as a blind man, while they could weave a path through it with ease. On one memorable occasion we set out to observe a troupe of lowland gorillas. After a long and hazardous hike—during which I narrowly avoided stepping on a highly venomous snake—the pygmies brought me to a clearing in the forest where a gorilla family was browsing under the protective gaze of a large silverback male. It was a remarkable sight—and a scene of great tranquility—but how the pygmies knew this group would be in this precise spot, I could not fathom.

On other occasions, I went with the pygmies to stalk bongo, the largest and heaviest of Africa's forest antelopes. Bongos are nocturnal, extremely wary and very elusive. Both males and females have spiral, lyre-shaped horns that resemble those of related antelope species such as nyala, sitatunga, bushbucks, kudu, mountain nyala, or eland (the common one and the larger Lord Derby variety). They have a hunched posture, holding the head up and the horns extended along the back. Bongos are considered among some of the most difficult of all the African game animals to hunt, primarily because of the terrain in which they live—the thick, almost impenetrable rainforest. The temperature hardly helps: it is usually over 30°C with 100 percent humidity and frequent rain. At times, at the rainforest-savanna margins, bongos are found lingering in open places along meandering streams that provide natural salt licks, called *bako*. (*Bako* means, in the Dioula language of Côte d'Ivoire, or the Bambara language of Mali, "behind the river": *ba* meaning river and *ko* behind.) Bongos, however, are hunted almost exclusively by tracking.

The pygmy trackers were friendly and cooperative and enjoyed hunting and the excitement of the hunt. Short in stature, they ranged from barely four feet to nearly five feet in height, making it more easy for them to walk and duck under, through and around the vines that are everywhere in their rainforest home. But what I found most interesting about working with the pygmies—a suggestion of the way our early ancestors may have lived—was studying the pygmy way of life, their practice of traditional medicine, the way they collected nuts, honey, and tobacco from the forest, their hunting methods, the way they build their huts from tree branches and leaves, and their traditional dances. The pygmies worship a forest spirit known as *jengi* (also called *djengi* or *ejengi*), whom they perceive as both a parental figure and a guardian and whom they celebrate through ritual dance. Each successful hunt is followed by a dance of thanksgiving known as the *luma*, accompanied by drumming and polyphonic singing.

The pygmies are often perceived as relics from the pre-Neolithic era, able to follow animals over all kinds of terrain and vegetation under almost any condition. With their unique forest skills, the pygmies can see things that are invisible to modern, urbanized humans. They have the ability to spot animals at some distance in extremely dense vegetation. They can live in places where it would be very difficult for "civilized" people to live. Their world is cloaked in a thick layer of green vegetation wherever you look; the humidity in the air is extreme; the tracks are mostly open and clear but strewn with obstacles like fallen trees or large roots at regular intervals.

Despite these conditions, the pygmies are some of the world's most skilled trackers. They know how to determine accurately the age of a track—essential knowledge before embarking upon a long tracking exercise through a highly inhospitable habitat. As I hunted with them, I realized that losing contact with them in the rain forest would be like being set adrift on an ocean with no reference point. Finding camp again would be impossible for me.

We pursued the bongo through thick jungle cover, the trees draped with liana and creepers, vines hanging from the branches. After a very long hike, getting increasingly wet and muddy while crossing streams and boggy areas, all hell broke lose without any apparent warning. There was a cacophony of noise, dominated by the barking of the dog that accompanied us. The pygmies pushed me in the direction of the noise at a run, some challenge given the low overhanging branches, creepers, vines, and lianas blocking my way. The barking of the dog grew louder. I felt my pulse rate increasing by the second. The forest I was pushing through seemed like an impenetrable green curtain in front of me. Then suddenly, I glimpsed an orange blur that moved. I froze; I was only a few meters from the man-dog-bongo circus. Now, I could make out the shape of the bongo and a small dog that was circling it, yapping incessantly. The bongo, head low, was trying to spear the dog with its horns. I had the sensation that time was standing still—and I made my shot...

Eidetic memory and art

Practice makes the sensory organs of "primitive" humans more highly developed than those of "civilized" humans; the Inuit and pygmies are exemplary practitioners of nature intelligence. But I maintain that we can recover and develop some of these capabilities, long since lost to us by our increasing urbanization, through hunting. Despite many generations of continuous separation from nature, it is still possible to reawaken and revitalize our dormant nature intelligence. Much of what comprises nature intelligence is the refinement of the senses: vision, smell, hearing, and even taste are qualities that many city dwellers have lost. Another feature of natural intelligence is an eidetic or photographic memory, the ability to recall images, sounds, smells or specific objects from memory with extreme accuracy. In primitive man this was responsible for the development of mythological and artistic traditions. Many of the artistic representations dating from the earliest chapters of human history depict wild animals and the hunt. They provide the strongest possible evidence of the central role played by hunting in primitive society and underline the powerful mystical and spiritual significance of hunting.

The most celebrated and vivid depictions of the hunt are the cave paintings at Lascaux in southwest France. Discovered in September 1940, the caves are decorated with about 2000 drawings and paintings of animals, human figures, and abstract patterns that many experts believe are accounts of past hunting successes or were created as part of a ritual designed to bring luck in future hunting expeditions. The artists who created these vivid images were hunter-gatherers of the Upper Paleolithic period who lived around 17,300 years ago.

But artistic representations of hunting date back much further, to the very earliest traces of prehistoric humans: cup marks and a meandering line etched into the wall of a sandstone cave in India two or three hundred thousand years ago; inscribed lines on bone, teeth and ivory of equal antiquity found at the campsites of our prehistoric ancestors and sculptures in the form of modified natural forms in the Near East are all believed to refer to hunting as a group. These all pre-date the emergence of modern *Homo sapiens* by as much as 100,000 years. Some experts believe that early hominids used larger animals for food almost two million years ago.[27]

From our exalted modern perspective, this all seems very old and very primitive. But consider the very short period of time during which *Homo sapiens* has existed on this Earth; and then consider the infinitesimal period in which we have supported our existence through agriculture, industry, and technology. It is no more than three or four thousand years. But for tens of thousands of years before that, humans lived entirely by hunting and gathering—as, indeed, some still do to this day. It is very easy to dismiss these time-honored activities as a relic of our long-forgotten history and condemn the desire to hunt as primitive, barbaric, and retrograde. But we as a species have not evolved so very much in the three or four thousand years since our forebears discovered agriculture and animal husbandry. The hunting instinct was bred into us over hundreds of thousands or even millions of years and it is still there, just beneath the surface. Moreover, it is not so deeply buried that it cannot rise to the surface and manifest itself not only in actual hunting but in other more subtle ways that blend readily into our sophisticated modern social behavior patterns—so easily that we barely notice them. If you doubt that this instinct still remains, then consider how easily a child can become fascinated by an activity such as hunting and fishing. Most children will take up hunting and fishing with uninhibited enthusiasm if they are only given the chance. Lacking the acquired sophistication and aloofness of their adult guardians, children can more easily access their latent nature intelligence before it withers away under the influence of civilization.

Technology

If hunting was the catalyst that sparked humankind's mystical and artistic awakening, it was even more directly responsible for our development of tools and technology. The simplest form of hunting—the pursuit and capture of small animals—requires no tools. But to hunt bigger animals our predecessors needed to find a way to magnify the strength of their bare hands and extend their reach beyond arm's length. As I mentioned earlier, the first weapons were almost certainly stones and sticks that could be used to bludgeon captured prey or thrown to bring down fleeing animals. Once the animal had been killed, the same tools could be used to help the successful hunter get to the meat, but it was only with the invention of cutting tools made from materials such as stone, bone and shell, that the first hunters learned to butcher their prey and make efficient use of it—for example, by removing and curing the skins and by shaping bone and antlers to make other tools. The more meat featured as a part of the human diet, the more tools began to play a more central role in the evolutionary process. Taking and exploiting the bodies of other animals added to humankind's nature intelligence and at the same time helped to raise our species above the rest of the animal kingdom.

From the invention of the wooden spear to the development of complex traps for large game, humans' ingenuity blossomed and rose to ever-higher levels of achievement. The big game hunters of old had many ways of hunting large prey and gradually modified various tools to help them do so. Cliffs, waterways, and natural corrals could be used to gain advantage over animals that could be killed with relatively primitive tools. For example, when hunting in a group for large herd animals such as aurochs, bison or mammoths, one common technique was to encircle the herd and drive it toward a cliff edge or into a bog where a few individuals would fall and could be stabbed, speared or stoned to death. The Inuit still obtain a considerable amount of their meat by intercepting large migrations of caribou and picking off a number on the fringe of the herd. The pygmies of Central Africa whom I have seen hunt in groups will drive small animals such as duikers—a species of small antelope—into nets. These techniques have their modern equivalents in the more stylized and ritualistic practice of driven pheasant- and grouse-shooting and the European practice of driving wild boar and other big game animals toward a line of waiting guns.

Around 15,000 years ago humans started to enlist the help of another species by domesticating wild dogs and establishing a symbiotic relationship with them. "Man's best friend" has also remained his main hunting companion to the present day. The most primitive method of hunting with dogs survives in the form of the traditional Spanish *monteria*, where packs of specially bred hunting dogs pursue and push the prey toward the hunters. The *monteria* would be instantly recognizable to those ancient hunters who used fire-hardened jabbing or throwing spears in exactly the same way.

Hunting as a symbolic activity

Foraging, scavenging, and hunting were our ancestors' principal means of obtaining food and clothing throughout the Paleolithic period. But eventually human society evolved to the point—around 10,000 years ago—where social groups abandoned their nomadic lifestyle to remain in one place. They were the first farmers. Living in permanent settlements where they could cultivate crops and keep domesticated animals made life safer and more secure for these

early farmers. No longer dependent on the luck of the hunt and no longer obliged to venture into the wilderness in search of food meant that life became less a matter of survival and more of subsistence. Hunting was no longer the main source of meat for the community, but nonetheless it remained important, not only as a way of supplementing the food supply but also as a social and cultural activity. Two trends began to emerge. First, hunting became a specialized activity carried out by a social elite—usually male and of the warrior class—who possessed special knowledge and equipment. Second, hunting started to acquire a recreational function among this elite group, who had the time and the resources to pursue it. Hunting persisted because it was fun. Tending a herd of domestic goats might put meat on the table but it was no match for the thrill of the chase. Hunting tested an individual's strength, courage and skill—it was exciting. This "sporting" element must have developed from the competitive pressure that drove early hunters to demonstrate their prowess in the field, maximizing productivity and earning kudos among the female members of the clan. Hunting also became a useful method of honing combat skills and acquiring the bravery that was needed in times of conflict with other groups.

Many higher mammals play because it stimulates the brain, exercises the body, and develops skills that are useful in other ways. Why does a domestic cat chase a piece of screwed-up paper? Why does it catch and bring home mice, rabbits, and birds when its food bowl is filled several times a day by a doting human? The answer, surely, is that the cat has evolved in this way and hunting is its natural behavior. It is the same with human beings. The instinct to hunt is in our genes and has stayed with us long after it ceased to become essential for our survival.

As hunting developed as a recreational activity it acquired strong social significance and hunting "tournaments" became highly organized and highly symbolic of the hunter's status in the community. They offered the opportunity for the powerful and wealthy to show off—evidence of which can be found in art galleries and museums around the world. The more dangerous the prey— lions, tigers, elephants, or wild boar, most of which were hunted on horseback or from the safety of a chariot or an elephant's howdah—the more prestigious and exclusive the hunt. Like most social pastimes, hunting soon became a badge of social class and in many instances hunting became an exclusive prerogative of the aristocracy that owned the land and the animals living on it. Hence the princes and senior functionaries of Assyria and Babylon hunted according to a well-established protocol: they could take leopards, aurochs (wild cattle), boar, deer, antelopes and wild asses. But lion hunting was the preserve of the kings and severe punishment lay in store for poachers who broke the laws of the land.

Similarly, in most parts of medieval Europe, the upper classes seized the sole rights to hunt in certain areas of a feudal territory. Game was preserved as a form of recreation for the aristocracy. This is illustrated to perfection in the legend of Robin Hood, where one of the principal charges against the outlaw is that he "hunts the King's deer." For the peasant class, hunting—or rather poaching—was less a matter of recreation (though no doubt it afforded plenty of excitement) and more a way of supplementing a meagre diet. But as the story of Robin Hood illustrates, peasants would routinely defy the law to shoot the "noble" game that trampled their crop or snare the occasional rabbit for the pot. Hunting as a recreational activity for the rich and powerful became a powerful symbol of inequality that persists today.

One of the first modern treatises on hunting, the *Livre de Chasse* (Book of the Hunt), written by Gaston Phébus, Count of Foix and Béarn in the late 14th century, offers a fascinating insight into how complex and formalized hunting had become among the ruling classes of medieval France.[28] It not only describes hunting methods and mores in great detail, but also is widely regarded as an important document of the cultural history of its time.

The book is divided into four parts, dealing with different types of game, the care and training of the hounds, methods of hunting stags and other wild animals, and a closing section on traps, snares, and crossbows. In addition, Phébus reveals an impressive knowledge of the natural sciences—long before the age of modern empirical science—with detailed observations on the various animal species.

Phébus portrays hunting as an expression of human social development and (a factor still important in contemporary hunting) also represents it as a form of theater. For Phébus, as for countless hunters through the ages, hunting implies the pursuit of the mythical and the magical as well as the corporeal. Phébus depicts the hunt almost as a kind of morality play in which the emotional and intellectual connections between the hunter, the natural world, and other humans are played out. In 14th century Europe hunting had evolved into a magnificent spectacle put on by and for the benefit of the aristocracy. For the kings of France, the hunting season was an orgy of killing and feasting. At the Chateau of Chambord, built in 1510, François I—the most famous of France's hunting kings—enclosed 13,000 acres of woodland game reserves within a stone wall measuring 30 km in length. The wall served not only to prevent trespass by the lower orders but also to prevent the escape of the vast numbers of red deer, roebuck, and wild boar with which François stocked his park. Here, on Europe's largest hunting estate, animals were pursued and killed in vast numbers by a class of people who had very little in common with the hunter-gatherers of the Paleolithic age. There was no need for much nature intelligence here. Hunting had become a crude expression of power and influence.

Since the Middle Ages, such "dramatic" hunts have remained popular with the ruling classes, reaching their peak at the turn of the 20th century. In Russia—a vast nation with a strong tradition of hunting—these recreational massacres were popular with the aristocracy. Large numbers of various game animals were rounded up, while the Tsar and his grand dukes with their retinue slaughtered them from concealed positions. The British aristocracy, too, were enthusiastic gluttons for slaughter. In 1911, King George V, during an imperial visit to Nepal, accounted for 39 tigers, 18 rhinoceroses, and four bears, employing thousands of beaters to drive the game toward his waiting guns.

Meanwhile in the United States, where there was no ruling elite that could claim ownership of the game, destruction on an even greater scale was visited upon the apparently inexhaustible populations of bison. Significantly, though, this slaughter was carried out in the name of commerce, not sport (and, it should be remembered, to deprive Indians of a valuable food resource). Very much helped by cattle diseases, the North American bison reached the brink of extinction. The passenger pigeon, due to the destruction of nesting sites, excessive hunting, and the clearing of forest to make way for agriculture, was completely wiped out. Giving an ironic twist to the role of hunting as a means of obtaining meat and skins, wild animals were again killed in order to promote the success and prosperity of the human population. By now, though, humans had developed an industrial society and hunting became an industrial process as much devoid of any nature intelligence as the bloated rituals of Europe's royalty. With this kind of "industrial" hunting, *Homo sapiens* had come a long way from the days when hunting was seen as part of the essential fabric of a healthy, functioning society.

⊨

Hunting in modern society

In today's world, these kinds of decadent hunting activity—frequently organized for social and political reasons—have become increasingly rare. The spread of democracy and the collapse of the ruling upper classes have made such spectacles less acceptable to society and our growing understanding of ecology has taught us that such activities are not necessarily the best way to manage wildlife populations. Nevertheless, they still occasionally take place and I have attended huge drives for small and big game, including driven shoots in Germany where, at the end of the hunt, more than 100 wild boar would be dead, laid out on fir tree branches, and lit up by flaming torches while the huntsmen sounded their hunting horns. In the UK, France, and Slovakia I have seen large numbers of pheasants driven over a line of guns with a loader standing by with a second gun ready so the shooter loses no time by having to reload. Although such hunts may test the hunter's shooting skills, they emphatically cannot be considered hunting. The birds are artificially reared and released in specific locations to ensure sufficient numbers for the guns. Neither the shooter nor the beaters who drive the game require much nature intelligence and there is none of the mystical connection with the natural world that true hunting can bring. In their defense, however, large formal shoots provide employment for the local community and are a real economic benefit to rural districts where

the soil is not suitable for any kind of agriculture. Dealers and wholesalers buy dead game, and the wealthy guns who pay serious money for a day's sport support the local community.

Some of these activities are similar to scenes from Jean Renoir's famous film, *La Règle du jeu* (The Rules of the Game)—a title with a double entendre. What rules are Renoir referring to? Societal rules? The rules of war? Hunting rules? Are the old rules no longer relevant? Is some massive change under way?

The events of this timeless movie take place in the country house of a marquis—a signifier of the decadence of the French upper classes. There are rules, even though they may be hollow. The guests play cards, have parties and put on skits; they have love affairs; they hunt—to them, all of life is a game. But what creates the tension in this film is our knowledge that everything is played out against a background of an approaching war. While the guests play, the rules and the game are never explicitly stated. But one thing is clear: there are no rules for what is coming. Life, for this frivolous, upper-class society—which has set up unspoken rules in order to hide behind them—is over. But none of the characters is prepared to take such a hard look at the truth.

The centrepiece of Renoir's complex story—the symbolic core of his critique of French society—is the hunting scene, which reveals the volcano that seethes beneath the ritualistic behavior of the characters. Renoir's camera shots throughout most of the film can run for a minute or more; in the hunting episode, there are 51 shots in less than four minutes, a mounting rhythm of cutting and movement that culminates in an awesome barrage of gunfire. When the guns finally stop, Renoir shows us the hunting field, littered with dead birds and rabbits. It is a brilliant prologue to the carnage of World War II, simultaneously a premonition and reminder of the slaughter to come. This scene has justifiably been called one of the most powerful scenes in all cinema. It is also a powerful illustration of hunting gone wrong—where rules have taken over from apparent purpose—making these kinds of activities rather questionable.

Types of hunting

Subsistence hunting is no longer a necessity for any but a few isolated tribes; hunting nowadays is regarded as a sport, although this is not a word I ever use myself in connection with hunting. The refer to hunting as "sport" degrades the complex emotional experience at the heart of true hunting, which I compare to a "calling." It is more appropriate to refer to hunting as an "avocational" or "lateral" activity, which is taken up as a counterbalance to our regular work or profession. Avocational hunters make up the bulk of the contemporary hunting community and although they earn a living through other means than hunting, I believe that they have much in common with subsistence hunters. They pursue the same interests; there is a cultural link that connects them.

Avocational hunters can be further sub-divided.[29] For example, there are those who hunt as a form of wildlife management and whose hunting is aimed at securing the welfare of a specific animal by preventing overpopulation. These hunters are often professional game wardens and to that extent, their hunting contributes to their livelihood. Then there are what we might call *utilitarian* hunters, people who hunt for food not because they depend upon it but because they derive satisfaction from taking control of the process. Wild meat is healthy and is not the product of agri-industrial mass production. Utilitarian hunters often live in the countryside and follow country pursuits, of which pot-hunting is a time-honored tradition. Other hunters might be described as *nature hunters,* individuals for whom it is important to maintain a connection to nature in a real, even visceral, sense.

Another group may be called *exposition-collector* hunters. Usually, these are people with far less experience of country life but who relish the opportunity to be in the wilderness, facing the challenges that nature presents to them. They like to test themselves. There is also a narrative aspect to their behavior—they like to talk to others about their success. The stories and photographs published in hunting journals such as *Safari Club International Magazine* or *Slam Quest* speak for themselves, and are indicative of what motivates this particular group of hunters. For some of these people, hunting also becomes a way of demonstrating their physical fitness—their ability to overcome the hardships that come with being in wild places. The tougher the conditions, the greater the satisfaction when the kill is made. No guts, no glory.

Finally, there are what I call *slob hunters*, a fringed group that damages the reputation of the others. These people have no respect for, nor understanding of, the natural environment and lack the patience and energy to subject themselves to any discomfort or risk in order to pursue their "sport." They prefer to shoot their quarry from the safety and comfort of SUVs, all-terrain vehicles, planes, or helicopters. In many instances, they just kill for the sake of killing and may even leave the carcasses in the field to rot.

⌐

The call of the trophy

In most respects, these forms of hunting are quite different from the hunting done by our Paleolithic ancestors. But a closer look reveals some common features. For most contemporary hunters, it is still important to get game for food; the same can be said for the animals' horns, skulls, and hides, which are used for utilitarian or ceremonial purposes, just as our Paleolithic forebearers did. Practically, they can be made into garments or utensils. Symbolically, they represent a sort of totem, a reminder of a deeply significant experience from the past.

This, in a modern context, translates into trophy hunting. For many avocational hunters (although they may not necessarily express the idea explicitly) being successful at a hunt is not enough; they need a tangible memory, a trophy indicating that they have been selective and successful in their endeavor. This is the world of the exposition-collector. Management hunters do not seek trophies—indeed, selective culling usually entails removing the poorer specimens from a population, leaving the best (for example, the stag whose antlers most trophy hunters would choose to hang on their wall) to continue contributing to the gene pool. However, a responsible trophy hunter will select animals carefully and there are times when the best specimen can be culled; for example, removing an old male will give one of the younger ones the opportunity to occupy the alpha position and improve the bloodline. However, an obsession with records and trophies (and humans are prone to such obsessions) soon dulls the hunter's appreciation of the natural world and the animals hunted.

Hunting for "sport"—especially trophy-hunting—is guaranteed to stir up very strong emotions. Killing an animal just to obtain another trophy is an outrage to people who consider hunting for sport or recreation unacceptable, and who argue that hunting can only be considered "sporting" if the animal has a good chance of winning. They question hunters' motivation and, not surprisingly, often conclude that people who hunt for sport do so in order to release some form of distorted urge for violence. A basic tenet of all arguments against trophy hunting is that the hunter is in pursuit of the rarest and most valuable specimens of a species and, as such, is responsible for the destruction of endangered animals. This is a misconception; exposition-collector hunting can be very beneficial for game management. There is such a thing as responsible hunting. The fees charged for taking out animals at the end of their life cycle can hugely benefit game management—and will financially benefit the local population that lives with these animals. Any wildlife policy that does not include the voice of the local population will be doomed. However, it is hard for the hunter's voice to be heard above the noise of opposition.

Responsible hunting might also be termed "fair chase" hunting. By fair chase, I mean hunting that is governed by strict game regulations and that requires a considerable effort to obtain the trophy. Fair chase trophy hunting is hunting in the service of sustainable development. Although some hunters will inevitably be preoccupied by size of skull or horn, for the vast majority of hunters—even those hoping to bag a trophy—this will be of fairly low importance. For most hunters, it is principally the outdoor experience that counts; and even trophy hunters most often enjoy eating what they kill. Trophy hunting can be an expensive occupation, so hunters play an important role in many local economies. Licence fees cost a considerable amount of money; guides and wardens must be paid and the willingness of people to pay to hunt means that animals that might otherwise be culled out of existence, so that their habitat can be replaced by livestock and crops, are guaranteed security and continued existence.

Nature's vicissitudes

It is almost impossible for somebody born in a city to imagine what life would have been like for our Paleolithic ancestors whose survival depended on their hunting prowess. Most of us who hunt today have very little idea of what it means to lack a reliable food supply and to have to spend every minute of the day in search of nourishment. We might wonder occasionally what time the shop closes—but we won't be fretting about whether we will be in the right place at the right time to intercept a migrating herd of reindeer. For primitive humans, however, the danger of starvation and death was ever-present. Modern humans have no problem accepting why these early people needed to hunt. But what about today's hunters? Put simply, hunting is not readily understood today. The origins of hunting lie buried in our unconscious mind—and so the psychological urge to hunt will always remain hard to explain. Hunting is not just about being able to kill and eat an animal; there are many other explicit and implicit factors at play. And although it may sound incredible to the non-initiated, hunting can become a near-mystical and highly emotional experience, a test of skill, perseverance, and courage—an opportunity to commune with nature.

I am often asked to explain why I hunt and others are sometimes surprised by the terms I use and emotions I evoke. For me, the act of hunting re-establishes a personal compact with nature. It is a kind of spiritual act, reconnecting me to my genetic history as a member of the human species. Hunting helps me in my search for meaning; it is a celebration of a deep-seated sense of self; it is a way to reaffirm my identity. And if that sounds rather solemn and complex, I should explain that hunting also brings me, simply, great pleasure and joy. It awakens the playful child in me; it makes me feel alive; it helps me recover from the stresses and strains of daily life and replenish my spiritual reserves in order to continue to function well. Hunting helps me to be more creative. That seems paradoxical and logically absurd to those who do not hunt—but as I hope to make clear throughout this book, hunting is not just, or even principally, about killing.

Although Paleolithic man is ancient history, his hunting legacy is still with us. Hunting is part of our instinct to tame nature and harness its power and it is a way of reaffirming a core element of our social identity. The American essayist, philosopher, and poet, Ralph Waldo Emerson, in his essay "Nature" observes:

"The lover of nature is he whose inward and outward senses are still truly adjusted to each other; who has retained the spirit of infancy even into the era of manhood.... In the presence of nature a wild delight runs through the man, in spite of real sorrows.... every hour and season yields its tribute of delight; for every hour and change corresponds to and authorizes a different state of the mind, from breathless noon to grimmest midnight.... I am the lover of uncontained and immortal beauty. In the wilderness, I find something more dear and connate than in the streets or villages. In the tranquil landscape, and especially in the distant line of the horizon, man beholds somewhat as beautiful as his own nature."[30]

Modern humans are seldom in such harmony with nature. Nature may have a better understanding of the order of things than present-day *Homo sapiens* may have. It certainly has this effect on me. Nature is my medicine; nature calms me down. Nature is part of my inner world on which I can draw in times of difficulty. I feel better when I remember beautiful lakes, streams, mountains, deserts, and seashores. I feel better when I recall natural smells, sounds, and silences. I feel better when I study clouds, and make sense of their ever-transforming imagery. I have a real sense of the healing power of nature.

Nature is also a great teacher and for me, a source of inspiration, a form of concentrated art that never goes out of style; the kind of art that can't be found in a museum. In the wilderness I sense the essential miracle of life, I deepen my understanding of the natural world, and I understand myself better. My goal in life is to do as the philosopher Zeno counseled, and "to live in agreement with nature."

13 — Ardrey, Robert. *African Genesis*. London: Collins, 1961, p. 9.

14 — Atkinson, Quentin D. "Origin of language," *Science*, Vol. 332 (6027), 2011, pp. 281–28.

15 — Johanson, Donald C. and Wong, Kate. *Lucy's Legacy*. New York: Crown Publishing, 2009.

16 — Dart, R. "Australopithecus africanus. The man-ape of South Africa," *Nature*, Vol. 115, 1925, pp. 195–199; Dart, R. *Adventures with the Missing Link*. Philadelphia: The Institutes Press, 1967.

17 — Wilford, John Nobel. "A New Ancestor Redraws the Human Family Tree," *International Herald Tribune*, Friday, October 2, 2009, pp.1, 4; Jamie Shreeve, Jamie. "The Evolutionary Road," *National Geographic*, 218 (1), 2010, pp. 34–67.

18 — Tirrell, M. "Wandering 9-Year-Old Stumbles Upon Unknown Human Ancestor in South Africa," *Bloomberg*, April 8, 2010.

19 — "Butchering dinner 3.4 million years ago," *Nature News*, August 11, 2010.

20 — McGrew, W.C., Baldwin, P.J., Marchant, L.F., Pruetz, J.D., Scott, S.E. and Tutin, C.E.G. "Ethoarchaeology and elementary technology of unhabituated wild chimpanzees at Assirik, Senegal," *Paleoanthropology* 1, 2003, pp. 1–20.

21 — Baumeister, Roy F. and Vohs, Kathleen D. "Sexual Economics: Sex as Female Resource for Social Exchange in Heterosexual Interactions," *Personality and Social Psychology Review*, Vol. 8, (4), 2004, 339–363; Hawkes, Kristen, O'Connell, J.F. and Coxworth, J.E. "Family Provisioning is not the only Reason Men Hunt," *Current Anthropology*, 51 (2), 2010, 259–264.

22 — Vaillant, John. *The Tiger: A True Story of Vengeance and Survival*. London: Sceptre, 2010, p. 114.

23 — Pfeiffer, John E. *The Emergence of Man*. New York: Harper & Row, 1978.

24 — Goodall, Jane. *The Chimpanzees of Gombe: Patterns of Behavior*. Cambridge, Massachusetts: Harvard University Press, 1986.

25 — Goodall, Jane. *The Chimpanzees of Gombe: Patterns of Behavior*. Cambridge, Massachusetts: Harvard University Press, 1986; Pruetz, Jill D. and Bertolani, Paco. "Savannah Chimpanzees, Pan troglodytes verus, Hunt with Tools," *Current Biology*, Vol. 17, 2007, pp. 412–417.

26 — Smith, David Livingston. *The Most Dangerous Animal: Human Nature and the Origins of War*. New York: St Martin's Griffin, 2007, p. 24.

27 — Bednarik, Robert G. "The First Stirrings of Creation," *UNESCO Courier*, April, 51(4), 1998, p. 4; Bower, B. "French Cave yields Stone Age Art Gallery," *Science News*, 147(4), 1995, p. 52.

28 — Brise, Gabriel. "Medieval hunting scenes: Illuminated manuscripts," in *The Hunting Book* by Gaston Phoebus, Paris: Miller Graphics, 1978.

29 — Kellert, Stephen. "Attitudes and Characteristics of Hunters and Antihunters," *Transactions of the Forty-third North American Wildlife and Natural Resources Conference*, 1978, pp. 412–423.

30 — Emerson, Ralph Waldo. *Nature and Selected Essays*. New York: Penguin Classics, 1982, pp. 38–39.

*How much more game he will see who
carries a gun, i.e. who goes to see it!
Though you roam the woods all your
days, you never will see by chance what
he sees who goes on purpose to see it. One
gets his living by shooting woodcocks;
most never see one in their lives.*
　　—Henry David Thoreau,
　　*The Journals of Henry
　　D. Thoreau, Vol. 8*

*No one but he who has partaken thereof
can understand the keen delight of
hunting in lonely lands. For him is the
joy of the horse well-ridden and the
rifle well-held; for him the long days of
toil and hardship, resolutely endured,
and crowned at the end with triumph.
In after years there shall come forever
to his mind the memory of endless
prairies shimmering in the bright sun of
snow-clad wastes lying desolate under
gray skies; of the melancholy marshes;
of the rush of mighty rivers; of the
breath of evergreen forest in summer;
of the crooning of ice-armored pines
at the touch of the winds of winter;
of cataracts roaring between hoary
mountain masses; of all the numerable
sights and sounds of the wilderness; of
the immensity and mystery; and of the
silences that brood in its still depths.*
　　—Theodore Roosevelt,
　　The Wilderness Hunter

*Alone far in the wilderness
and mountains I hunt,
Wandering amazed at my
own lightness and glee,
In the late afternoon choosing a
safe spot to pass the night,
Kindling a fire and broiling
the fresh-kill'd game,
Falling asleep on the gather'd leaves
with my dog and gun by my side.*
　　—Walt Whitman,
　　Song of Myself

*After the first week in Alaska I began to
realize that the object of sheep hunting
was to intentionally deprive yourself
of all the comforts of normal life.*
　　—Pam Houston,
　　Cowboys Are My Weakness

THE TRAIL LESS TRAVELED

In the previous chapter, I described how the ability to hunt played a pivotal role in *Homo sapiens'* development. Hunting had a great impact on the evolution of humankind; it came to define our identity and to determine how we relate to the world. Hunting provided us with a sense of meaning and created the foundation of concepts such as family structure, social organization, social movements, and social systems.

I am aware that, however I present it, people who oppose hunting are likely to abhor the idea that hunters seem to respond to a deep-seated, archaic call (a predisposition we all possess) that has been handed down to us by our prehistoric ancestors. Yet whether we like it or not, and whether we practice it or not, hunting is hardwired into our collective identity. Although memory traces of our lingering "hunting instinct" are buried deep in our unconscious, they are easily revived—the content of our dreams and fantasies is a vivid reminder of this. And when we are put in a wilderness situation, these archaic memories and instincts return rapidly. The novelist and hunter Robert Ruark described this phenomenon:

> "The hunter's horn sounds early for some. For some unfortunates, imprisoned by city sidewalks and sentenced to a cement jungle more horrifying than anything to be found in Tanganyika, the horn of the hunter never winds at all. But deep in the guts of most men is buried the involuntary

response to the hunter's horn, a prickle of the nape hairs, an acceleration of the pulse, an atavistic memory of his forefathers, who killed first with stone, and then with club, and then with a spear, and then with a bow, and then with a gun, and finally with formulae. How meek the man is of no importance, somewhere in the pigeon chest of the clerk is still the vestigial remnant of the hunter's heart; somewhere in the nostrils the half-forgotten smell of blood. There is no man with such impoverishment of imagination that at some time he had not wondered how he would handle himself if a lion broke loose from a zoo and he were forced to face him without the protection of bars or handy, climbable trees."[31]

Strange as it may sound, when I am hunting I can imagine how our Paleolithic ancestors would have felt in those ancient days; I find myself in another world as the primitive in me awakens, a world of daydreams, fantasies, illusions, imagination, and passion. These sensations are approximations of what I felt during the games I played as a child, when I entered a transitional space—a place of make-belief, a twilight zone between reality and fantasy,[32] and engaged in a fanciful pretense dominated by the primitive in me. In my imagination I went to a place where, like my early Paleolithic ancestors, I was the ultimate predator. In these wild places of my mind, I would stalk lions, leopards, tigers, or bears. All my senses were on high alert. The predator in me, conjured by hard-wired, prehistoric memories, would return.

Perhaps it is thus unsurprising that, when I hunt, I feel as though I am participating in an ancient sacrament—a conscious and unconscious attempt to reach out to the primitive part within me. A salient part of the hunting avocation is its ritualistic elements, pregnant with overt and covert meaning. This also explains why I do not kill for the joy of killing, a common accusation made by anti-hunters. In fact, it is quite the reverse: every true hunter feels remorse when taking the life of an animal.

I hunt to participate in the timeless dance of life and death between the hunter and the hunted. Hunting is fraught with symbolism. It enables a fusion of inner and outer reality; it makes me feel truly alive, and part of the mystical, ecological cycle of life. I can imagine how my Paleolithic ancestors felt stalking their prey—or their fear of themselves being the prey, of being stalked by a dangerous predator. But hunting is not merely evolutionary memories in action. The fog covering all these impressions is the aesthetic appreciation of being in the wilderness.

Hunting in the wilderness gives joy and meaning to my life. I have eidetic memories of the pleasure of looking at African sunsets, of hearing the mating song of woodcocks during a Siberian spring, of observing the dance of black cocks in the Austrian heather, of seeing a mass of butterflies dancing at a saltlick in the jungle of Central Africa, or of spotting a band of Marco Polo sheep high in the mountains of the Pamir.

City dwellers may find it strange, but hunting and fishing are among my experiences of the sublime. For me, the strange tension between what is desirable and what is threatening in nature creates a feeling of unity, a sense of being connected to wild places. And in those wild places, I often arrive at metaphysical insights about the meaning of life, the human condition, and my totally insignificant place in the universe. I also discover different, creative ways of looking at things. From this perspective, hunting is also an anti-depressant—a way of overcoming the difficulty of dealing with the fact of our transitory existence—and is intimately woven with a love for the wilderness. The Russian novelist Ivan Turgenev, in *Sketches from a Hunter's Album*, described these feelings very poetically:

> "Has anyone save a hunter experienced the delight of wandering through bushes at dawn? Your feet leave green imprints in grass that is heavy and white with dew. You push aside wet bushes—the warm scent accumulated in the night almost smothers you; the air is impregnated with the fresh bitter-sweet fragrance of wormwood, the honeyed scent of buckwheat and clover. Far off an oak forest rises like a wall, shining purple in the sunshine; the air is still fresh, but the coming heat can already be felt..."[33]

I strongly subscribe to Turgenev's idea of nature, with its sense of measure and harmony, and its obedience to eternal laws. Nature has its own logic; it moves at its own pace; it takes what belongs to it; and despite what urban dwellers might argue to the contrary, *Homo sapiens* is an intricate part of the natural cycle of life. Our ease with nature constitutes an essential part of our true self—the more spontaneous, original part. For Turgenev (and for me), hunting always seems to be a means to an end, a way to understand nature better, to arrive at a sense of community with the world around us, and to feel at one with wild animals and their environment.

I, like Turgenev, want this communion with nature for myself. It is not a spectator sport; I'm not interested in being a detached observer, watching a nature program on my television, computer, iPhone or iPad. I want to be part of it in the flesh. Whether I am predator or prey, I want to be part of the cycle of life, the context in which experiences are deepest and emotions most intense.

I have tried the more sublimatory activities related to hunting but they are pale and stale. When I am hunting, whether it's for pheasant, duck, antelope, or dangerous game like cape buffalo, my senses sharpen. I feel more alert; I am totally focused on what I plan to do. It is just not the same with a camera in my hand instead of a gun.

But how can I explain these feelings to people who have never had these experiences? Most people acquire a romantic sense of nature from wildlife programs on television; but being really immersed in nature as a hunter gives you a totally different perspective from the rose-colored, two-dimensional view you absorb from the comfort of your sofa.

In reality, nature makes many people who are born and raised in urban centers distinctly uneasy. Literature, drama, opera, cinema, and paintings provide endless examples of people caught out or lost in the dark in wild places, their mind playing tricks, imagining endless, unnamed, horrors and threats, encouraged by unfamiliar sights, sounds, and smells. In contrast, people brought up in the country are less susceptible; although they, too, are aware of the threats implicit in nature, they are more robust in the outdoors.

I came of age in the countryside, and was a hunter from childhood, which I believe gave me a real sense of the forces of nature. For some reason, one that I cannot completely explain even to myself, when I hunt I assume an identity that I sense brings me closer to my prehistoric roots. I re-discover my "nature intelligence." But there is no equally spontaneous eagerness to shed blood. The idea of killing is far from my thoughts. I am not driven by the wish to spoil or destroy; quite the opposite. I hunt for the joy of living, to search for meaning, to be part of the cycle of life, to affirm my connection to the land. Hunting helps me to acknowledge and work through all that is primitive about me. It is my way of feeling whole. It helps me to accept my archaic roots, to recognize the aggression within me, and to reconnect with my inherent nature intelligence.

These may seem very personal statements but I believe they are applicable to our species, *Homo sapiens*, as a whole. As far as the "kill" is concerned, I always temper my killing out of respect for the game that I am pursuing. I see the animal I am after not merely as something to possess, but also as a living creature that should be honored, and that deserves respect in life and in death. Theodore Roosevelt, US President (1901–1909), hunter, outdoor romantic, and eminent conservationist concurred:

"In hunting, the finding and killing of the game is after all but a part of the whole. The free, self-reliant, adventurous life, with its rugged and stalwart democracy; the wild surroundings, the grand beauty of the scenery, the chance to study the ways and habits of the woodland creatures—all these unite to give to the career of the wilderness hunter its peculiar charm... The wilderness hunter must not only show skill in the use of the rifle and in finding and approaching game, but he must also show the qualities of hardihood, self-reliance, and resolution for effectively grappling with his wild surroundings. The fact that the hunter needs the game, both for its meat and for its hide, undoubtedly adds a zest to the pursuit."[34]

Woodcraft

I view woodcraft as the art of finding my way in the wilderness, the ability to survive against all odds, knowing how to use nature's bounty. The naturalist and hunter Vladimir Arseniev, whom I mentioned earlier, wrote, "He who has dealings with nature and wishes to enjoy her gifts must learn to commune with her even when she is not in a caressing mood."[35] Some "salon" wilderness dreamers don't realize that wild places can be very dangerous. I have encountered many of these dreamers in the north of Canada or Alaska, all hoping to carve a living out of this wild country. But the wilderness is no Garden of Eden. It can be a thoroughly thorny place and casual visitors better beware. It is exceedingly difficult to find the food you need to survive in wild places.

One man who failed to realize that nature can be a fearful place was Christopher Johnson McCandless, who grew up in an affluent suburb of Washington DC. McCandless dreamt of making an "Alaskan Odyssey," living off the land, far away from civilization. Jon Krakauer's book *Into the Wild* (later made into a movie) is an excellent portrayal of the difficulties encountered by someone who tries to live off the land without really understanding what that implies.[36] In this case, the unfortunate McCandless decided to hike into the Alaskan wilderness with little food and equipment, hoping to live the simple life. His city background had provided him with no woodcraft or other survival skills, and he resisted the advice of others who recognized that he had no sense of the reality of the Alaskan environment. It added up to a disastrous equation. Almost four months after McCandless entered the wilderness, he died of starvation. He was too much a product of the asphalt jungle, and did not have even the most rudimentary woodcraft skills.

In the *pas de deux* between hunter and hunted, I do not mind being outwitted and out-maneuvered by my quarry. Failing at the end of the day is fine; there always will be another day. As I like to reiterate, the outcome of the hunt should never be a certainty; if it is, it is unethical and shouldn't be called hunting. There needs to be fair chase. I also believe in sustainability, and view myself as a steward of the land and its resources. We need to strive to create continuity. As the dominant species on our planet, we should make every effort to do the least harm.

In his highly influential book, *A Sand County Almanac*, the hunter and conservationist Aldo Leopold reflects on the mystique of hunting. Here, he laconically describes how not getting the quarry (in this case a grouse) didn't decrease his enjoyment of hunting:

"My dog, by the way, thinks I have much to learn about partridges, and, being a professional naturalist, I agree. He persists in tutoring me with the calm patience of a professor of logic, in the art of drawing deductions from an educated nose. I delight in seeing him deduce a conclusion, in the form of a point, from data that are obvious to him but speculative to my unaided eye. Perhaps he hopes his dull pupil will one day learn to smell.

Like other dull pupils, I know when the professor is right, even though I do not know why. I check my gun and walk in. Like any good professor, the dog never laughs when I miss, which is often. He gives me one look, and proceeds up the stream in quest for another grouse."[37]

⊣

Hunting and identity

Much of hunting is a strictly personal, subjective experience, making the interpretation of its inner meaning and significance to non-hunters, and even to fellow hunters, fraught with difficulties. To me, hunting is more than a casual pastime. Hunting and fishing are passions that make up a large part of who I am. And as I stated earlier, hunting has become one of my ways of communicating with nature. The difference, however, with other forms of immersion with nature (including fishing, where there is a practice of "catch and release") is its finality. Its cut-and-tried nature gives it greater gravity. Whenever we deal with themes of life and death, in any context, the impact is much more intense. Having the choice between life and death is highly significant.

Looking back over the many years I have been hunting, the times when I have decided to pull the trigger have been far fewer than the opportunities I have had to do so during the hunt. Deciding not to shoot is an interesting test of character. I remember once sitting in a blind in a pine forest in eastern France. It was the beginning of the day and the sun was making an effort to penetrate the haze that enveloped the trees. Suddenly, from nowhere, almost gliding out of the fog, a majestic red stag appeared. I was struck with a sense of awe. I had the stag in the cross hairs of the scope on my rifle, but I lowered my gun and watched, as the animal seemed slowly to evaporate into the mist. How often has a bear, deer, moose, or chamois come close, and I merely admired the animal?

People who do not hunt or know little about hunting may find it difficult to understand the point I am making. How can I explain the contradiction between truly appreciating wild, living things, but being prepared to kill them at the same time? How to explain this great ambivalence that occupies the inner world of fair chase hunters? And how can I convey the thrill of the hunt? Experiential activities are always hard to understand for people who have never participated in them. It's like trying to explain colors to a blind person, or the Internet to a tribesman in the jungles of Brazil.

My non-hunting friends have asked me numerous times, why not let the animals live? Why kill what you love? Why don't you just carry a camera instead of a gun? They cannot understand (especially given the type of work I do), why "blood sports" like hunting and fishing interest me. They believe that taking photographs of animals would be as good, or even be a much healthier approach to communicating with nature. But going into the wilds merely to take pictures is an experience of a very different magnitude from hunting. And I truly know; I have done it. Taking photographs does not evoke the same emotional experience. It does not have the same degree of gravitas—at least for me. Moreover (and as an aside), photo safaris are harder on the land and animals than we might think. As a specialist on the matter, Margaret Kinnaird of the Mpala Research Center and Wildlife Foundation, says: "The idea that you can replace a profitable cropping program with ecotourism is absolutely false."[38]

Hunters make life and death decisions; they make a commitment. Photographers remain much more detached. To me, taking photographs feels like playing poker with plastic chips, gambling without real money. What makes all the difference is having the potential to throw the dice of life and death. Death needs to be an intrinsic part of the age-old ritual of the hunt, and its natural end—a proof of conquest and skill. Carrying a gun instead of a camera means that I am part of the play. I am not merely an observer, I become one of the actors. And once I have decided to aim my rifle or shotgun and pull the trigger, I know that there is no going back. Facing this kind of dilemma creates an

unusual kind of suspense, composed of anxiety, tension, and suspension of disbelief. Hunting, as I have stressed is not merely killing; but if you take away the ability to kill, you take automatically away most of the enjoyment of hunting.

I have described how the hunting avocation evokes symbolic associations with our evolutionary and contemporary nature; yet there is the physical element as well. The meat, horns, and hide of the animals I kill are an accordant reminder to me of having been successful in the hunt. Their use, in some kind of "animistic" (almost religious) way, can be viewed as a sign of respect for a worthy opponent in this game of life and death. In particular, when the quarry has been difficult to obtain—in pitting the skills of woodcraft and marksmanship against the animal's ingenious survival skills—I feel a sense of accomplishment, a reaffirmation of a sense of self. Later, seeing and touching the horns and hides refresh these memories.

Unheimlich

We live and act in the familiar, or *"Heimlich."* Hunting is *"unheimlich,"* that is to say that it evokes the uncanny, uncomfortably strange feeling that something is both familiar and foreign at the same time. I am sure I transmit this *"unheimlich"* quality to others, who are troubled by the association between hunting and death. During the hunt, the true hunter is engaged in a subliminal dialogue with the quarry. And perhaps this secret dialogue is my way of dealing with my ambivalence about death.

We all find it very hard time to accept the fact and inevitability of death. We know, we don't know, we don't know what we don't know, and we don't want to know what it is all about. The act of killing that accompanies the hunt can be seen as a way to triumph momentarily over death. Thus hunting becomes a way of dealing with themes that were once *"heimlich"* (familiar) but also *"unheimlich"* (uncanny), experiences pertaining to our Paleolithic heritage.

The desire to hunt can also be seen as an instance of inverse bonding between our aggressive disposition and our affectionate tendencies, an exploration of the mysterious relationship between sex and aggression. Through hunting, however, feelings of aggression and attraction attain a clarity not muddled or distorted by the forces of repression or sublimation. Perhaps this goes some way toward explaining how I can kill the things I love. Hunting becomes a transcendent communion between man and beast—an attempt to rebel against death through its administration—a communion with high stakes.

The risks attached to this game of life and death fill me with a sense of mystery, rapture, and wonder. I can imagine that it is a state of mind that duelists may have recognized, just before the duel took place, or (in a very different context) that of a matador facing a bull. The matador loves the bull, but will also try to kill it (or vice versa). Like in a duel, the stakes are high. Would the *faena*—the final act of the bullfight—attain its full dignity if the bull did not die? Having real "chips" in the game is what makes a bull fight such a deeply emotional and even disturbing experience. Like the matador, the hunter has a "moment of truth." Strangely, it is the presence of death in this age-old ritual of hunter and prey that makes us feel truly alive; the contrast has to be part of the experience. The defining part of the hunt—that an animal may die or that you might die yourself (as has almost happened to me on a number of occasions in Alaska, Kamchatka, Africa, and even Europe)—creates very powerful feelings. There can be no real comparison between having your finger on the trigger of a rifle or on the button of a camera.

We can all understand the pleasure, excitement, and attraction of unpredictability and suspense. After all, why do we take the time to read an entire novel instead of going straight to the back to see how it ends? Why do millions of us watch football games, rather than look at the results later in the newspaper? A major part of the thrill of participating in these activities is the suspense, the excitement of not knowing the outcome. In a soccer match, what

we enjoy most are the moments when the ball is in the air and the hero's fate remains uncertain. We are easily enthralled by the suspense that comes with uncertainty.

This desire to surmount life's uncertainties—to play with the dice of life and death—may be a derivative of our evolutionary biological development, part of our genetic make-up. It may be an archaic form of behavior that arose with our ancestral predecessors. Perhaps the willingness to take risks was a signal to members of the opposite sex of an individual's bravery; perhaps it gave that particular person an advantage in the mating game. Engaging in risky behavior may have been a way of communicating superior skills and abilities; most importantly, of being a better provider. Of course, in taking risks—hunting for meat—our ancestors were playing for high stakes. From an evolutionary point of view, they could lose out big time with the opposite sex (and produce no offspring), or they could win big, in fitness terms, and produce many offsprings with several different partners.

The kill

I have been trying to explain that hunting is a journey. The destination, the kill, is just a sideshow; like life, most of the enjoyment comes from the journey. But, as I have stressed, if we remove the ability to kill, we take away much of the special nature of the activity. Although the kill bothers me, it does not diminish the primitive sense of triumph I feel after the kill. As the philosopher Ortega y Gasset noted:

> "To the sportsman the death of the game is not what interests him; that is not his purpose. What interests him is everything that he had to do to achieve that death— that is, the hunt. Therefore what was before only a means to an end is now an end in itself. Death is essential because without it there is no authentic hunting: the killing of the animal is the natural end of the hunt and the goal of hunting itself, not of the hunter. The hunter seeks this death because it is no less than the sign of reality for the whole hunting process. To sum up, one does not hunt in order to kill; on the contrary, one kills in order to have hunted."[39]

But should human beings have this power over life and death? Should the hunter have the power to make final judgments? Aren't hunters involved in repeated massacres of the innocents? Isn't hunting a primitive response by emotionally crippled human beings unready to fully accept the responsibilities of contemporary society? Isn't hunting a sort of retro-machismo, flaunted by bearskin rugs on floors and walls bristling with antlers?

These are the kinds of questions that can be expected in our increasingly urbanized society, and they are not always easy to answer. Taking another perspective, I could also ask: are people who eat meat insensitive individuals who fail to realize that for every steak or chicken wing, a living creature has to be killed? I don't think so. There is a basic truth here: if we are to live, something has to die. But having said all this, another important truth remains for me: the act of taking a life should always be accompanied by a twinge of uneasiness.

⌐

A hunter's trajectory

Another question, often posed by people who question or are mildly amused by my desire to go to the wild, is whether hunting isn't really a retro-activity that we should have out-grown in our post-modern society? The naturalist and philosopher Henry David Thoreau (no stranger to hunting) thought that, from an evolutionary point of view, people would ultimately outgrow the need to hunt. Over time, Thoreau came to view hunting as a rather regressive experience, comparing his compulsion to hunt with his sexual drive, both of which he felt belonged to the lower orders of creation.[40] I must admit that I have never seen it this way.

From my earliest years I have been a keen observer of flora and fauna, and I have always been fascinated by the behavior of insects, fish, birds, amphibians, and animals. I have even dabbled (and still do) in lepidopterology (butterfly collection). I often bring my butterfly net along on hunting trips, to the great amusement of the locals (the rain forests of Central Africa or Asia are exceptional areas for success).

I have explained that, for me, hunting is a logical extension of my interest in wildlife and nature. But it is also part of my heritage—as I had mentioned before, it was my father's brother, Jaap, who introduced me to the more formal aspects of hunting, which was his life's passion. My father also hunted but was not as keen as my uncle; hunting had a more social value for him. However, the chance to get closer to my father was an important incentive for me to take up hunting. We had few opportunities to see him, as my brother and I lived with my mother after our parents divorced when I was only five years old. My brother Florian never showed any interest in hunting, which I have often regretted. Now we have reached another stage in life, and it could have been a powerful means of spending more time together.

I grew up in the countryside, and from a very young age I saw hunters doing what hunters do, making hunting seem a normal and very desirable pursuit (at least to me). I was always acutely aware where meat and fish came from; I knew they didn't grow on trees, wrapped in plastic bags. I knew what needed to be done to have a steak or a fish on our plates. We lived close to farms and by the sea and I saw farmers slaughtering their livestock, and fishermen killing fish, and many of the people I knew were hunters and fishermen. At the time I was growing up, hunting was an old tradition, even in an increasingly urbanized country like Holland.

⌐

Origins

My first actual encounter with hunters must have been when I was about seven years old. I was playing in the fields of heather and woodland that surrounded our house outside a small village, when I heard shots. Very soon after, a hunting dog came running by at full speed, followed a little bit later by two hunters. One of the hunters had wounded a hare, and the dog was trying to retrieve it. The dog flushed the hare one more time, and one more shot was heard. I saw the dog retrieve the dead hare, and take it to the two hunters, and I was curious, so ran up to get a closer look. There was a moment of silence when the two hunters and I all looked at the still body of the dead hare. Without anything being said, I understood that we were paying homage to the animal, to the end of this hunt. It was a good example of the feelings experienced by hunters engaged in fair chase. They had gone to great lengths to recuperate the hare. I realize now that their silence suggested a last respect, a final greeting. It was a ritual pertaining to death, remorse, and farewell. Many decades have passed, but I still retain a very strong memory of that episode. I can easily recall the specific scene of the hunters and their prey. I strongly believe that at that moment I understood their sense of ambivalence at having made a decision about life and death.

My uncle Jaap was renowned in Dutch hunting circles. Each time I saw him, he would tell me about his latest hunting exploits, recounting truly fascinating stories. I think he liked having such a very receptive audience—Uncle Jaap was no stranger to narcissism. Once, for my birthday, he gave me an air gun, a spontaneous gift to the son he had never had. My mother, with her strong memories of World War II and fear of any kind of weapons, promptly confiscated it. But I never stopped thinking about that gun. I managed to sublimate this setback by saving enough money to buy a Sami hunting knife (the kind traditionally used by the Lapps). I can still remember the terrible row when my mother discovered and confiscated my knife. As a child, I was given to outbursts of anger. The Dutch have a nice term for that kind of child: "*drift kikker,*" literally meaning "quick-tempered frog." Although I have become better at controlling my temper, aspects of it are still very alive within me.

As I didn't have a rifle or knife, the next best thing was to create surrogate weapons in make-believe games. Rifles started to play an important role in my inner world. I wanted more than anything to be an explorer and a rifle would be one of the essential accessories I would need. As a child, I was deeply influenced by the novels of the German author Karl May, who wrote travel and adventure stories and became one of the world's all-time best-selling fiction writers. May wrote about American Indians in the Old West and Desert Arabs. For the novels he set in North America, he created the characters of Winnetou, the wise chief of the Apache Tribe, and Old Shatterhand, the author's alter ego and Winnetou's white blood brother. Winnetou rode a horse called Iltschi (Wind) and had a famous rifle called the *Silberbüchse* (the Silver Gun), a double-barreled rifle whose stock and butt were decorated with silver studs. It was easy for me to enter Karl May's world, reading the stories of his hero's adventures time and time again. (I learned only later that Karl May himself must have had a very rich fantasy life, as he did not set a foot in America until most of these stories had been written.)

Influenced by these stories about cowboys and Indians, and the importance of the hunt in their lives—but having no rifle—I tried to capture animals by building what I thought a trap would look like. I found the prototype of my trap in a Donald Duck magazine—not exactly the most reliable source for such a construction. Unfortunately, I never had much of a mechanical bent, and that, combined with my cartoon style guide, meant my traps were amateurish, to say the least. I put a large carrot in one of these contraptions, hoping to attract a squirrel, hare, or rabbit. In bed that night, I fantasized excitedly about success, despite my non-existent trapping skills. Unfortunately, no animal was ever dumb enough to step into one of the phantasmagoric creations that I (and Disney) imagined an animal trap would look like.

As I mentioned earlier, we all dwell at times in that transitional space between fantasy and reality—a place of make-believe where everything might be possible. The Karl May stories and hunting became part of this make-believe world. It was not too much of a stretch to believe I was a hunter-explorer, roaming wild places as I played in the woods, meadows and fields of heather close to home. I built more traps to catch animals; I made dams in the little stream and pond close to our house to encircle fish. Although success was rare, I was unstoppable. But my successes didn't go beyond the capture of a few sticklebacks, frogs, lizards, and salamanders, which were duly put in the pond at the back of our house. Later, when we moved to the coast of Holland,

I played with children of my own age in the sand dunes that surrounded the village. There, as a teenager, I would regularly find snares set for rabbits by the local poachers. Once, I found a live rabbit in one of the snares; it was unharmed and I set it free.

My fascination with explorers and hunters continued as I grew older, transplanting me to imaginary, far away places where I, like a Walter Mitty, was the star in exciting hunting adventures. I would find myself in tropical jungles, pursuing dangerous animals like tigers, leopards, lions, buffalos, rhinoceros, and elephants. I would trek through the tundra after bears, wolves, and caribou. Or I would climb mountains in India, Iran, Tajikistan, Kazakhstan, Afghanistan, Outer Mongolia, Australia, or New Zealand, going after wild goats and sheep, endangering my life while hanging from steep cliffs. I would have very different encounters than the more urbanized ones of my daily life.

How passionately I wished, at the time, that these fantasies would turn into reality! Would there ever come a time when I would be able to really act them out? Fantasy or reality, these childhood activities were the basis for my becoming a hunter—and something of an explorer. And I am sure that my story isn't very different from that of many other people who are passionate about exploration, hunting, and fishing.

My passion for hunting fish and game was a logical extension of the kind of hunter-gatherer mindset I was developing. I was born during World War II, and food had been scarce when I was very small. I overheard many of my mother's stories about the infamous winter of 1944 when there was almost nothing to eat in Holland. The Nazis occupying the country had taken most of the food away. My mother had grown up in Germany during the period of hyperinflation that followed World War I, when there was never enough food in the house. As a result, the rule in our house was that you ate what you "caught." Food always had a special quality. I can still hear my mother's voice in the background telling tales of how difficult it was to find food during the war—and at other times. She would say, if I was reluctant to clear my plate, "Think about all these starving people…." This tune is still resonates with me.

Predictably, gathering the bounty of the forests and lakes—berries, wild mushrooms, and fish—was highly appreciated, particularly by my mother. I grew up with a conviction that taking and eating game (and fish) was an essential part of growing up into a well-rounded individual. The excitement I felt when finding a grove with edible mushrooms (chanterelles, parasol mushrooms, meadow champions, or various boletus), I would be able to bring something home to my mother and make her happy, is hard to describe. My personal sense of triumph at bringing mushrooms, berries, or fish to my mother would probably have been familiar to the earliest hunters: it must have been very exciting to bring something back from the forest or lake, and ask for it to be cooked. My mother always gave an enthusiastic reception to whatever I brought; she was certainly a great cheerleader in that respect. Every time I come home with game today, that old memory is still very much with me.

At times, my mother, brother, and I would go out into the forest together. It was our mother who first taught us about edible berries and mushrooms, fish, and game. I firmly believe that this upbringing contributed to my attitude to nature and helped me to develop a deeper, closer relationship with the natural world.

Unsurprisingly, biology turned out to be my favorite subject at school. I was a superstar in the subject. The biology teacher told me once that to mark me fairly, he would have to give me 12 out of 10. Otherwise, most of the other children in the class would fail. I sometimes wonder what would have happened if I had studied biology at university. I would probably have spent most of my life in wild places, studying animals. But my parents did not see biology as a viable career option, although they never said so explicitly. Once I understood that my primary interest was not seen as economically viable, hunting turned into a sideshow, an avocation, to harness my interest in the natural world.

Of course, like most future hunters, I finally managed to save sufficient money to buy an air gun. My mother was no happier about this one than she had been about Uncle Jaap's present. Her experiences in World War II, during which she took in and cared for many fugitives, haunted her for the rest of her life. She was always very proud of the fact that she had been honored by the State of Israel as a "righteous gentile," the title given to non-Jews who risked their lives to save Jews during the Holocaust.

In hindsight, my mother may have been right to forbid me having an air gun at such a young age. In the fatherless house where I grew up, I may have been too excitable a boy. But it is often the case that we covet what is forbidden. As I grew older, it became more difficult for my mother to stop me. The first victim of the air gun was a sparrow. When I walked over to the dead bird, touched its soft feathers, and felt its warmth, I was filled with a feeling of sadness. I had taken a life for no purpose at all. After that experience, the main purpose of the air rifle became target practice.

I had a lot to learn about the hunting game. Several years later I found myself on a small sailing boat with my childhood friend Erik on a lake near the village of Vinkeveen. We had been eying the large number of mallards that were everywhere on the water. As our financial resources were limited, and our food supply basic (cans of sardines were the staple), cooking a duck seemed to us as the height of luxury. We fantasized about eating duck à l'orange. But getting a duck (shooting one without a hunting license was illegal) was a different matter altogether. Looking at the lay of the land (or rather the lay of the lake), the two of us made a plan. We would try to approach one of the ducks stealthily very early in the morning before the lake attracted any tourists. The plan was that I would place myself in the front hatch of the boat with my air gun until we came within shooting range. At the right moment I would dispatch one of them.

Early the next day, before there was any movement on the lake, we (the two future Nimrods) set out, trying to keep out of sight of the many pleasure boats anchored in the reeds. Using the outboard motor, we moved closer to a number of unsuspecting mallards. I was ready for the hunt. When I thought that we were close enough, I aimed and (amazingly) hit one of the ducks. But what followed was unforeseen. Instead of having a dead bird for our projected duck à l'orange feast, we found ourselves in the middle of a duck circus. Silencing a wounded duck, which was making an enormous racket, flapping its wings on the water, encouraged by the quacking from its (no longer so close) companions, was anything but easy. We panicked, fearing that the duck row would wake up everyone on the lake and that we would be caught. Although I am usually the last person to welcome cold water, this time—without hesitation—I jumped overboard to swim to the duck, and to silence it. Surprisingly, despite being a poor swimmer, I managed to get hold of the duck. But what was I going to do with this quacking bird now? I made a valiant effort to drown it. But that too was far from easy. Ducks are not that easily drowned—people are. The duck was doing a much better job in the water than I was. Clearly, ducks are much better at holding their breath under water than humans. But there was one comfort. At least, under water, the duck didn't quack. The spectacle continued for a while as—busily engaged in this endgame—I eyed the neighborhood anxiously, fearful of bystanders who might cause trouble. I finally managed to put the duck out of its misery. The next step was to prepare our long-awaited meal.

We moored the sailing boat at a quiet place inside the reeds where I could pluck the bird. I put its feathers in a bag, added a stone, and let the debris sink to the bottom. We didn't want to leave any evidence of our crime. Finally, we could relax and prepare the infamous duck *à l'orange*—a challenge, given the very elementary utensils to be found on the boat. Unfortunately, while I was busily preparing the duck in a small frying pan, the weighted bag—meant to sink to the bottom—burst without warning, and all the feathers came up, floating on the surface. The evidence of our crime was clearly visible all around. The only thing we could think to do was to start the outboard engine and make an extremely rapid exit. There was too much evidence of our duck adventure drifting about. We managed to get away without being caught. The duck was rather tough, and nothing like how we had imagined it would taste. I told myself, rather unnecessarily, never to do anything like that again, however appetizing fantasy ducks may look. It was my only poaching adventure, although in my defense I should add that a considerable amount of water on the lake was owned or leased by my father for its hunting rights. Looking back now, I realize that my 'poaching adventure' must have occurred on home waters.

Learning the ropes

While my amateurish entry into hunting taught me something about duck behavior, I deepened my understanding of animal behavior (having had an early start) by accompanying my uncle and later my father as a beater when they went to hunt. I spent many hours with my uncle, acting as a "bearer" for the game he had shot. And he was a spectacular shot—one of the best in the country, attested to by the many prizes he won at shooting contests. Uncle Jaap was really the person who taught me the basics of hunting. He taught me about the behavior of animals, and, very importantly, the rules of the game—the etiquette I had to respect while hunting—and gun safety. Uncle Jaap was quite a stickler for the ethics of hunting. Given his pleasure as having me as "his" bearer, I do wonder, at times, whether, consciously or unconsciously, he may have stretched my time in that role. In hindsight, he could have given me permission to carry a gun much sooner. The length of my apprenticeship was quite exceptional for the customs of the time.

Apart from wandering through forests and fields with gun and dog, these hunts in Holland were often "shoots" for small game such as pheasants, Hungarian partridges, ducks, geese, wood pigeons, hares, and rabbits. Although I might complain about the length of my apprenticeship without a gun, the good thing about being a beater is that you are always right in the middle of the action. I would enthusiastically cry "Partout" or "Tiro," depending on whether the beast was running or flying, to warn the hunters that game was coming their way. The most exciting form of beating I experienced was participating in a wild boar drive with my uncle in the center of Holland. I still remember crawling through thick stands of snow-covered fir trees—where the wild boar liked to bed down during the day—and almost being run over by one of them. In the evening, cold and wet, and covered with snow, I felt awed looking at the many dead boar that were the result of the hunt.

Being a beater was a thorough way to learn more about the behavior of game—and the behavior of hunters. It may even have created the foundation for my interest in personality theory and leadership. How people behaved while being at "shoots" appeared to me a good predictor of their general behavior. Although it is not the kind of personality test found in serious psychology books, it taught me quite a bit about people's personality make-up—how these individuals engaged in a non-work activity would operate in their daily life. For example, there were the "shooters," hunters with very little or no respect for the game. These people were out to kill—they were not very subtle about the way they managed their aggressive disposition. I used to wonder what kind of bullies they made at work. For some, the social event was most important. These "social butterflies" used the hunt as a form of networking without having a real interest in what it stood for. Others would act out their acquisitive nature in the field. They were the "greedy ones" who were highly competitive about numbers of game shot. For these people, the overriding purpose of such "shoots" was to end up with the most animals. After a drive, they had the bad manners to spend a considerable amount of their energy counting dead game, and telling others how many they had shot. They would be sure to claim a bird as theirs if more than one person had shot at it. They also maneuvered to obtain the best places during a drive.

Another category was the "dangerous ones," hunters who handled their weapon carelessly and (out of greed or ignorance) were likely to shoot too low or too close when birds flew over. These people had very little self-control. Once the game warden (whom I knew very well) had seen them in action, they would quickly end up somewhere in "left field," where they couldn't do much damage, without even realizing what was happening.

Then there were the "gentlemen" who would pass on very good chances, and offer other hunters opportunities. My role model of a true ethical hunter was a tall, sturdy Dutch farmer, Kees Blauwboer (whom I mentioned in the Introduction). Kees Blauwboer represented to me everything that was ethical about fair hunting. He was a very good shot, but would leave most of the chances he got during these drives to others. He was very eager that the other participants should have a good time.

This long apprenticeship as a beater taught me much about ethical hunting, the standards and conduct of behavior that hunters need to follow if they want the activity to be fair chase. It is worth remembering that most hunting is unlike team sports where referees watch for infractions of the rules, and equally unlike individual sports where judges sit on the sidelines and assess points or penalties. With hunting, most of the time—collective hunts with beaters being the obvious exception—the hunter will be all alone, which necessitates the self-policing of ethical behavior. It is up to the hunter to take such a responsibility.

My uncle and other hunters would give me suggestions about what was right and what was wrong. Most important, of course, was to follow their example. There were endless temptations to deviate from the straight and the narrow. In this context, I recall what the noted naturalist Aldo Leopold wrote about his first experiences as a hunter—and the ethics instilled in him by his father:

"When my father gave me the shotgun, he said I might hunt partridges with it, but that I might not shoot them from trees. I was old enough, he said, to learn wing shooting.

My dog was good at treeing partridge, and to forego a sure shot in the trees in favor of a hopeless one at the fleeing bird was my first exercise in ethical codes. Compared to a treed partridge, the devil and his seven kingdoms was a mild temptation.

At the end of my second season of featherless partridge hunting I was walking, one day, through an aspen thicket when a big partridge rose with a roar at my left, and, towering over the aspen, crossed behind me, hell-bent for the nearest cedar swamp. It was a swinging shot of the sort the partridge hunter dreams about, and the bird tumbled dead in a shower of feathers and golden leaves."[41]

In this small passage, Leopold makes clear the need for voluntary limitations when we hunt. The hunter has to act out of personal conscience—in his case his father's admonitions loomed large. There is no mob of onlookers present to cheer him on, or disapprove. Hunters have to respect the environment in which they operate, as well as to consider the question of what is legal and what is ethical.

It is difficult to conceive a situation in hunting where committing an illegal act could be considered ethical. The inverse, however, is not only possible, but also quite common. Hunters may engage in unethical activities are nevertheless within the confines of the law. For example, they might kill a female wild boar that has young. In many countries, shooting such an animal would be legal, but would it be ethical? Unfortunately, there may be as many definitions of hunting ethics as there are hunters defining them. A cynic might define hunting ethics as "the way hunters behave when nobody is watching."

Hunting ethics are strongly tied to societal mores. Historical accounts of hunting show how hunting ethics have changed over time as society and its values have changed. Furthermore, hunting ethics are culturally determined. What is viewed as ethical in one country can be viewed as unethical in another. For example, in Holland, professional duck hunters (*"kooikers"*) once used a

very effective technique of obtaining large numbers of ducks by leading them into a funnel, encouraged by life-like decoys. A dog (called a *"kooiker"* dog) was also brought in to stimulate the fowls' curiosity and lead them far enough up the trap to enable the decoy man to cut off their retreat back to the lake or river they came from. Today, this way of capturing ducks is highly illegal in Holland. It is only used for ringing studies, to build a knowledge base for water bird movements. Another traditional practice, now illegal in my country of birth, is catching plovers (or, for that matter, any animal) with nets. In the Pyrenees of the Basque Country (the backcountry of Biarritz and Saint Jean de Luz), in October and November, the migratory wood pigeon (ring dove or *"palombe bleue"*) flies above the mountains during its annual migration from northern to southern Europe. In France, hunters use nets to catch wild pigeons—a practice that is illegal in other European countries. And I could go on.

As hunters, we need to show respect to animals and wildlife in general. This need has become more important than ever with the rise of the avocational as opposed to the subsistence hunter. I very much doubt whether Paleolithic man gave much thought to whether pushing mastodons over a cliff could be considered ethical behavior. Very few of the market hunters for bison in 19th century America are likely to have had second thoughts about the fact that they were exterminating the herds.

The transition

After long exposure as a beater (my uncle kept repeating that being a beater was the best training for becoming a hunter), I was finally allowed to acquire a hunting license and a gun. Hunting legislation is very strict in Holland, and you cannot just go to a drugstore and buy a hunting license, as you can in North America. You have to go through a grueling and challenging theoretical and practical hunting exam (and I know what I am talking about—I have done hunting exams in three different countries) that tests your knowledge of various biotopes, animals, gun safety, guns, and shooting ability. This exam is much more than merely learning about gun safety—the kind of exam I had to do when I lived in Quebec, for example. The Dutch exam deals with agriculture, forestry, flora and fauna, weaponry, and wildlife management. As most European countries don't recognize each other's hunting exams, I had to do another much less complicated exam when I later moved to France.

As well as passing a hunting exam, to be able to hunt in Holland you have to lease hunting rights from a farmer or other landowner. This tradition—a long-term proposition of stewardship of the land—is an effective antidote to the kind of greed and thoughtlessness I have often seen among North American hunters, far too many of whom have the mentality of "take as much as you can before it's used up." The European outlook creates a much more sustainable attitude as it is in the hunter's interest to keep enough breeding stock for the next season. Such legislation contributes to a more responsible ethic about land use. For example, in severe winters, hunters will do anything to help the game. In Holland, where there are regular floods and much of the land is below sea level, hunters are always the first to save game from drowning.

Finally, I had transcended the stage of being a beater. I recall that it coincided with my success in passing a major exam at the university where I was studying. Passing that specific exam had become the marker of whether or not I would be able to hunt. I had a hunting license but without land, as I didn't have the means to rent a territory, I was dependent on the kindness of strangers—in this case, my father and my uncle, both of whom had hunting territories. This meant, however, that I was dependent on their favors, and as I was the youngest retained a position in the pecking order somewhere in between hunter and beater. During beats, I would walk with the beaters, and was more than strongly advised only to shoot at game that turned back in the drive. The more senior members of the hunting party were given preferential treatment.

I still remember, like yesterday, the first game animal I shot—legally. I was walking in line with a number of beaters in a field of sugar beet in one of the polders in Holland. Holding a shotgun for the first time while hunting, I was

tensed up. Finally, after so many years of waiting, the moment of truth had arrived. I was no longer the one carrying a stick to rattle the trees or making lots of noise to push the game. I was no longer a second-class citizen. I had a real weapon in my hands. I was responsible for the safety of others. I was expected to make instant life and death decisions.

Just as I reached the middle of the beet field, a hen pheasant suddenly flew up, turning backwards. In a reflex movement, I put my gun up into the air, aimed, pulled the trigger—and the bird fell down. I still remember running to the still warm pheasant, touching its feathers, and feeling very pleased with myself. I also remember that for the rest of the day I couldn't hit a thing. I had the bird mounted and for decades it graced my mother's apartment.

From then on, I did a lot of hunting for small game in Holland. In those years—my studies at the University of Amsterdam were not very demanding—I had a lot of free time, and hunted extensively. Occasionally, during these hunts, some rarities would pop up like a fox, woodcock, or goose. I shot my first goose, sneaking up on a flock through a ditch with a few other hunters. I recall how surprised the geese were when we stuck our necks out of the ditch. I was quite sure that I killed one of them, but one of the other hunters claimed it. Since I was the lowest in the pecking order, it was better just to shut up, and let it be. I had to keep a low profile with all those seniors around.

Hunting in Holland was often a very social activity for which I feel great nostalgia. There was an enormous amount of camaraderie among the hunters. Most of the time we hunted as a group and there was a real sense of belonging. There was an intense interchange between the local beaters and hunters. Together, blocks of forests and field were beaten to get the game moving. Occasionally, however, the hunting party was made up of only a few people and a dog. Lunch, which sometimes took place in the middle of the field, made a very nice interlude, a time to recount what had happened, for spinning various "war" stories, and for telling jokes. I tended to keep quiet, ever the junior member, but I drank it all in. Many tall tales were told in the hunting cabins I visited.

My father, in particular, enjoyed the social scene, which was much more important to him than the actual hunt. And it was in the hunting hut that he exercised his culinary talents, although his cooking efforts were more gourmand than gourmet. He was famous in Dutch hunting circles for the quantity and quality of the food he served. My father only seemed to be happy when people staggered out of the door, completely stuffed.

ⲧ

Going out into the world

In 1966 I moved to North America to continue my studies at Harvard University. The environment in Cambridge was not exactly hunting-friendly but I found a few people who shared my passion. At times, there was a sense of camaraderie, but it bore no comparison to the hunting scene in Holland. In the US, there was less emphasis on small game hunting. Big game hunting was the thing and unlike the hunting I had done in Holland was a much more solitary activity.

Initially, I found many North American hunting regulations—like the obligation to wear orange—quite strange. And then there were disturbing crowd scenes. The first day I hunted in Massachusetts for small game, on the opening day of the season, I was amazed by the hustle and bustle in the field. With the American friend who had introduced me to hunting in North America, I found myself in a patch of wood where, as was explained to me later, the local game wardens had just released some pheasants. Obviously, the release of the birds must have been public knowledge, and had attracted the crowd. All of a sudden, I found myself surrounded by far too many people for my liking, all dressed in orange, who raced into the field to find *the* pheasant. Who was going to get *the* pheasant? Where was the hot spot? After a lot of commotion, a friendly pheasant flew up ("friendly" because the bird was not much of a flier). Not only was the bird slow, but it also stupidly flew directly over the line of shooters, who saluted its passage with a barrage of gunfire. After something like ten shots the bird tumbled down, to initiate an argument among the many shooters who claimed ownership. I had held back and discovered I was standing next to the local game warden, who was observing this circus intensely. I commented there were too many "sound shooters"—people shooting at anything that moved without identifying what they were aiming at. The warden agreed. I found the scene quite amusing, but decided that it was too risky for me—I could easily get shot in the field surrounded by so many trigger-happy people. Hunting had always been a more solemn event for me. Later, during my stay in the other States, I had much better, solitary experiences, hunting for snowshoe hares, grouse, and squirrels in Vermont and Maine.

My hunting bug was better dealt with when I moved to Montreal to take on a professorship at McGill University. Hunting in Holland was just for sissies compared with hunting in Canada. I hunted with a good friend, Jack, who lived in Alberta, where the daydreams of my youth began to come true. In Northern Alberta I was really in wild country, the kind of wilderness where wolves, coyotes, cougars, black and grizzly bears, mule and whitetail deer, wild sheep, mountain goats, caribou, elk, and moose roamed. Seeing some of these animals for the first time filled me with excitement and exhilaration.

Jack was an excellent hunter and (like my uncle) a fantastic shot. In hindsight, I realize that he must have been quite amused by the enthusiasm of this young man from Holland but we hit it off the moment we met. I went all over Alberta with Jack, discussing the meaning of life while we looked for places where there was game. I was very enthusiastic and my hunting excursions with Jack became a yearly—sometimes twice-yearly—pilgrimage. For me, Western Canada was the Promised Land; it was paradise. More concretely, these hunting trips to Western Canada transformed me into a big game hunter, even if duck and grouse did remain part of the menu.

On one outstanding trip, Jack and his wife, Esther, invited me to join a horseback elk hunt in British Columbia. We had to do a lot of riding to get to base camp and I learned firsthand what saddle sores were all about. My backside and knees got a real hiding, spending all day in a saddle—pain that recurs every time I climb back on a horse. But, as I keep reminding myself, sitting on a horse beats climbing.

One day, almost at dusk, a bull elk showed itself, just over a ridge that was very close to the front of the camp. Seeing the elk step out into the alpine meadow was a magical moment. As had happened many times before (and has happened since), I became over excited, aimed, shot, and nothing happened—no dead elk. Instead, it turned round in a stately fashion, and went back where it had come from, disappearing out of sight. I may have missed the elk but I'd hit something: the scope of my first rifle, an unpleasantly kicking Weatherby .300 Magnum, had split my eyebrow, causing considerable damage, and blood was pouring down my face.

Later I couldn't sleep. The disappearing elk haunted me all night. I blamed myself for having missed what might be the only opportunity to get the elk of a lifetime. Would I ever get another chance? I replayed the scene over and over again in my mind. How could I have screwed up such an opportunity? The outfitter told me later that he thought I had flinched when I pulled the trigger. He felt (probably rightly so) that I was afraid of the kick of the gun. But he seemed to have a plan.

The next day, we climbed the Octopus Ridge, a steep range so named because of the many lateral ridges worming their way deep into the mountain. It was an extremely tough climb that gave Esther long-lasting knee problems. But we continued higher and higher. Suddenly, an elk jumped up in the middle of a bunch of low-standing fir trees—it was the same bull I had tried for the previous evening. I shot, shot, and shot once more. Just as it seemed the animal would vanish into the dense forest and disappear yet again, it lost its balance, and crumpled. The still life of my first big deer was a sight I will never forget. And although many people condemn the habit of displaying deer heads on walls, every time I look at this elk—which, after many moves, now hangs on the wall in my house in the South of France, and which (for reasons I forget) was baptized Willie by the children—I am flooded with memories of this adventure. Looking at Willie takes me back to that special time in my life in the Rockies. And when we skinned out the elk, we found my bullet from the previous day. I had not missed; the shot had been too high. I was glad that I had put the animal out of its misery.

On another hunt with Jack, a few years before the elk hunt, we were trying to get a moose. Elk are already quite impressive beasts—but moose are really, really big. Shooting a moose is very different from shooting a European roebuck or chamois. After I had shot and admired the enormous moose, I was faced with a problem. How to get it from where it was lying in the woods to the truck? I tried to push the dead animal, but couldn't move it even fractionally. It was then and there that I learned the hard way that, while moose hunting is comparatively easy (at least compared to hunting wild sheep or goat), the real work starts afterwards. Cutting such a big animal into manageable parts, then carrying the hide, meat, and rack out of the bush, is the kind of exercise that makes you think twice before hunting for one again. In that respect, hunting on horseback for elk was a much easier proposition. The horses did most of the work.

We were lucky that the moose was not very far from the road. But, even after all these years, I can still feel my sense of exhaustion. Jack mumbled that next time I shot a moose, it would be a good idea to have some body-building trappers and horses available. A year after this experience, we encountered a rather demented moose very close by the road. We looked at each other silently, and then I picked up a stone and threw it at the beast, hoping that would teach it to be more wary of people. The "body-building" Canadian moose first graced my father's office, and was a real tourist attraction, the Dutch not being familiar with such an imposing animal. Later, I gave the trophy to my friend Erik who hung it on one of the walls in his house, where it became a conversation piece.

My initial Canadian adventures were followed by a hunting trip to India. Sudhir, a very close friend who had been at Harvard the same time I was there, suggested that I visit him. Joking over the phone, as I sat at a café in Harvard Square, I said, "Only if you arrange a tiger hunt." (At that time hunting for tigers was still possible in India.) Soon after, I received a telegram from him, saying that the tiger hunt was arranged, and that I should come. Nowadays I am much more familiar with Sudhir's organizational talents; then, I should have known better. But excited by the prospect of the imagined tiger hunt, I decided to give it a go. Taking a shotgun and a rifle with me, I set out on my safari. In those innocent days, before the introduction of endless security measures, you just took your weapons to the plane and handed them over to the captain. On arrival in Mumbai, I missed my connecting flight to Ahmadabad. The police at the airport had been too excited (in a positive way)—and took their time checking out my weapons.

Having arrived in Ahmadabad, the next question was: what about the hunt? Of course, very little had been arranged, least of all a tiger hunt. But at the Indian Institute of Management where my friend Sudhir was a professor, there was a student hunter, who knew a local enthusiast—a multi-talented individual, who also supplied the neighborhood (including the management institute) with liquor, an activity explicitly forbidden in the state of Gujarat. With my new guides, I went off to endanger the local wild life. On that expedition, I took some ducks, black partridges, a nilgai antelope (blue bull), and a female black buck.

India has a diversity of wildlife—but I began to realize that hunting with "Cocaine Jim," as I had nicknamed my hunting partner (who seemed to have an addiction), was not a very smart move, from a legal point of view. I learned much later that he died in a gunfight with a competitor in the liquor business. I have, however, a strong memory of freezing to death with him on an endless drive through a desert, at night, in an open jeep. We were lost. The next day, I woke up in his heavily guarded "fortress" in the inner city, and was served blackbuck garamasala.

In Gujarat, I also hunted with an acquaintance of Sudhir—a young man who was trying to elude his mother's efforts to find him a suitable marriage partner. We drove all night in a new car to a place where we picked up some local guides who would help us to locate a nilgai. After some fruitless efforts I finally got one. We butchered the animal and put the mess of bloody meat in the trunk of the car, which by now was looking thoroughly beaten-up: we had been assured that the road was a flat as a billiard table. The car's owner did not appreciate its condition when we returned.

It finally dawned on Sudhir that his hunting connections in Ahmadabad were not very encouraging. True, I had learned a lot about the countryside and the habits of the local population but it was not the kind of hunting I had come so far to find. It was only then that Sudhir remembered a great-uncle who had once been the mythical hunter in the family. This uncle had a place in Nainital in the foothills of the Himalayas, the area where the famous hunter Jimmy Corbett used to go after man-eating tigers and leopards. We were on our way. The hunt was finally becoming serious.

After a highly uncomfortable, but interesting journey, we arrived at Mr. Khanna's place. The enormous stuffed head of a gaur—the largest bovine in the world—welcomed us in the hall as we entered. According to Mr. Khanna, this gaur, which he had hunted in the central Indian state of Madhya Pradesh, was actually a "baby"—I could not tell if he was serious. Mr. Khanna said he had rented a hunting block for me and had asked a local man, Kathar Singh, to act as my guide. This time, the hunting was very different, jungle hunting at its best. I hunted for chital and hog deer, peacock, black partridge, jungle fowl, and even jungle cats. But large wild cats were never a real option. Getting a tiger would necessitate beaters and elephants or hunting with bait from a *machan* (a wooden platform built between trees), none of which I had the means for at that time. The closest I got to a tiger was seeing a few fresh tracks. Little did I know that just five years later, in 1972, hunting would be banned in India due to excessive poaching, and more particularly the destruction of the animals' habitat. As it is, I have donated quite some money to help protect the tiger, but with the increase in population and poaching, whatever is done, conservation continues to be an uphill struggle.

After my marriage, I would spend every summer at my in-laws' summerhouse in the heart of Sweden. The estate they owned consisted of farmland, with intermittent patches of forest, bordering a lake. As the summers went by, I got to know the lay of the land very intimately. I knew where I would meet *the* hare or *the* roebuck that lived on the property. Looking back, I realize now the extent to which I re-enacted my childhood fantasies at my in-laws' property. I once even saw a moose on their land. My first moose hunt in Sweden, however, contrasted sharply with the difficulty of taking a moose out of the forest in Canada. The moose hunt was organized on a large forestry domain in the east of Sweden. The professional hunter who was guiding us told me that he had to take out more than a hundred moose to control the ever-expanding population. Not only did the moose damage the young forest growth, they were also a traffic hazard. In the northern countries in Europe, many people are killed each year in road accidents caused by moose.

During this moose hunt, we used a Nordic spitz dog (the true descendent of the Vikings' hunting and herding dogs) to "place" the moose. I recall this hunt vividly. There was the constant barking of the dog, followed by a "tiger" crawl through the dense fir trees to get closer. When I saw the moose, it was almost impossible to shoot because of the dog that kept circling and barking at the animal. Finally, I saw a window of opportunity, and managed to get off a shot. For the people in Sweden—sensibly—moose hunting is all about the meat. Although European moose are smaller than both the Canadian moose and the Shiraz moose, they are big enough. The one I got had a miserable set of antlers but the animal was good to eat. To get the enormous beast out of the forest, we used a kind of "moose mobile," a mechanical contraption with a winch and a small engine that could maneuver the moose between the trees. This machine made getting moose out of the forest much easier, and with the numbers of game the forestry authority had to deal with, was indispensable.

While I was at my in-laws' farm, I was an extremely busy person, putting out nets for fish, collecting mushrooms and berries and—highly appreciated by everyone when the season started—catching crayfish in the lake. Rowing in the dark all night, placing and lifting crayfish pots was an activity filled with excitement. The experience of lifting a net, and feeling the resistance of a struggling fish, or raising a crayfish pot, admiring my latest capture, remain very vivid, but bitter-sweet memories, as it is now many years since that property has last been in the family.

But my activities in Sweden were mostly about fishing on the lake, and differed greatly from my hunting in the Volga Delta (on both the Kazakhstan and Russian sides). This landscape is an ideal habitat for waterfowl but wild boar can also be found living in the reeds. The first time I went to the delta it was truly a haven for an incredible variety of water birds. There were many more kinds of duck than to be found in Holland. The tactics for getting at them, however, were similar. Of course, in Holland, there was not the fringe benefit of eating the caviar of delta sturgeon. The first time I was there, I overdosed on caviar. Believe me, caviar for breakfast, lunch, and dinner can be too much.

I have always loved duck hunting. I am always amazed at the aerial maneuvers ducks can make. Hunting ducks in a blind is an exercise in hide-and-seek, hiding from the birds until the last moment—than getting up and surprising them. The speed of teal especially is a sight to behold. When they see the hunter, they literally jump in the air—then go into overdrive. And then there are the geese. The rich, musical honking of geese and the quick wing-beats of ducks who fill the sky are sounds no hunter easily forgets.

Eventually, when I could afford it, I began to make hunting excursions to Russia (and the countries that used to be part of the USSR) and Africa. With Africa, it was love at first sight. There is an old saying that "once you've drunk the waters of the Zambezi River you have no choice but to come back," and for me at least that is true. The smells, the sounds, the scenery, and the incredible variety of wild life were, for me, a revelation.

Of all the game available in Africa, buffalos became one of my favorites. I am not completely clear why. Perhaps it has to do the mystique surrounding the danger of hunting these animals. Old Dagga Boys (older, no longer breeding bulls who have distanced themselves from herds and are solitary or form small bachelor groups) can be quite dangerous. They may charge unprovoked if the hunter is spotted by chance. And they are among the most dangerous animals when wounded. Often they seem not to know that they are dead. Many a hunter has had a narrow escape, and some have even been killed going after them. Robert Ruark wrote:

"I don't know what there is about buffalo that frightens me so. Lions and leopards and rhinos excite me but don't frighten me. But the buff is so big and mean and ugly and hard to stop, and vindictive and cruel and surly and ornery. He looks like he hates you personally. He looks like you owe him money. He looks like he is hunting you."[42]

In Zimbabwe once, driving through the long grass early in the morning, checking a place that had been baited for leopard, we suddenly found ourselves face-to-face with three Dugga Boys. One was very good looking, with a good spread, and a heavy, solid boss (the base of the horns). When the buffalo saw us, they stampeded, running away toward the local national park. The next day we went back to the same place and, seeing fresh tracks, decided to track them. After a relatively short stalk—at times I have been after buffalo for many very long, and very hot, sweaty hours—we caught up with them. I aimed at the oldest buffalo with the best boss, shot, and the animal fell down. The other two buffalos were leaving the scene as fast as they could. But when they realized their leader had deserted them, to my great surprise, they turned back. Using their horns as levers, they tried to lift the badly wounded animal. I had heard of such behavior with elephants, but not buffalo. The injured buffalo stumbled up and started running again, joined by the two others. I managed to get off another shot that finished it off. I heard the death bellow of the animal and at that sound, the other two disappeared. When I approached my quarry, I was silent. I felt a real melancholy about what I had done. But every time I see this buffalo—it is now hanging on the wall in my apartment in Paris—I think about the solidarity of the other two. Until now, from a trophy point of view, it has been my best buffalo.

Buffalo hunting grows on you. My first African safari was in Zimbabwe and I recall it as a very good hunt. Everything was new; there were so many impressions to absorb. But I also remember that I had difficulty getting an old buffalo on that particular trip. Over-the-hill buffalos were hard to get, and our first three stalks panned out. So when one morning I found the fresh track of a solitary buffalo we decided to give it one more try. This was the occasion when I learned how difficult it is to see anything in the thick Mopani bushes, including animals as large as elephants or buffalo, which seem just to vanish in the background. After a three-hour stalk with the track winding all over the place (and at times crossing our own tracks), we spotted, at very close quarters, an ancient buffalo—obviously kicked out of the herd—with a partially broken horn dozing away under some Mopani bushes. We crawled closer, then closer still. Eventually, we were so close that we could hear the swishing of his tail as he tried to get rid of the flies we could clearly see coming and going. Finally, we were so close that we were sharing the same flies. Perhaps the buffalo heard something because it suddenly stood up—at which moment I aimed, and fired my gun. Although (as I later learned) I had hit the buffalo right in the heart, it kept on running—luckily away from us. My guide, Dirk, shot at its vanishing shadow; it was dead, from an anatomical point of view, but didn't seem to have realized it. We found its body not too far away. My wife and I stayed with the animal while Dirk hiked back to get the truck; it was like holding a wake. This was the first time I enjoyed the delights of the Mopani flies (which are actually bees) that crawled all over my face, driving me crazy.

As I mentioned, buffalo hunting is addictive; it makes you want more. Perhaps it is this that makes people addicted to bull fights? The bull-leaping frescos (dating from the 15th century BC) that once adorned a wall at the Great Goddess Sanctuary at the palace at Knossos are world famous. They show an acrobat grasping the bull's horns as the animal charges him, then somersaulting onto its back, and jumping off. We know that young Minoan men and women would jump over bulls as a test of their athletic prowess. Bulls are the arch-representative of male power, of virility. Is that the reason so many people love to hunt them? Or is there more to it?

Bulls have always been symbols of strength, power, passion, bravery, freedom, and fertility. There is an ancient belief that after sacrificing a bull, new life would start. Bulls can be unpredictable—and buffalo even more so. There is always the chance that the hunt will turn sour. There is the thrill or wondering whether you will be still alive after the exploit. The need to hunt African buffalo may be a window into my inner theater. Whatever it tells about me, I will keep on going after *mbogo*.

⌐

On pigs and men

Buffalo hunting has an obvious element of danger, but many other forms of hunting also evoke archaic memories of hunting and being hunted—of taking part in the dance of life and death. Even wild boar hunting can fall into this category. I have hunted wild boar all over the world including India, Germany, France, Tajikistan, the Czech Republic, Sweden, Russia, and Iran. I have also gone after wild hogs in California, Florida, Australia, and Mauritius. I remember I took part several times in an elegant boar hunt in Germany when everyone was put on a low *"Hochsitz"* (hunting stand), while the wild boars were driven to the hunters by beaters with dogs. A "turbo" boar (it proved to be the largest of the day) came running out of the forest at full speed, and I managed to have a shot at it. Soon after, a smaller one came streaking by, but I didn't know if my shot was true as a small hill was blocking my sight. Then a little dachshund appeared out of nowhere, disappeared over the small hill, and started yelping desperately. The barking went on and on, until I couldn't stand it any longer, got down from my stand, put my gun on safety, and took a few steps in the direction of the noise, to find out what the racket was all about. There was a lot of mud and some snow, and it was very slippery. In a ditch behind the little hill where the noise came from, two wild boar were lying, one very large and very dead, and the other much smaller and not dead. This was what the dachshund was barking at. I had hunted dangerous game such as bears, lions, leopards, and buffalo and had never paid much attention to stories about how dangerous wild boar can be. But when the small boar saw me, all his bristles went up, and before I realized what was happening, he had run toward me with such speed, knocking me off my feet, that I didn't even have time to get my safety catch off. Seconds later, I was lying dazed and spread-eagled in the mud. It all happened so quickly I had no time to feel fear. Still flat on the ground, the first thing I did was to check my limbs. Apart from having lost some of my dignity, my body felt intact; my arms and legs seemed okay. I looked around, and saw my rifle lying in the mud, not very far from me. The wild boar, which was small in comparison to the very dead monster lying in the ditch, had returned to the same spot, and was eying me suspiciously. The dachshund had renewed his concerto. It was as if nothing had happened. But lying in the mud was no mirage; it was very real. Carefully, very carefully, I managed to get hold of my rifle, checked there was no mud in the barrel, took it off safety, and ended this strange ordeal. Since then, I have treated wild boar with a considerable dose of respect.

A more amusing boar incident occurred in Arnhemland, the northern part of Australia, while I was hunting for water buffalo. My guide and I were standing close to a water hole. It was the middle of the day and extremely hot. Suddenly, a parade of wild hogs came out of nowhere, obviously making for the water hole. The guide told me to shoot the lead boar, which looked like the biggest one of the sounder. I aimed, shot, and the animal fell stone dead. Most of the pigs ran away squealing, frightened by my rifle shot. However, one of them, against all odds, saw some kind of opportunity (the alpha hog being dead) and decided to mount one of the sows. It was a remarkable sexual performance—until then I had always thought that safety would be the highest priority for animals.

I once hunted wild hogs in Florida—an interesting experience, as they were to be found in the middle of the day, cooling off in a swamp in the terrain that I was hunting. To get to the spot through the swamp, we had to use an amphibious contraption build on extremely large wheels—a "hog mobile." The guide and I had a dog with us to sniff out the hogs. As soon as we saw a hog, the dog jumped out of the hog mobile, ran at the hog, and circled it, while the boar tried very hard to kill the dog. Suddenly, to my amazement, the guide jumped on top of the hog—it was not a very big animal—tied its legs, and got me to take a photograph. After that he let the animal go. It was quite some act of bravura. When he was trying to show me his acrobatics another time, an extremely large hog that had been hiding in the swamp got up, and tried to sneak away. I managed to shoot it—and it turned out the biggest one they had ever seen in that hunting territory.

There are also wild hogs in California. Like those in Australia and Florida, most of these are descended from feral domestic pigs that showed up with the first settlers and explorers in the 1700s, and have populated most of the region. In the 1920s, wild boars from Europe were released at various places in the US to enrich the "mix." Hunting these hogs was a case of spot-and-stalk, which I did from a truck. Driving along one day, I spotted not far off the head of a hog slowly rising in the middle of a field, then immediately dropping down again. The pig, no doubt grown blasé about the sound of trucks, had decided I was nothing to bother about. I snuck up on the animal, and met a very surprised hog, black with white spots.

I have also hunted the whole spectrum of the pig family in Africa, with the exception of the wild boar of Northern Africa. The most elusive animal of the pig family that I have hunted on that continent is the giant forest hog, the largest wild member of the pig family. The scientific name (*Hylochoerus*) is derived from the Greek words *hule*, meaning a mole or wart and *khoiros*, a pig or hog. The animal is mostly black, although the hairs nearest to the skin of the animal can be deep orange. Its ears are large and pointed, and its tusks are much smaller than those of the warthog but bigger than that of the bush pig. Frankly, the giant forest hog is anything but an attractive animal. I have been told that males can reach as much as two meters in length and 1.1 meters at the shoulder and have been known to weigh as much as 600 pounds. They live in the dense forested areas of various equatorial African countries. They are mostly nocturnal and are active for about four to eight hours a day between dusk and dawn. They can live in large sounders of up to 20 animals. Interestingly enough, although known to native peoples of tropical African forests, giant forest hogs were not scientifically classified until 1904. To detract even further from their mystique, they can be extremely ferocious.

I tried for a number of years to see and obtain a giant forest hog. Eventually, it became something of an obsession. My first effort to get one was with an outfitter in the Central African Republic who turned out to be totally unreliable, and even incompetent. I don't think he had ever seen a giant forest hog; he just fantasized that it could happen. I tried again the next year with Matthieu Laboureur, a remarkable guide whom I knew well—a true connoisseur of African wildlife and nature.

Since forest hogs live in very thick rain forest, the best chance of getting one is to sit in a *mirador*, or blind, high up a tree at the edge of a *bako*—an open place in the jungle that often contains a natural salt lick. There we sat, and waited, and waited, and waited some more. We made good use our time in killing the occasional tsetse fly, which fortunately were not frequent visitors to the blind. And we saw many animals and birds—a whole parade of colobus monkeys that descended from the trees to eat the salt, with faces like wise old men, a large herd of female bongos that lingered at the salt lick, and a beautiful male that visited for a long time.

From the *mirador* we could see a forest sitatunga nibbling at the vegetation in the swampy terrain in front of us. The animal was moving around the middle of the papyrus, and its unusually wide feet made it look as though it was dancing on the water. One moment, we would see it, the next it would be gone. I was thankful to see it, as it is a very unusual to be able to watch such a rare antelope for such a long time. I let it be; I had hunted sitatunga before and had had the good luck to obtain two nice specimens. But no giant forest hog made a cameo appearance, despite the many tracks to be seen. One day, when we had pretty much given up, we decided to have a final visit to the blind where we had spent so many fruitless hours. When I reached the top of the *mirador*, I saw a giant forest hog 200 meters away. Thoroughly overexcited at seeing this mythical animal, I shot too quickly and blew it. As it turned out, I had wounded the animal (fortunately, not seriously). We tried to follow the tracks, crawling through thorns and brambles, but it was mission impossible. I thought, "That's it, for forest hogs." I had let myself down. I felt extremely bad about the situation. All hunters make mistakes, but still…

The next day, Mathieu decided that we should visit another blind at another *bako*, with smaller and less lush than the first. But again, there were a few fresh tracks of the elusive giant hog. I had not been sitting in the blind for long when another parade of colobus monkeys decided to visit the salt lick. Still no giant hog. I started to zone out, thinking about a Japanese animation, *Princess Mononoke*, that I had seen fairly recently. The film portrays the epic struggle between the guardians of the forest and the humans who take its resources. It begins with the young hero saving his village from a vicious assault by a hideous wild boar covered in writhing worms, an animal that is actually the giant boar god Nago. The boar is corrupted by rage, and is threatening the lives of the villagers. The animal symbolizes the hatred of the beast gods toward the civilization that has brought deforestation, but the film also contains imagery of hope and rebirth.

While I was daydreaming about this, I saw a sudden flash of movement at the edge of the bushes at the *bako*. I came to my senses, unsure whether I had seen was a *fata morgana*, a mirage. Soon after, I saw a snout cautiously stuck out of the bushes, and disappear once again. Then there was that snout again, and there it wasn't. It was quite a spooky experience. Suddenly, two animals came out into the clearing. In their ugliness, they looked like the nightmare wild boar I had seen in that Japanese movie. After all the years I had waited to get my hands on this animal, I wasn't going to wait any longer, and decided to take a shot. That giant forest hog is one of the animals I will not easily forget. The whole camp ate meat for a long time.

More recently, I hunted for another kind of wild boar, also called a *"cochon marron,"* on the island of Mauritius. I was really hunting for rusa deer, which originate from the Indonesian island of Java; their presence on the island is linked to the need to resupply the old sailing trading ships. In November 1639, the Dutch Governor Adriaan Van der Stel's boat anchored in Mauritius. On board were sugar cane plants, as well as a veritable Noah's ark of chickens, rabbits, pigeons, lambs, monkeys, and these Javanese deer. Following the demise of the poor dodo bird, the cargo was intended to provide the early settlers with fresh meat. The governor could not have suspected that the degree of success he would have. Today, there is an overpopulation of this rusa deer on the island. There are also numerous *cochon marron* (a cross between a wild boar and the domestic pig). Although I was after rusa deer, I was also lucky to shoot (according to my guide) one of the biggest *cochon marron* on the island—actually, not that big if compared with a real Russian boar. But the pig I shot did have sizable teeth. My guide Lionel jumped a meter in the air out of sheer delight when he saw the dead pig.

Hunting and creativity

It is not easy to write about the sounds, smells, and images evoked by these hunting experiences. Writing can be only a pale reflection of what the actual experience is like and can only rarely bring out the real passion felt in the moment. However, writing makes me think of the tragic transience of things and recalls many bittersweet memories of times that have passed. It is sad, too, to remember the people with whom I have hunted, and who have gone to the "Happy Hunting Grounds." My nostalgia is compounded by the fact that it is a very long time since I have hunted in Holland, my country of birth. My inertia—I haven't really made any effort to do so—is probably because I am wary of the power of the memories. Too much has changed.

But I still do hunt. I am still eager to have new hunting experiences. And each time, at the aftermath of a hunt, I return home with a feeling that something out of the ordinary has taken place. As I said earlier, it doesn't make much difference to me whether I have been successful in the hunt; what counts is the experience of having hunted. Theodore Roosevelt once said that the days a man spends fishing or hunting should not be deducted from the time he's on earth. In so many ways (and as I have said before), hunting is important for ones mental health.

I realize that, in this day and age, the kinds of experience I have had are increasingly uncommon. Urbanization continues its unstoppable march; most people are brought up in cities; parks and zoos present feeble reflections of what life in the wild is all about; nature documentaries cannot convey smells, sounds, wind, rain, snow, cold, or heat. I find this development pretty depressing. We have to pay a high price for civilization and urbanization. Growing up and living surrounded by constructions of steel and concrete makes for a very different experience from living close to forests, rivers, lakes, and mountains—experiencing nature at close quarters.

Hunting will always remain a controversial subject, not least because, for some people, it reminds them of parts of themselves they are not comfortable with. Seeing hunters in the field may remind them of things they worry about within themselves. Watching the pursuit of game forces them to acknowledge deep-seated, primitive drives inside themselves that they fear may run out of control. More precisely, this discomfort touches on fears that they may not be able to manage the aggression within.

There is a lot of violence in our world. We only have to open a newspaper or watch the news to see the evidence. War is a prime example of aggression unbound—in the context of war people do inconceivable things and otherwise "normal" people start to behave abnormally. But is putting the shadow side of ourselves into a box and closing the lid the answer? Are there no better ways of dealing with the aggression within? Shouldn't we try to understand it better? Aggression that is not understood, or dealt with, functions like a serious contagious disease. The way societies channel violence is one of their greatest challenges. The films of director Sam Peckinpah are famously preoccupied by violence and the corruption of violence in human society. Peckinpah once said, "There is a great streak of violence in every human being. If it is not channeled and understood, it will break out in war or in madness."

31 — Ruark, Robert. *Use Enough Gun*. London: Gorki Books, 1972, p. 41.

32 — Winnicott, Donald. "Transitional Objects and Transitional Phenomena," *International Journal of Psychoanalysis*, 34, 1952, pp. 89-97.

33 — Turgenev, Ivan. *Sketches from a Hunter's Album*. London: Penguin Books, 1990, p. 385.

34 — Roosevelt, Theodore (1893). *The Wilderness Hunter*. New York: Irvington Publishers, 1993 ed.

35 — Arseniev, Valdimir K. *Dersu the Trapper*, (Trans. Malcolm Burr). Kingston, NY: McPherson & Company, 1996, p. 213.

36 — Krakauer, Jon. *Into the Wild*. London: Pan Books, 2007.

37 — Leopold, Aldo. *A Sand Country Almanac*. New York: Oxford University Press, 1949, pp. 63-64.

38 — Martin, Glen. *Game Changer: Animal Rights and the Fate of Africa's Wildlife*. Berkeley: University of California Press, 2012, p. 89.

39 — Ortega y Gasset, José. *Meditations on Hunting*. H. B. Wescott (transl.).Belgrade, MT: Wilderness Adventures Press, 1995, pp. 96-97.

40 — Thoreau, Henry David. "Walden," 1854, in *The Writings of Henry David Thoreau*, Vol. 2. Boston: Houghton Mifflin, 1906.

41 — Leopold, Aldo. *A Sand Country Almanac*. New York: Oxford University Press, 1949, p. 121.

42 — Ruark, Robert. C. *Horn of the Hunter*. Huntington Beach, Cal: Safari Press, 1999, p. 285.

*For the wild animal there is no such thing
as a gentle decline in peaceful old age. Its life
is spent at the front, in line of battle, and
as soon as its powers begin to wane in the
least, its enemies become too strong; it falls.*
    —Ernest Thompson Seton,
    Lives of the Hunted (1901)

*If sentimentalists were right, hunting would
develop in man a cruelty of character. But
I have found that it inculcates patience,
demands discipline and iron nerve, and
develops a serenity of spirit that makes
for a long life and a long love of life.*
    —Archibald Rutledge

*Serious sport has nothing to do with fair
play. It is bound up with hatred, jealousy,
boastfulness, disregard of all rules and
sadistic pleasure in witnessing violence. In
other words, it is war minus the shooting.*
    —George Orwell

*It is nearly impossible for modern man to
imagine what it is like to live by hunting.
The life of a hunter is one of hard, seemingly
continuous overland travel… A life of frequent
concerns that the next interception may not
work, that the trap or the drive will fail, or that
the herds will not appear this season. Above
all, the live of the hunter carries with it the
threat of deprivation and death by starvation.*
    —John M. Campbell,
    The Hungry Summer

THE "AGGRESSION WITHIN"

Once when I was hunting for bear with my old friend Jack in Northern Alberta, high up in the North Country, we found a small farm at the border of a provincial park. It looked a very likely spot for game. The fields surrounding the farm were planted with oats—a cereal that many of the farmers in the region tell me is like candy to bears. The only break in the panorama was a small strip of wood at the back of the farm that ran from one side of the forest to the other. I assumed that the strip had been left there to give the farmhouse a modicum of protection against the icy northern winds. But leaving this narrow strip of wood standing had had consequences. Any bear wanting to go from one side of the forest to the other and keep out of sight could use this little strip of wood as a short cut. In fact, this short cut—combined with the attraction of oats—had turned into a tempting super highway for the numerous black bears (and occasional grizzly) that populate the region. And unfortunately, the strip of wood also ran closely past the yard at the back of the farmhouse.

Although it may give you the exciting feeling that you are living smack in the middle of the wilderness, there are disadvantages to having bears hanging around your backyard. It can be distinctly unnerving when you have small children playing there. The farmer's wife had made it clear to her husband that she wasn't happy finding a bear on the back porch, or having one bang at her kitchen window while she was baking bread, and the farmer was taking no chances. Bear encounters of the close kind had to be prevented at all costs.

The obvious solution to this problem would have been to cut down the infamous strip of woodland. However, this was something the farmer was not prepared to do. He wanted to retain the windbreak—and I suspect he didn't really mind seeing bears. Life on these farms, far north, can be quite boring. Sneaking up on bears (or vise versa) adds a frisson of excitement to sitting on a tractor for hours. Consequently, his more surreal and non-wildlife-friendly solution was to shoot on sight every bear that came within the vicinity of the house. At the time, this was a legitimate option for farmers in Alberta. Bears were classified as vermin in farming areas and if they caused trouble could be disposed of, at any time.

Unfortunately, taking this option created even more problems. Now the farmer was faced with having numerous dead bears in his backyard. He didn't mind eating bear meat occasionally, but how many bears can you eat? And, actually, moose meat, rather than bear meat, was the family's favorite source of protein. He needed to find a way to get rid of some of the dead bears. But bears can be heavy—they aren't easily dragged away. With the help of his tractor, however, the farmer disposed of these carcasses at his junkyard, which was not very far from his house—and also within the strip of woodland. This solution, however, rebounded on him: bears don't mind eating their own and many cannibalistic bears found those rotting cadavers quite irresistible.

I crept quietly through the strip of wood to get closer to the spot where the farmer had dumped the dead bears, to assess the situation. I found one very live bear, happily digging into the stomach of one of its defunct relatives. Watching the scene—although I could empathize with the farmer's concern for his kids—I wondered whether there was really no better way to deal with his dilemma, although he had assured me there wasn't. His was a very unsatisfactory and rather violent solution. In this case, human aggression—or even better, thoughtlessness—exacerbated the animals' cannibalistic behavior. Intra-species (between members of the same species) and interspecies (between two different species) aggression seemed to be combined.

What I was witnessing wasn't exactly the kind of imagery we find in Walt Disney or nature movies, like Jean-Jacques Annaud's *L'Ours (The Bear)*, a very successful feature film that tells the story of an orphaned bear cub that is befriended and protected by an adult male grizzly—a totally unrealistic, anthropomorphized story of grizzly behavior, as male grizzlies (like black bears) have the unfortunate habit of eating cubs whenever they get the opportunity.

⌐ᴴ

Aggression and its vicissitudes

"Aggression" is a key concept in the study of human behavior, and an expression in daily use. Frequently, however, the words "aggression" and "violence" are used interchangeably. For our purposes, to better understand *Homo sapiens* the hunter, I suggest that "aggression" refers to a thought (a state of mind or a verbal display) while "violence" refers to an aggressive action. Violence is a result of aggression acted out physically, with the intention to hurt someone or damage something. In these terms, violence is a real assault on other people or other things, which results in serious injury or serious material damage. In contrast, aggression refers to the *intention* to damage or hurt somebody in a physical or verbal way. So, when I talk about violence, I can use the term aggression. But when I talk about aggression, I can't use the term violence. In everyday conversation, however, we tend to use the terms aggression and violence interchangeably.

Aggression can take many forms. At times, it can be appropriate and self-protective, even constructive (as in healthy self-assertiveness), or inappropriate and destructive when it transforms into uninhibited aggression and violent action. Aggression may be directed outward, against others, or inward, against the self, leading to self-destructive or even suicidal actions.

Although hunters (or pseudo-hunters) are often singled out as an aggressive bunch of people—as we can extrapolate from the unusual bear story with which I began this chapter—violent behavior can be observed in every living animal (including humankind) on earth. The potential to kill seems to be written in our genes. As a species, *Homo sapiens* can be extremely dangerous to one another. And even the most animal-"loving" of the anti-hunting groups are no strangers to aggression. Some of these groups are so violent that it raises questions about the personality make-up of the people that belong to these pressure groups. Unfortunately, as far as human aggression is concerned—if we compare ourselves to other members of the animal kingdom—the sad fact is that we (*Homo sapiens*) are one of the cruelest and most ruthless species that has ever walked the earth.

⌐ᴴ

Is biology destiny?

In my search for an explanation for the aggression within, there are a number of schools of thought to explore. Some people consider aggression an instinct—an inborn pattern of behavior that is characteristic of a species. The instinct theory of aggression argues that it is an innate biological drive, similar to sex and hunger. Others view aggression as a predictable reaction to violent stimuli, that is, not an innate predisposition. The central supposition is that aggression is a predictable reaction to a defined stimulus—frustration. Pursuing this line of thought, we can understand why some students of this topic argue that aggression is socially learned behavior rather than an automatic response to aggression or any other stimulus. According to them, in the process of growing up we learn that aggressive behavior can pay off.

These different theories about the origins of aggression leave me wondering what aggressive behavior is really all about. Is it genetically determined or environmentally learned? Unsurprisingly, this question has been an endless source of debate. Many theories have been proposed, supporting the idea that aggression has a genetic link in humans.

Reflecting on the various theories of aggression, I can place them on a continuum where, at one end of the spectrum, aggression is seen as a consequence of purely innate, instinctual factors and, at the other, it is determined by external factors. In fact, much of the discussions about aggression can be framed within a more general "nature versus nurture" debate. Obviously, in the context of hunting, anti-hunting proponents are likely to argue that hunting is the unfortunate outcome of learned behavior. They try to negate the power of unconscious processes; they prefer to ignore the dynamics of our internal world, and our phylogenetic heritage.

The behavior of our closest relative the chimpanzee (described in Chapter 1) is indicative of the fact that a penchant for group violence may have been genetically bred into us over millions of years of evolution. The hypothesis is that we are biologically hardwired for aggressive behavior—and this hypothesis is supported by archaeological records rife with prehistoric and historic evidence of Homo sapiens' talent to make war. Throughout history, humankind has been unequaled in practicing violence. Ironically, the more successful we have been in defending ourselves against predators, the more dangerous we have become to each other.

To understand better the reasons why we behave as we do, we need once again to return to our origins. And here evolutionary biology may help us find explanations. Our evolutionary past may help us understand why, and under what circumstances, the human animal turns violent. We soon discover that some of the explanations for man's violence assume the form of a cost-benefit analysis about food and sexual selection. Other explanations are derived from social learning theory.

As Jane Goodall, Diane Fossey, Frans de Waal, and other well-known primatologists have observed, chimpanzees will carry out "raids" against other chimps in a purposeful manner. Like *Homo sapiens*, chimpanzees go to war. These to all appearances peaceful great apes systematically hunt smaller primates, such as colobus monkeys, for meat. As well as killing for food, some female chimpanzees will also kill the young of other females in their own troop in an effort to maintain dominance. And as in human society, there are in-groups and out-groups; under certain circumstances, male chimpanzees will kill members of neighboring groups—most commonly chimpanzees caught alone. These animals are no strangers to intra-species aggression.

Since we are genetically very similar to chimpanzees, such behavior suggests a common inherited (developed) source of aggression within.[43] If we are to believe what many evolutionary biologists tell us, the potential for violent behavior is found within ourselves—buried deep in our evolutionary past. Taking this evolutionary perspective implies that aggression can be viewed as an innate part of human behavior.

Once, a bear decided to let me live

I was walking on a high mountain plateau in the Aleutian Peninsula. On one side was the sea; on the other side was tundra, alders, and snow-covered mountains. I was on a bear hunt, and trying to find a sign of them. My guide and I had decided to split up and go in different directions, so we could glass a much larger area.

I had been sitting on a rock for a while, trying to ignore the relentless arctic wind that was sweeping down the plateau. I glassed through my binoculars, drank some water, and ate a chocolate bar. The only living things I could see through my binoculars were a few caribou, looking like hazy figurines far in the distance. Fairly close by a red fox was hunting, probably for willow ptarmigan or mice. In the water I could see the movement of harbor seals and Steller sea lions. Earlier in the day I had seen a number of killer whales. A flock of cackling geese flew overhead. There was a lot of action but no bears to be seen. On the next mountain range, I could make out bear tracks in the snow—but the tracks petered out into nowhere.

I was getting colder. While this wasn't the arctic climate of the Alaskan inner territory to the north, I knew the winds on the Aleutian Peninsula from hard experience. If I stayed put, there was a good chance I'd get hypothermia. I needed to get warm. It was time to move to the other corner of the mountain plateau. From there I'd get a different

---

view of the valley. Since I was going to have to come back to where I was—and to minimize the weight I had to carry—I decided to leave my backpack and rifle on the rock where I had been sitting. I was pretty sure it would be safe to do so; there was no way I'd meet a bear so high up the mountain.

It was when I was walking to the other side of the plateau that I heard the unmistakable sound—that woof, something between a grunt and a bark, that a bear makes when it wants to let you know it knows you're around. I stopped abruptly but I couldn't see anything. Then there was some movement behind the alders and the grizzly sow appeared. She must have gotten my scent. When she saw me, she froze too. She looked me over. She sniffed the air. Time stood still. We tend to give bears human attributes, because they seem to have moods, much like we do. They can be shy, curious, pushy, but also very aggressive. Standing there frozen, I wondered what the bear was thinking. What would she decide to do? Fight or flight? I knew that most bear attacks are caused by too-close encounters, and I was in the middle of one now. I was well inside her comfort zone. I also knew that most bears usually opt for flight. But this bear had been surprised and was threatened by my presence. And I knew, too well, that a female with cubs would be especially aggressive and defend her cubs at any provocation.

I cursed myself for leaving my rifle behind. There were no escape routes. There were no trees so far north, so nothing to climb. The alders wouldn't do. Running would be suicidal. It would trigger an aggressive response—and bears can outrun any human uphill or down. I had read that others who had found themselves in this kind of situation had played dead. Playing dead would show the bear that I wasn't a threat. But could I do that? Could I really roll myself into a ball with my face on the ground, protecting my vital parts, for as long as it took while I wondered all the time what was going on? Not really. I forced myself not to panic. Having exhausted all the options, the only thing I could think to do was to stare her down. And that is what I did.

Impossible to know what was going on the bear's mind. She must perceive me as a threat? She was facing me with an aggressive posture that I recognized signaled a charge. Or did she see me for what I was: harmless—at least for now? She was swinging her head from side to side. Did that mean she was reluctant to charge—or the opposite? Was she waiting for me to withdraw? She didn't pop her jaws, which I knew would be an imminent signal of attack. I shut my mind to what might follow; bears don't necessarily kill their prey before they eat it.

My thoughts were racing, one obsessively: what I would do if I had my rifle with me? I would have tried to kill her if she had come for me. But I would have done so very reluctantly. It would be self-defense. Defenseless, I decided to back away slowly, speaking in a low voice, telling her that I understood she was upset; that I wasn't supposed to be here; that I was in her domain. I tried to present a one-down position and appear submissive; I tried to get out of her way. After what felt like an eternity, the bear turned slowly away; her two cubs joined her, and she ambled off down the mountain.

She had decided to let me live. That encounter is still with me. It will be there for the rest of my life. Human aggression had not been reciprocated.

As I discussed in Chapter 1, once upon a time, our relatively defenseless hominid predecessors lived in mortal fear of the great carnivores. Death could strike at any moment because our forefathers tried to steal meat from their kills (very like the behavior of hyenas, jackals, or vultures toward lions). Gradually, due to the evolutionary processes I described earlier, our ancestors grew not only larger but also smarter, and (given their brain power) began to subdue these dangerous carnivores using various successful stratagems. In the process, they learned—a characteristic that had evolutionary advantages—to keep their aggression within tolerable measures. With the march of time, *Homo sapiens* became the most feared and effective predator of them all. Taking an evolutionary, historical perspective, we can assume that prehistoric humans— like their close cousins the chimpanzees—were no stranger to aggression: they could behave violently among themselves and toward others.

We can infer from behavior of chimpanzees that much human violence (if it didn't revolve around food) may have originated in male-male competition for the favors of the opposite sex. Other factors, such as competing with other species, defending and expanding territory and other resources, and feeding and protecting offspring may have also played a role. Even the need to obtain food through hunting—particularly when it was scarce—may have contributed to this evolutionary aggression equation. Most probably, these early hominids viewed the availability of food and sex as a zero-sum-game. For the purpose of survival (when resources were scarce), a clan of our ancestors needed to be able to stir its warriors into a killing mood against all outsiders. Territoriality was important, a required violent action. To quote the anthropologist Robert Audrey:

"Investigations revealed the obligatory dependence of territorial defense upon social order, and the exquisite relationships of social order to acceptance of responsibility by the dominant hierarchy, to acceptance of domination by the rank and file, to division of duties and communication between social partners, to the minimizing of sexual conflict, to the development of a dual code of behavior—amity for the social partner, hostility for the territorial neighbor—and to the enlarging role of the female as sexual specialist to counteract the tendency of social males to be preoccupied with activities other than reproduction."[44]

Returning to the question of causality in the history of violence, the more aggressive specimens among our Paleolithic ancestors would have more reproductive opportunities than their less aggressive kin. Their success as providers of food and as defenders in battle would have made them more attractive to the females in their communities. We can infer that the children of these unions would have inherited some of the violent temperament of their fathers as—generation after generation—the genes for violence proliferated within the population. Therefore, our disposition toward violent behavior that is something that we need to accept as part of our evolutionary heritage. Humans cannot be labeled simplistically as good or bad; many of our behavior patterns are products of nature, having strong and rooted biological foundations regardless of the value judgments, lamentations, and appraisals of moralists. I need to accept that the taste for violence is bred into me; it is written in my genes. All human beings have the potential to be hideously cruel and destructive to one another. Our predilection to wage war with each other is symptomatic. To quote the philosopher David Livingstone Smith:

"Like it or not, war is distinctively human. Apart from the raiding behavior of chimpanzees... and the so-called wars prosecuted by certain species of ants, there is nothing in nature that comes anywhere near approximating it. Despite this, we often describe warfare as *brutal* (literally 'animal-like') or *inhuman*—conceiving of it as something remote from our true humanity. Another distancing tactic is to treat war as a social illness, a deviation from the naturally peaceable state of humankind, a strange cyclic malady like fever that causes us to periodically shed the garments of civilization and fall prey to the wild beast within (Leonardo da Vinci called it '*bestialissima pazzia*', 'the most bestial madness')."[45]

David Livingston Smith also noted:

"Mark Twain concisely described the principle almost a century ago: 'We're nothing but a ragbag of disappeared ancestors.' We inherited our warlike nature from prehistoric bands that were able to kill their neighbors and acquire their resources. These groups flourished while the pacifists withered on the evolutionary vine. Another likely reason why war became part of our nature is its intimate relationship with sex. Not only do warriors acquire females as booty, warrior heroes also have an aura of glamour that makes them especially desirable mates. As a result, they have mating opportunities denied to other men. A penchant for war enhanced men's reproductive success, which is why it was selected into our behavioral repertoire."[46]

Violent behavior seems to be bred into us—with all its consequences. Violence injures, paralyses, and kills. And in spite of the long march of civilization we have retained our bloodlust. It doesn't take much—as the many wars in our history show—for us to regress to violent behavior. The extent of the biological basis of our behavior may be indicated by the ease with which children become interested in fishing, hunting, fighting, and war games.

Take a snap shot at any point in the history of humankind and you will find that aggression has always been an inescapable aspect of the human condition, just as it is now and (most assuredly) always will be. I have to conclude that our Paleolithic ancestors were anything but "noble savages." Starting from our genesis, we have never been much of a loving kind. What's more, the transition of *Homo sapiens* from hunter-gathers stage to farmers did not imply the disappearance of the aggression within. It continued to be an intricate part of the human condition. Human aggression (and its derived violent behavior) continued its wayward march at every stage of our evolutionary history. To survive in the harsh world they lived in, our forebears needed to be primed to express the aggression within effectively. But, importantly, they also had *to learn how to manage* this aggressive predisposition.

☞

Lessons from the pundits

One prominent scientist associated with the aggression-as-instinct school was the psychoanalyst Sigmund Freud, who considered aggression to be a consequence of a primary instinct that he called Thanatos—an innate drive toward destruction. He postulated that all humans possess this aggressive drive from birth, and that, together with the sexual drive, it contributes to our development as individuals, and is expressed in our behavior. Although not very knowledgeable about evolutionary processes, Freud made the rather hard-nosed statement that:

" . . . men are not gentle creatures, who want to be loved, who at the most can defend themselves if they are attacked; they are, on the contrary, creatures among whose instinctual endowments is to be reckoned a powerful share of aggressiveness. As a result, their neighbor is for them not only a potential helper or sexual object, but also someone who tempts them to satisfy their aggressiveness on him, to exploit his capacity for work without compensation, to use him sexually without his consent, to seize his possessions, to humiliate him, to cause him pain, to torture and to kill him. *Homo homini lupus* [man is wolf to man]. Who in the face of all his experience of life and of history will have the courage to dispute this assertion? As a rule this cruel aggressiveness waits for some provocation or puts itself at the service of some other purpose, whose goal might also have been reached by milder measures. In circumstances that are favorable to it, when the mental counter-forces which ordinarily inhibit it are out of action, it also manifests itself spontaneously and reveals man as a savage beast to whom consideration towards his own kind is something alien."[47]

A fellow Austrian, the ethologist Konrad Lorenz, concurred and also sug-gested that aggression was innate, an inherited instinct, as significant in humans as it is in other animals. Lorenz defined aggression as the fighting instinct in beast and man that is directed against members of the same species. He related his observations to Darwin's notion of the "struggle for existence." What drives evolution forward is the competition between near relations, because it is always favorable for the species if the stronger of two rivals takes possession of the territory or the female. From his animal studies Lorenz noted a shared instinct to defend territory from encroachment by an animal of the same species, to defeat a rival for a female, and to protect the young and defenseless of the species. He found that such aggression serves the animal kingdom well in that it brings about a balanced distribution of animals of the same species over the available environment.[48]

These two giants in science—coming from two very different perspectives—also shared a belief that we have a reservoir of aggressive energy within us. Their observations suggest that aggression can be viewed as a universal, externally directed drive, possibly connected to a survival instinct, which humankind has in common with the animal world. The suppression of aggressive instincts—a necessary condition in human societies in order for people to live together—means these instincts build up, occasionally to the point where they are released in episodes of explosive violence. According to Freud and Lorenz, this force, which builds up all by itself, needs periodically to be drained off—for example, by participating in (or looking at) competitive sports or even fishing or hunting—lest the human animal explodes into violence. But they also observed that aggression should not merely be seen as a negative force; it is a part of human nature that energizes our relationships, acts as an impetus for psychological development, and enables us to master our world.

⊐

Learned aggression

Returning to the aggression-as-instinct theory, many psychoanalysts and social scientists found Freud's and Lorenz's observations about aggression too speculative. They queried their proposition that aggression should be viewed as a primary drive. Instead, some of them gave more credence to developmental processes and suggested that aggression might be a reaction to the frustration of primary needs. Thus the second theory of aggression moves from innate, evolutionary predispositions (nature), to external stimuli (e.g., frustration), to learned behavior that contributes to aggression (nurture).

Advocates of learning theory point out that the work of many anthropologists totally debunks the aggression-as-instinct school.[49] They maintain that the instinct explanation is insufficient, given the different levels of violent behavior found in various societies. They argue that other explanations are needed, of which nature is the most obvious. The central idea of the developmental (nurture) proposition is that aggression is learned behavior.

Albert Bandura is a major researcher, theorist, and exponent of the social learning theory of aggression.[50] His experiments have shown, for example, that children who observe aggressive adult behavior models reproduce the same kind of behavior, even in new situations, while children in a control group do not do so. Bandura and other psychologists contend that children and adolescents are vulnerable to media portrayals of violence, particularly in film, video games, and on television. They also point out that anonymity may facilitate aggression: when individuals are part of a large group, they are more likely to engage in violent behavior, through a combination of de-individuation and the dehumanizing of their opponents. Essentially, when de-individuation occurs in a group context, a person no longer acts as an individual in his or her own right. This condition is characterized by diminished self-awareness and individuality, and an individual's self-restraint and normative regulation of behavior are reduced.

According to advocates of this way of looking at things, the main cause of violent behavior is believed to originate in early childhood. When humans are subjected to violent environments, they are significantly more likely to behave aggressively themselves. If children are abused or witness abuse, they are more likely to be abusive in adulthood, quite apart from the immediate adverse effect of the violence on them.[51]

Aggression "bound"

These various research streams suggest that a multitude of factors play a role in the genesis of aggression and the manifestation of violence. In a rather oversimplified way—based on the evidence available—I suggest that, like most matters concerning the functioning of the human animal, both nature *and* nurture are at work in the ontogenesis of aggression. People don't act in a specific way on instinct alone. We may be hardwired, but other drivers enable the hardwiring. As human beings *we can have a choice.* Violent acting out is not a question of being on automatic pilot. People may act in particular ways because of their culture, or the way they were brought up; we are all "wired" to some degree—but we are not completely "hardwired" for aggression. *Homo sapiens* are what we are, due to a combination of instinctual, environmental, societal, and cultural variables.

To take an extreme example, in the past a number of tribal groups practiced cannibalism in the Amazon Basin, Africa, Fiji, and New Guinea, usually as part of rituals connected to tribal warfare. This apparently violent behavior may be abhorrent to us, but in a number of primitive cultures, eating an enemy meant gaining his or her strength. It was a cultural artifact. It was a way of paying respect.

All of us have a disposition toward aggression, but this kind of violent behavior—cannibalism—is not merely a question of nature; it is also a question of nurture. It is learned behavior that plays an important role in the way these societies used to function. To quote the anthropologist, Robert Ardrey:

"The miracle of man is not how far he has sunk but how magnificently he has risen. We are known among the stars by our poems, not our corpses. No creature who began as a mathematical improbability, who was selected through millions of years of unprecedented environmental hardship and change for ruggedness, ruthlessness, cunning, and adaptability, and who in the short ten thousand years of what we may call civilization has achieved such wonders as we find about us, may be regarded as a creature without promise."[52]

Beyond determinism

Given the darker side of Homo sapiens, how do we manage the aggression within? How do we prevent violent behavior? Is violent acting out the only way? Is the pharmacological or surgical route our best hope for dealing with the aggression within? Or are there other ways to deal with unbound aggression?

Self-evidently, evolution is not for sissies. The biological processes that drive evolution are relentless. I have already mentioned that the hominids that were most successful in obtaining food and sex were those favored by natural selection mechanisms. Given our evolutionary history, the proclivity to aggression is deeply ingrained in our psyche. However, it as also important for Paleolithic man to belong to a group (again, for reasons of survival). Being a member of a group offered greater protection against predators and hominids outside the group. Other members of the group provided sex, and enabled the continuation of the species. Group members shared food. Hunting was the glue that bound the group; and it was also a way to channel violence.

In Chapter 1, I described how, throughout most of our history, humans have used hunting as a subsistence strategy. A visit to any anthropological museum shows us that. As humans we are made to hunt; it in our DNA; it is part of our mental makeup. Our carnivorous evolutionary development means that the pursuit, killing, and consumption of animal have always been with us. When our ancestors first decided to try meat, they altered the nature of the species. This act had a profound effect on behavior. Without this bold move, Homo sapiens may never have turned out the way it has. Obtaining meat necessitated language development, symbolic learning, long-term planning, and better communication, all of which contributed to brain development.

Evolutionary psychology attempts to explain that mental and behavioral traits are functional products of natural selection. Distinct mental functions—such as perception, reading other people's intentions, responding emotionally to potential mates—are underwritten by different neurological "circuits," which can each be conceived as mini computer programs selected under environmental pressure to solve specific problems of survival and reproduction typical in the original setting of human evolution. Taking this perspective, we can see how far our hunter-gatherer heritage has influenced our behavior as a human species. Our aggression within, expressed through hunting, has been a central factor in assuring the survival of our species.

But *Homo sapiens* also came to realize that "unbounded" violence would lead to the destruction of the species. Without cooperative behavior, the human species would not be able to survive. Evolutionary psychologists suggest that this understanding began to prevail when early hominids realized it was easier to accomplish tasks critical for survival if they worked as a group. Although our hunter-gatherer ancestors may have seen the benefits of violent action, they also discovered the benefits of cooperation. To survive, they needed to learn how to live together. The "survival of the fittest" had to be combined with the "survival of the nicest."

The quintessential example of fitness and niceness at work together is group hunting; wolves and wild dogs hunt in packs because they will end up with a portion of larger game than the small game they could catch on their own; a pride of lions will hunt a large animal like a buffalo, Lord Derby eland, giraffe, or even elephant. Our hunting ancestors did the same, organizing big game drives to stampede game into swamps, over cliffs, or into nets or pits, where large animals would be killed. For our Pleistocene predecessors, hunting in groups yielded more highly valued protein in the form of meat, thus promoting stable patterns of cooperation and exchange.

As I have mentioned before, hunting also provided males with a currency that they could exchange for sexual favors. From an evolutionary perspective, human males may have evolved the kinds of psychological attributes that make hunting a highly satisfying and rewarding experience, despite its many risks. Although it is open to debate to what extent the hunting "instinct" is part of the male *Homo sapiens'* heritage, the fact remains that while both men and women hunt, in the vast majority of human societies hunting is still a predominantly male activity. To be a successful hunter, it was in *Homo sapiens'* interest not only to have a solid dose of aggression within, but also to develop a cooperative predisposition, negating the expression of unbounded violence. In the struggle for survival, we can identify two powerful evolutionary forces that operate simultaneously: aggression and attachment.[53] An innate aggressiveness is born of our need to fight for food, shelter, and the right to breed; innate attachment is based on our human craving to belong to a group.

Taking these push-pull forces into consideration, we are not completely stuck in the deterministic abyss of aggression; there is a glimmer of hope. We have been so successful as a species not only because we are like violent animals but also because we are very social animals. If clan members had spent all their time busily killing one another, they wouldn't have been able to present a united front against an enemy, and overcome the violence without. I believe they exerted choice. As the learning theorists argue, notwithstanding our harsh evolutionary past, we learned how to set boundaries to control our innate violent inclinations.

Taking a historical perspective, our prehistoric ancestors triumphed over much stronger adversaries because they established social communities. Powerful barriers against in-group violence were needed for these to work adequately. Natural selection not only favored aggression, but also favored cooperative behavior. Both of these forces assured a better chance of survival by obtaining food and dealing with danger. Coordinated actions and altruistic behaviors characterized within-group interactions, and violent competition characterized between-group interactions. In the interest of self-preservation they directed aggression toward the "other." *Homo sapiens* needed to learn to channel their aggression. The result of these evolutionary developments has been that we are the most ferocious but also the most cooperative animal that ever inhabited the planet.

From an evolutionary point of view, hunting is an activity full of contradictions. Hunting has become far more than a means of killing animals to put food on the table. It has contributed to an essential part of our socio-cultural development. A violent form of action, it was also essential to the way our ancestors learned about cooperation. And as a practice it has itself evolved; it has become an activity full of symbolic meaning.

Many social and symbolic values—like virility, manliness, resourcefulness, or courage—have become attached to the hunt, which turns into a platform on which these various social forms are enacted. The cultural meanings associated with hunting evolved into ritual, memory, narrative, and symbol and became a powerful signifier of personal identity and socialization within a culture. In our post-industrial society, however, this kind of symbolism no longer reverberates with large sections of society, not without consequences.

⌐

Societal implications

Notwithstanding *Homo sapiens'* ability to be socially cooperative, violence is still an innate part of our behavioral repertoire. Indeed, despite the so-called progress of civilization, the aggression within has continued to haunt the human experience. Thousands of years of warfare have not dampened the human race's disposition toward aggression and violent behavior. What we have seen instead is human intelligence coupling with our capacity for aggression—a deadly combination in an era of nuclear and biological weapons, growing international terrorism, ethnic cleansing, genocide, and state-sponsored, state-organized warfare. In comparison, hunting looks like a state of innocence.

A review of the history of our species shows that our violent, aggressive nature has withstood the march of time—in spite of the forces of cooperation that began with Paleolithic man. Whatever culture we look at, its history has been one of violence. Very, very few of the world's rulers, across time, have been paragons of peacefulness. We have been highly creative in devising ways of treating each other violently—and we still are today. Present-day *Homo sapiens* is a violent species and, helped by more effective killing technologies, has raised the level of violence to astronomical heights. Our history might be titled "A History of Violence."

In today's media-saturated world, we are constantly confronted with accounts of aggression and violence, ranging from sports brawls, rapes and murders, revolutions and wars, terrorist attacks and suicide bombings, to genocide. The apparent universality of aggression seems to support the notion

that humans are "naturally" violent and that aggressive behavior is part of our normal condition. Mankind is still a hunter whose natural instinct is to kill.

Aggression, violence, and population density appear to be intricately linked. *Homo sapiens* are as territorial as the lesser beasts on the evolutionary scale. Again, the trigger for aggression is control over resources. Studies of crowd behavior have shown that population density does not bring out the best in people.[54] Activated by population growth—creating a territorial imperative—a large part of the world is vulnerable to social instability, induced by rising food and energy prices, failing states, water scarcity, climate change, desertification, and increasing migration. These worrisome developments have contributed to a wide range of violent activities that are expressed in various micro and macro ways. The opportunities for us to demonstrate our talent for violent acting out seem unlimited. We see it in the form of child abuse and neglect, youth violence, battered partners, suicidal behavior, sexual violence, the mistreatment of the elderly, self-directed violence, and collective violence. In particular, city life—with its special constraints—can be a prime forum for violent, gang-based behavior.

Whenever I turn on my television or open a newspaper, I see how, all over the world, one group of people is inflicting violent acts on another. Every minute of the day, someone, somewhere, somehow, and in some form, experiences a violent death. And violence hurts individuals, families, communities, and societies. Violence can be individually motivated, the consequence of group actions, or state-sponsored—genocide being its most vicious example. And, unfortunately, in spite of an outer veneer of civilization, state-sponsored violence reached a peak in the 20th century. During its wars, more people were killed than ever before, and the middle and later years were marked by examples of horrifying violence, including the Armenian genocide, Hitler's "final solution" for the Jews of Europe, Stalin's Gulag Archipelago, Mao's Cultural Revolution, the genocide committed by the Khmer Rouge in Cambodia, the Bosnian conflict, and genocide in Rwanda and Darfur, the civil war in Syria. An endless march of violence characterizes our world.

The media do not merely report violence: they intensify it through entertainment—Hollywood films that portray very explicit killing and the proliferation of violent video games. This sorry parade suggests we have a love affair with aggression and violence. Unbounded aggression not only contributes to violence within families, ethic groups, and society, it also contributes to depression, anxiety, and alcohol and drug abuse. Our disposition to unbounded aggression has been the bane of mankind.

A pas de deux with the mujahedeen

Despite the march of civilization, intra-species aggression thrives in this world of ours—and Afghanistan is a good example. As many invaders or "pseudo-invaders" can testify, nobody wins a war in that country. The Russians were in Afghanistan for just over nine years, between 1979 and 1989, and I met several members of their armed forces on my hunting trips in the region. Roasting potatoes outside a tank while you are guarding Dushanbe airport in Tajikistan is not a job for sissies but it is a safer assignment than pursuing the mujahedeen in the mountains of Afghanistan. Also, sleeping in a tank is not exactly the height of luxury. Luxury, however, has never been a reason for enlisting in the Russian army. In fact, the conditions in which these soldiers had to live and work were miserable. The only positive news they could give me was that their war with Afghanistan was winding down. That might have given the new recruits some hope, but it was little comfort to the colleagues and families of the wounded or dead. From the border in Tajikistan, I watched Russian artillery pounding the Pamir mountains. There were plumes of smoke everywhere, the last signs of a war that had gone nowhere. Was the pounding having any effect? Or was it just an exercise in vindictiveness? I wonder. Maybe it helped raise the morale of the people mourning their loved ones.

I have a series of disconcerting, eidetic memories of that trip. One was of returning to the camp we had left the day before after a successful hunt. The way back involved a long, hard, dangerous hike through those same mountains, and not just because of the terrain. There were also human dangers. It was dark before we got close to the camp, which made walking very difficult. I was forbidden to use my flashlight because of the risk of alerting the mujahedeen and at one point I almost fell into a deep hole. For the last few hundred meters, we crawled toward the fire in the distance. There was no question of walking in; we had to check that the mujahedeen had not cut the throats of the people we had left behind. In the end, we found the happy sight of "our" mujahedeen roasting a porcupine on the fire.

I also remember our return to Tajikistan during the night. Suddenly, out of nowhere, a piercing light forced our small, Russian, four-wheel drive bus to an abrupt stop. Blinded, I tried to figure out what was happening. It turned out to be the light on a tank that was preparing to shoot us to smithereens. Fortunately, we had a Russian colonel in the Special Forces with us, who jumped out and screamed something to the men

> in the tank. It had the required effect: they let us go. But we were as close to being killed as I have ever been. The Russian losses in that war had been heavy and in those last days they must have been very much on edge.
>
> Then there was the return flight from Dushanbe to Moscow, which provided an almost surrealist cameo that is burned on my memory. My friend Shahin had managed to convince the Armenian-Russian captain of a transport plane—a gigantic machine—to take us on board. Every square meter on that plane was full and among the cargo were ambulances full of wounded that had simply driven on board. Soldiers sat playing cards on top of the vehicles. *Homo hominis lupus...*

The Milgram experiments and their aftermath

We cannot comfort ourselves by arguing that most violence is due to the actions of especially disturbed, psychopathic individuals. It is simply not true. In the early 1960s, the social psychologist, Stanley Milgram conducted a classic yet controversial experiment on obedience to authority. The results of his experiments demonstrated people's reluctance to confront those who abuse power—and confirmed the existence of the "aggression within." To prove that ordinary people are no strangers to violence, Milgram recruited subjects for his experiments from various walks in life. Respondents were told the experiment would study the effects of punishment on learning ability. "Teachers" (the recruited subjects) were asked to administer increasingly severe electric shocks to the "learners" when they answered questions incorrectly. The experimenter instructed participants to shock a learner by pressing a lever on a machine each time the learner made a mistake on a word-matching task. Each subsequent error would lead to an increase in the intensity of the shock in 15-volt increments, from 15 to 450 volts. In fact, no "learners" were shocked at all. The only electric shocks delivered in the experiment were single 45-volt sample shocks given to each "teacher" at the beginning of the experiment, so that they would get an idea of the strength of the jolts they thought they were discharging. To everyone's dismay, the experiment showed that 37 out of 40 participants (92.5 percent) were willing to progress to the maximum (deadly) voltage level.

Milgram's study demonstrated that the most ordinary individuals could be induced to act destructively even without physical coercion, and humans need not be innately evil or aberrant to act in ways that are reprehensible and inhumane. His experiment provoked a flurry of discussions about the mysteries of human nature and led to profound revisions of some fundamental assumptions about humanity.[55]

⌐

Lupus est homo homini

Can we assume that hunter-gatherer social structures contained much less organized violence and violence against local ecologies than agricultural and industrialized societies? Quite apart from the obvious differences in magnitude, it is hard to answer this question. Has the industrialization of society caused a reallocation of the forces of interpersonal and group violence elsewhere, either directly (through violence on an industrial scale) or internally, through repressive mechanisms? Is the latter an explanation for the dramatic rise of psychosomatic and mental illness? There may be some truth in these questions but there are no cut and dry answers.

Of course, Paleolithic man was no paragon of peacefulness. Our ancient ancestors did not necessarily live in primordial harmony.[56] Anthropological studies of ancient graves indicate high rates of violent death in hunter-gatherer societies. We should not romanticize the behavior of the "noble savage" who remains uncorrupted by the forces of civilization; our ancestors were much more ignoble savages. There is no reason to glorify primitive cultures; they were not inherently "good." The idea that, in a state of nature, human beings are naturally good is a hoax.

However, there is a difference between us and the imaginary noble savage. Nowadays, much of our violent behavior has been sanitized. There is less one-on-one and more detached violence. Fighter pilots, or commanders of drones, do not see their adversary. They don't see burned bodies and body parts; they don't see blood. They are engaged in violence on an anonymous, distant scale. Had these people been hunters—and more sensitized to the direct act of killing— would they be less likely to engage in such activities? Would hunting give them a dose of reality about what violence is all about? Again, these are not easy questions to answer.

⌐

Are hunters more bloodthirsty?

I frequently wonder whether modern man has been able to make the proper transitions necessary for modern living. Have we been able to really move beyond our Paleolithic origins? Are we more civilized in the 21st century? From what we can tell, the notion of *"lupus est homo homini"*—man is a wolf to his fellow man—is still very much with us. Despite the developmental progress we have made, we still prey on each other and notwithstanding our civilized veneer, it would not take much to effect a retrogressive metamorphosis from human to Paleolithic man. In this respect, ontogeny seems to follow phylogeny, meaning the development of each individual seems to be a repetition of the evolutionary history of a race. How successful have we really been in transforming our violent roots?

A good example of this easy metamorphosis into aggression can be seen in James Dickey's 1970 novel, *Deliverance,*[57] in which four middle-aged, suburban men take a weekend canoe trip through the wild hills of northern Georgia, hoping to get away from their sanitized, humdrum lives. But as the novel (and film) shows, not much is needed to bring out their Paleolithic side. They get into danger, and primitive man soon comes to the surface.

The heroes of *Deliverance* are presented as decent, ordinary men forced to confront the violence in nature and their aggression within—a take on modern man versus nature and the need to survive. It is a metaphoric study of civilization and its relation to the environment, in which civilization can be interpreted as destructive, and nature inhospitable and vengeful. The novel describes the transformation of the characters, and their symbolic loss of virginity as they are forced to kill and lie.

The film adaptation of the novel stars Burt Reynolds as the macho Lewis Medlock, a man full of bravado. Obsessed with Hemingway-like notions about establishing true masculinity by challenging nature, Lewis persuades three of his friends, Bobby, Drew, and Ed, into joining him on a white-water canoe trip down an uncharted river in the Appalachians. The locals that Lewis hires to drive their cars downstream warn them about the difficulty of the journey, but this only make the men even more eager to prove themselves. The first day goes smoothly as the men learn how to shoot through the rapids, and they are left feeling exhilarated. On the second day, Ed and Bobby become separated from the others and reach a landing point ahead of them. Two hillbillies suddenly appear from nowhere and decide to hold the two men at gunpoint—this marks the starting point of the trip's downward, regressive spiral. One of the hillbillies sodomizes Bobby. When it is Ed's turn to be raped, Lewis happens by and kills one of the men with an arrow. The other hillbilly manages to escape.

The four men now find themselves dealing with violent sexual assault, serious injury (the super-confident Lewis is incapacitated when he breaks his leg), murder, a cover-up, more murder, and deceit. The psychological angst of the novel is played out in the figure of the narrator, Ed Gentry (played in the film by Jon Voight), as he learns the ways of nature in his fight for survival. But Ed gains the upper hand in the survival game, and in the process matures, discovering a new self-confidence as he matches his wits against a primitive antagonist. As he accepts his more "primitive" state of mind, Ed finds he feels grateful for this opportunity to live life to its fullest. He comes to the realization that when you venture into places where you aren't supposed to go, remarkable self-discoveries can be made.

At the end of the narrative, each man has learned to face his own demons. Drew is dead. Bobby is confused about his sexuality and has lost the self-assurance that he can handle nature. Lewis is humbled and diminished by his injury and has no choice but to relinquish control to Ed. And Ed overcomes his fear of drawing a weapon and striking a live target with the intention to kill. And he has changed: he realizes that continuing to live his comfortable, laid-back, suburban, middle-class existence is no longer an option. He has become more attuned to his inner self and nature—and more comfortable with the aggression within.

Dickey's novel is a cautionary tale of how to manage the aggression within. It is a poetic narrative concerning four naive city dwellers who are confronted with the harsh realities of unforgiving wilderness and ever-present violence. It also shows that civilization is only skin deep. The canoe trip that Ed and his friends take echoes the river journey into the horrifying heart of Africa in Joseph Conrad's classic novel, *Heart of Darkness*. A weekend jaunt turns into a reluctant progress toward the darkest, most violent side of human nature in the course of which the protagonists confront more than they ever bargained for. The Appalachian wilderness and the events that take place there symbolize a moral darkness, an evil that can easily swallow us up. This darkness represents a spiritual emptiness at the center of our existence; but above all it is mystery itself, the mysteriousness of the kind of behavior that will emerge under extreme circumstances. *Deliverance*, and Milgram's experiments, highlight that we all have a shadow side—one filled with savagery that we prefer not to recognize.[58] It is this aggression within that haunts anti-hunting campaigners. But, ironically, as this story and experiment show, scratch a human and you will find a hunter.

Many of us wrestle with this shadow side within ourselves: we try to subdue it, only to learn that it is a never-ending struggle. Perhaps we can only become a whole human being when we own, rather than repress, our shadow side. To quote the psychoanalyst Carl Jung:

> "Unfortunately there can be no doubt that man is, on the whole, less good than he imagines himself or wants to be. Everyone carries a shadow, and the less it is embodied in the individual's conscious life, the blacker and

denser it is. If an inferiority is conscious, one always has a chance to correct it. Furthermore, it is constantly in contact with other interests, so that it is continually subjected to modifications. But if it is repressed and isolated from consciousness, it never gets corrected."[59]

Hunting has always been the matrix occupying a central space in explaining the behavior of the human species. Throughout our evolutionary history, hunting has been our default pattern, an immutable part of our natural state. It has been symbolic of the equilibrium between violence and cooperation. And *Homo sapiens*—until more recent times—has lived with the awareness of our hunting heritage. This aspect of our make-up has been at the center of much of our behavior, and expressed in many different forms, some functional, some extremely dysfunctional. In this context, it is interesting to quote the anthropologist John Pfeiffer's study *The Emergence of Man*:

"Men deprived of hunting as a major source of prestige, deprived of wild species as a major force of aggression, began playing the most dangerous game of all. Men began to go after other men, as if their peers were the only creatures clever enough to make hunting really interesting. So war, the cruelest and most elaborate and most human form of hunting, became one of the most appealing ways of expressing aggression—war has always been more exciting than peace, robbers than cops, hell than heaven, Lucifer than God."[60]

Throughout most of our history, humans have lived with the awareness of the symbiotic relationship between themselves and animals that needed to be killed or protected. Hunting—as the characters in *Deliverance* discovered the hard way—is part of our natural state. Primitive man, apart from embarking on cooperative activities, channeled much of the aggression within into hunting. It was a prime, and socially acceptable, outlet through which to express an aggressive disposition.

Many people, however, have great difficulty in accepting the human disposition toward violent acting out. They prefer to remain in a mist of denial. Yet negating this shadow side of our make-up may mean we lose the very essence of who and what we are. There are reasons why our ancient ancestors bequeathed this propensity for violence to us. It is an important legacy, intended for the purposes of survival.

Realizing the presence of the aggression within can be very disturbing. Some people react very harshly when they recognize in others what they fear in themselves. It becomes the proverbial red rag to a bull; and for some, the red rag is hunting. Anti-hunters frequently accuse hunters of being engaged in a regressive activity that has a negative contamination effect. They believe that, at our evolutionary stage, humankind should only engage in non-violent, higher-level activities. But because they are caught up in their own self-delusion—fearing the aggression within themselves—they violently attack what hunters stand for. From "Psychology 101" we all know that we have a tendency to project on others what we most fear in ourselves—to project and externalize internal problems. Anti-hunters view hunters as part of a regressive spiral, bringing out the worst in humankind. They even go so far as to say that hunters bear most responsibility for contemporary violence, and that people who hunt are more violent than other. Yet these defensive reactions may imply an unwillingness to face that specific part of their own inner make-up.

⌐

Hunting for mental health

How valid is it to say that hunters as a group are more violent than non-hunters? Are hunters really more bloodthirsty? Is the average human being less aggressive than the average hunter? Are hunters very different from that group of middle-aged, suburban men depicted in *Deliverance*? Do hunters have a more violent group disposition?

It would be very convenient for anti-hunting organizations if the answer to all these questions were "yes." However, there is no scientific evidence for these allegations. Hunters are no more violent or bloodthirsty than the rest of the population. The argument that hunting is a breeding ground for aggression is a false one. Specifically, no academic studies have ever shown that hunters have more personality disturbances than the general population.[61] In spite of the false propaganda disseminated by anti-hunting groups, there is no relationship between hunting and poor mental health. Of course, it is always possible to single out certain people with specific psychological disorders who are more violent than others—but not hunters as a group. The difference between hunters and non-hunters may only be in the way in which they direct or sublimate their aggression.

I wonder, in fact, whether there has been sufficient time for *Homo sapiens* to make the adjustments necessary for life in modern society. From an evolutionary perspective, have we truly progressed? Are we managing the aggression within in a proper way? Will there be fallout if we over-control our aggressive disposition? I could hypothesize that the need to repress our instinctual nature is one of the explanations for the dramatic rise of psychosomatic and mental illnesses over the last 100 years or so. As post-industrial humans have, to all appearances, become far removed from our prehistoric roots (including our familiarity with nature), we can speculate that this detachment from our origins may have a high prize tag attached. The price we are paying for increasing urbanization may be much greater than we think. We may have underestimated its social impact. The traditional routes to managing the aggression within—like hunting—have been cut off for the urbanized population, which may contribute to a higher degree of crime and violence. I would go as far as to say that the aggression within—externalized in the hunt—has transmuted into the hunting of men.

The allegations made by anti-hunters that hunters are more violent beg the question of causality, as there is little or no physiological or behavioral evidence to suggest that predatory aggression (hunting) has much in common with intra-species aggression. It is a false association: they might just as well say the same about other activities, such as sex, or running a business, both pursuits that can also have violent consequences. And false associations produce absurdly reductionist equations in which rising crime rates are connected to guns and hunters—conveniently leaving drug dealers and other criminals out of the picture. As a consequence, hunting accidents or poaching incidents receive a lot of media coverage, while the very extensive conservation work done by hunters is generally ignored.

It is true that in the past extensive overhunting, commercial and recreational (in combination with other factors, such as habitat loss and introduced predators), made many species of game animals in the US and elsewhere (passenger pigeon, dodo, Caspian tiger) extinct or nearly extinct but recovered due to hunting conservation efforts (American bison, wild turkey, wisent). It is hunters rather than anti-hunting groups that have been the pioneers in designing game laws and wildlife refuges to save game animals and birds from extinction, and acknowledged the need for sustainable development. Anti-hunting groups are very good at crying wolf but are not known for their generosity in sustaining wildlife, with the exception of their financial generosity toward their own leadership.

Compared to intra-species aggression, inter-species hunting is a much more natural, healthy outlet to cope with the aggression within. Ironically, while hunting has been ostracized in "civilized society," in the inner-city jungle and the theater of war, extremely violent actions have become new avenues of expression. Has the industrialization of society caused a reallocation of the forces of interpersonal violence elsewhere? Compared to the violence common in cities, the incidence of inappropriate behavior by hunters is minuscule.

I am very much aware of the extent to which hunting evokes strong reactions from others, particularly given the work I do. Over the years, my identity as a hunter and fisherman has constantly been viewed with suspicion by the uninformed and misinformed. At times it makes for very awkward and adversarial conversations. Hunters—at least, hunters living in urbanized, Western societies—are increasingly asked to justify their existence. In spite of the evidence to the contrary, anti-hunting advocates continue to condemn hunting as a sadistic, bloodthirsty activity. The psychoanalyst Erich Fromm commented on this in his book *The Anatomy of Human Destructiveness*:

> "The psychology of hunting, including that of the contemporary hunter, calls for extensive study, [but]....there is a considerable body of information about still existing primitive hunters and food gatherers to demonstrate that hunting is not conducive to destructiveness and cruelty...Sadism (which has been alleged to be characteristic of modern hunters by some anti-hunting activists) is much more frequently to be found among frustrated individuals and social classes who feel powerless and have little pleasure in life."[62]

Hunters are not sociopaths; on the contrary, most are peaceful people who have a deep love for nature and wildlife. In all the time I spent with tribal peoples like the pygmies, penan (a nomadic aboriginal people living in Borneo), Inuit or Kirgizian tribesmen, I never witnessed excessive cruelty. Not only is there no evidence that primitive hunters had a deep need to destroy, but the opposite is also the case—there is far more evidence of hunters having affectionate feelings for the animals they pursued. To quote the anthropologist, Colin Turnbull:

> "I am also not convinced that hunting is itself an aggressive activity. This is something that one must see in order to realize; the act of hunting is not carried out in an aggressive spirit at all. Due to the consciousness of depleting natural resources, there is actually a regret of killing life. In some cases, this killing may even bear an element of compassion. My experience with hunters has shown them to be very gentle people, and while it is certainly true that they lead extremely hard lives, this not the same thing as being aggressive."[63]

From the dawn of man, apologies have been made after the killing of an animal. Affection for the animal created feelings of remorse that were—and still are—an intricate part of the hunter's journey.

Contrary to the vitriolic accusations presented by anti-hunting organizations, sadistic and violent behavior is not a characteristic of hunters; I could make a strong case for the opposite being true.

Hunting has always been a "natural" way of dealing with the aggression within—a ritualized way of channeling aggression. Sadistic behavior is less common among hunters than in a random sample of the general population. From my observations I know that if we take children hunting or fishing (as I have done in Canada or Outer Mongolia), they are much less likely to get into trouble.

Children who are taught to hunt responsibly are generally more mature and saner adolescents in "the wilds" of modern life.[64] We should remind ourselves that the forces of cooperation and sharing are just two of the legacies of *Homo sapiens* the hunter.[65] Through hunting, respect, responsibility, and self-control become an intricate part of their personality make-up.

Sport activities versus hunting

There is much evidence that indicates that the hunting experience can be incomparable for helping young people develop into responsible adults who respect life and take responsibility for the world they live in. If we can believe the stories of numerous hunters, myself included, the hunting experience—the escape from the tensions of daily life, by being in fields, climbing a mountain, crossing a river, or walking in the desert—has a calming effect and reduces our aggressive inclinations. And while I do not consider hunting a "sport," comparisons with sports are inevitable.

There are, of course, many other ways than hunting to deal with the aggression within, one of which is sports. There must have been sport-like activities since humankind's earliest days—we only have to watch young children play to know that. But the evolution of sports took a significant step forward with the Olympic Games that started in Greece in 776 BCE. In Roman times these activities became more "refined." During this period, gladiators competed for their lives in amphitheaters comparable to modern day stadiums. These were deadly activities, as gladiators were pitched against each other, wild animals, and condemned criminals, while bloodthirsty spectators egged them on. Over the march of time, these two precursors of modern day sporting events have been refined and made more civilized—but sporting activities can still be viewed as a way of sublimating the aggression within. What else explains why billions of people around the world spend an irrational amount of time watching, playing, reading about, or training for sports?

As anyone who has been to a significant sporting event will know, it is sometimes difficult to draw the boundary between "aggression unbound" and "aggression bound." It may not be fashionable to say so, but many of our most popular sports thrive on violence to attract crowds. Boxing is the most obvious but ice hockey is a prime example, as its sticks and pucks are frequently used to inflict bodily harm. Violent acting out is written into the DNA of sports like rugby or American football. Although at first sight soccer seems comparatively non-violent, soccer fans "help out" with their hooligan-like behavior. In the context of violence in sport, whatever violence can be attributed to hunters, they appear to be distinctly minor league players. However, I haven't yet heard anti-hunting groups condemn any other sporting activity as regressive on the evolutionary scale.

Transcending carnivorous denial

I am prepared to argue that if more people hunted, violent acts toward others (including animals) would not be an abstraction—people would not become desensitized to the origin of their meat or fish. It would bring a greater dose of reality to the fact that humans are primarily carnivorous. What's more, the closeness hunters experience with the game they pursue is very different from the attitude of someone buying a Big Mac, veal chops, or a lobster. Closeness makes for identification, compassion, empathy, remorse, and guilt, reflected in the many rituals associated with the hunt that continue to this day. It has led to many prohibitions about the killing of animals and created the conditions for "fair chase."

Can the same be said about righteous meat- or fish-eating people, or even vegetarians, who condemn hunting—forgetting the impact of large-scale agricultural ventures on the natural world? Or cat owners, who talk about the cruelty of hunters while the exterminating machines they own are killing birds and other creatures, night after night? In comparison, the hunter-gather lifestyle is more compassionate to animals as a whole. In large-scale animal farming the outcome is inevitable: all these animals are going to be slaughtered to provide human food. Breeding and raising and keeping animals purely for consumption has many (suppressed) ramifications—this is the underbelly of our post-industrial world that we don't like to dwell upon. Hunting, on the other hand, brings chance into equation; there's a fair chance that the animal hunted will get away. Surely this is far less abhorrent than creating an animal assembly line of death?

Is it really feasible to insist that obtaining meat through hunting is crueler than going to the butcher to buy milk-fed lamb? Does no one ever trace a Big Mac back to the slaughterhouse? And what about "finger-lickin' good" fried chicken? Anyone who has ever visited the huge agro-industrial farms that supply these fast-food outlets very quickly gains an understanding of animal misery. If people with modern sensibilities took care to source their own meat, they might be more wary of taking human life. Instead of stimulating violent acting out, it may do just the opposite.

The march of civilization—despite our talent for violence—has been accompanied by an increase in ambivalence about our hunting heritage. At times, the level of negation has reached the height of absurdity. For example, in his essay "Vindication of a Natural Diet," the English poet Percy Bysshe Shelley argued that vegetarianism was ethically and medically superior: human beings, according to Shelley, started as gatherers of vegetable food and only later took to eating meat, which brought with it violence and disease. He claimed that the depravity of the physical and moral nature of man originated in his unnatural habits, and made it a rule "to never take any substance into the stomach that once had life." [66] It is clear Shelley should have stuck to poetry. He was no scholar of biology, anthropology, evolutionary psychology, or nutritional science. He seems to have been quite ignorant of the materials necessary (in the form of food) to support life. His simple cause-and-effect analysis showed no understanding of complex, interrelated bio-systems.

Shelley's wistful view of the superiority of vegetarianism has not been backed up by anthropological studies. The remains of *Homo habilis* (the forerunner of our own species, who lived more than two million years ago) have been found along with butchered animal bones. As I mentioned in Chapter 1, it is most probable that these pre-humans were scavengers rather than hunters, eating meat from carcasses killed by other animals. But *Homo erectus*, who flourished around half a million years ago, was almost certainly a hunter; and by the time our species, *Homo sapiens*, emerged, human beings were carnivorous, meat-eaters who got their meat through hunting.

⊨

Acknowledging our hunting heritage

Given *Homo sapiens'* extremely short history on Earth, we may need to ask ourselves how much humankind has really changed. Are we really that civilized or is our civilization only skin deep? And I have already questioned whether we are so different from our Pleistocene ancestors? Well over 99 percent of our species' evolutionary history has evolved living as hunter-gatherers in small nomadic bands. In this life-long "camping trip," our ancestors had to detect and avoid predators, develop alliances to defend themselves against aggression, obtain food, and select mates, all ultimately for the purpose of the survival of the species. We can confidently say that the need to hunt is bred into the bones and blood of all of us. It is one of the most fundamental elements of human nature. It is part of our identity as a human being.

Natural selection is a slow and imperfect process that occurs at a glacial pace. In many cases, our brains are better adapted to solve the problems faced by our ancestors on the African savannas that those we encounter in contemporary society, in the classroom, or at work. Something that was a successful fit in the past might contribute to maladaptive behavior in the present. We could even argue that we are faced with problems for which we are not properly equipped. But is denying our evolutionary roots—that rich storage of knowledge of man, the hunter—the answer?

The anthropologist Robert Ardrey noted: "For millions of years we survived as hunters. In the few millennia since our divorce from that necessity, there has been no time for significant biological change—anatomical, physiological or behavioral. Today, we have small hope of comprehending ourselves and our world unless we understand that man still, in his innermost being, is a hunter."[67] The mental mechanisms designed to serve the needs of our ancient ancestors—for whom hunting was a major preoccupation—continue to exert a subtle and powerful influence on human thought and behavior today. William Laughlin, another anthropologist, concurred and added: "Hunting is the master behavior pattern of the human species. It is the organizing activity which integrates the morphological, physiological, genetic and intellectual aspects of the human organism and the population who comprise our species."[68]

Hunting has made a major contribution to transforming our primitive ancestors and to the development of civilization as we know it. Apart from fulfilling a basic need for meat, it contributed to the creation of complex networks of social interaction, as I discussed in greater detail in Chapter 1. It created the basis for culture and led to the sophisticated frameworks on which contemporary society has been built. Moving from necessity to choice, the remnants of our hunting instinct are expressed in many different ways, of which violent intra-species behavior is one of the more destructive.

Considering all the alternatives—and reflecting on what is happening in contemporary society—hunting retains an aura of relative innocence. Many stories of hunting celebrate togetherness in nature and togetherness with people close to us. The desire to hunt can be explained as the modern vestige of an evolutionary trait of utmost adaptive significance to early humans.

However, I realize that notwithstanding any of the arguments I make, anti-hunting groups will have great difficulty understanding or accepting *Homo sapiens'* hunting origins. Their incomprehension is not helped by the fact that most antis have never lived in the country or spent time in the outdoors. How can people born and brought up in cities really understand that killing and death are part of the cycle of life? These people never leave their urban deserts and never experience nature. Given their background and their indoctrination through sanitized nature movies, they have a somewhat idealistic way of looking at the way animals interact. I would not be surprised, however, if deep down, they know the truth of it—but denial, and an unwillingness to be involved in the messy business of obtaining meat, is a much easier option. Animal behavior is not like Noah's Ark, with lamb and lion living peacefully side-by-side. On the contrary, inter-species violence is a fact of life. In this context the science writer Edward Ricciuti writes:

"The impasse between hunter and anti-hunter is to some extent a measure of how much and what kind of contact people have with wild animals. Most naturalists, biologists, and zoologists I have met hunt, or if not, have no objection to people who do. People who blindly oppose hunting, on the other hand, very often have limited exposure to wild animals—perhaps only at the zoo, or when feeding squirrels in the park, for instance. The ranks of anti-hunters also are filled with people whose ideas about the way animals live in the wild have been colored by the antics of the humanized beasties of the boob tube."[69]

Many of these people have lost touch with their core identity as *Homo sapiens* the hunter. They have found other outlets for dealing with the violence within—and, ironically, targeting hunters is a favorite one. But in their ardor to vilify hunters, they attack a significant part of their own selves and negate a central part of their own identity. Perhaps one of the more understandable reasons why they act the way they do may be that the wars of the 20th century have made us more sensitive to violence and less able to endure the idea of killing as an activity. At the same time, modern life has so cut us off from the natural world that few of us get any closer to wild animals than as onlookers, like television viewers for whom nature has become merely a spectacle. The outcome has been that it upsets us even to see animals killing each other. We have become far removed from the hunter of antiquity, the medieval huntsman (let alone the prehistoric hunter-gatherer), and from the processes of life and death.

In closing, I ask myself once again whether the degree of violence in cities is an unfortunate aberration of an archaic need to hunt. Can crime and other forms of violent behavior be viewed as twisted manifestations of this need? Can crime be the consequence of the fact that many young people living in cities don't know about hunting—or sport— as a sublimatory way of working through their violent predispositions? Given our lineage as a predator, and the role of the hunt in the formation of social identity, these questions are worth further exploration. We have to find better ways to deal with aggression unbound.

While "aggression unbound" can destroy a society, "bounded aggression," in the form of hunting (or other activities), may have the opposite effect. Innumerable people hunt because they enjoy it. Hunting offers a physical and mental sublimatory outlet that is hard to replicate. The opportunity to reconnect and reaffirm our identity with our historic past improves our mental health. Being one with nature makes us feel better about ourselves. Unfortunately, for far too many people, this link with our historic origins has been lost, largely through urban living, contributing to unbounded violence. Playing computerized war games or watching violent movies offers excitement to many. These activities evoke memories—in perverted form—of their true, archaic self. By comparison, peace comes across as extremely boring. Wouldn't outdoor activities, such as hunting and fishing, offer a much more constructive solution to the aggression within?

43 — de Waal, Frans. *Our Inner Ape*. New York: Riverhead, 2005.

44 — Ardrey, Robert. *African Genesis: A Personal Investigation into the Animal Origins and Nature of Man*. London: Collins, 1961, pp. 18-19.

45 — *Ibid*, p. 6.

46 — *Ibid*, p. 81.

47 — Sigmund, Freud. *Civilization and Its Discontents*. New York: W. W. Norton & Company, 1989, p. 58.

48 — Lorenz, Konrad. *On Aggression*. New York: Harcourt, Brace & World, Inc., 1966, p. ix.

49 — Fromm, Eric. *The Anatomy of Human Destructiveness*. Greenwich, CT: Fawcett Crest, 1973, p.17.

50 — Bandura, Albert. "The Social Learning Theory of Aggression." In R. A. Falk and S. S. Kim (Eds.), *The War System: An Interdisciplinary Approach*. Boulder, CO: Westview Press, 1980.

51 — Kets de Vries, Manfred F.R. *Lessons on Leadership by Terror: Finding Shaka Zulu in the Attic*. Cheltenham: Edward Elgar, 2004.

52 — Ibid p. 348.

53 — Lichtenberg, Joseph. *Psychoanalysis and Motivation*. Hillsdale, NJ: Analytic Press, 1989.

54 — Hayes, Nicky. *Foundations of Psychology*. 3rd ed., Andover, Hampshire: Cengage Learning Business Press, 2000.

55 — Milgram, Stanley. *Obedience to Authority: An Experimental View*. New York: Harper and Row, 1974.

56 — Ancient Warfare Fighting for the Greater Good http://www.newscientist.com/article/dn17255-ancient-warfare-fighting-for-the-greater-good.html

57 — Dickey, James. *Deliverance*, New York: Dell Publishing, 1970.

58 — Kets de Vries, Manfred F.R. *Lessons on Leadership by Terror: Finding Shaka Zulu in the Attic*. Cheltenham: Edward Edgar, 2004.

59 — Jung, Carl G. "Psychology and Religion". In *Psychology and Religion: West and East. Collected Works* (Vol. 11). Princeton: Princeton University Press, Bollinger series, 1938, p.131.

60 — Pfeiffer, John E. *The Emergence of Man*. New York: Harper & Row, 1978.

61 — Swan, James A. "Hunting and Mental Health," *IWMC World Conservation Trust*, 2005 http://www.iwmc.org/IWMC-Forum/JamesSwan/041024-01.htm

62 — Fromm, Eric. *The Anatomy of Human Destructiveness*. New York: Fawcett Crest, 1975, p. 160.

63 — Turnbull, Colin. M. *Wayward Servants, or the Two World of the African Pygmies*. London: Eyre & Spottiswood, 1965, p. 72.

64 — Konner, Melvin. *The Tangled Wing: Biological Constraints on the Human Spirit*, 2nd ed. (original 1982). New York: Times Books, 2002.

65 — Flynn, Clifton P. "Hunting and Illegal Violence Against Humans and Other Animals: Exploring the Relationship," *Society and Animals*, 10, (2), 2002, pp. 137-154.

66 — Shelley, Percy Bysshe. "Vindication of a Natural Diet," 1813. http://www.animal-rights-library.com/texts-c/shelley01.htm

67 — Ardrey, Robert. *The Hunting Hypothesis: A Personal Conclusion Concerning the Evolutionary Nature of Man*. New York: Antheum, 1976, p. 187.

68 — Laughlin, William S. "Hunting: An Integrated Biobehavior System and its Evolutionary Importance," In *Man the Hunter*, Irvin DeVore and Richard Lee (eds). Illinois: Aldine, 1968, p. 304.

69 — Ricciuti, Edward R. *Killer Animals: The Menace of Animals in the World of Man*. Guilford, Delaware: The Lyons Press, 2003.

When some of my friends have asked me
anxiously about their boys, whether they
should let them hunt, I have answered, yes—
remembering that it was one of the best parts
of my education—make them hunters.
    —Henry David Thoreau, *Walden*

The wild life of today is not ours to do with
as we please. The original stock was given to
us in trust for the benefit both of the present
and the future. We must render an accounting
of this trust to those who come after us.
    —Theodore Roosevelt

Harmony with land is like harmony
with a friend; you cannot cherish his
right hand and chop off his left.
    —Aldo Leopold

Emotional occasions, especially violent
ones, are extremely potent in precipitating
mental rearrangements. The sudden and
explosive ways in which love, jealousy,
guilt, fear, remorse, or anger can seize
upon one are known to everybody,... And
emotions that come in this explosive way
seldom leave things as they found them.
    —William James

FEAR, ELATION, AND REMORSE

One late afternoon, close to Lake Kariba, in Zimbabwe, my wife and I took a wilderness hike following a dry riverbed. The plan was to hunt for kudu, which at that time, I had been unsuccessful in obtaining. I guess everyone (and I was no different) wants a kudu once. Ever since Ernest Hemingway published his semi-autobiographical book, *The Green Hills of Africa*, the kudu has been at the top of the wish list for almost all (at least first-time) African hunters.[70] Without a doubt the greater kudu, with its white-striped coat, black-and-white neck ruff, brilliant white nose chevron, and marvelous horns, is the most recognizable of all African antelopes.

The walk turned out to be very memorable, full of exciting encounters. First, we met a bull elephant "midstream," if such a word can be used while walking on a dry riverbed. Lone bull elephants are easily riled: We just got out of the way of one before it had the chance to lose its temper and charge. The next high point was crossing the fresh tracks of a pride of lions. As our timing was off, and the light was fading fast, this added a dose of excitement to our little odyssey. But there was more to come. Clearly, the lions were following a herd of buffalos that had to be nearby, because we could smell them. This emotionally stimulating walk ended dramatically when we almost fell over a fresh leopard kill that was sticking out of some kind of grotto—we had had to come to a screeching halt, as we realized we were in very close proximity to the backsides of a herd of elephants. Did I like it? I certainly did. Would I do it again? No question about it. Unlike my usual walk in the Jardin du Luxembourg in Paris, close to where I live, this "little" hike in the African wilds touched something deep inside, and lingers with me still.

Although hunting plays an important role in helping us to get in touch with our core identity (as I have emphasized before), the activity has always been characterized by a great deal of ambivalence. For the hunter, the emotional feelings associated with the hunt are a mixture of elation and remorse, thrill and regret, reason and unreason. As I have stated repeatedly, I am always in two minds at the prospect of killing an animal, engaged in a wordless inner dialogue in which remorse and regret play an important role. The essayist Barry Lopez, in his book *Arctic Dreams*, describes this state of mind very well:

"Hunting in my experience—and by hunting I simply mean being out on the land—is a state of mind. All of one's faculties are brought to bear in an effort to become fully incorporated into the landscape. It is more than listening for animals or watching for hoof prints or a shift in the weather. It is more than an analysis of what one senses. To hunt means to have the land around you like clothing. To engage in a wordless dialogue with it, one so absorbing that you cease to talk with your human companions. It means to release yourself from rational images of what something 'means' and to be concerned only that it 'is.' And then to recognize that things exist only insofar as they can be related to other things. These relationships—fresh drops of moisture on top of rocks at a river crossing and a raven's distant voice—become patterns. The patterns are always in motion. Suddenly the pattern—which includes physical hunger, a memory of your family, and memories of the valley you are walking through, these particular plants and smells—takes in the caribou. There is a caribou standing in front of you. The release of the arrow or bullet is like a word spoken out loud. It occurs at the periphery of your concentration."[71]

Unio mystica

Although the conditions may have changed, the many emotions that drive the archaic desire to hunt (not necessarily a conscious process) are undeniable. As I have previously indicated, this desire is an essential part of our human identity and evolutionary heritage. The inclination to join in the seasonal ritual of the hunt derives from basic motivational need systems that are far removed from prosaic arguments for or against hunting. In spite of many evolutionary developments, the love of being in wild country still thrills most of us. Being in hunting mode only intensifies these feelings. The echoes of our archaic, forgotten past resonate within all of us, and particularly the hunter. To a true hunter, the joy of hunting is intimately woven with the love of the great outdoors, the love of nature, the love of wildlife, and the love of the chase. For many hunters, the beauty of woods, valleys, mountains, rivers, and skies has a positive effect on their mental health. The quest for game only intensifies these feelings of energized focus, and full involvement. It relates to a feeling of *unio mystica* (mystical union), a state of boundlessness in which the individual seems to merge with the universe.

This *unio mystica* can be viewed as the cognitive and affective merging of the individual consciousness with a superior, or supreme, consciousness. It implies the pursuit of communion and identification with, and conscious awareness of, an ultimate reality, divinity, or spiritual truth. It means liberation from the fetters of finitude, which is itself made up of a multitude of strands: one is human and consists of an array of emotional, psychological, and physical layers; the other is nature, in all its complexity.

Many hunters experience this feeling of *unio mystica*. As I mentioned in the introduction to this book, for the ethical hunter, the key to the joy of hunting is not killing; first and foremost, it is the journey, the appreciation of the outdoors, the subtle contest of skills, and the use of resourcefulness in survival. It is the satisfaction that comes with applying "nature intelligence," the ability to read and live off the land. True hunters count their achievements in proportion to the efforts involved and the fairness of the hunting activity. At the risk of repeating myself, the "kill" is only one element in this mysterious equation.

I associate hunting with solitude, scenery, aesthetics, physical ability, courage, resilience, and independence. As hunting is part of our living heritage, and of our core identity as human beings, a mysterious aura remains attached to it, largely because the reasons behind the desire to hunt are so multifarious. For those who are seduced by the sirens of hunting, no further explanation is needed. And, unfortunately, no explanation will ever be good enough for those who don't hunt and are strangers to nature. If asked why they hunt, most hunters (including me) will talk about the magic and poetry of the hunt, of having caught the fervor at a very early age, and usually of being brought up in the great outdoors or on a farm—something that is less and less common in our post-industrial age. People who cannot live without "wild things" often have great difficulty expressing this need to those who can. It is very hard to put into words the very intense experiences that come with being in nature. How do you describe ecstasy? Because being ecstatic is part of the nature experience.

Ecstasy, a word derived from ancient Greek, means to be outside ourselves, being in an altered or trancelike state of consciousness. When ecstatic, I transcend ordinary consciousness—and as a result have a heightened capacity for exceptional thought, intense concentration on a specific task, extraordinary physical ability, and an expanded mental and spiritual awareness, frequently accompanied by visions, hallucinations, and even physical euphoria.

Sometimes we don't understand these ecstatic feelings ourselves, and prefer not to talk about them, even though they may drive our very souls. When I talk about my feelings about nature and wildlife with people who know nothing about hunting, or worse, oppose it, I often wonder whether it wouldn't be better to just shut up and not bother with explanations. Why talk about our evolutionary origins? Why mention the joys of being in the outdoors? Why refer to hunting as part of our core identity, our primary heritage, as human beings— as being part of our true self? Why talk about a hunting "instinct" or the theme of "bounded aggression?" I have learned from experience that however I try to explain my need to be in the outdoors, I rarely supply the kinds of response the people who are ignorant about hunting (or fishing) are looking for. Those exchanges fail to bridge the different mindsets.

But putting any psychological explanations aside—at least for now—when I am hunting, I feel different than I do in my "normal," more humdrum life. As a hunter, I am immersed mentally, physically, and even spiritually in an ancient predator-prey relationship similar to those that exist in the animal world. Obviously, in normal circumstances, I do not need to kill to survive—although I really enjoy and appreciate eating game. But, to paraphrase Ortega y Gasset once again, I kill in order to have hunted. I hunt to feel alive.

To non-hunters, many of these observations will appear quite contradictory and even puzzling. But, at times, hunting brings us into a metaphysical terrain, and exposes us to inherent or universal elements of reality that are not easily discovered or experienced in our everyday life. Hunting becomes a paradoxical search for meaning. Hunting helps me to go beyond the "manic defense"—the various ways we all use to fend off the depression that comes with the realization of our mortality. Hunting gives me the opportunity to reflect on what life is about. It brings me back to the joy that can be found in the moment; the silence of the hunt brings me peace, introspection, and renewed energy. Reflection offers me the chance to reconnect with the people important to me—something too easily neglected in our busy daily life.

This touch of the metaphysical makes an in-depth examination of what hunting is about difficult, as it touches on the existential question of why we are here. To quote the writer James Swan, "Hunters these days ultimately hunt memories as much as much as meat to put on the table. Memories feed dreams, and hunters must have dreams to keep them motivated. When you lose your dreams, you lose your mind."[72] Again, matters of hunting and mental health become intertwined. Hunting helps me with the difficulties of living. After all, without memories, there is no life. My hunting memories sustain me in difficult moments and recharge me when times are tough.

🐾

A communion with nature

In his essays on the outdoors, the highly influential American environmentalist Aldo Leopold attempts to describe his personal relationship with his natural surroundings. He writes about his childhood, growing up hunting, and exploring the environment where he lived. One of his most moving passages describes a stretch of water once known for its excellent canoeing, and teeming with wildlife. Sadly, over time, more and more cottages and urban sprawl disturbed the wildlife that lived there until eventually only a small, protected span remained. Leopold concludes regretfully that tomorrow's children will probably never know what it means to canoe down a river watching wildlife, and so will not even miss it. He observes:

> "For unnumbered centuries of human history the wilderness has given way. The priority of industry has become dogma. Are we as yet sufficiently enlightened to realize that we must now challenge that dogma, or do without our wilderness? Do we realize that industry, which has been our good servant, might make a poor master? Let no man expect that one lone government bureau is able—even though it be willing—to thrash out this question alone...
>
> ... Our remnants of wilderness will yield bigger values to the nation's character and health than they will to its pocketbook, and to destroy them will be to admit that the latter are the only values that interest us."[73]

Three themes stand out in Leopold's meditations: pleas for an appreciation of ecology, conservation ethics, and culture.[74] He suggests:

> "Conservation is a state of harmony between men and land. By land is meant all of the things on, over, or in the earth. Harmony with land is like harmony with a friend; you cannot cherish his right hand and chop off his left. That is to say, you cannot love game and hate predators; you cannot conserve the waters and waste the ranges; you cannot build the forest and mine the farm. The land is one organism. Its parts, like our own parts,

compete with each other and co-operate with each other. The competitions are as much a part of the inner workings as the cooperations. You can regulate them—cautiously—but not abolish them."[75]

Much of what Leopold writes is in the context of hunting. Although he doesn't refer to the concept of our core identity as a hunter, Leopold argues that people hunt in order to maintain their connection with nature—to stay in touch with their origins. As only a hunter can, he identifies the hunter's reverence for nature. The power of his book, *A Sand County Almanac*, is that it helps us see in many different ways that the land is an organism, a circulating system, of which we are but a minor part. If and when we tinker with the land, we must exercise great care. According to Leopold, we do the right thing when we preserve the integrity, stability, and beauty of the existing ecological system—and the wrong thing when we don't.

In one passage in *A Sand Country Almanac*, Leopold reflects on an encounter with wolves:

"In those days we had never heard of passing up a chance to kill a wolf. In a second we were pumping lead into the pack, but with more excitement than accuracy: how to aim a steep downhill shot is always confusing. When our rifles were empty, the old wolf was down, and a pup was dragging a leg into impassable slide rocks.

We reached the old wolf in time to watch a fierce green fire dying in her eyes. I realized then, and have known ever since, that there was something new to me in those eyes—something only known to her and the mountain...I thought that because fewer wolves meant more deer, that no wolves would mean hunters' paradise. But after the green fire died, I sensed that neither the wolf nor the mountain agreed with such a view.

Since then I have lived to see state after state extirpate its wolves. I have watched the face of many a newly wolfless mountain, and seen the south-facing slopes wrinkle with a maze of new deer trails. I have seen every edible bush and seedling browsed, first to anemic destitute, and then to death.

...I now suspect that just as a deer herd lives in mortal fear of its wolves, so does a mountain live in mortal fear of its deer. And perhaps with better cause, for while a buck pulled down by wolves can be replaced in two or three years, a range pulled down by too many deer may fail of replacement in as many decades."[76]

Leopold's point that "a mountain lives in mortal fear of its deer" is very well put. I wonder if he was familiar with the Inuit statement, "The caribou feeds the wolf, but it is the wolf that keeps the caribou strong," which encapsulates their awareness of the phenomenon of symbiosis in the natural world. We *need* to take a systemic view of the natural world and to understand these complex interrelationships. In *The Origin of the Species*, Charles Darwin famously wrote:

"I have very little doubt, that if the whole genus of bumble-bees became extinct or very rare in England, the heartsease and red clover would become very rare, or wholly disappear. The number of bumble-bees in any district depends in a great degree on the number of field-mice, which destroy their combs and nests...more than two-thirds of them are thus destroyed all over England. Now the number of mice is largely dependent, as every one knows, on the number of cats... Hence it is quite credible that the presence of a feline animal in large numbers in a district might determine through the intervention first of mice and then of bees, the frequency of certain flowers in that district!"[77]

The English biologist Thomas Henry Huxley, a great admirer of Darwin's work, dramatized the need for a more systemic view of nature, and extended Darwin's example, through his (tongue-in-cheek) hypothesis that the success of the rapidly expanding British Empire depended in fact on "old maids" who sat quietly at home. Huxley argued that the economy of the Empire was based on the roast beef eaten by its soldiers, who made the British expansion into other lands possible; the source of the beef was cattle that grazed on red clover. Red clover is pollinated by bumble bees whose proliferation depends, as Darwin showed, on the number of field mice. In a roundabout way, cats protect the bumblebees because they eat the mice that prey on their honey. "Old maids" are the most likely people to keep cats—so, Huxley concluded, the continued expansion and success of the British Empire was dependent on a number of cat-loving, elderly, unmarried ladies.[78] Clever as Huxley's example is, however, he forgot another systemic reality: Cats eat other living things than mice and in fact cause major ecological disruption as the number one killer of birdlife in areas where they proliferate.

Darwin and Huxley's examples help us to understand the highly complex, intense, personal, and interdependent relationship between the hunter, its prey, and the environment in which the hunt takes place. Hunting—and with it humanity—will be endangered if it doesn't take care of the precious resource that is nature.

My personal experience is that my desire to hunt or fish is to some extent a reaction against the sterility of modern living and the ugliness of urban life. The need I feel to participate actively in the bio-system—a system formed by the interaction of a community of organisms with their physical environment—reaffirms an archaic impulse within myself. It requires me to acknowledge that I am an intricate part of nature, and that I share the grave responsibility of maintaining its sustainability. As a hunter, I am a steward of nature, part of an early warning system, and as such I have to be prepared to take action when things are not right. Hunting is also my way of dealing constructively with the "aggression within," as described in Chapter 3. Living in an urban setting has removed me physically and spiritually from nature; hunting helps me to re-establish a bond that has always been there but has been pushed aside or neglected. Hunting is also a deceptively simple way of getting back to basics and reflecting on the meaning of life.

Journeys into the wild

I will never forget the first time I hunted for wild turkey. It was in the Fall and I was with my father, who had been invited by one of his clients to hunt on a small island on Lake Ontario. I was delighted to be one of the guests. At the time, I was a post-doctoral fellow at the Harvard Business School and didn't have many opportunities to hunt. But more important was the opportunity to be with my father—I didn't see him very often, as we were living on two different continents.

On the island we hunted for pheasants (which were plentiful) and shot a few ducks but there were no turkeys to be seen. On the last day of the hunt, I was hanging on to an open truck on our way back to the lodge when I saw a flock of wild turkeys cross a side path. After having been so good for so long at hide-and-seek, the turkeys were now in the wrong place at the wrong time. I jumped off the truck, and snuck up after them, managing to my great surprise to get two. As the only member of the hunting party to have wild turkey to his record, I was not Mr. Popular. But this particular hunting experience taught me to respect these large birds. Many years later, I still remember how good that turkey tasted, very different from the dry turkey meat we get from farmed birds.

Luckily there were more occasions to hunt wild turkey. The most memorable was in Florida. One early spring morning, I was sitting on wet grass in the middle of a Florida swamp, the mist dimming my vision, but experiencing a sense of

peace despite the rising damp. Close by, I heard the sound of a woodpecker, noisily hacking at a dead stump. Suddenly, I picked up, far away, the distinctive, piercing, and eerie call of a pair of whooping cranes performing a duet, or unison call, to advertise their breeding territory to others. For me, cranes are an awesome representation of the wilderness and a symbol of our untamable past. I had seen these very rare birds the previous day while stalking for alligators. As we drew closer to them, they protested our encroachment with great fervor, standing their place and refusing to fly away.

I knew that somewhere in one of the tall palmetto trees not far from me, a solitary male gobbler was roosting. I also knew that his harem would be resting lower down on the ridge of the creek bank, where he could keep an eye on them. The question was how to get that gobbler within range. It was a real challenge because turkeys (contrary to all the derogatory jokes) are anything but stupid.

This particular turkey seemed to be quite content to stay where it was. While I was lying low, and trying to deal with the cramp in my legs, the silence was broken by a faint gobble in the distance. To me, at the time, it sounded like one of the wildest of nature's calls. My guide gobbled back. Soon after, a female turkey came running in our direction, almost crashing straight into us. Afraid that I would make a mistake, my guide hissed at me, "Don't shoot." The scene made me tense up: It was like a foretaste of what was to come. The hen turkey disappeared, probably having a nervous breakdown after having come so close to humans. Again, there was a very silent silence. The guide gobbled again, and swore silently to himself—he felt we had come, seen, and failed to conquer. Suddenly, out of nowhere, the "long beard" appeared, strutting through the reeds, puffed up and blue in the face. The copper and bronze of his feathers were quite a sight and his fanned-out tail another marvel. I was motionless—no game species in the world detects motion as well and reacts as quickly as a wild turkey. The lord of the swamp came closer, looking in our direction, stretching his neck to see where the sound had come from. He wanted to know where the intruder was so he could give it the evil eye. But the moment of truth had come. A big, feathered gobbler approaching in full strut is an unforgettable sight. The predator in me was fully awake, tensing up as the turkey, its head wagging, stalked toward us. I was ready....

As this Florida hunt illustrates, it doesn't take much to reawaken the hunter inside us. In my case, I had just arrived from Paris, having taken a plane to Miami. I had spent a day with a group of entrepreneurs talking about personality types, effective leadership behavior, innovation, teams, and high performance organizations. I had played the role of the professor. But 24 hours later, I was quite some sight, covered in mud, turkey blood dripping down my trousers. It hadn't taken much to bring me back to basics. I couldn't help wondering what my entrepreneurs would have said if they could have seen their professor at that moment.

Aside from the beautiful sunrises (and sunsets), the incredible vistas, and the invigorating exercise in mountains, tundra, prairies, swamps, rain forests or savannas, what attracts me to hunting is that it takes me out of myself into a slightly altered state of consciousness. While hunting, the concerns of day-to-day living are put to one side; in wild country, they are no longer relevant. As a hunter, I enter a very different realm, a space of make-believe or limbo, between play and reality.

There's nothing quite like following the track of an animal, spotting its silhouette in the distance, and trying to get closer. It is a transformative experience: I become the predator inside me. I enter a more right-brain state of mind, and while in the "flow," all my senses are turned to their maximum capacity to execute my objective. It is hard to describe this experience to people who have never been in a similar situation; even as I write this, I can see that some people reading it will think I have lost it. But as an educator, I firmly believe that some activities can only be understood experientially. We need to go through them to really make sense of them. I once participated in fire walk. How can I explain or convince others that walking on glowing coals doesn't hurt at all? It sounds quite unbelievable, even, in hindsight, to me—and I did it.

The prey-predator bond is very close because it is a relationship that can easily go either way. For example, I was once fly-fishing for golden mahseer in Corbett Park in Utter Pradesh, a state in Northern India. The park was named in memory of Jim Corbett, the Indian-born Irish hunter, naturalist, and conservationist, famous for his accounts of hunting man-eating cats, who had helped in marking out its boundaries and setting it up.

Corbett Park is notorious for its tigers. Just before my arrival, two people had been killed and partially eaten by tigers, one of them a servant collecting firewood, and the other an English birdwatcher who hadn't followed the park rules: he was taking photographs on foot. Nobody is permitted to walk in the park, precisely in order to prevent such incidents: you have to be in a car or on an elephant. I had myself seen a tiger while safely seated on an elephant. It stepped into a clearing in the dense jungle epitomizing the scene I always envisage when reading William Blake's famous poem:

"Tiger, tiger, burning bright
In the forests of the night.
What immortal hand or eye
Dare frame thy fearful symmetry?"

It happened so quickly that I hadn't even enough time to alert my wife and daughter, who were sitting back-to-back with me on the same elephant, and so looking in a different direction. By the time they had turned round, the tiger— like a phantom—had disappeared into the jungle.

You cannot fly fish from a car or an elephant, of course, so because of that, and because of my very personal relationship with one of the ministers in the Indian government at that time, I had permission to fish in the park (on foot) as long as I was accompanied by one of the park rangers (armed with a very old Lee Enfield rifle whose operational usefulness looked highly doubtful) for protection. I was fishing for golden mahseer, a giant member of the carp family that looks more like a salmon. I was very excited to be allowed to fish but having the ranger with me at all times defeated my quest for solitude. I also rapidly discovered that his company was not simply useless, it was actually disturbing, as he was not very observant. I decided—irresponsibly—to tempt the gods and fish alone.

Fly-fishing in the wilderness of Corbett Park was more amazing and very different from fishing in Canada, where I was living at the time. Langur monkeys stared at me from the other side of the river. Beautiful birds—ultramarine flycatchers, long-tailed broadbills, little and spotted fork tails, brown dippers, long-billed thrushes, and common green magpies—flew everywhere. A fish eagle soared overhead, looking for action. Close to me, I could see shy, wild, and colorful jungle fowl scratching the earth for insects. Their presence reminded me of my early days of hunting in India (before hunting was banned), when getting a chance at these jungle fowl was a real challenge. Less shy were the wild peacocks, a sight to behold, particularly when they decided to fly. I even caught a glimpse of a rare sambar deer crossing the river some way off and a few, now endangered, gharal crocodiles. There was also real danger from wild elephants, of which there were a great many, making a great racket, trumpeting to warn me to get out of their way. And all the time the big mahseer circled in the almost transparent water, totally uninterested in my flies. Obviously, I didn't have the right stuff.

But in the middle of all this aesthetic beauty, there were times when I felt not only like a predator, but also like prey. I may have been hunting the mahseer, but I was very aware of the fact that I could also be hunted. Each time I fished, I found large, fresh pugmarks made by tigers at the river's edge. Clearly, they were patrolling both sides of the river as part of their daily (or more probably nightly) routine. Although I am not easily disturbed by the presence of predators—usually, the opposite is true—these signs worried me. After all, I was unarmed apart from a fishing rod, which wouldn't be much help. What was the probability that I would become the prey?

I remembered a terrifying story our mahout—the person who looked after the elephant we had been riding—had told me. Several years previously, deep in the jungle, he was crouched low in a tree, cutting leafy branches for his elephant, when he was attacked by a tiger. He hadn't seen it coming as he was attacked from behind. (Allegedly, tigers don't like tackling humans face-to-face.) The mahout fell out of the tree, and to the consternation of both him and the tiger, he landed on top of the animal. The tiger tried to give the mahout the *coup de grace*, but in his desperation, the mahout managed to get hold of the tiger's tongue, while pummelling the animal in its face with his other hand. This was enough to confuse the tiger, and delay the kill, although the tiger did manage to scalp him in the scuffle. Fortunately, the cavalry, in the shape of his elephant, came to the rescue. With a lot of trumpeting, the elephant drove the tiger away, lifted the wounded mahout onto its back, and returned to camp. The mahout was immediately rushed to the nearest hospital. He obviously survived his ordeal but a turban now covered his scalped skull. This story gave me a lot to think about as I fished alone, beside the tiger tracks.

One morning, I noticed a set of pugmarks that were more than fresh—they still had nice, crisp edges that hadn't yet been rounded off by the wind. I realized that a tiger had passed by just minutes before me and must be lying somewhere, close by. I thought of something I had once read in Corbett's best-known book, *The Man-Eaters of Kumaon*: "Tigers do not know that human beings have no sense of smell, and when a tiger becomes a man-eater it treats human beings exactly as it treats wild animals, that is, it approaches its intended victims up-wind or lies up in wait for them down-wind."[79] I was up-wind, a situation that made me pretty unhappy, and my predicament was made even more exciting by the ample high elephant grass at the edge of the river—an ideal place for tigers to hide. I knew that tigers at times (particularly when the tiger is infirm), will eat people and the recent events in Corbett Park were not encouraging. I wasn't ready to be the next victim.

I decided to wade deep into the river in the places where there were patches of elephant grass. The possibility that there might be a tiger crouching in the grass while I waded meant that I constantly, and somewhat anxiously, watched my back. But strangely enough, despite the danger, the new situation I was experiencing, of being hunted rather than the hunter, was exhilarating.

Jim Corbett's tales about his encounters with man-eating tigers and leopards had fascinated me as a child. In spite of the dangers he faced, his responsible, fair-chase attitude always impressed me. He was a very ethical hunter and very respectful to nature and its inhabitants—even man-eaters. He wrote:

"There is a point on which I am convinced that all sportsmen—no matter whether their point of view has been a platform on a tree, the back of an elephant, or their own feet—will agree with me, and that is, that a tiger is a large-hearted gentleman with boundless courage and that when he is exterminated—as exterminated he will be unless public opinion rallies to his support—India will be the poorer by having lost the finest of her fauna."[80]

In his later years, Corbett became an increasingly vocal advocate of conservation, and predicted as early as 1950 that strict plans were needed to save the tiger and other creatures of the Indian jungle from human encroachment on their territory. He lectured at schools and other institutions to stimulate awareness of the environment, and the need to conserve forests and their wildlife. He helped create the Association for the Preservation of Game in Uttar Pradesh, and the All-India Conference for the Preservation of Wild Life. The park that was eventually named after him was India's first national park—a singular honor to bestow on a non-Indian.

This was not the only time I experienced the role reversal between hunter and hunted. It also happened while I was hunting Kodiak bear on the Alaska Peninsula, close to the Pavlof volcano, the most active, and dangerous, volcano in the Aleutian arc. From a cinematographic point of view, the place where I was standing was remarkable. A Super Cub bush plane equipped with gigantic tires had put me down on the beach at low tide. As we approached, I had been fascinated to see the multiple, crisscrossing paths these giant brown bears had made over centuries of use. I even spotted a bear that rose out the alders to look at our plane as we passed overhead. However, our welcoming committee on the beach consisted out of a lone wolf that glared at us from a comfortable distance, and then disappeared down the riverbank. In front of me was the Bering Sea. As I walked along the water's edge, I could see sea lions and seals popping up and looking curiously at me. There was even a pod of killer whales making a commotion, their position given away by some noisy seagulls. In the middle distance were the Aleutian Islands.

If you love bad weather, the Alaska Peninsula, where the wind can blow you away in a literal sense, would be difficult to beat. I reckon it's the place where

bad weather is born. Because of the strong winds, the sparse tree growth ends up totally stunted. Apart from the soggy tundra, the countryside is mainly covered by alders that grow into an impenetrable maze. The area sustains caribou, wolves, foxes, wolverines, and ptarmigans. But walking on the beaches, you find the imprints of the king of them all: *Ursus Arctos Middendorffi*, the great brown bear of coastal Alaska. With the possible exception of Kamchatka, the Alaska Peninsula is the domain of some of the largest brown bears in the world.

Our home from home (my 'long-suffering wife' was with me on this excursion) turned out to be a minimalist spike camp, a tent construction that was reinforced with wood against the ferocity of the wind. The tent was devoid of creature comforts; there was barely enough place to sleep. As we occupied it, it did occur to me to wonder why our guide had pitched our tent so close to what appeared to be a heavily used bear trail. Bears must have been cruising that beach trail, at the edge of the sea, for thousands of years. If we didn't find the bears, perhaps the bears would have an easier time finding us, with our tent so perfectly positioned as bait.

Every day the guide and I would climb to the top of a mountain, and look for bears through an onslaught of rain, hail, snow, and slush. (Most of the time, my wife chose to stay in the tent, and kept herself warm by collecting firewood.) During that period, we had scarcely a glimpse of the sun. I remembered a well-known Alaskan saying: "It didn't stop raining until the snow came." We spent many hours on top of that mountain, looking for any form of life. But, if we could believe the fresh tracks, the big boars were only moving during the night. During the daytime, we only saw a number of sows with cubs, puttering by a long way off. Every day, we returned to our tent totally exhausted.

One day, I saw two bears walking majestically on the tundra some distance away. After some thought, we decided to take a closer look. For those who have never done it, I can assure you that walking in the tundra is very difficult. It is like walking in treacle or on a trampoline; each step has a strange bounce to it and the soil tries to pull you back. As we got closer, the bears disappeared into the alders, where they were very difficult to spot. It was quite stressful to walk there not knowing where they were, but also knowing that they couldn't be far away. My wife (who had no gun with her) stuck very close to me during that trek. Our little excursion was just the latest in a series of unnerving experiences.

On the day we arrived, the large bear tracks, as big as dinner plates, we found at the edge of the sea had made a deep impression on my wife—so she was not entirely amused when I left her standing there alone (with a double rifle for security) while I ran after a large covey of ptarmigans higher up the shore. The birds were not very well camouflaged, as they were only half-white. I shot a number of them for the pot, while she stood fretting and wondering when I would return—it got darker and darker, and every shadow was transformed into a bear.

On another night, at around five o'clock in the morning, a strange banging woke my wife. The guide and I were fast asleep, exhausted after a long, fruitless hike the previous day. She was reluctant to wake us up and, remembering the phantom bear shadows, kept wondering whether she was imagining things. But the banging on the wood that reinforced our tent intensified. Something was out there wanting to get in—and this time it wasn't the wind. A bear, making its rounds at the edge of the sea, must have smelled food. As there were no trees, our guide had left our food box at the side of the tent—not his smartest move. Of course, we were acutely aware that, quite apart from the food in the box, we also represented an attractive food source.

I opened the zipper of the tent and what I saw before me woke me up. Five meters from me was what looked like a relatively young bear, sitting on its behind and glaring at me. Although it was young, it was big enough to warrant my full attention: it looked impressive, particularly as it was so close—and not separated from us by steel bars, as it would have been in a zoo. The whole scene was surrealistic: Two people lying flat in a rickety tent, a sitting bear, and me crouching.

I had two guns with me: a double rifle that I couldn't reach (it was under a mess of clothes) and my Weatherby .300 Magnum. I fumbled for the Weatherby, looked through the scope—and saw nothing. I had forgotten, in my drowsy state, to take the storm flaps off the scope. I did that, looked again, but still couldn't see anything that looked like bear. I had also left the scope at its maximum magnification. I only saw a brownish blur: hair. Looking over the scope, I could see that the bear was getting restless. Would it move away, or join us in the tent? Time was running out. However, I didn't want to shoot a young bear. I decided that the only thing to do was to make lots of noise and shoot my rifle in the air to frighten it off. The alternatives—a dead bear in front of our tent, or a wounded bear looking for revenge inside it—were not very attractive. When the shot went off, the bear disappeared into the alders, not to return. Hunter had turned into hunted but in this instance we were lucky. And to be honest, in most instances it is the other way around. The person with the gun is usually in the driver's seat.

On this particular hunt, we also ran out of food. One of the bush planes passed by one day and dropped some Hershey bars and a few apples—not much of a selection. Because of the strong wind, the plane was unable to land—in fact, at one point it looked to us on the ground as if it was actually going backwards. The weather was so bad that hunting was almost impossible. I never got a bear on that trip, but at least the outfitter eventually got us out of there.

This was my second hunt for brown bear on the Alaska Peninsula. On the first, I had an equally memorable encounter. That time, I was hunting in the spring, and the weather at that time of the year is usually rather better than in autumn. The sun came out regularly—a miracle. It was my first serious brown bear hunt and, not knowing better, I wanted to get a "big" bear.

I should say at this point that I have rarely been a "lucky" hunter—lucky meaning coming home with something. I often come home skunked, as far as game is concerned, but richer in experiences. This particular hunt seemed unlikely to be any different. Every day my guide and I followed the same routine, climbing high up the mountains to glass the landscape below for any bear movement. We did see a number of bears, and even went on a few stalks to get closer to them, but without much success. Usually, we saw females with cubs and a few immature males.

All our daily efforts to reach the top of the mountain and get a panoramic view yielded poor returns; not much was going on. More often than not, all our glassing efforts revealed were a number of caribou far off, a few ptarmigan, or a fox. No elderly, retiring male bear made its presence known, ready to give up. One day, however, at a considerable distance, I spotted two bears on another mountain plateau. It was quite bare and hardly a place to go to find something to eat. I remember that Stravinsky's "Night on Bald Mountain" went through my mind. However, the bears were too far away to make a stalk for them. The next day, while glassing, I saw them there again, and for several days afterward. I became increasingly curious to know what those bears were doing.

One day, after another lengthy but fruitless stalk, we found ourselves relatively close to the bears' bald mountain. I suggested to the guide that we climb up to find out what was going on. The wind, of course, was blowing hard, straight into our faces, and the climb was very tough.

We had almost reached the top of the plateau, and were peeking over the last knoll, when we saw the bears lying closely together. I realized immediately that they were a mating pair. It was such a very special sight that I decided to take a photograph. I reached quickly for my backpack, to get my camera. A mistake: my sudden movement caught the attention of the larger of the two bears. Its reaction was dramatic. All its hair stood on end, just like a cat's does when it is scared. The bear jumped to its feet, and went into overdrive, coming straight at me. I dropped my camera and aimed my rifle: it all happened so fast that I didn't have time to be scared. When the bear was about seven meters from us, and showing no sign of slowing down, the guide started to scream. The sound stopped the bear in its tracks. It veered off and disappeared in the alders. We then had the luxury of time and hindsight to be frightened. Perhaps the animal had realized that we weren't competitors for the attention of the female after all. An Alaskan told me later that the bears on the Alaska Peninsula are not very aggressive—adding, however, that on the average, one out of a hundred will decide to take you for a meal.

Early in the morning on one of the last days of that first Alaskan bear hunt my guide and I decided to do something we had been putting off—crossing the glacial river next to our spike camp. Our side of the river had not delivered bears; we might have better luck on the other. We stripped down to our short underwear—the wind, as usual, was blowing at maximum force—and tried to keep our balance as we crossed the fast-flowing river with bare feet. Crossing an icy stream littered with sharp pebbles is quite painful: the water was coming directly from a glacier.

But we made it across safely, shoes and clothes tied around our necks and rifles held high. Shivering with cold, we dressed and continued our journey on the other side. We now had a new beach and new mountains to explore. While we were slugging along on the beach, I suddenly saw a beautiful, golden colored bear lumbering in our direction. I looked urgently at my guide, who was marching on without giving any sign that he had seen the approaching bear, and realized he must be half-asleep. I made frantic signals to warn him of the danger until finally he came out of his trance, and stopped. I looked at the bear through the scope of my rifle and decided he was too young. He deserved more years to grow. I often wonder since whether I should have taken him, because I remember vividly how he looked. The bear, who also seemed not quite with it that morning, eventually saw us too. He stopped, looked at us for a while, took a leisurely shit, and marched off. We moved on, away from the beach, and decided to climb the highest mountain in sight. When we reached the top, we saw far below the dark silhouette of a bear, walking slowly in the direction of the sea. It was the last day of the hunt and we decided that this bear was going to be it.

We ran down the mountain to intercept the bear but when we got close to where we had last seen it, it was nowhere in sight. We looked everywhere but finally assumed that the animal must be sleeping in a patch of alders not far from us. But which bush and where? To find out, we decided to start a mini bear drive. The plan was that I would station myself in front of the patch of alders while my companion circled the alders higher up the mountain, and made his way down. Our hope was that the bear would smell him, leave the alders, and move in my direction.

I watched my guide climb, then climb some more, until he was above the alders. I thought that the bear must have had his wind by now, if he was in the alders as we thought—but still nothing happened. By now, the guide was really close to the patch of alders where we expected the bear to be—still nothing. Then all of a sudden there was a noise like a truck being revved up in the bushes. Branches were breaking, and faster then I thought possible, the bear was powering out of the alders. Its speed took me completely by surprise. Needless to say, seeing such a big animal coming straight toward me was somewhat intimidating. As the bear ran past me (I don't think it was running at me), I shot—but immediately realized that my aim had been too far back. Before I could shoot again, the wounded bear disappeared into the alders. Now we had a real problem on our hands, one I had read about but never wanted to be involved in. We had to follow the wounded bear into the scrub, find it, and end its suffering.

When I tell this story, people ask me whether I was scared. Not really—I was in the flow; I had become a predator, like the bear. But trailing a wounded brown bear, crouched on your hands and feet, through a thick scrub of alders that prevents you seeing anything more than two meters away, is no walk in the park. The track was easy to follow, however. My bullet had done a lot of damage.

We crawled on, expecting the bear to rush us at any time, and then saw a dark shadow not far off. It was the bear, which was clearly no longer going anywhere. Quickly, I gave another shot, and put the beast out of its misery. To quote the well-known outdoor writer Russell Annabel: "One of the reasons why bear hunting is a great and fascinating activity is that it is full of surprises. For instance, you can never tell how a bear—any kind of bear—will react to a set of circumstances."[81]

Another bear paradise is Kamchatka, in the Far East of Russia. Like Alaska, getting to Kamchatka is not exactly a turn round the block; it's a formidable trip. After the usual flight from Paris to Moscow, I continued to Petropavlovsk, was collected by an elusive helicopter (the only way of getting there: there are no roads in Kamchatka), and delivered to the camp—a number of primitive tents with stoves. My first meal there was a capercaillie soup (capercaillie is the biggest grouse in Siberia).

After a snowstorm that must have put at least a meter of snow on the ground, my guide and I began to look for tracks or other signs of bear in this pristine but forbidding landscape. We saw the fresh tracks of a wolverine, a few foxes, and a number of snowshoe rabbits, but that was all. No sign of bear. The day went by, until at one point, high on the mountain, the guide spotted a bear. He kept on looking at it but didn't move as the bear was very high up, and the snow was very deep. Finally, after a number of hours, I suggested in sign language (my knowledge of Russian is rudimentary) that we should stalk the bear. I tried to point out the obvious: we were here and the bear was high up and evidently not coming down.

Easier said, even in sign language, than done. We started the climb and I swiftly realized why the guide had been so hesitant. He was a giant of a man, and I am anything but large. He must have eyed me up and decided that it was doubtful I would be able to make that climb. And he was right—but he didn't know anything about my persistence.

The very deep snow made it a truly grueling climb. To save energy, I tried to step in the guide's footsteps. At times, we were up to our waist in the snow, struggling to get a hold on the slippery slope and avoid sliding down. But we climbed, and climbed, and climbed some more, in this totally silent, white landscape, taking one exhausting step after the other to get closer to where we had last seen the bear. When we were approximately a hundred meters off, a raven appeared out of the blue. It circled above us, breaking the silence with its loud noise.

At my level of exhaustion, the racket made by the raven triggered a whole stream of thoughts. Ravens have always fascinated me. In most traditions, the bird is associated with death—highly appropriate at that particular moment. In Norse mythology, two ravens accompanied Odin, one of whose many titles was *Hrafna-Gud*, the God of the Ravens. In many western traditions the raven represents darkness, destructiveness, and evil. Both witches and the Devil were said to be able to take the shape of a raven. Some Native American tribes believed the raven was a trickster; others saw it as the bringer of light. All this flew through my mind even as I swore silently at this particular raven, willing it to shut up—to me, at that moment, the trickster was the right denomination, as the bird was ruining our stalk. I was increasingly worried that the bear would be spooked and that our expedition up the mountain would be in vain.

When we looked over the rim of a dip in the mountain where we had spotted the bear, all we saw were its footprints. As I expected, the raven had spooked the bear. Just as I discovered it was gone, the raven stopped squawking and flew off to the side. I looked after the disappearing bird, with no very friendly thoughts—and caught a glimpse of the bear disappearing into the trees. In another few seconds it would be completely out of sight. I don't know how I did it, but I managed to aim and shoot while lying in the snow and, to my great surprise, my bullet hit true. The bear crumpled and rolled ten meters down the snow—then all was quiet. I approached its body with awe and sadness. There is something majestic, almost sacred, about looking at and touching a dead *ursus horribilus* (horrible bear). That evening we ate bear tongue and paws, while I admired the hide. But the raven was still with me. What had that mysterious bird been doing? I felt more inclined to give credence to all the stories I'd heard about its magical power.

"Was sich liebt, das neckt sich"

Because I am interested in the life of primitive tribes, I have accompanied them on bear hunts for many years. I have learned a lot about the how these people deal with this adversary—and I have learned that bears can be extremely unpredictable. Although they are formidable in appearance, most will run away. But you never know if one will charge you; you can never be quite sure that you are not going to be its next meal. By participating in this hide-and-seek game of proximity as a hunter, and by understanding the behavior of the prey, I have developed a great deal of affinity with them. For me, bears are an archetypical symbol of the wilderness and strange as it may seem, given the number I have killed, I feel close to bears. I admire them, respect them, and am afraid of them. In a way, the bear is my totem animal. Again, this factor may be difficult to understand for non-hunters. In hunting, there is always this paradox: the affinity with the object of the hunt, and the desire to possess and even kill it.

Aggression and affection, what does it all mean? In German, there is an expression—"*Was sich liebt, das neckt sich*"—that roughly translates as "lovers' quarrels strengthen love." We tend to be both more aggressive toward the people we are close to—whereas we are usually polite to others—but also more conciliatory. The Japanese have a similar saying, "*Ame futte ji katamaru,*" which means literally, "ground that is rained on hardens," implying that adversity builds character. There is a fine line between admiration and aggression. The same applies to hunter and the hunted.

Hunting has done a great deal to improve my "nature intelligence." It motivates me to know everything there is to know about the behavior of the animal I am pursuing. I want to know more about its habitat and its role in the cycle of life Thomas Huxley described so well in his story about the old maids

and bumblebees. When I hunt dangerous animals, I become especially aware of my participation in the eternal cycle in which life and death play their part. During the hunt, hunter and hunted merge. They are engaged in a dance that transcends the ages.

When I am hunting, I assume some of the behavior patterns of the game I am pursuing. Something similar happens when I embark on a clinical interview with someone. What do I need to do to understand what the other person is all about? What makes her tick? I have to observe her carefully; I try to get under her skin. I need to think the way she does. The parallels between what I have to do during a clinical interview and what I have to do when hunting are striking.

When I hunt, I go to great lengths to understand the modus operandi of the animal I am after—why it behaves the way it does, what I can do to get closer. This game of proximity reminds me of a painting I once saw of Indians hunting buffalo. They had covered themselves in wolf skins or buffalo hides and were sneaking up to the herd, waiting for the right moment to get to the animals. They had to be careful not to make the buffalo stampede. In the same way, when hunting deer, many tribesmen wear the head of a deer that was caught in an earlier hunt. Wearing this disguise, they hide in tall grass or bushes and wait for the deer to get close enough to shoot with a bow and arrow. For centuries, hunters have worn animal disguises, and still do so today. Disguises put hunters in a transitional zone between hunter and hunted.

This imitative behavior extends to copying the sounds that animals make. When I hunted in the rainforest in Central Africa with the pygmies, I admired their way of blowing through their nose to make the sound of a wounded duiker, luring other duikers out of the shadows of the forest to see what was going on. From nowhere, these duikers would come. I have used the same technique when trying to call in a wild turkey, and I have used an animal's distress signal to call in predators like bears, coyotes, foxes, or bobcats.

Memorably, a guide did the same when we were hunting for moose in British Columbia. These legends of the fall would emerge from the shadowy black timber of the forest like ghostly monsters following instinctual longings. We were hunting them during the rut, when the calm of nature would be shattered by the primordial scream of wild, tribal-like celebrations. Before the noise started, all that could be heard was the eerie call of a loon far off on a nearby lake, or flocks of geese flying overhead on their way down south. We had had tough going in a canoe against the stream to reach the hot spot where we hoped to find moose. In the last part of the trip, the guide, my stepdaughter Eva, and I had had to drag the canoe upriver because the water was too shallow to paddle.

When we arrived at the hot spot, a steamy mist was rising from the water as the crisp morning air stole any remaining warmth the stream. My challenge was to locate a bull moose in an endless landscape of alders. The silence was broken suddenly by a cracking sound, not far away. A branch snapped. What was doing it? Moose, or bear? More noises sent shivers down my spine. It *must* be one or the other. Not far away, I could hear trees and brush being thrashed to pieces, and then as if nothing had happened, silence descended again. My guide started calling, imitating a moose cow—and the silhouette of the forest giant appeared out of nowhere. I tensed up. My heart started to pound—it felt as though it was coming out of my chest. I was trembling and made an enormous effort to control myself. I tried to blend into the landscape as the moose came closer. I steadied the rifle on a branch of a tree and prepared to shoot. I was ready. But would I do it? Would I take that animal's life?

70 — Hemingway, Ernest. *Green Hills of Africa*. New York: Scribner, 1996.

71 — Lopez, Barry. *Arctic Dreams: Imagination and Desire in a Northern Landscape*. New York: Bantam Books, 1989, pp. 199-200.

72 — Swan, James A. *In Defense of Hunting*. San Francisco: Harper Collins, 1994, p. 42.

73 — Leopold, Aldo. "A Plea for Wilderness Hunting Grounds," *Outdoor Life*, November, 1925. Reproduced in David E. Brown & Neil B. Carmony, (eds), *Aldo Leopold's Southwest*. Albuquerque: University of New Mexico Press, 1990, pp. 160-161.

74 — Leopold, Aldo. *A Sand County Almanac, and Sketches Here and There (1948)*. New York: Oxford University Press (1987).

75 — *Ibid*, p. 145.

76 — *Ibid*, p. 140.

77 — Darwin, Charles. *The Origin of the Species*. Philadelphia: University of Pennsylvania Press, pp.120-121, 2006.

78 — Huxley, Thomas Henry. *Conditions of Existence as Affecting the Perpetuation of Living Beings*. Project Gutenberg, 2001.

79 — Corbett, Jim. *Man-Eaters of Kumaon*. Long Beach: Safari Press, 1991, p. 54.

80 — *Ibid*.

81 — Annabell, Robert. "Now you Take a Bear," *Field & Stream*, 1943.

The Great Spirit is in all things, he is in the air we breathe. The Great Spirit is our Father, but the Earth is our Mother. She nourishes us; that which we put into the ground she returns to us...
　　—Big Thunder (Bedagi),
　　Wabanaki Algonquin

We believe that the Sun Spirit is all-powerful. For every spring he makes the trees to bud and the grass to grow. We see these things with our own eyes, and, therefore, know that all life comes from him.
　　—Blackfoot

A human being is a part of the whole called by us universe, a part limited in time and space. He experiences himself, his thoughts and feelings as something separated from the rest, a kind of optical delusion of his consciousness. This delusion is a kind of prison for us, restricting us to our personal desires and to affection for a few persons nearest to us. Our task must be to free ourselves from this prison by widening our circle of compassion to enhance all living creatures and the whole of nature.
　　—Albert Einstein

We need another and a wiser and perhaps a more mystical concept of animals... In a world older and more complete than ours they move finished and complete, gifted with extensions of the senses we have lost or never attained, living by voices we shall never hear. They are not brethren, they are not underlings; they are other nations, caught with ourselves in the net of life and time, fellow prisoners of the splendor and travail of the earth.
　　—Henry Beston

From my rotting body, flowers shall grow and I am in them and that is eternity.
　　—Edvard Munch

ANIMIST THINKING

When I am hunting, I regard nature as a very special, almost sacred place. It is a realm of both finite and infinite space. During my hunting ventures, I am acutely aware that I am part of the great, eternal cycle of life. Hunting forces me to recognize that, in nature, everything breaks down and gets rebuilt: we come from dust and to dust we must return. Hunting encourages me to reflect on eternal cyclical patterns, how generations of species (including *Homo sapiens*) have succeeded each other. It makes me realize the extent to which life is a perpetual circular process. It makes me accept the omnipresence of death. Black Elk, the holy man of the Oglala Sioux, noted:

> "Everything the power of the world does is done in a circle. The sky is round and I have heard that the earth is round like a ball and so are all the stars. The wind, in its greatest power, whirls. Birds make their nests in circles, for theirs is the same religion as ours. The sun comes forth and goes down again in a circle. The moon does the same and both are round. Even the seasons form a great circle in their changing and always come back again to where they were.
>
> The life of a man is a circle from childhood to childhood, and so it is in everything where power moves. Our teepees were round like the nests of birds, and these were always set in a circle, the nation's hoop, a nest of many nests, where the Great Spirit meant for us to hatch our children."[82]

Life on Earth is a cycle of birth, infancy, childhood, adulthood, old age, and death. There are also circadian rhythms, a roughly 24-hour cycle in the biochemical, physiological, or behavioral processes of all living things. The seasons are cyclical, as are changes in the tides, night and day, and the weather. Our planet, moon, and sun are all spherical and move in apparently circular orbits. From the earliest times, hominids must have struggled to make sense out of these cyclical phenomena—the regular alternation of light and darkness must have been an equally mystifying process to Paleolithic man.

ᛁ

Into that darkness

Darkness is the main feature of the foreword to universal mythology. The book of Genesis (1:1–2) tells us, "In the beginning God created the heaven and the earth. And the earth was without form, and void; and *darkness* was upon the face of the deep." Being surrounded by darkness must have been uncanny and disorienting for our ancestors, just as it can be for us today. The coming of darkness highlights our impotence vis-à-vis the forces of nature. Darkness has always had a menacing quality. Light, its opposite, is coupled with clarity. Images of light and darkness animate our sense of the opposing forces of good and evil within us and in the outside world; each draws its meaning and power from the presence of the other. We talk about people's "darker" qualities and portray evil as a product of darkness. In many cultures, the stereotypical villain wears dark clothes, while the stereotypical hero or heroine wears bright colors, reminiscent of the light. The Devil, the personification of evil, is called the "Prince of Darkness." The drama of the human story lies in the possibility of overcoming these forces of darkness.

It is not fanciful to assume that the first great natural adversary recognized by primitive humans was darkness—the constant and eternal enemy of the light. Predators would attack most successfully during the hours of darkness, so the association between darkness and danger is understandable. Compared to large predators, we are quite defenseless: we have no venom, spines, claws, or large teeth; we cannot outrun them, we can't fly, and we have no camouflage. And most importantly, we can't see very well in the dark, making us especially vulnerable at night, so darkness has always represented an especially dangerous time for our species. Until we had fire, and later, artificial lights, we had very little idea what might come for us out of the darkness. From our earliest origins, the odds of being killed in the dark have always been much higher than being killed in daylight.

I once hunted for hyena in an area that had ample buffalo, elephants, lions, and leopards—and for that, we had to sneak around in the dark on bare feet, trying to get closer to a place where we knew lions had left the rotting carcass of a buffalo. The hyenas had become pests in the camp, because they considered the meat the hunters had collected as legitimate food. I assume that, consciously or unconsciously, my keenness to get them was influenced by the hyenas' poor (and actually unwarranted) reputation. The hyenas' impressive dental structure, formidable hunting tactics, and nocturnal habits are intimidating, and explain why they are often cast as hysterical and unhinged villains in numerous movies and tall tales. They also appear (at least to many) hideous, of course, but much of the folklore (and ignorance) about hyenas may stem from the physical similarity between males and females. The genitalia of female hyenas so closely resemble those of the males that it is not easy to distinguish between the two sexes. Thus this sexual confusion may also add to the animal's negative imagery—it might be a catalyst for our concerns about our own gender identity. Their reputation is not enhanced by African tribal superstitions that hyenas are owned and ridden by witches. In popular folklore, hyenas have a long association with cruelty, treachery, and greed. More specifically, in the African backcountry you often meet people with deformed faces, the result of hyena bites. A hyena that comes across someone who has passed out in the bush after an alcoholic binge thinks that it has found the ultimate bonanza, an easy meal. Given the extraordinary strength of a hyena's jaws, the inevitable hangover would be the least of the victim's concerns.

As I drew closer to the buffalo carcass, I almost jumped in the air at the sound of the unnerving call of one of these icons of the African landscape. I had listened before to their noises at night, and had realized that hyenas have a variety of vocalizations, including wailing calls, howling screams, and the well-known "laughter," differentiating calls that are used to alert other troop members that food is available.

This barefoot stalk in the darkness was uncomfortable on many levels. I had to get used to the shadow play of moonlight on the dry riverbank, which was quite disorienting. It didn't help that I had seen lions in the area the previous day—including one with a real attitude problem—and that I was intensely aware that my eyesight was not good enough to see what was really going on, unlike the animals I was hunting. In the end, my nocturnal expedition produced nothing but several very blue and bleeding toes, from the sharp rocks I had bumped into in the darkness. I failed to get any pesty hyenas.

As my rather sorry tale shows, our fear of the darkness does not just spring from the imaginary dangers it represents. On the contrary, it is reality-based; for prehistoric man, it was a literal experience—a real danger materialized in the dark. With the passing of generations, however, darkness has come to be associated with a fear of the unknown. We are scared of what we do not know, of what could be lurking in the darkness. Darkness becomes a symbolic representation of our helplessness and vulnerability in face of the unknown.

Over time, our fear of the dark was transformed into a metaphorical, moral, or spiritual ordeal accompanying the irrational fear that darkness would swallow the light. Our forebears, seeing night fall, might have thought, "Who knows? Maybe this is the time when darkness will finally triumph, with all its dreadful consequences." No wonder that our ancestors in bygone eras—most prominently the Aztecs—invented rituals urging the sun to rise every day.

To the Aztecs, there was no guarantee that every sunset would be followed by the promise of a new dawn. Nothing was sure, so measures had to be taken to ensure the return of the light. And the Aztecs were not alone: solstice ceremonies were performed in many cultures around the world. At the root of all of these practices hovered the ancient fear that the failing light would never return unless humans intervened with anxious vigils or wild celebration.

It is hard for us today to imagine how life must have been without electricity and other means to make light. The period before our ancestors were able to make fire—the time before they were able to bring light into darkness—must have been truly trying. No wonder that the mastery of fire gave early humans such a new source of vitality; the power to create light and heat was a seminal milestone on our evolutionary path, exemplified in the myth of Prometheus. According to the myth, after Prometheus had stolen fire from the hearth of Zeus and given it to mortals, humans no longer shivered in the cold of the night, and wild animals (which feared fire) were no longer such a threat.

Our early predecessors, of course, left no records of their fears and travails against the dark and the predators that roamed in it. But we can get an inkling of their feelings from more contemporary accounts, like John Henry Patterson's book, *The Man-eaters of Tsavo*.[83] Patterson was an engineer who arrived in East Africa in 1898 with a brief to build a railway bridge over the Tsavo River. This apparently simple engineering assignment soon assumed tragic and macabre dimensions as Patterson's largely Indian workforce began to be systematically killed by a pair of lions that had turned man-eaters. Very soon, their predations brought the bridge-building project to a complete halt. Patterson described the lions' nocturnal reign of terror and his own attempts to kill them—no easy task, as the lions turned out to be pure killing machines. Over a period of nine months, more than 100 workers were taken by them.

In Chapter 4, I mentioned Jim Corbett (1875–1955), an Indian-born British hunter, conservationist and naturalist, who was famed for taking out a large number of man-eating tigers and leopards in India. Corbett was nominally

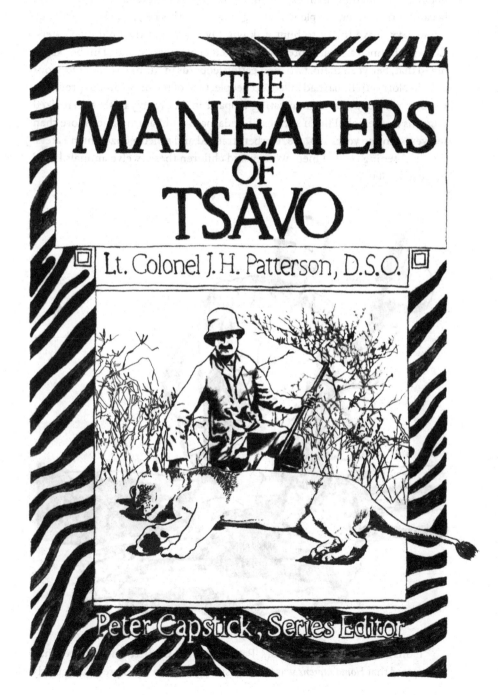

THE MAN-EATERS OF TSAVO

Lt. Colonel J.H. Patterson, D.S.O.

Peter Capstick, Series Editor

a British civil servant, but devoted much of his time to protecting the local population from these man-eating night prowlers. Whenever a tiger or a leopard became a man-eater, people would beg Corbett for his help, and he would take a few days' leave to try to hunt it down. Over years of tracking man-eaters, Corbett obtained a great appreciation of their cleverness. In one of his books, he noted that, between them, two man-eating leopards in Kumaon (a mountainous state in Northern India) had killed 525 people. One of the most famous predators Corbett recorded was a man-eating leopard in Rudraprayag that terrorized pilgrims to the holy Hindu shrines of Kedarnath and Badrinath for more than ten years. In the years 1907–38, Corbett tracked and killed a dozen man-eaters. The frightening total of men, women and children these twelve animals killed exceeded 1,500. [84]

I imagine that the predators Patterson and Corbett encountered had discovered that *Homo sapiens* was much easier to kill than other prey, particularly where shelter was inadequate and their targets had no security fences, guns, or other measures to protect themselves. Corbett's description of his adventures in hunting these night prowlers, in particular, gives us a very accurate idea of how our prehistoric ancestors must have felt when carnivores developed a taste for human flesh. He wrote:

"During the day, people went about their lives as usual. Trade and commerce, transport and all other transactions went about their normal way. But as evening approached, there was a marked change in their behavior. Pilgrims rushed toward their night shelters, businessmen closed shops abruptly, and people scurried toward their homes for relative safety. No curfew was more strictly imposed. No orders to remain indoors were observed as faithfully."[85]

Fire offered a degree of protection against these feared nightly visitors. Outside the ring of fire, however—in the darkness—predators would be prowling. Listening to their sounds, Paleolithic man would cower around the fire in primeval community and threw flaming sticks into the dark to drive away the threatening beasts. We can speculate that feeling relatively safe close to the fire, they would talk about the dangers of the dark and discuss strategies for dealing with them. These exchanges in a safe place may have been an early step in the creation of social structure—patterns of causal interconnection and the recognition of interdependencies. Through story telling our early ancestors tried to make sense of the unpredictable world that surrounded them in any way they could. Mysteries surrounded them. There was so much to explain. Why were they so fearful at the end of each day, as darkness descended? Why was the natural world around them so capricious? Why did the weather change? They would puzzle over the movement of animals, where and when they were coming and going. How would they deal with all these uncontrollable, incomprehensible forces of nature? Their fear of what awaited them in the dark made them truly appreciative of the daily miracle of sunrise.

In our fear of the dark, as with many things in life, psychology interfaces with physiology. As indicated before, unlike predators, our eyes are not adapted to night vision. When a light is switched off, the human eye takes an unusually long time to adjust to the change in visibility. We are literally momentarily blind and start to lose our bearings. And when the mind's eye also becomes blind to the light, we doubly feel the darkness and the unknown.

Given *Homo sapiens'* prehistory, our primal fear of darkness could be seen as an instinctive reaction dating back to when we were relatively defenseless, diurnal creatures (to some extent we still experience these feelings today). Predictably, with a physiologically determined day-night schedule, prehistoric man would be most vulnerable during the night, when predators were out hunting, and they were trying to catch some sleep. The sight and sounds of cave bears, cave lions, wooly rhinoceros, and other formidable creatures must have struck deep into the imagination of Paleolithic man. From an evolutionary perspective, fear of the dark would be beneficial for survival purposes. But as the evolutionary process took its natural course, these behavioral adjustments were introjected into the human psyche.

Presumably, once humans became intelligent enough to go beyond simplistic cause-and-effect thinking, and were able to engage in flights of fancy, the purely practical fear of the night took on an extra dimension of fantasy, and the darkness became populated with all sorts of imaginary dangers. Things that are actually quite innocuous in daylight can turn into threatening apparitions in the dark.

As we don't have cats' eyes, we try to make sense out of what we can't see. In the dark, we let our imagination run wild; we can imagine things so vividly that they almost become real. Hence it is easy to go from the fear of predators, to a fear of ghosts and supernatural beings. The imagination of primitive man would attribute mishaps, losses, and pain to a web of mysterious entanglements that took place in the dark. I have lost count of the times I have sat in a leopard or lion blind or other hidden structure, and begun wondering whether the tree stump that had been clearly visible in daylight had not transformed into a bear, lion or leopard in the dark. In that situation, you have a sharp sense of the fears our Paleolithic ancestors must have felt. And those noises under the bed that used to terrify you as a child? Well, suddenly you are hearing them in the brush all around you.

With the exception of people who hunt dangerous game, few of us now have to worry about animal enemies at night; only the fantasy elements remain. Yet all these feelings are ultimately based on a biological, evolutionary imperative. Our fear of the dark is here to stay, exacerbated by stories told to intimidate and create fear—stories of ghosts, bogeymen, and evil spirits that would come to haunt us if we failed to obey the rules. These stories added a developmental dimension to an evolutionary one.

⌐

Lord of the flies

Down the millennia, our fear of the dark has retained its sting. Despite our evolutionary progress, we still go into the dark with a great deal of apprehension. This is an ingrained reaction, as the behavior of small children signifies. In infants, we can observe an inborn fear of the unknown and the unfamiliar. Children are often fearful that something catastrophic will happen when the light goes out. Their inability to see their surroundings, coupled with a healthy dose of imagination, fuels that fear of the dark, where something sinister may be lurking, waiting for its moment to strike. There *are* monsters in the closet. To quote the naturalist, John Vaillant:

> "As long as they are carnivorous and/or humanoid, the monster's form matters little. Whether it is Tyrannosaurus rex, saber-toothed tiger, grizzly bear, werewolf, bogeyman, vampire, Wendigo, Rangda, Grendel, Moby Dick, Joseph Stalin, the Devil, or any other manifestation of the Beast, all are objects of dark fascination, in large part because of their capacity to consciously, willfully destroy us. What unites these creatures—ancient or modern, real or imagined, beautiful or repulsive, human, or god—is their superhuman strength, malevolent cunning, and above all, their capricious appetite—for us. This, in fact, is our expectation of them; it's a kind of contract we have. In this capacity, the seemingly inexhaustible power of predators to fascinate us—to 'capture attention'—fulfills a need far beyond morbid titillation. It

has a practical application. After all, this is the daily reality of many savanna baboons, and it has been ours as well. In southern Tanzania, in the Sundarbans of Bangladesh, and in many zones around the world, it still is."[86]

For a time when I was a child, we lived in the beach village of Zandvoort in Holland. I often played with my friends in the dunes, digging caves in the sand. The play of light and darkness in our little shelters would evoke strong feelings of secrecy and mystery. Entering the small cave was exciting, but would also create an uncanny feeling, a fear of darkness. To us, caves were both threatening and alluring; they represented the forbidden and the dangerous. Caves could also be very seductive places. It was as if these caves were beckoning us to test and overcome our fears.

Our early hominid ancestors found shelter in caves, which gave them a modicum of protection against the various dangers they faced, including the vagaries of the weather. But these caves would also incite feelings of apprehension, as they were a permanent twilight zone between light and darkness. In the primary process language of dreams, caves easily became centers of mystery. Caves can be compared to incubation chambers—the wombs of our imagination.

Our beach in Holland contained more than our own caves. Other, more elaborate, but also more dangerous man-made caves had been left by the German occupiers of Holland, who had built a series of fortifications that bored deeply into the dunes in anticipation of an invasion from the Allies during World War II. After their defeat, they left these elaborate constructions in various states of disrepair. The Dutch authorities, fearful that explosives had also been left behind, had put up signs forbidding anyone from entering them. But the forbidden is too tempting, the illicit far too attractive. Naturally, my friends and I ignored these warning signs and went in anyway. Our adventures were made even more exciting by the need to avoid the police, who patrolled the bunkers at times.

What with all the warnings I had been given by my mother and others, entering these bunker-caves for the first time was a real adventure. The descent from light into darkness aroused mixed feelings of fear, curiosity, and danger. Just as (I imagine) Paleolithic man before me, I had a lingering fear (never directly expressed) that fearsome monsters would be waiting for me in these dark places. Matches, candles, and flashlights helped me to penetrate deeper and deeper into these underground structures. Eventually, as I got to know these caves well, I managed to deal with most of my fears. Making a fire deep down in the bunker also helped me to master my fear of the dark. Returning to the light, however, always filled me with a sense of relief. It is only when we are in the dark, that we truly appreciate the importance of light.

These caves became very significant outlets for make-believe activities. When my brother, my friends and I became more confident about going into them, the caves became meeting places for our "secret" explorer society. Many of our discussions would center on inclusion and exclusion—who was going to be included as a member of our primitive tribe; who was going to be left out because they didn't have what it took. We made decisions about these (to us) very important matters. Over time—like primitive man—we created a set of complex, almost shamanistic initiation rites for new members.

During our "tribal" meetings, we would discuss "hostile" outsiders—meaning children from other parts of the village—and the best ways of dealing with them. At times, even low-grade xenophobia (of a village nature) raised its ugly head. We were no strangers to the notion of what has been termed the "narcissism of minor differences." To strengthen the bond between each other, we needed to have in-groups and out-groups. Identity formation, 'us', is often established in reference to the other, 'them', which explains the need to have enemies.

These games were played out on the beach and in the dunes, where we would imagine ourselves as great adventurers and hunters. There would be "wars"—small skirmishes—between the various groups in the village. And there was a need to establish a pecking order—who would be the leader of the pack for our raids and hunting parties? Who would be second and third in command? Who would be the shaman? I remember that I was definitely not a pushover when it came to deciding the leadership position. To reaffirm our tribal identity—and to mark shamanistic rites of passage—we had placed various "treasures" in the cave. As well as the seashells that we found on the beach, we accumulated another kind of shell—rusty live ammunition that had been abandoned by the Germans. Unexploded bombs were among our more exciting forbidden treasures.

Without knowing it, we were acting out a milder version of the well-known novel (and later film) *Lord of the Flies.*[87] According to the author, William Golding, we all have an evil inner nature that is poorly disguised by a social veneer. As the film *Deliverance* also dramatized, when societal mores are removed, elements of our inner nature may emerge and chaos and lawlessness are likely to erupt. Contemporary man can quickly regress to a much more primitive state, in which hunting is the master pattern. It doesn't take much to make us change from civilization to primitivism.

In our childish imagination and creation of a tribal society, we were trying to manage conflicting impulses toward civilization: living by the rules, in peace and harmony, versus the lust for power and domination. Our cave-based exploits also echoed Freud's classic work, *Totem and Taboo*, on a much smaller scale.[88] Isn't it true that "savages," neurotics, and children have many characteristics in common? As far as shamanistic rituals were concerned, I played a very active leadership role—a sign of things to come; an indication of the shamanistic role I would assume later in life in my eventual career as a psychoanalyst and leadership specialist.

Clinical experience tells me that to understand adult behavior, we often do well to study the kinds of games children play. The games we played in those caves can be seen as a re-enactment (albeit unwitting) of the shamanistic practices of primitive man. These practices were all about protecting territory and hunting, and assuring the supply of food. There was a sexual element, too. What was sex all about? How could we approach girls? How could we deal with these mysterious creatures?

I realize now that being in the dark enhanced our pseudo-regressive behavior. We created these primitive rites to overcome our real or imaginary fears. In many ways, we were behaving exactly like our early hominid ancestors: in the darkness, whatever remnants of prehistoric man remain inside us were being revived to help us cope with the fears that emerged from our collective unconscious—closely associated with the dread of the predators lurking at night, in the dark.

Tricks of darkness

In Zimbabwe once, I sat in an open blind, at ground level, as darkness fell, close to a zebra bait we had tied to a tree to attract lions. A male lion permit had been issued as a pride of lions had moved in too close to a local village to become livestock killers. The male lion had been particularly aggressive, threatening some villagers. He needed to be stopped. As the dusk intensified, a lioness stealthily passed the blind at very close quarters and fed quickly on the bait. It was clear the animal was not at ease; she continually looked round nervously as if she expected to see another animal arrive. After a very hasty meal, the lioness stopped eating and disappeared out of sight. With the growing darkness, her behavior made me feel uneasy. Perhaps she had felt our presence? Or were there other dangers around? What was she up to? Soon after, the lioness reappeared on the other side of our blind, sliding out of the thick Mopani bush. She came very close, gave us the evil eye, and then moved slowly away. Did she want fresher meat? Katharina (a close friend of mine who was with me at the time), became scared and grabbed my rifle, aiming it at the lioness. I was rather amused by her fear, but assumed that if the lioness were really interested in us, she would be back in the dark.

There is something wonderful at seeing a lion so close up but it is also frightening and sinister. It is not surprising, given their majestic nature, that lions symbolize power in many different contexts. This situation was no different; our lioness inspired fear, but she was also strongly attractive.

I had to remind myself that I was not in a zoo; that there were no steel bars separating us safely from her in the Mopani forest. I remembered something I once read by the novelist Robert Ruark: "A lion is life in its simplest form, beautiful, menacing, dangerous, and attractive to the ego. A lion has always been the symbol of challenge, the prototype of personal hazard. You get the lion, or the lion gets you."[89]

Sitting in the blind, I realized that lions look much bigger uncaged, particularly when they are only six meters away. My apprehension increased because the light was now disappearing fast and the lioness was the one with the cats' eyes; I was disadvantaged. I reflected on how primitive man would have felt in this situation without the modern weaponry that I was carrying. Who would get whom?

Now it was almost dark. The magic moment had come when the fading light started to play tricks on us. Were those stumps in the distance really lions? Than I heard a lion roar in front of us, and a reply from another behind the blind. There was the short "peet" sound of a nightjar. Then silence. Suddenly, not far off, there was a rustling of leaves. What was going on? Clearly, the lioness was not alone; she had company. Would the lions come for us? Would we hear or see them in time? In this small, open blind, we were in an extremely vulnerable position. As darkness finally fell there was more roaring. I reckoned we were surrounded by a large pride of lions. Even armed, it was not hard to imagine ending up as a meal.

With the last shimmer of light I saw a male lion emerge from the bushes. I tensed up, aimed, and pulled the trigger—after the shot, there was once again dead silence. The darkness was complete. We would need the lights from our truck to find out what had happened—but to get to the truck we had to walk through tall elephant grass. Making this journey in darkness was a sober reminder of our vulnerability. Where was I now in the cycle of life—in the middle or at the end? Was the process about to be accelerated by one of the lions we had just heard?

As we drove the truck up to the baited tree, all I could see were eyes, and more eyes, lit up in the headlights. It was a very intimidating sight. But there was no sign of the male I had shot. Our guide thought I had missed or, worse, wounded it. He even began to doubt that I had aimed at a male. But it was very clear from the comments of the professional hunter who was with us that even if there was a dead lion somewhere around, there were too many other lions coming to its funeral. He had become increasingly uncomfortable in the dark and was plainly fearful for his and our safety. It was time to go.

Lying in my bed in the rondavel at the camp that night, I rehearsed the experience. I had been quite sure when I pulled the trigger that my aim was right on—and that I had seen a male lion. But now, I was no longer so sure. Why couldn't we find the animal? He should have fallen on the spot. If you hit them properly, lions aren't difficult to kill. It was a mystery why the animal wasn't there. What had happened? My assurance was shaken: had I really taken a male lion? Maybe our guide was right, and I had shot a lioness in error.

The darkness had played tricks on me. Our failure to find the lion, combined with the guide's doubts, made for a poor night's sleep. Images of unapproachable lions haunted my dreams. Every time I came close, the lions seemed to evaporate. I heard them roaring. When I woke up, I realized that it was my birthday. But would I have got my lion? Was the guide right, and I had blown it?

At first light, we went back to the blind. Two other guides came along as back up in case we found a wounded lion. But we found his body right where I had first seen him. The lion had fallen exactly at the place where I had shot it. I couldn't understand how we had failed to see him the previous night. Another trick of the darkness—human eyesight has its limitations.

Animism

Animism is humankind's oldest spiritual belief system. Anthropologists and archeologists have found evidence for animism going back at least 50,000 years. Some scholars believe that the origin of animism may even be much older, and date back to the Paleolithic age. Whenever it originated, it was here to stay. Animism predates and permeates the belief structures of most modern religions and cultures.

The term animism comes from the Latin *anima* (meaning mind or soul), and refers to a belief in the existence of personalized, supernatural beings that are supposedly endowed with reason, intelligence and will; these spirits inhabit both inanimate objects and living beings and govern their existence. An "anima" can help or harm people, including the souls of the dead—the ancestors. In the animistic world, animals are also viewed as our predecessors (this is still the case in hunter-gatherer societies today) and regarded as kin from whom much could be learned.

Dersu, the protagonist in Vladimir Arseniev's narratives (see Chapter 2), had an animist outlook on life. He believed nature was pervaded by spiritual forces and attributed conscious life to natural objects or phenomena. Mountains, woods, forests, rivers, and lakes were all thought to possess spirits. For example, the Plains Indians used to describe trees as standing people, birds as flying people, animals as walking people, and fish as swimming people. To true animists, human existence is inseparable from the plants, animals, earth, and sky that comprise the great mystery of life. *Homo sapiens* is just one more participant in this animistic world, neither apart from it nor superior to it.

I have suggested that prehistoric man was completely "in the dark" about natural phenomena. And there was a lot to be scared of. What caused earthquakes, storms, and floods? Why were there eclipses, thunder and lightning, comets and so on? Why was there a daily alternation of light and darkness? What if the light would not return? There was the fear of sickness and the fear of falling victim to predators. The most important source of anxiety, however, was whether there would be game. Without game, starvation would follow. An animistic worldview was an attractive way of explaining all these mystifying phenomena. Just as I acted out shamanistic games in the Dutch sand dunes, our archaic predecessors looked for ways to create an illusion of certainty in a highly unpredictable world. An animist attitude enabled our ancestors to explain the inexplicable and make sense of nature's volatility.

From what we understand about the development of the mind, animism is a very "natural" way of making sense of the world around us. It is a much more spontaneous way of interpreting our experiences than the more dogmatic theories, beliefs, and practices found in most organized religions. Looking back at the dawn of mankind, I would argue that we began as animistic children and for most of our evolutionary history grew into animistic adults, turning eventually to organized religion. In time, animistic thinking was overwritten by the rationalistic objectivity of sustained, prolonged, and pervasive formal education, more typical of contemporary society.

Most animists hold on to the belief in spirits (souls) that are separable from bodies, and the notion that these spirits survive physical death. Predictably, the major world religions have maintained that tradition of belief. Animists believe that if certain "rules" are followed, spirits pass to an easier world where there will be an abundance of game and ever-ripe crops (the infamous "Happy Hunting Grounds"). But if things are not done properly, spirits remain on earth in the form of (often malignant) ghosts. It is vital that the soul journeys to the spirit world without becoming lost, and does not end up as a ghost. For animists, it is important to maintain the cosmic balance—people, animals, and inanimate things, must all be at peace with one another. Rituals and rules are essential for survival—ways of winning the favor of the spirits responsible for the provision of food, shelter, fertility, and health. [90]

The dreaming

I like to think that many of these animist beliefs may derive from dream processes—a special form of primary process thinking. Dreams are an intricate way of transcending the ordinary conscious human experience and entering wider realms of life. Dreams represent a synthesis of our being, manifested on a physiological and a psychological level. The symbols and metaphors presented in dreams have been used since the beginning of time to explain our connection to the sacred. And I can find striking similarities between animist and dream logic.

Dreams, like waking language, are representational, and are made up of symbols connected to latent unconscious thoughts. While the symbols that constitute waking language are largely verbal and only partly unconscious, those that constitute dreams tend to be more disguised, needing an associative process of decoding and interpretation. During the dream process, memory and intuition, fact and fiction, intermingle without the interference of normal censure processes. Issues are presented in a metaphoric sense. I imagine that primary process thinking lies at the origin of animism—the kind of unconscious thinking that uses symbols and metaphors, and disregards traditional logic. When traditional logic no longer applies, the dreamer crosses the boundary between what is human, animalistic, and inanimate—an interface that is experienced as real. The messages found in dreams contain information relating

to both animate and inanimate objects, such as trees, stones, mountains, rivers, and oceans. This imagery is then incorporated into conscious logic and used as a reliable guide for future action. I speculate that our prehistoric animist ancestors (and even the animist of today) used their dreams as a source of information for important decisions, like what to hunt, where, and when, and how to overcome possible dangers. For some tribal people like present day Aborigines, the Dreaming continues to play an essential role for establishing the structures of society, rules for social behavior, and the ceremonies performed to ensure continuity of life and land.

History, sacred writings, and tribal lore record events in which dreams and their interpretation played major roles. Specific animals frequently take prominent positions in these nighttime revelations. It has been speculated that some ancient cave paintings of animals may represent the dream images of cave dwellers whose lives were mostly spent chasing, hunting, and taming animals. The kill would activate primary process imagery that would be reflected in their dreams.

I am speculating about times long past, drawing on observations of clients in my clinical work, who often present me with accounts of dreams in which animals play a significant role. Some of these dreams are nightmarish; in them, the dreamer is pursued by animals or various kinds of monsters. Animals that play a significant role in dreams are often representations of the more untamed and uncivilized aspects of our nature that we repress in daily life. In dreams, through animalistic imagery, we may be exposed to issues that we try to push away in daily life. Analogous to what was important to our early hominid predecessors, it is my responsibility as a psychoanalyst or coach to understand the messages that these dreams are trying to convey. And although today we can simply ignore this kind of imagery (unless we are interested in making sense out of the language of dreams), this casual neglect was not an option for primitive man, who could not distinguish between the realities of the dream world and the physical world. Their dream life would be vital to maintaining the connection of the spirit world with the physical world.

I am convinced that there are remnants of this mystical, animist world inside the mind of contemporary hunters, although we are not necessarily consciously aware of it. Like our ancient predecessors, while I am hunting I have to accept that death—killing the prey—is just one more event in the cycle of life, one mode within a pattern of deconstruction, decay, and resurrection. Hunters, more than other people, are acutely aware that we are an intricate part of this cycle of life.

To illustrate, I was once fly-fishing for West Coast salmon—another form of hunting. It was late in the season and many salmon were ready to spawn and had begun to discolor. Returning to the river a few weeks later, most of these salmon were dead or dying. Their decomposing bodies lay everywhere. As I looked at the scene, I realized that these salmon carcasses would bring crucial nutrients to the rivers and forests and provide food for the young fry that would hatch in about six months' time. The carcasses would also be food for the many animals that prowled the river during the spawning season. The life cycle of the salmon symbolizes the cycle of life; and *Homo sapiens*, too, can be considered part of this gigantic ecosystem, of which our life cycle makes up an infinitesimal part—and over which we have little or no control.

ᖰ

Shape shifting

For animists, human-animal relations lie on a flexible continuum; each entity can become and not-become the other. In this interconnected worldview, *Homo sapiens* is viewed as merely another animal. Personhood is ascribed to non-human creatures such as the animals they hunt as well as the spirits that inhabit their world. Hunters are considered to be both human *and* the animals they hunt.

Remember that in the animist world, there was no clear distinction between the spiritual and the material. People would seek deliverance through a wide range of shape-shifting spirits. But hunters were also shape shifters; they too could move back and forth between the world of their prey, and the world of the predator. In Rane Willerslev's book *Soul Hunters*, in which he describes his observations of the Yukaghirs (a little known group of indigenes from the Upper Kolyma region of north-eastern Siberia), we meet one of the hunters, "Old Spiridon." According to Willerslev:

"Watching Old Spiridon rocking his body back and forth, I was puzzled whether the figure I saw before me was a man or elk [Willerslev wrote elk but must have meant moose]. The elk-hide coat worn with its hair outward, the headgear with its characteristic protruding ears, and the skis covered with an elk's smooth leg skins, so as to sound like the animal when moving in the snow, made him an elk; yet the lower part of his face below the hat, with its human eyes, nose, and mouth, along with the loaded rifle in his hands, made him a man. Thus it was not that Spiridon had stopped being human. Rather, he had a liminal quality: he was not an elk, and yet he was also not *not* an elk. He was occupying a strange place in between human and nonhuman identities.

A female elk appeared from among the willow bushes with her offspring. At first the animal stood still, the mother lifting and lowering her huge head in bewilderment, unable to solve the puzzle in front of her. But as Spiridon moved closer, she was captured by his mimetic performance, suspended her disbelief, and started walking straight toward him with the calf trotting behind her. At that point he lifted his gun and shot them both dead. Later he explained the incident: 'I saw two persons dancing toward me. The mother was a beautiful young woman and while singing she said: 'Honored friend. Come and I'll take you by the arm and lead you to our home.' At that point I killed them both. Had I gone with her, I myself would have died. She would have killed me." [91]

Moving like a moose, with a moose-hide coat and moose-like headgear, making sounds like a moose, Old Spiridon no longer resembled a human being. With a rifle in hand, he was unmistakably a hunter. But, according to the rules of his animist world, he was also more than that. To ensure the continuation of his success as a hunter, he also needed to live in a "hall-of-mirrors" world—a territory inhabited by humans, animals, and spirits, all of whom were understood to be endless mimetic doubles of each other. In this animist world, human beings would inhabit an in-between state of individual selves and reincarnated others, assuming a variety of forms, of which the human form was only one.

In the world of our early ancestors, hunters were engaged in a process that can be described as "participation mystique."[92] In other words, hunters would linger (to use clinical terminology) in the twilight zone between projection and projective identification[93] Using this very primitive, pre-verbal, interpersonal mode of communicating and relating, an "I am you" connection would be established between hunter and prey.

I recognize these feelings when I am hunting—walking in the footsteps of my ancient predecessors. To master the hunt is to understand the character and soul of my prey. To capture an animal is to first enter its world by way of mimesis, to recognize not only the soul in every animal, but the capacity for self-transformation in all humans. I try to do the same in a more modernistic manner, in the form of animal calls and camouflage clothing. For example, while moose hunting, like Old Spiridon, I have imitated their sounds. If I were to mimic a bull moose I would squeal, grunt, or bugle; if I was a cow or calf, I would make chirping-mewing sounds. Imitating moose would not only help me locate them but also bring them to me. I could bring them even closer by using antlers to simulate two bulls sparring. While I engaged in these activities I was in a world between playing and reality.

⌐⌐

The covenant

A complication for animists is that when they eat the animals they hunt, they are eating their souls, or spirits. As a result they worry constantly whether these spirits will avenge themselves on the hunters who have taken away their body. The animists need to appease these spirits for having taken their lives, and to ask them for forgiveness. As "eaters of souls," they need to create a ritualized form of restitution, a way of handling the inherent dilemma of killing other living creatures for the purpose of their own survival. If these rituals are not followed appropriately, the spirits may retaliate, and even take the hunter's soul.

Our animist ancestors had various strategies for warding off such dangers. Some tribes would create the illusion that someone else did the killing. Others would create the illusion that the animal gave itself up. However, the most common way of dealing with this dilemma was to make some kind of offering to the spirits. Whatever procedures had to be, these rituals were closely connected to sustainability—the preservation of the game they were hunting. Nothing was more important than ensuring that the animals they hunted would be willing to die again when needed for food. For primitive man—as it should be for ethical hunters today—sustainability took pride of place.

⌐⌐

Shamans

Shamans brokered the relationship between hunter and hunted, bridging the divide between world of the living and the spirit world. They ensured that the ceremonies and rituals that needed to be performed to appease the spirits were carried out appropriately. Shamans were the explorers of that magnificent hidden universe that lay beyond the visible world.

There are many similarities between the role of the shaman and that of people in the helping professions today (psychiatrists, psychotherapists, psychoanalysts, and even coaches, counselors, and consultants). Small wonder that, as a psychotherapist, psychoanalyst, coach, and consultant, I have always been fascinated by shamans.

It was assumed that shamans, as shape-shifters, could ascend the sacred tree that connected heaven and earth, transform themselves into animals, and know how to converse with them. What's more, shamans, as mediators between the hunter and the animal spirits, would know how to pacify the "Animal Master."

They would know how to atone for the death of an animal; how to appease the "Animal Master" for the "offenses" against the animals hunted. Shamans knew what rituals were needed to influence the behavior of the animals. The famous psychologist Carl Jung described the significance of Native American shamanic rituals as such:

> "First come the dances, he must dance hunting, whip himself into the mood of hunting until he is thoroughly filled with the idea. He identifies also with the animal he hunts, he becomes his own buffalo and he is the hunter at the same time. The red Indians wear the skin of the buffalo and they *are* buffalos; they represent them as grazing in the pastures, but each buffalo carries his own arrow by which he will be hit, they are both the hunter and the hunted one."[94]

To be able to make these spiritual journeys, shamans had to dance and sing songs for the animals that were hunted; they needed to think like them, imitate them, and thank them for sacrificing their lives. Animists believed that if these rituals were done properly, and if the meat, skin, and bones were treated reverently (not violating the souls of the animals), the Animal Master would take the souls of the slain back to the dark womb of Mother Nature where they could be regenerated, and a new cycle of life would be initiated. If the proper rituals were not followed, the harmony of the natural world might be broken, with dire consequences.

I suggested that the shaman was the exemplary inhabitant of an intermediate realm lying between the human and beyond-human worlds, the primary strategist and negotiator in dealings between the two. Using rituals, trances, ecstasies, and "journeys," shamans ensured equilibrium in the relationship and the natural forces that made up the order of things. They became the guardians of the tribes' myths and concepts of the world.

I once visited the underground Trois Frères (Three Brothers) cave in Ariège, in Southern France, which contains an important group of late Paleolithic paintings and engravings. There is evidence that this awe-inspiring, cathedral-like cave was used over thousands of years by primitive man as a shrine to transformation and rebirth. One figure in particular, the Sorcerer (boxed in the following image), is one of the most striking images in prehistoric art. This mythic being has the full beard and dancing legs of a man, owl eyes, the antlers and pricked ears of a stag, and the paws and phallus of a lion. Surrounded by a herd of 30 bisons, ten horses, four ibex, and a reindeer, this part-human Animal Master seems to be directing the herd's movements. He is controlling the hunt and responsible for the continuation of game.

I can imagine how this Sorcerer, painted more than 16,000 years ago, might have served as a mediator between life and death, between humans and the animal "kin" they venerated. It is believed to be one of the first depictions of a shaman performing a ritual to ensure good hunting. The Sorcerer (and a long line of shamans who followed) may have created supersensory experiences by means of altered consciousness (often induced by psychedelic drugs) to gain knowledge of the animal world—the world of the ancestors. I and other contemporary hunters can testify that this combination of human and non-human is not limited to the early prehistoric period. Horn- or antler-crowned shamans are still represented in many places in the world today.

Archeological finds have revealed that there have been shamans since the dawn of mankind. For example, in Iraq there is evidence of shamanistic practices dating back 60,000–80,000 years. Evidence from an ancient grave in Shanidar, Iraq, where the ritualistic burial of nine bodies was discovered, suggests that the Neanderthals demonstrated a belief in an animist or spirit world. The artistic act of painting or drawing, combined with other means of expression, was a medium for Paleo-shamanic rituals and practices. The need to influence the course of life through the creation of images, like cave art, has persisted from the San artists (the hunter-gatherers, also called bushmen, of southern Africa) to contemporary artists. I think it's safe to assume that through their complicated ceremonies and rituals, primordial hunters were coming to terms with the strangeness of a world in which they needed to kill in order to live.

᠆

Beyond consciousness

Shamans were masters in the art of ecstasy, a psychological state characterized by a feeling of wonder, amazement, bliss and, at times, alienation. These states of ecstasy contributed to a special kind of perception, a heightened or visionary state of expanded consciousness, during which they gained knowledge and power for themselves or their communities. Shamans would beat drums and engage in an elaborate and frenzied dance, clothed in a distinctive dress that was often decked with snakes, stripes of fur, and little bells. The dancing and chanting not only recounted the long journey to be undertaken by the shaman, it also led to a self-induced trance state that enabled the shaman to start the journey.

The ability to move consciously beyond the physical body was the specialty of traditional shamans, who developed techniques for lucid dreaming, and what we today call out-of-body experiences. The call to shamanism is often directly related to a near-death experience, such as being struck by lightening, a fall from a great height, a life-threatening illness, or a lucid dream experience in which the candidate dies or loses and replaces a major organ and so is reborn. Survival of these initial inner and outer brushes with death provided shamans with personal experiences that would strengthen their ability to work effectively with others. Having had a near-death experience, or something similar, a shaman was more likely to understand what must be done to correct a difficult condition or situation. Knowledge of other realms of being and consciousness, along with the ability to ward off dangers, is the basis of shamanic power.

I had one of these near-death experiences myself while hunting (described in the Preface to this book), and through it I gained a sense of what a shamanic trance is like. When I broke my spine on the summit of a mountain during a bear hunt in Kamchatka, in the instant the accident happened, I believed I had died. On impact, I experienced a magical review of my life and when that experience passed, felt a great sense of peace. After my blackout, and even though I was very seriously injured, I felt less pain than I was to experience later. During the very long sleigh ride down the mountain to my tent, I was in a trance-like state. I had become, to quote the psychologist William James, "twice born."[95] James used the term to describe people who are given a new lease of life. Once they have undergone fundamental moral and spiritual upheaval (such as my near-death experience), they are more prepared to transcend their self-limitations. Like shamans, "twice-born" people actively use these difficult experiences to help them come to peace with their inner demons.

With appropriate words and acts, shamans used their power to envelop people in a kind of protective amour so that evil spirits would become inactive or inoffensive. So as well as negotiating with animal spirits to assure the continuity of game, shamans were also able to heal the sick, foretell the future, and change the weather. They could discover the cause of sickness, hunger, and disgrace, and prescribe an appropriate cure.

Shamans also guided their disciples' personal development, assisting them in their journey of self-discovery. Shamans encouraged them to go beyond not knowing, helping them uncover whom they really were. The shamans' need to help, together with their progressive accumulated experience of dealing with others, gave them wisdom about the vicissitudes of life. Thus shamans, as prehistoric psychiatrists, psychoanalysts, psychotherapists and coaches, engaged (or were engaged) in similar activities as contemporary ones.

I was once present at a shamanistic dance at Shaman rock, Olkhon Island, the sacred land of the Buryats at Lake Baikal in Siberia. The shaman put himself into a trance by playing a drum. As I listened, I realized that I was also being hypnotized by the rhythm. My mind drifted off... The Sorcerer in the Trois Frères cave... the bear tracks I had seen while I walked on the rocks by the lake... As a psychoanalyst, to what extent am I a shaman, a guide in in-between states, trying to help others find answers to the difficult questions in their lives?

82 — Neihardt, John. *Black Elk Speaks. The Life Story of a Holy Man of the Oglala Sioux as Told to John G. Neihardt*, http://www.lesekost.de/biograf/hhlb13.htm

83 — Patterson, J. H. *The Man Eaters Of Tsavo And Other East African Adventures*. London: Kessinger Publishing, 2004.

84 — Corbett, Jim. *Man-Eaters of Kumaon*. Long Beach: Safari Press, 1991.

85 — *Ibid.*

86 — Vaillant, John. *The Tiger: A True Story of Vengeance and Survival*. London: Sceptre, 2010, p. 191.

87 — Golding, William. *Lord of the Flies*. New York: Penguin, 1999.

88 — Freud, Sigmund. "Totem and Taboo," *The Standard Edition of the Complete Psychological Works of Sigmund Freud*, Vol. XIII, Transl. James Strachey, London: Hogarth Press and Institute for Psychoanalysis, 1913.

89 — Ruark, Robert. *Use Enough Gun: On Hunting Big Game*. London: Corgi Books, 1972.

90 — Tylor, Edward B. *Primitive Culture*. 2 vols., 7th ed. New York: Brentano's [orig. 1871], 1924.

91 — Willerslev, Rane. *Soul Hunters: Hunting, Animism, and Personhood among the Siberian Yukaghirs*. Los Angeles: University of California Press, 2007, p. 1.

92 — Lévy-Bruhl, L. *How Natives Think*, Translated by Lilian A. Clare, London, 1926.

93 — Ogden, Thomas H. *Projective Identification and Psychotherapeutic Technique*. London: Karnac, 1992.

94 — Douglas, Claire. *Visions: Notes of the Seminar given in 1930-1934 by C.G. Jung*, Volume 1. Princeton: Princeton University Press, 1997, p. 988.

95 — James, William. *The Varieties of Religious Experience* (1902). New York: Touchstone, 1997.

*The frog does not drink up the
pond in which he lives.*
      —Native American Proverb

*One touch of nature makes
the whole world kin.*
      —William Shakespeare

*My profession is always to be alert,
to find God in nature, to know God's
lurking places, to attend to all the
oratorios and the operas in nature.*
      —Henry David Thoreau

*To see a world in a grain of sand,
And a heaven in a wild flower,
Hold infinity in the palm of your hand,
An eternity in an hour.*
      —William Blake

*What is man without the beasts? If all the
beasts were gone, man would die from a
great loneliness of the spirit. For whatever
happens to the beasts, soon happens
to man. All things are connected.*
      —Chief Seattle

*Let children walk with Nature, let them see
the beautiful blendings and communions
of death and life, their joyous inseparable
unity, as taught in woods and meadows,
plains and mountains and streams of our
blessed star, and they will learn that death
is stingless indeed, and as beautiful as life.*
      —John Muir

WORSHIPPING NATURE

Our early ancestors had a deep sense of awe and wonder about natural phenomena. They had to make sense of nature's unpredictability, decipher nature's hidden qualities and forces, and work out their "fit"—their place in the cosmos. Paleolithic man was anything but a detached observer of nature, as most of us are today. Our hominid ancestors spent much time and energy pondering the mysteries of their relationship with the natural world, of which they were an integral part. Storytellers wove magical tales to make meaning from their experiences with nature. They worshipped the land, in the widest sense of the word. Their love of the wilderness was an expression of loyalty to the Earth that had borne them and would feed them.

Primitive humans worshipped the natural phenomena they could not understand—storms, thunder, lighting, floods, earthquakes, landslides, volcanoes, fire, heat, and cold. Their sense of helplessness in the face of these forces of nature compelled them to find ways to live harmoniously with them, through rites, rituals, ceremonies, and other practices that affirmed and celebrated the sacredness and interconnectedness of life. Their belief systems were based on their fears and their attempts to understand the mysteries occurring in the world around them.

Early man attributed spiritual dimensions to the animals that crossed their path. As I mentioned before, they assumed that animals had souls and as "eaters of souls" they had a responsibility toward them. Their awe of these animals and interdependency with them motivated the need to worship; and to find ways of atonement for taking their lives. To better understand what these creatures were all about, they would go through lengthy processes of identification in which imagery of humans and animals became conflated. This kind of belief system suggests the perception of continuity between humans and nature.

To explain this need for veneration, we have only to remind ourselves that animals have qualities that we either lack or possess to a much lesser degree, such as strength, power, cunning, smell, hearing, vision, or speed. The desire to possess these qualities would be a strong motivating force for worship. No wonder that animals, in both fantasy and reality, created the base for the evolution of belief systems.

In Chapter 5, I discussed rock art, the most basic form of expressing belief systems. The wall paintings in the ancient caves where our early predecessors lived demonstrate the degree to which the animals they pursued (or were pursued by) were regarded as sacred. The caves were sites of ceremonial rituals where Paleolithic artisans incorporated art with the mystical beliefs of their people. They created many of these paintings as a magical way of ensuring a successful hunt. The murals of bison, horses, and the hunt depicted both the everyday life and the symbolism of their prehistoric world.

While I lived in Canada, I went to the north, on the coast and inland, to understand the landscape of the Arctic Circle better. The panoramas I was exposed to were harsh but awe-inspiring. These visits taught me something about the interdependencies between humans and animals. In an increasingly urbanized society, city dwellers may find it difficult to understand the depth of the dependence of inland Inuit communities on caribou for their survival and identity. Caribou hunting has evolved over thousands of years and is still central to the life and survival of the Inuit who winter in the Arctic interior.

The Caribou Inuit in these remote corners of North America have sustained themselves culturally and physically over generations on the caribou herds that are still plentiful today. Their population varied depending on the movements and numbers of the resident and migratory caribou herds they followed. Some of the older Inuit told me that starvation had been a regular phenomenon in their communities when they were children—and for them, the danger was still real, despite modern means of communication and transportation. Each community member seemed to be familiar with harrowing tales of hardship and starvation, passed down in stories that had been told by many generations. The Caribou Inuit lived in constant fear of the uncontrollable, due to the harshness and randomness of life in the Arctic, where a streak of bad luck could destroy their entire livelihood.

Beseeching potentially angry, vengeful, but unseen powers for their help in surviving another day was one way of creating an illusion of control over their environment. The Caribou Inuit were animists, and believed the caribou had souls. This belief, and their interdependence with the caribou, meant that the animal was the most respected spirit in their cosmology—but at the same time their dependence on caribou for food made them extremely vulnerable. As one Inuit expression put it, "The great peril of our existence lies in the fact that our diet consists entirely of souls." No wonder that they constantly asked themselves whether the spirit of the caribou would be merciful. Their caribou fetishism led them to believe that they drew the special energy of the caribou into themselves.

The hunt for food at the end of summer and beginning of autumn was vital to the survival of the Inuit during the winter months. Rituals were used to ensure the timely arrival of the herds; divine beings were invoked to send them. But these divine beings could be fickle. They could be angry, and withhold their help. To the Inuit, the non-arrival of the caribou was an ever-present danger.

For the animist Caribou Inuit, special rituals, rules, and taboos had to be observed before and after the hunt to ensure that the great caribou spirit would not be offended. Any hunt that failed to show the appropriate respect and customary supplication invited retribution—meaning that the great migrations would not be intercepted. They had to show remorse for what they had done. The provisions of the Caribou spirit had to be honored. Engraved in the minds of these Inuit also was that game populations should never be abused. As true hunters, they were guardians of the land and its bounty. Interestingly enough, some of these rituals are still practiced, and remain an important part of their culture even today.

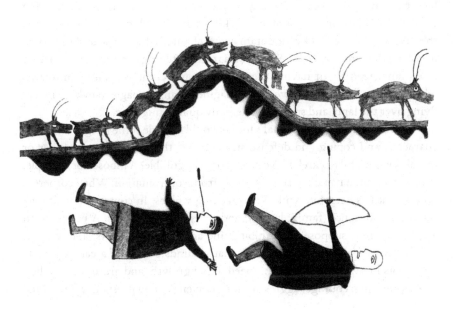

Totem and taboo

In the spiritual world of the animists, animals are associated with healing or inspirational power. Like the Inuit, for each clan, tribe, or group of people that predated modern man, specific animals would be adopted and worshipped as totems. Behind the designation of an animal as a totem was the more-or-less hidden desire for the animal's qualities (power, speed, intelligence, etc.). This totemic symbol represented a direct, specific kinship and relationship between these animals and the people. And to ensure their support, our early ancestors (and some tribal people today) would carry or wear carvings of these animals or birds (fetishes) as a reminder of the wisdom, experience, understanding, and medicinal power of their totem animal. Because they are often regarded as a companion and helper with supernatural powers and as such are respected and occasionally venerated, many of totem animals cannot be hunted.

These totem animals not only referenced our more primitive ancestors' dealings with the spirit world; they also defined relationship patterns in everyday life. The chosen totem provided a window of insight into the tribal groups' way of interacting with their world. However, while a certain totem would be sacred to specific individuals or a specific group, it was not necessarily sacred to others.

As a hunter I empathize with this need for animalistic identification. There have been many occasions—having reached a state of total exhaustion in trying to scale an almost insurmountable rock formation—when I would marvel at the ease with which Rocky Mountain goats, chamois, ibex, or wild sheep could negotiate the same obstacles. Sitting on a rock, watching their acrobatics, I have often fantasized about having their stamina and climbing ability. Similarly, when glassing for game, I have often imagined being an eagle, hawk, or raven, flying over the land, and spotting where my quarry might be.

Understanding an individual's totem would provide some insight into their character, and coping and defense strategies. Is the totem slow to anger or impulsive? Careful or careless? Very wily or very gullible? A moose, for example, is very tolerant. It usually just walks away from confrontation. When cornered, however, it has been known to kill attacking wolves. In contrast, a wolf may stand for endurance, family loyalty, and a degree of wiliness. A person with a feline totem is supposed to exhibit feline actions, movements, and traits as well as that indefinable "something" that reminds people of a cat. A gazelle represents knowledgeable action, speed, rapid growth, and grace, while a lion evokes cunning, courage, aggressiveness, nobleness, and prosperity. Presented with danger or challenge, a gazelle will fly from danger whereas a lion will meet a challenge head on, often with much noise and gusto.

My totem animal has always been the grizzly bear, a brute of an animal that can show gentleness, but can also be extremely fierce. Traditional names for the grizzly bear include "king of the forest" and "grandfather," both of which show the respect that the bear inspires in traditional shamanic cultures and probably add to my sense of identification. The grizzly bear stands for courage, strength, protection, and life—a symbol of invincibility, self-contained and strong willed. My identification with the bear is possibly also related to the fact that bears hibernate in the cold months of the year, allowing them access to the forces of the unconscious, emerging with answers to spiritual dilemmas.

Totems also identify and symbolize a group that shares common interests—particularly an interest in the protection of kin—in societies that have no other agency or mechanism for performing this function. Indeed, the term *totem* is derived from the Ojibwa Indian word *ototeman*, meaning "one's brother-sister kin." The grammatical root, *ote*, signifies a blood relationship between brothers and sisters who have the same mother and who may not marry each other. Hence, in many tales of origin, descent may be traced to a totemic ancestor, which becomes the symbol of the specific clan or tribe.

Although totemism is not a religion, totemism is certainly imbued with religious elements. The relationships that exist between clans, tribes, and their totems may very well grow into one of worshippers and gods, leading to the establishment of religious ceremonials to allay the totem's righteous anger, or secure its continued protection. Totems could transform into deities, while totemic practices can be seen as a form of magic, predating the emergence of more organized religion.

Totemism is still practiced by many primitive cultures throughout the world. For example, remnants of these traditions can be found among Australian aboriginal groups, Native American tribes, the Inuit, in parts of Asia, and especially in Africa. Even in contemporary society, we can find various belief systems about animal reincarnation, or transmigration as it is sometimes called. All these ideas have their origin in belief systems that began with the delicate dance between hunters and hunted—the success or failure of the hunt being the ultimate determining factor.

The totemic animal of the Maasai people of East Africa is the lion, a symbol of strength, bravery, and savage beauty since time immemorial. This totem can be killed, however. The way the Maasai hunt lions is very different from trophy hunting. It is a rite of passage—a way of demonstrating their fighting ability. As the Maasai depend on livestock (cows, sheep, and goats) and do not eat game meat, only three products are used from the lion: the mane, tail, and claws.

After a successful lion hunt, the mane is beautifully beaded by Maasai women, given back to the one who makes the kill, and worn over his head on special occasions. To the Maasai, lions are part of their life and culture. Without them they cannot truly be Maasai.

A less formidable remnant of totemistic practices is the great obsession about the ways and wanderings of the whitetail deer in North America, where there is also a great cult around wild turkey hunting. It is very clear to me, living in Paris, that people who hunt in France are fascinated by wild boar. The favorite food of, the fictional character from the popular French comic book series *Astérix*, is roasted wild boar. As long as there is the promise of wild boar, one of the cartoon heroes of the book, Obélix, will do anything.

A totemistic bestiary

While hunting for banteng and water buffalo in the Coburn Peninsula and Arnhem Land in Northern Australia, I was told about the special relationship of the Aboriginal Australians with the crocodile. For thousands of years, crocodiles have been intimately involved with aboriginal culture and traditions, figuring prominently in their stories and myths and reflected dramatically in their ancient rock art. Most coastal aborigines have always regarded these enormous amphibians as sacred animals or totems and viewed them with awe, fear, and respect. They know the crocodile intimately; they know its habits; they have learned how to avoid being eaten by them. It explains their Dreaming stories, songs, and dances about the crocodile.

To many aboriginal communities the crocodile is so sacred that it cannot

even be hunted, a law they have respected for thousands of years. Perhaps they learned from experience that attempting to kill crocodiles was an open invitation to be killed themselves. They may have decided that it was much wiser to establish a mutually respectful relationship. Looking at the size of the drag marks I saw made by crocodiles at some of the billabongs in Arnhem Land and the Coburn Peninsula, I could easily understand this sense of awe. The Australian estuarine crocodile is the largest, heaviest, and one of the most dangerous of all the crocodile family. It can grow to anything between four and seven meters. In the museum in Darwin, a very famous stuffed crocodile, named "Sweetheart," is displayed. This "salty" was a 5.4-meter male crocodile famous for its habit of attacking the outboard motors on local fishing boats that strayed into its territory in Sweet's Lookout billabong. Eventually, Sweetheart was trapped by the Park Rangers but finished up in the museum because it did not survive the trapping. Ironically, Sweety seems to have drowned.

I remember how once, on one of the beaches on the Coburn Peninsula, the most northern part of Australia, I was taking a break from hunting banteng and wild hogs, and looking for shells. While walking I came across one of these salties, looking at me. A close encounter like that certainly makes you think twice about taking a swim in the sea. My guide once told me, while fishing for barramundi, "The only thing I put in the water is that lure you are holding." In Arnhem Land, I once shot a wild hog that had a leg missing. It must have had an unfortunate encounter with one of these huge reptiles but somehow managed to get out of its jaws.

To the Australian aborigines, looking after the crocodile means they are looking after the land in the same way their ancestors did. In their complex religious set of beliefs—their Dreaming—they had learned that their crocodile ancestors had made parts of their land. They were related. Each Aboriginal community had its own stories about the crocodile, the land it inhabits, and its spirits.

From totemism to deification

In pre-modern societies, totemism could evolve into animal worship. This was reflected in animal deities, or animal sacrifice. In the case of animal worship, an appropriate animal—the epiphany, or incarnation of the deity—would represent the sacred power of the deity. In contrast to totemism, in which animals or birds were special to certain individuals, animists see sacred animals as sacred to the gods, and thus to everyone. Our ancestors worshipped animals that had inimitable traits and because they believed that everything in nature had a soul.

I can imagine that many old deities were either the predators or the prey of man. In many pagan religions, the veneration of animals derived from the primitive notion of kinship and ultimate identification with all forms of life. To animists, every living thing was a member of one large family: the four elements (earth, air, fire, water), and the plant, animal, and human worlds were connected to each other in often complex and sophisticated ways. And this identification with animals (as the belief system of the Caribou Inuit illustrates) has continued until the present.

In Chapter 5, I described how early man looked at animals as their equals and didn't differentiate between the animal and the human kingdoms. Gods could be worshipped via a representative animal, which made animal cults and totemistic practices part of Paleolithic man's psychological landscape. Many archeological excavations suggest that primitive man performed a host of animal rituals, ranging from the glorification of animal deities, to animal sacrifice, or simply showing great respect for specific animals.

For example, horned animals, particularly the ibex, were worshipped as icons in the prehistoric Near East; they are portrayed on pottery dating as far back as 5500 BC. One explanation given for this worship is that it derives from the goat's remarkable sex drive. Generally speaking, goats have always been viewed as symbols of fertility. Goats and rams were also worshipped in Ancient Egyptian cities. For example, in the city of Mendes, Ptah, the Egyptian god of magic, knowledge, and wisdom is represented by a species of wild goat with long, outwardly curling horns. In early Babylonian times the god Ea, protector of its people and the bringer of knowledge and civilization to humanity, was portrayed as a goat. Excavations in Central Asia (predominantly Afghanistan) have revealed ancient, ritualized goat-burial practices that demonstrate the religious significance of the goat. The Greek horned and hoofed goat-god Pan was commonly associated with fertility and the goat was closely related to the god Dionysus during the Roman era. Thor, the hammer-wielding Norse god associated with thunder, lightning, storms, strength, destruction, fertility, healing, and the protection of mankind, was worshipped before the other gods of Valhalla. Some say this deity existed as early as the Stone Age. Thor drove a great chariot, pulled by two gigantic and powerful goats—symbols of thunder and lightning. Some medieval legends maintain that the Devil created the goat. Satan himself was often depicted with goat horns, and was said to change his shape into that of a goat.

The fearsome qualities of some animals could be the cause of worship. Unlike present-day city dwellers, our ancestors were well aware that they lived in a world where every creature fed on was, in turn, food for some other creature. The predators that roamed their land reminded our hominid ancestors of their limitations and vulnerabilities—but they learned to co-exist with these dangerous creatures. They developed a deep respect for the lions, leopards, tigers, bears, crocodiles, and poisonous serpents with which they shared the land. The need to worship these animals was made even more pressing by the fear that the soul of these animals, if they were slain, would take vengeance on the hunter.

For example, serpent worship is still practiced in some parts of the world. Snakes are erotic, phallic, mysterious, and often deadly creatures. No wonder that, in the dance between nature and culture, the snake became a potent player in religion, folklore, and dreams. The Ancient Egyptians worshipped a number of snake gods, including Apep and Wadjet. Even earlier, the Sumerians had a serpent god. In India, carved representations of cobras can be seen throughout India. Human food and flowers were offered to these serpents and candles burned before their shrines, signifying the exalted position snakes held in Hindu mythology. Some of the First Nation tribes in North America revered the rattlesnake, as it supposedly had the power to provide fair winds or provoke tempests.

In West Africa, I was told about the cult of the leopard. Among the Ashanti, a Ghanaian tribal group, leopards were linked to divine kingship. The Ashanti believed they shared a common ancestry with the leopard, which they were forbidden to kill. In that region there were leopard societies, secret organizations that were also active in Sierra Leone, Liberia, and Côte d'Ivoire. Leopard men (or "were-leopards") would dress in leopard skins, waylaying travelers with their claw-like weapons. They ritually mutilated their enemies in emulation of the beasts into which they claimed they were able to transform themselves. The victims' flesh was cut from their bodies and distributed to members of the leopard society. They believed that the ritual cannibalism they practiced would strengthen the members of the society and by extension their entire tribe.

There are numerous other examples of the ways in which our ancestors honored an animal's superior strength, speed, vision, and fertility. Unsurprisingly, given man's general fear for them, lions have been worshipped in many societies. These great carnivorous cats have been revered in myth, legend, fable, and folk tale since the times of Paleolithic man. Lions are almost universally regarded as the embodiment of strength and power and because of these associations, lion imagery has often been used to represent royalty. The ancient Nubians (inhabitants of Sudan), Egyptians, and Persians deified lions. Apedemak, "the lord of royal power," was a Nubian lion god, and the relief at the Apedemak Temple at Naqa shows Apedmak being worshipped by the royal family. The same relief shows the enemies of the king being subdued, and in some cases devoured, by lions. Kings were always seated upon lion thrones and lions were kept in the Lion Temple, as living symbols of Apedemak.

Tamed lions would sometimes accompany kings into battle to confer their beneficence and protection on the entire army, and to represent the physical presence of the great lion god. It's likely that worship of the ancient lioness goddess Sekhmet was originally introduced to Egypt from Sudan. Sekhmet was not only a great guardian, but also represented the pharaoh as a goddess of battle, retribution, and war. The Pharaohs kept tame lions as symbols of power and sometimes took them into battle for the same reason— to inspire awe and dread in the minds of the opposition in a little pre-emptive psychological hype.

In Egypt, the lion was associated with the Egyptian god Ra (the sun), while the god Mahes had the head of a lion. In Babylon, lions were the symbolic protectors of cities as well as symbols of royalty. Lions were regarded as sacred in Phoenicia; the Greeks sculpted lions as royal symbols; the pre-Islamic Arabs had a lion-god, Yaghuth; the ancestral god at Baalbeck, in Lebanon, was worshipped in the form of a lion; and there are frequent references to lions in the Old Testament—for example, the lion was the symbol of the tribe of Judah, one of the tribes of Israel. Yet the lion's closest royal association will always be in Africa, with Haile Selassie, the revered former ruler of Ethiopia. Thirty lions roamed his palace grounds freely as his personal bodyguards. Haile Selassie's proudest title was, fittingly for a truly great Emperor-King, "The Lion of Judah." In modern Africa lion-idolatry exists in many tribal groups, including (as mentioned earlier) the Maasai.

Elsewhere in the world, the tiger was worshipped as provider, protector, guardian, and an intermediary between heaven and earth. Like lions, tigers have always been regarded with a mixture of awe and fear. Throughout history, people have worshipped tigers to avert disaster, regenerate life, and increase fertility. India's mythology is full of references related to tiger worship. Not only were tigers treated as gods by many of the forest-dwelling peoples on the sub-continent, tiger images and legends featured (and still occur) in Hindu-dominated areas. Many temples and shrines were constructed to worship the tiger.

The earliest known images of the tiger in India appeared on the famous Harappan seals, which date from about 2500 BCE. These images are presented as top figures whose front half is a woman and rear half a tiger. The tiger is also associated with the Hindu deities Shiva and Durga. The goddess Durga relied on a tiger to guide her through the million obstacles on the battlefield of her perpetual fight against evil. With the tiger's help she was able to destroy evil, and bring light to earth. Even today, the image of Durga riding her tiger is highly visible in every corner of India. The destroyer god Shiva rides a tiger and wears a tiger skin. In Rajasthan, in Northern India, there is a primitive community of tiger-worshippers known as Baghel Rajputs. Legend has it that their chiefs derived their origin from a child who appeared to them in the form of a tiger. The Baigas of Central India worship tigers; in Bihar there is a tiger-god called Vanaraja. Followers of Buddha rode tigers to demonstrate their supernatural ability to overcome evil. Sumatran followers of Islam believed tigers punished sinners in the name of Allah. There are also many legends about "were-tigers," people who could turn themselves into tigers. In Pokhara in Nepal people hold a tiger festival where celebrants dance disguised as tigers and prey. Tiger-gods can also be found in Hanoi and Manchuria and the vestiges of tiger worship can still be observed among many of China's ethnic minority groups.

Apart from venerating the deadly, there was another good reason for worshipping animals—they were an important source of food. In Hinduism, the cow retains sacred qualities and cannot be slaughtered. Cows represent the entire animal kingdom and link mankind to the animals of Creation. By respecting the cow, respect is shown for all living things.

The magic of horns

My ultimate hunting fantasy—or "worship"—started at a hunting show in Paris, when I saw for the first time the spectacular horns of the Marco Polo sheep (*Ovis ammon polii*) and vowed to visit the countries where these animals roam. I was obsessed about getting a set of these magnificent horns. It took a lot of effort, but in the end I succeeded.

The Altai argali (*Ovis amon amon*) of Outer Mongolia and the Marco Polo sheep of the Pamir Plateau in Tajikistan are the largest members of the sheep family. The horns of the Marco Polo sheep have the widest spread (each horn can be as much as 1.7 meters long), while those of the Altai Argali are the most massive (weighing up to 35 kg). The Marco Polo sheep is named for the explorer, who described the species during his crossing of Pamir (ancient Mount Imeon) in 1271.

Ovis means sheep and *ammon* is a derivative of Amun, the ancient Egyptian god who was depicted as ram-headed, with curved horns. For much of the history of ancient Egypt, Amun was honored as the supreme god in the Egyptian pantheon. Just as the gods of Egypt loomed larger than life, the sheep of Central Asia still stir the same devotion among hunters—a fact I can testify to. For the contemporary hunter, these sheep have attained almost mythical status because of their horns. I now own several of these, which I have either picked up or hunted on expeditions in Tajikistan with Yuri Matison, the legendary, formidable but also amiable owner of Badakhshan Scientific Expeditions. The horns, which hang in my office and apartment in Paris, are reminders of a landscape I have visited many times, a terrain of strong contrasts—stark beauty with the ever-present threat of death. I look at them with undiminished awe and respect. In a strange way, I have also become a sheep "worshipper."

On one expedition in the Pamir Mountains, I found myself climbing a rocky animal path, at night, at a height of over 5,000 meters, without oxygen but with a considerable wind-chill factor, in pursuit of Marco Polo sheep. This effort certainly fell into the category of walking with a purpose and also threatened to be an impossible quest. Yuri Matison, who is probably the best guide in the Pamirs, had pointed out the sheep to me the day before, a large band of about 70 in a valley some way below. Yuri had looked from them to me transmitting an unmistakable message: "We're here, and they're there. How do you suggest we close the gap? How are we going to get closer with all those eyes staring at us?"

There was only one way: to get above them while they couldn't wind us. I wasn't entirely happy about tackling the staircase of rock in the dark but Yuri had said that this band of sheep had the most capital horns in the world. We had already spent the previous day lying behind some rocks, watching the sheep and hoping that they would come down closer to us—but no such luck. They were much better at hide-and-seek than we were and the rams clearly sensed that something was very wrong, even though we thought we were well hidden. We were lying flat and motionless for so long, waiting for a chance to get closer, that at one point a few lammergeyer vultures began to circle above us, probably hoping they were in for something good. But we weren't quite dead yet, despite the cold. We were so still, that at one point a weasel in winter coat crawled right over me without paying me the slightest attention.

The climb was exhausting and nerve-wracking but at first light I found myself at a steep drop. Below us, the sheep were circling nervously. Again, they must have known that something was up. I was lying prone, aiming my rifle, and looked at Yuri for the sign to go ahead—but he waited, then waited some more. At one point, I whispered to him that something had to be done soon as my trigger finger was getting frozen. I had to make a heroic effort to control my trembling. The icy wind felt colder and colder. Finally, Yuri pointed at a ram that he wanted me to shoot. After the shot, the ram fell, but Yuri thought he saw a second animal run away wounded, probably injured by a ricochet, as my shot had been made at a very steep angle and the sheep were closely bundled together. It took us a long time to recover the sheep—it is not easy to estimate distances accurately in the clear mountain air. My altitude meter told me we were at 5,500 meters and at the end of a day spent running after the injured animal I was totally exhausted. But resting—even standing still—was not an option in the freezing cold, especially at night. If we stayed in the open, the cold would kill us. One of the guides, Mansur, who doubled as our camp cook, encouraged me to keep going. The relief I felt when I saw the silhouette of a mounted Kirgiz shepherd, who lent me his horse to return to our yurt, was inexpressible.

I like to think that over time I have become more realistic, although perhaps not always much wiser, about sheep and ibex hunting, which is about creating as much discomfort as possible. The first time I was pursuing the mythical Marco Polo sheep, it was December, much later in the season than the climb I described earlier, and this, combined with the wind-chill factor, made for extreme cold. It didn't help that there was deep snow on the ground and we had no snowshoes or skies. Just as before, we couldn't get close to the sheep in daylight, so decided to try at night. Our little band of hunters began tracking through deep snow, heading into the wind that was howling down the open valley we were in. I rapidly named our absurd quest "the battle of Pamirgrad," as it became obvious we were attempting something bold but impossible, and something I would never want to do again. It was the most grueling hike of my life, in thin air and a temperature of minus 30°C, with a wind-chill factor that was truly horrifying. After a long trek, we set up our small tent on a frozen river. The next morning there was ice around the "breathing hole" of my sleeping bag, and it took a long while for the little gas stove to defrost my boots, due to the lack of oxygen. Engaging in normal biological activities in the extreme cold was memorable; we certainly didn't hang about doing whatever needed to be done. In spite of all our efforts to ambush them, the sheep were victorious: they saw us, and spooked. But it was an experience I will never forget.

As I have noted, primitive man believed that their ancestor-spirits gave them access to supernatural powers that could be used for good or evil and that gods, demons, and land-spirits could intervene in human affairs. However, they liked to have some control over this interchange. They practiced sorcery, divination, and healing to establish contact with the spirit world, and believed spirits made their presence known through sacred masks, dances, dreams, and prophecies.

As animists, our ancestors didn't see themselves as superior to the animal world; they thought of themselves as rather like older brothers. Animists did not differentiate between animals and people. They believed souls of their ancestors could become embodied within a particular animal. This reasoning appears to dovetail with the belief that animals were humans' ancestors, or viewed as gods who were ever willing to come to the aid of man, and thus had a right to their own cult.

ᡓ

Ape-like creatures

Among our early ancestors (and still observable in some primitive tribes) there were innumerable myths about our animal origins. If we can believe crypto-zoologists, human-like creatures are still supposed to roam the earth today. These humanoids—allegedly sighted in the more remote, wooded, or mountainous regions of North America, South America, Russia, China, Australia, or Africa— were (and are) believed by some anthropologists to be a two-footed mammal that constitutes a kind of missing link between humankind and the great apes.

Sightings of monstrous ape-like creatures lurking in the shadows of forests and wild mountainous regions of the world have been reported since ancient times. For example, a widespread Asian myth (which has proved more than a myth) told that people descended from apes. Certain tribes from the Malaysian peninsula trace their ancestry to a pair of white mountain apes. This legend reflects a Buddhist myth about the origin of flat-nosed tribes in Tibet, who were supposed to be descended from two miraculous apes. In the same way, the Jaitwas of Rajasthan claim they are descended from the ape god Hanuman and that their rulers have an elongated extension of the spine, a kind of vestigial tail, to prove it.

There are many sexual fantasies attached to these ape-like creatures. The image of the ape as rapist and kidnapper has been a common theme in the artistic imagination. The film *King Kong*—a huge hit when it appeared in 1933 and equally popular as an award-winning remake in 2005—depicts the kidnapping of a woman by a giant ape. In China, where monkeys are a very common sight, there are many stories where the differentiation between man and monkey is blurred. "The White Monkey," a story dating back to the Tang dynasty, tells of a woman kidnapped by a white monkey, an affair that ends with the conception of a child.[96] Monkeys have always had both positive and negative imagery projected on them. "Monkey," a popular Chinese saga based on a real pilgrimage to India undertaken by the 7th-century monk Hsuan Tsang, is probably the best example of this;[97] the monkey is portrayed both as a devilish rapist, and as an ordinary person stumbling through life.

And somewhere in the mountains and woods in North America, the Sasquatch, or Bigfoot, is supposed to live—a creature some people maintain is a relative of *Gigantopithecus*, an extinct Chinese primate. The Sasquatch is known by many regional names, including Arulataq (Alaska), Grassman (Ohio), Momo (Missouri), Oh-mah (California), Old Yellow Top (Ontario), Skunk Ape (Florida), Windigo (Quebec), Woods Devil (New Hampshire), Wookie (Louisiana), Nuk-luk, or Nakani (North West Territories) or simply Bushman. Before Europeans came to North America, the Sasquatch was the subject of First Nations' mythology and verbal history from Alaska to California. This large hairy humanoid creature was first described by European settlers in 1811. Since then, there have been hundreds of reported sightings and encounters.

When I was hunting in the Rocky Mountains of Alberta some years ago, I met and had a long conversation with René Dahinden, a Swiss national who had come to Canada in search of the Sasquatch. At the time, his collection of "eyewitness reports" from North America to Russia had made Dahinden one of the leading authorities on the Bigfoot mystery. During a long evening in a gas station café in the neighborhood of Hinton, he showed me and my old friend Jack casts and photographs of Sasquatch prints. When we retruned to our camper that night, and looked at the shadows on the mountains, his stories began to run more and more true.

The Himalayan cousin of the Sasquatch is the Yeti, which means "magical creature." The earliest references to this darling of crypto-zoologists can be found in the *Ramayana*, an ancient Sanskrit tale whose earliest version date from the 4th or 5th century BCE. The Yeti has been allegedly sighted regularly since 1832 and was dubbed "The Abominable Snowman" by western newspapers that fed their readers stories of the terror the creature supposedly caused in the valleys, crevices and glaciers of the Himalayas. Sir Edmund Hillary, who conquered Mount Everest in 1953, reported seeing huge footprints during his time in the Himalayas; but he and his co-climber, Tenzing Norgay, who had grown up hearing stories of the Yeti—not least from his father, who claimed to have seen the creature twice—returned with nothing more substantial than a fur hat fashioned in imitation of the Abominable Snowman's scalp.

The ambiguity inherent in the belief and legends about these crypto-hominids makes it all but impossible for the folklorist to presume to know the "truth" about Bigfoot. All assertions are likely to be subjective at root, and draw folklorists into the legend debate, a process they would do better to observe than to participate in. The existence of these creatures cannot be readily accepted because of the lack of evidence; the little there is lacks detail and does not help with the verification or denial of the existence of these creatures. Reflecting on these mythical creatures many years ago, I wrote:

"The sightings of Sasquatch and Yeti are most likely of a delusionary, illusionary, and hallucinatory nature and, as such, the projections of conflicting images of people living in isolated environments under conditions of severe stress. The actual presence of bears and apes probably played a major role in the creation of these creatures considering the process of condensation and distortion operating in dreams, delusions, and hallucinations. Many rituals and tales dealing with apes and bears support this contention. I have emphasized the great similarities in mental processes among children and primitive man and have used this to explain these institutionalized animal-like phobias. I do, however, also realize that many of the more recent sightings of these creatures (especially in the case of Sasquatch), have been made by 'modern' man. I suggest that in these instances, conditions of severe stress mobilized defenses and subsequently more primitive psychological processes became operational. Sometimes the behavior of primitive and modern man seems to be not far apart."[98]

Whatever the source of these sightings, its signals must be filtered through human consciousness and perception, which shape these manifestations and make them conform to certain archetypal forms that are both strange and yet oddly familiar to us—strange, because they appear supernatural or extraterrestrial, but familiar because, in a sense, we have created them ourselves. Dream work plays a major role in this process.

Female hunting deities

In the context of hunting, having moved from animals, to ape-like creatures, to human representations, it is interesting to see that some of the most important images of hunting involve female figures. Women were generally assumed to be handicapped in the hazardous business of chasing large game animals (given the likelihood of their being in an advanced stage of pregnancy, or having to take care of small children). However, in many instances women have turned out to be active hunters and scavengers. I would even go so far as to suggest that throughout history women (compared to men) might have been the more consistent providers in the family. Vegetables, fish, and small game—usually harvested by women—made up the bulk of the Paleolithic diet.

Although men usually assumed the role of hunter, in the human imagination, the bounty of the earth came from the great Earth Mother, which explains why women played such an important role in religious beliefs about hunting. The

Earth Mother symbolized the earth's fertility and was typically the mother of all other deities and the patroness of motherhood. This association probably derived from the perception that the earth was the source from which all life sprang.

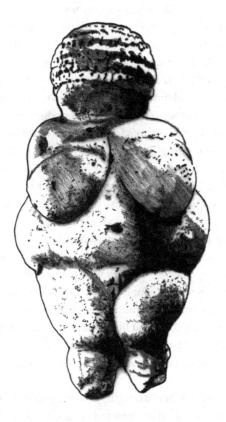

The Earth Mother appears as a motif in many mythological stories. In ancient Middle Eastern religions, she is referred to as the Great Mother of the Gods. Gaia, the primordial deity in the Greek pantheon, is often portrayed as the Earth Mother, representative of a general fertility deity—the bountiful embodiment of the Earth. She was worshipped under various names in different cultures, including Astarte (Syria), Ceres (Rome), Cybele (Phrygia), Demeter (Greece), Ishtar (Babylon), and Isis (Egypt). In fact, the worship of the Mother Goddess may have started in prehistoric times. For example, several small, corpulent figures have been found during archaeological excavations of the Upper Paleolithic period, of which the Venus of Willendorf is probably the most famous. The figurine is estimated to date from approximately 24,000–22,000 BCE. Given the importance that Gaia, the Earth Mother, played in the human imagination, it is not surprising that a female goddess also represented the hunt.

Diana: the goddess of forest, hills, and wild animals

Given the preeminent role that men assumed in hunting, particularly big game, it is ironic that Diana is considered the patron of what is generally perceived as a highly masculine activity. Diana represents nature in all its beauty, ferocity, and chaos. She is the protector of woodlands and wild animals, but she also hunts them down and kills them. In addition—something that can be an irritant in patriarchical societies—Diana is highly independent of men. Men are unable to control her. She remains indefinable in her relationship with the "stronger" sex. She destroys anyone who tries to compromise her dignity.

The cult of Diana was widespread in antiquity. Throughout ancient Greece she was worshipped as the goddess of forests, hills, and wild animals and associated, paradoxically, with both chastity and childbirth—because numerous myths recounted that Diana once assisted her mother in the delivery of twins. In early descriptions, Diana was also associated with Hecate, the primal, pre-Olympian feral goddess. Later, she was identified with the Greek goddess Artemis, though the Diana cult was Roman in origin.

In Roman and Greek mythology, Diana/Artemis is presented as the most independent of all the goddesses—a deity who thrived on challenges. As a child, sitting on the knee of her father Jupiter/Zeus, Diana asked him to grant her a number of wishes. Among her requests were to have a bow and arrow and a knee-length tunic (so that she could hunt); to have 20 nymphs as handmaidens to watch her dogs and weapons while she rested; to rule the mountains; to have the ability to help women in the pains of childbirth; and to remain eternally a virgin.

Diana was adored for her strength, athletic grace, beauty, and hunting skills. As a goddess, she is often depicted in gender-neutral clothing; while her robe is feminine, her belt is identifiably masculine, as is her weapon of choice, the bow and arrow. She is usually portrayed accompanied by a deer and sometimes with hunting dogs, as well as several nymphs (her requested aides). Diana also earned the title of "the triple goddess"—maiden, protector, hunter-destroyer. Sculptors occasionally depicted her with three heads, those of a horse, a dog, and a boar. These statues were usually displayed at crossroads where three tracks met.

Diana was also associated with fertility rites and the Great Earth Mother. She ruled the wilderness, the untamed frontiers of nature. But the association between Diana and the wilderness—symbolic of her untamed spirit, and her need to protect her own sanctity and that of others—meant that, intentionally or otherwise, she could be very threatening to men. This perception was

corroborated by myths in which Diana defended powerless (women) against unjust treatment at the hands of the Olympian patriarchy.

Diana's nature was as varied as the associations people had about her. Her character as a goddess was highly changeable and unpredictable. As goddess of forests and hunting, she was considered pure and virtuous; yet she could also be arrogant, prideful, extremely vengeful, and occasionally unforgiving and bloodthirsty. (This characterization may have arisen from the fact that there is no forgiveness in nature.) As a moon goddess, she was also a symbol of chastity and those who menaced her chastity would feel her terrifying wrath. She would also kill any of her companions who lost their virginity.

Artists often depicted Diana hunting or bathing in secrecy with her band of nymphs. Many myths recount that Diana protected her privacy ferociously. For example, when the hunter Actaeon came upon her—and saw her bathing naked—she shot him with her bow and arrows, then turned him into a stag, whereupon his own dogs turned on him and tore him to pieces.

The cult of Diana was so pervasive among pagan tribes that early Christians perceived her as their major rival, and despite Christian opposition, and its association with witchcraft, the cult continued to attract followers for centuries. In fact, Diana is still worshipped today by women practicing the religion known as Dianic Wicca (or Dianic Witchcraft or Dianic Feminist Witchcraft).

Diana, like the Hindu goddess Kali, is a creature of contradictions. She can be loving and creative, but also fierce and destructive. And like Kali, Diana's opposing characteristics create a whole, representing the complete circle of creation and destruction in the world, and emphasizing that our universe is an apparent collection of dualities. In many ways, the mythology surrounding Diana deepens and enlightens our insights into the human experience, even today. Diana personifies many conundrums, including our ambivalence about hunting, and the eternal riddle of the duality of life and death.

Women who hunt

Women have always played a varied and active part in the evolutionary struggle for survival. The psychologist Carl Jung realized that the traditional hypothesis—men developed hunting and fighting skills to protect women and children, while women gleaned and tended the hearth—is far from accurate. Women have hunted since Paleolithic times. I showed in Chapter 1 that the female apes among our earliest predecessors hunted and killed. In many primitive tribes, like the pygmies of Central Africa, women also hunt. The story of our evolution demonstrates that both sexes share the legacy of our peripatetic hunting, gathering, and fighting ancestors.

True enough, in certain societies, over the march of time, women were assigned the role of home keepers, while hunting became the preserve of men. But a paradoxical development has been taking place in post-industrial society as the old stereotypes about proper feminine behavior have broken down. While hunting has fallen significantly into disrepute because of the rise of animal rights and gun control ideologies, it has become increasingly popular among women. My own experience, having hunting women around me, bears out the trend; many women take up hunting after meeting outdoorsmen. For example, it is estimated that about a third of female hunters are taught about hunting by their fathers, while about half learn about hunting from husbands or boyfriends.[99]

Until very recently (ignoring our early evolutionary history), women didn't engage in many outdoor activities. They may have done a bit of camping with the family or taken part in other outdoor activities, but they didn't bother to pass hunting exams or buy hunting licenses or actively do what men were doing. We could blame socialization practices for some of these differences; it used to be much more common for boys to be asked to join their father, grandfather, or uncle on a hunt than for girls. But these stereotyped roles have been changing over the past 20 years and currently there is greater re-engagement with hunting by women, who aren't satisfied with being bystanders; they want to engage in these activities themselves. One explanation for this change in the hunting population may be the increase in the number of single mothers, who want their children to be involved with activities that their fathers would have taught them. And women's increased interest in hunting may be a sign of the further liberation of the sexes.

Many anti-hunters are unwilling to accept that nature overrules ideology and that women share the fundamental human drive to hunt. The author and huntress Pam Houston goes further and describes hunting as an essentially female activity:

> "[W]hen I remember that time in my life, I try to think not only of the killing, but also of the hunting, which is a work of art, a feat of imagination, a flight of spirit, and a test of endless patience and skill. To hunt an animal successfully you must think like an animal, move like an animal, climb to the top of the mountain just to go down the other side, and always be watching, and waiting, and watching. To hunt well is to be at once the pursuer and the object of the pursuit. The process is circular, and female somehow, like giving birth, or dancing. A hunt, at its best, ought to look from the air like a carefully choreographed ballet."[100]

Hunting still presents a challenge to some feminists, who see the language of hunting as a discourse of patriarchy, associating hunting with the hunting of women. They read an intimate connection between female and animal oppression. For many feminists, hunting stands for the reinforcement of patriarchical values, contributing to the suppression of women. For these people, the association of women with weapons is problematic. In fact, most of the stories of women who hunt emphasize the pleasure of being in the field, sitting and patiently watching for game, rather than the kill and possession.

But why should we suppose that men should be more susceptible than women to the deep, empirical learning that hunting can teach about the interconnectedness and interdependence of all life? Strict separation of the roles of the sexes can be highly artificial. We need to accept that every individual has both masculine and feminine characteristics.[101] In Jungian terms, the anima refers to "feminine" personality traits that are repressed in the male unconscious, while the animus refers to "masculine" traits that are repressed in the female unconscious. This fluid mixture of masculine and feminine energies is part and parcel of human biological and psychological development.

Diana symbolizes this gender dualism, as well as the polarity that defines our natural world: death and birth, the twin faces of life. All hunters—men and women alike—have to deal with the Diana inside us, the interplay between anima and animus, our femininity and masculinity. The Diana within us requires us to respect our nurturing and aggressive disposition, and to care about our natural heritage.

The Wild Hunt

Throughout the ages, humankind has struggled to come to grips with this duality of affection and aggression. Aggression often triumphed. The myth of Actaeon may be behind stories about the Wild Hunt, in which Diana would lead her dogs and female companions on a savage hunting trip. Over the ages, this wild scene became transformed and Diana started to figure in European myths about the Wild Hunt, in which she took along people who had died violently or before their time.

The Wild Hunt became a force of evil in folklore, the huntsmen gods who had been forsaken by their worshippers and joined the hunt to take out their anger on the world. In most tales, the hunt was led by the monstrous Wild Huntsman, a giant with antlers growing from his head. The Wild Hunt and its phantasmal leader haunted the skies, accompanied by a hideous cacophony of hunting horns, pounding hooves, the howling of coal-black hounds, and raging winds. In other tales, the rider was headless.[102] In violent winds, people fancied they heard and saw the Wild Huntsman leading his train of mounted huntsmen and baying hounds.

The idea of the Wild Hunt might have grown from collective memories of past conflicts, raids, or times of plague. Certainly, sighting the Wild Hunt was thought to presage a catastrophe, like war, illness, or the death of the witness. As a child, I remember being told stories of the Wild Hunt, in which good or evil befell those who witnessed it, depending on how they responded. Mortals who got in the way of the hunt or followed it could be kidnapped and taken to the land of the dead, so the prudent traveler took pains to avoid such an encounter altogether. If the Wild Huntsman was treated with respect and reverence, or witnesses demonstrated ingenuity, they might be well rewarded. But anyone who had the audacity to mock the Wild Hunt was snatched away and never seen again. There are numerous folk tales of people whose lives were taken by the Wild Hunt, their souls traveling as part of the hunt for eternity.

Dichtung und Wahrheit

The idea of the Wild Hunt may also have grown out of the fear of thunderstorms and other disastrous natural phenomena in ancient times. It may also have been based on beliefs that the spirits of people who died before their time (warriors, criminals, and suicides) would have to remain on earth, suspended between this world and the next. There are references to the Wild Hunt in Ovid and Tacitus and in Scandinavian mythology, the Norse god Odin rushes through the skies astride his eight-legged steed, Sleipnir, accompanied by furious winds, lightning, and thunder, taking with him the souls of the dead. Odin was supposed to prefer hunting during Yule, the period around the end of the old year, when the winds blew fiercest and the days were shortest, before hope began to return with the lengthening days of the new year.

The Wild Hunt was also a common theme in Germanic countries, where female deities supposedly led it. I believe that these European hunt goddesses, who were increasingly associated with agricultural and domestic fertility in the

Middle Ages, can be seen as alter egos of Diana, as can the stag-horned Herne from British folklore, who wore the antlers of a great stag, carried a horn and bow, rode a mighty black horse, and was accompanied by a pack of baying hounds.

But Diana may only be a latecomer. It is not difficult to find similarities between the Wild Huntsman and the figure of the Sorcerer in the Trois Frères cave described in Chapter 5. Similar cave paintings have been found in South Africa and elsewhere. It seems that European immigrants brought the Wild Hunt to northern America, in the shape of the Ghost Riders, a band of cursed cowboys, forever chasing the devil's herd across eternal skies.

Many aspects of the Wild Hunt tradition can still be traced in Nordic and Germanic countries. Until the beginning of the 20th century, young men in Norway enacted the Wild Hunt at winter solstice in a kind of "trick or treat." Mounted, masked, and costumed, they would punish neighbors who had transgressed, usually by stealing beer and livestock. If the riders were given food and drink, however, they promised their neighbors prosperity. In the Alpine areas of Austria, Frau Perchta was said to appear on Earth at the turning point between the old year and the new (the time of the winter solstice, Christmas, and the Scandinavian Julfestival). Young men ("*Perchten*") would dress up as evil spirits to banish those that accompanied her. Today, wooden animal masks called *Perchten* are still made for traditional Austrian holidays and festivals (such as the *Fastnacht* carnival).

Der Freischütz

The cosmic struggle between good and evil represented by the Wild Hunt has also inspired many artists, and the theme seems to have a perennial fascination. Perhaps the most striking example is Karl Maria von Weber's opera *Der Freischütz* (1821), based on an old German folk tale about a marksman who makes a pact with the devil, exchanging his soul for seven bullets that will unfailingly strike their target. The first six bullets will go where the marksman wants, but the seventh is the devil's own. Despite this unpromising premise, good triumphs over evil in the end. Weber's opera was a stupendous hit across Europe, and aroused so much frenzied admiration that people talked about *"Freischütz Fieber,"* (*"Freischütz* fever").

Saint Hubert

On 3 November every year, the town of Saint-Hubert in the Ardennes honors the patron saint of hunting, Hubert, after whom the town is named. The focal event of the impressive celebration is a solemn high mass, held in the basilica, an event full of pomp and drama that attracts people from far and near.

St Hubert, or Hubertus, was born in around 656, the son of a nobleman who nevertheless became the first Bishop of Liège and was known as the "Apostle of the Ardennes." The story goes that, as a young man, Hubert led a superficial life consisting of the pomp, pleasure, and vanity of court life—but above all hunting. When his wife died during childbirth, he gave up all pretense to be interested in anything else. On the morning of Good Friday, the holiest day in the Christian calendar, when everyone went to church, Hubert turned his back on them and went hunting.

The legend goes on to describe Hubert's epiphany. He had been pursuing a wonderful white stag when it turned and he saw between its antlers a glowing golden crucifix. A voice told him that he would be damned if he did not turn to God and continued his worthless life. When Hubert begged for guidance, the voice told him to go to the Bishop of Maastricht for instruction, and Hubert took his first steps on the path to sainthood.

The cult of St Hubert was very popular in medieval Europe and it is rather ironic that he became the patron saint of hunters as he stopped hunting after his conversion. Once again, as in the Diana myths, we recognize the duality that hunters need to manage: bounded aggression.

Today, 3 November, St Hubert's day, usually marks the formal opening of the hunting season in Catholic Europe. I once went to the St Hubert's Mass in Saint-Hubert and it was like going back in time. Many people had brought their dogs to the basilica and during the High Mass, the hounds howled whenever the huntsmen, resplendent in their green or red hunting jackets, sounded their horns—a primordial sound that was fundamentally moving. At the end of the Mass, the priest went down the aisle, and another note was played, after which the dogs rushed out of the church into the yard. There the priest, having blessed special St Hubert's bread, water, and salt, administered them to the dogs—an old ritual that harks back to the belief that St Hubert could intercede in cases of rabies.

Hunting rituals

This celebratory Mass is one of the more spectacular rituals inspired by hunting. Other cultural traditions are more restrained. Take clothing, for example. Although modern breathable fabrics and fleece have snuck into the hunter's wardrobe, traditional dark green—the prime color of the hunting world—is the only color most hunters in Europe will consider wearing. European hunters are very keen to maintain a variety of ancient traditions.

One popular ritual is the "last bite." When I killed my first chamois in Austria, the gamekeeper with me gave it the last bite—the final honor paid to the dead animal and a symbolic act in which the hunter joins with nature. Three twigs, roughly the length of a man's palm, are taken from a leafy tree, preferably a pine, close to the place where the game died. The first twig, the "last bite," is put in the mouth of the animal as a mark of respect and remorse for the kill. The second is put on the game's side of the wound, and the third is lightly dipped in the game's blood.

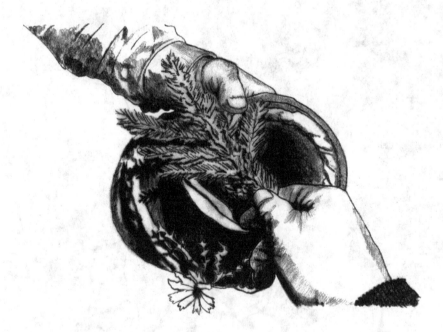

The gamekeeper offered me the blood-dipped twig on his hat, saying *"Weidmannsheil"* ("Good hunting"), and I replied, *"Weidmannsdank"* ("The hunter thanks you"). I then fastened the twig to the right-hand side of my hunting hat so everyone could see I had been successful in the hunt. This ritual is observed for most game, except birds. The hunter keeps the branch as a memento of days gone by.

I also remember being asked to bend over a deer I had shot in the Czech Republic, and receiving a number of blows on my behind with pine branches as punishment for shooting such a beautiful animal. The deer's blood was smeared on my forehead before it received the last bite. Another traditional ritual, marking respect for the dead animal, is to give a specific call on the hunting horn to indicate what kind of animal has been killed.

In the polder, where I used to hunt in Holland, each time the hunt ended all the game would be laid out in front of my father's hunting cabin for the hunters to pay their respects. The beaters would stand on one side, the hunters on the other, and all would remove their hats. Tradition required someone to stand in front of this tableau and play the hunting horn, making the ritual sounds that designated the animals killed: birds, hares, rabbits, and foxes. I was the only one who knew how to play the horn; in fact, I was so passionate about the various sounds that I even knew some that hadn't been heard in Europe for generations, like "wisent dead," and "bear dead." The last sound was the *hallali*, the signal made at the end of the hunt—and usually played at the funeral of a hunter.

The persistence of these traditional rites, in which hunters atone for the kill and assuage their guilt, indicates that the duality of the Diana figure still endures. I began by describing how ancient man viewed hunting as a covenant between the animal and human worlds. They hunted, killed, and ate with reverence the sacrifice of the animal. As well as reinforcing the belief that they lived in harmony with other creatures, their rituals were also a way of apologizing (as I have done many times myself) for the death of an animal. And this tradition continues. In life, there are hunters and hunted, and we are lucky enough to be at the top of the food chain. Do we still retain primordial memories of what it was like to live as an animal, foraging for food, living day to day in fear of being eaten? In hunter-gatherer societies there has always been a certain amount of guilt associated with killing animals.

The level of guilt may even be greater when it comes to killing an animal that is seen as being more human-like or rare. The greater the guilt, the deeper the reverence. For example, Northern people still have a huge number of superstitions connected with bears, based on their profound respect and fear for the animal. Bear ceremonies evolved to pacify the animal's vengeful spirit and there is evidence that bear sacrifices were carried out more than 50,000 years ago; early 20th-century German excavations of the Wildenmannisloch (Wild Man's Cave) and other caves in the High Alps uncovered altars dedicated to bears, with skins and skulls ritually treated in exactly the same way as found in the Arctic. These echoes of ancient practices may explain my own reverence for and fascination with bears. Whenever I am in an area where there are bears, I feel that intermingling of guilt and respect. The mountains, valleys, and woods become more sacred and I feel even more intensely alive at the prospect of the hunt.

96 — Anonymous. "The White Monkey," In *Dragon King's Daughter: Ten Tang Dynasty Stories*, Honolulu: University Press of the Pacific, 2001.

97 — Ch'eng-en, Wu. *Monkey: Folk Novel of China*. New York: Grove Press, 1994.

98 — Kets de Vries, Manfred F.R. Abominable Snowman or Bigfoot: A Psychoanalytic Search for the Origin of Yeti and Sasquatch Tales, *Fabula: Journal of Folktale Studies*, 23 (3/4), 1982, pp. 246-261.

99 — Houston, Pam. *Women on Hunting*. New York: Norton & Co, 1996.

100 — *Ibid*, p. x.

101 — G. Jung, Carl G. *The Archetypes and the Collective Unconscious*. London: Routledge, 1996.

102 — Yolen, Jane. *The Wild Hunt*. New York: Harcourt Brace, 1995.

My paw is sacred. All things are sacred.
   —Sioux bear song

Of the strength and ferocity of the grizzly bear the Indians had given us dreadful accounts. They never attack him except in parties of six or eight persons, and even then are often defeated with a loss of one or more of their party.
   — Meriwether Lewis and
   William Clark,
   The Journals of Lewis and Clark

Bears keep me humble. They help me to keep the world in perspective and to understand where I fit on the spectrum of life. We need to preserve the wilderness and its monarchs for ourselves, and for the dreams of children. We should fight for these things as if our life depended upon it, because it does.
   —Wayne Lynch,
   *Bears: Monarchs of the
   Northern Wilderness*

One of the reasons why bear hunting is a great and fascinating sport is that it is full of surprises. For instance, you can never tell how a bear—any kind of bear—will react to a set of circumstances.
   —Russell Annabel

Bears sleep by day. At night they stay awake to chase away bad dreams.
   —Anonymous

The primitive man's belief that the bear dance will inevitably bring the bear to the hunt depends on...[an] unconscious identity, for the bear and man are felt to be a continuum. And it must be admitted that sometimes the bear seems to feel it too, since reliable observers have stated that the bear does come when so called.
   —Esther Harding

ARCTOLATRY—BEAR WORSHIP

I have already written about my fascination with cowboys and Indians while I was growing up, so it will come as no surprise that I have always been intrigued by the life and deeds of Theodore Roosevelt, who was one of my role models during my childhood. I like to think that, having read his life story, I was impressed that the 26th President of the United States was such a political change agent. But in truth what really appealed to me was Roosevelt's reputation as an outdoorsman and conservationist—even a visionary, when it came to the protection and preservation of the country's natural resources. That, and his "cowboy" image.

Born on October 27, 1858, in New York City, Roosevelt came from a wealthy and politically prominent family. His childhood was clouded by illness but his love of the outdoors helped his health to improve. In his early twenties, he headed West, attracted to the Dakota Territory by alarming reports that three years of relentless hunting had almost destroyed the massive buffalo herds of the northern plains. Roosevelt was determined to add this symbol of the American West to his trophy collection before it was too late—clearly, fair chase and conservation were not yet his major concerns. But Roosevelt fell in love with the landscape and the strenuous life of the plains and bought a ranch in the Dakota Badlands before returning to New York, marking the beginning of a life-long preoccupation with game management in general.

Just a year later, in 1884, the Badlands ranch provided a refuge for Roosevelt as he mourned the deaths of his young wife and his mother, both of whom died on Valentine's Day. A lesser loss, but one that left him at a loose end, was the defeat of his reformist faction at the Republican National Convention. The Badlands wilderness offered him space for reflection and writing—something that later contributed significantly to his popular appeal. Roosevelt published 35 books on natural history, the American frontier, and political and naval history. His autobiography included accounts of his life in the wilderness.

During his time in Dakota, Roosevelt recorded daily life at the ranch and his hunting adventures. These records show an astute observer of nature and wildlife, which he remained throughout his life. Whenever he was outdoors, he always observed from the dual perspective of hunter and naturalist—although the passionate hunter usually had the upper hand. Roosevelt hunted for a wide variety of game all over the world, from birds to big game animals like elk, bear, sheep, lion, and elephant. He even explored the Amazon jungle to make an account of the exotic flora and fauna in that region. During these exploits he survived lion charges, and buffalo and elephant attacks, as well as encounters with anacondas, piranhas, and caimans.

But even though I am myself a hunter, it is not Roosevelt's reputation as a hunter that impresses me most: I consider his conservation efforts to be his greatest achievement. In the "Wild West," people went out and shot anything that moved. Before the introduction of hunting tags, licenses, and conservation, senseless slaughter was the order of the day. Thanks to powerful people like Roosevelt, conservation legislation was enacted that aimed specifically at preserving American wildlife for future generations.

Roosevelt was ahead of his time in realizing the need for federal regulation to ensure environmental conservation. At the urging of Gifford Pinchot, first chief of the US Forests Service, Roosevelt used the 1891 Forest Reserves Act, which empowered the President to set aside public lands as national forests, to increase federal land reserves. Roosevelt was also responsible for the establishment of the Boone and Crockett Club, which was founded in 1887 and promoted hunting in "wild and unknown areas of the country." This club became a powerful lobbying group in support of wildlife preservation and well known for its "fair chase" hunting philosophy. It took a leading role in eliminating market hunting, creating wildlife reserves, and establishing conservation-based hunting regulations. The Boone and Crockett Club was soon followed by the Sierra Club in 1892 and the National Audubon Society in 1905. During Roosevelt's administration (1901–9), federal land reserves increased from 45 to 195 million acres; 18 national monuments were created (including Niagara Falls and the Grand Canyon); five new national parks were established; and 51 wildlife refuges designated.

In November 1902, Theodore Roosevelt was in Mississippi trying to settle a boundary dispute between that state and Louisiana. The president never missed an opportunity be outdoors, and he took time out on this trip to do some hunting. But he hadn't any luck. One of the guides, trying to be helpful, captured a bear, tied it to a tree, and invited Roosevelt to shoot it. This was very far from what Roosevelt thought hunting was all about, and he set the young black bear free.

Roosevelt's refusal to fire at a helpless target inspired a famous political cartoon by Clifford K. Berryman that appeared in the *Washington Star*. The cartoon was captioned "Drawing the Line in Mississippi," and played on the two ways Roosevelt was drawing a line in the region—a reference to the somewhat overshadowed border dispute.[103] The cartoonist originally drew the bear as a fierce animal (it had just killed a hunting dog) but later tuned the bear into a cuddly cub. The cartoon and the story behind it captured the public's imagination. Back in Brooklyn, New York, a Russian-Jewish immigrant called Morris Mitchcom and his wife Rose had for some time supplemented the income from their candy store by making stuffed toys. Inspired by the bear cub story, they started to make toy bears that they named "Teddy's Bear," with his permission, in the president's honor. They copied the cute cuddliness of the cub in Berryman's cartoon—and "Teddy's Bear" became an instant sensation. The Mitchcoms founded the Ideal Novelty and Toy Company on the strength of it, a company that was eventually subsumed into Mattel in 1997.

Meanwhile, in Germany, Richard Steiff was working for his aunt Margarete's stuffed toy business. He often visited Stuttgart zoo to sketch animals, and his drawings of bear cubs were used for the design of a new toy bear that the Steiffs produced in 1902—the same year the Mitchcoms introduced "Teddy's Bear." The Steiffs showed their new bear at the Leipzig Toy Fair in March 1903. There was little interest from European buyers, but an American buyer, aware of the growing interest in toy bears in the States, ordered three thousand. At the World's Fair in St Louis the following year, the Steiffs took orders for a further 12,000 bears and won the exhibition's gold medal. It was the start of teddy bear fever in America, and of phenomenal success for the Steiffs. It is hard to decode why these early teddy bears were so instantly attractive. It may be that the form of its face—similar to that of human infants—triggered a protective reflex in both children and adults.[104]

Like many other children, I had a teddy bear. There is photographic evidence that it was extensively handled: in early photos of me, the bear looks much the worse for wear. Taking a simplistic, developmental point of view, a child psychologist might suggest that my fondness for this teddy bear may have set the seeds of my fascination with bears. Of course, that explanation is only one among many. My mother took me regularly to Artis (the Amsterdam zoo), and although I have no conscious collection of these excursions, I imagine that they had their own impact. Certainly, I still visit zoos wherever I am in the world. Whatever the origins of it, I can't remember a time when I didn't have this fascination for bears. To me, they are the arch symbol of the wilderness. Seeing a bear walking on the tundra or at the edge of a forest always fills me with a sense of wonder and excitement.

A Dutch childhood digression

So I had my beaten-up teddy bear, to which I was very attached. It was clearly a "transitional object," a physical object that substitutes for the mother-child bond. Most children have one and the most common examples are dolls, blankets, and soft toys. Later on I was fascinated by Dutch children's stories about Bruintje de Beer (Bruin the Bear); but my real passion was reserved for another bear.

Olivier B. Bommel was a fictional anthropomorphic bear and one of the two principal characters in a series of comic books by Marten Toonder, who was the most famous and influential Dutch cartoonist of his time. Olivier B. Bommel's companion was Tom Poes, a wily cat who complemented the bumbling bear and usually got him out of trouble.

At first, Olivier B. Bommel was just a supporting character, but he quickly became the main character in the series, as most of the action in the stories depended on the antics of the bumbling bear. Olivier B. Bommel lived in his castle at Bommelstein, where his butler Joost took care of his needs. Although he was well off, he dressed plainly and drove a solid and reliable rather than flashy car, maintained that money was "of no consequence," and was generous to his friends. Yet despite his good intentions, he had a remarkable capacity to get himself into trouble, and when things went wrong he was prone to tantrums. Olivier B. Bommel was given to acting without thinking, and he was not faultless—he also had a bad habit of blaming others for his own mistakes. It was easy to identify with Olivier B. Bommel's character and his "bumbling"—yet there was also a longing to be part of his adventures that fed into my fantasies of being an explorer. There were many days when I would curl up on the sofa or in bed and lose myself in the stories of this wonderful bear.

Although the adventures of Olivier B. Bommel were translated into many other languages, at heart he was a very Dutch bear. He never achieved the international reputation of A. A. Milne's Winnie-the-Pooh or Rudyard Kipling's Baloo, both of whom were immortalized by Walt Disney. Baloo plays a key role in Kipling's *Jungle Book* stories about the abandoned "man cub," Mowgli.

The bear symbolism in these cartoon series and films must have influenced the subconscious images of bears in the minds of generations of children in many different countries. Certainly, it affected the way I look at bears, which to this day remain highly attractive, fascinating, mysterious, but also dangerous creatures to me. This may explain why I am so curious about bears and, ironically, my need to observe and hunt them.

I also remember, as a child, reading William Faulkner's story *The Bear*, now recognized as one of the greatest American hunting stories of the 20th century. *The Bear* is set in the late 19th century, just after the American Civil War, and is a classic rite-of-passage story, describing the initiation of the young Ike McCaslin into adulthood as he accompanies his father and friends on their annual hunt in the wild country of the Tallahatchie River region.

Ike is instructed in woodcraft and how to handle a gun by a veteran hunter, Sam Fathers, the son of a Chickasaw Indian and an African slave. Fathers gives him the hunting skills he needs if he is to have a chance of killing Old Ben, a legendary bear with a maimed foot that constantly eludes hunters. Ike has heard tall tales of how Old Ben kills and devours pigs and calves, mauls and kills dogs, and is impervious to shotguns and rifles fired at point blank range. But, as Sam Fathers says, "Somebody is going to it, some day."[105]

The story follows Ike as he makes this annual hunting trip for the sixth time, as obsessed as ever with Old Ben. On the tenth day of the hunt, the dogs begin to make a very different sound and the hunters realize that they are chasing something very different than deer. It is Old Ben. This time, the party has an exceptional dog with them: a massive Airedale cross called Lion. With the dog's help, Old Ben is killed, but not before the animal fatally wounds Sam Fathers and Lion.

I assume that Faulkner intended Old Ben to symbolize the wilderness—huge, intimidating, primitive, but maimed and ultimately destroyed by man. According to Faulkner, you are either a true hunter, in tune with the wilderness, or part of that section of society that has been corrupted by the forces of industrialization and urbanization and estranged from nature. Hunting is the only way to build this deep connection to nature. When people organize a hunting party, they re-establish fundamental ties that bind them to what life was like before civilization pervaded every element of it. Hunting gives them the opportunity to reconnect with the prehistoric man within.

The death of Old Ben is not the end of Faulkner's story. He goes on to describe the steady desecration of the wilderness, including the site where Lion and Sam Fathers are buried, as the railroad and loggers move in. His theme is that once we lose our sense of common heritage, and our understanding of the laws of nature, we condemn the wilderness to death. The combination of civilization and technology has its advantages but as we move further away from nature through the process of industrialization and urbanization, we steadily disown our roots. Only a few, like Ike, don't.

When I first read this story, I totally identified with Ike's obsession with Old Ben. Bears are the arch symbol of unspoiled, untamed wilderness and they resonate with the wild, more primitive part of me. Bear hunting is an intensely emotional way of establishing and re-establishing a deep relationship with nature. Killing a bear is merely a sideshow. The preliminaries are what really count.

Bear histories

Sadly, I am only familiar with the black bear (in its many color phases, including "blue") and the brown or grizzly bear. I did a lot of climbing in Tajikistan while searching unsuccessfully for *Ursus arctos isabellinus*, the white-clawed sub-species of the grizzly bear, but was never lucky enough to see one. I have only seen spectacled, sloth, moon, polar, and panda bears in zoos, although I have been in areas where sloth, moon, and polar bears roam.

It is now many years since I first saw a black bear, at the edge of a farm in Peace River country in the wilds of Northern Alberta. When I saw it, I got—to use an American expression—"buck fever." All those years of fantasizing about bears, and then actually seeing one in the wild, must have been too much for me. I got overexcited and bungled the shot. Theodore Roosevelt once said, when asked, "No, I'm not a good shot, but I shoot often." I had great fellow feeling for him at that moment—even though I have become parsimonious in my shooting.

The farmer had told me that bears love oats. According to him, you could bet your life if there was only one field of oats in bear country, all the bears in the neighborhood would assemble there. He was fed up with the highly visible damage the bears were causing to his fields. Huge areas of the land looked as if earth-moving machinery had been through it. On the day I saw my first bear, I was sitting on a small protrusion in the oat field, to get a better view of approaching bears. I was staring in the direction from which I expected bears to come, given the evidence of numerous tracks. I was prepared. Then I heard a slight noise behind me. I turned my head, and there was a bear, not more than 30 meters behind me. To say I was confused is an understatement. I shot too quickly, a genuine case of "Ready, Fire, Aim." At the noise, the bear disappeared into the undergrowth and I was left with nothing but a great sense of disappointment. I had a lot to learn about the unpredictability of bears.

Six months later I was back in the same oat field trying to redeem myself. Spring had sprung in Peace River. This time I was sitting more strategically at the edge of the forest, against a tree on an active bear trail, waiting for a bear to show up. In front of me was the half-frozen stubble of a partially harvested field of oats. I stayed in position for several hours, watching geese fly over, a coyote scurrying by, and amused by a great gray owl that sat on the ground close to me, and far from being frightened away by my presence, just occasionally turned its head toward me as if in disgust at my intrusion.

I still remember that I had a book with me—*The Double Helix*, Nobel Prize winner James Watson's description of the discovery of the structure of DNA. While reading, time passed quickly. Suddenly some additional sense made me look up from the page I was reading to see a bear emerge from the thick brush at the edge of the forest. I was as excited as I had been in the Fall, but this time managed to pull myself together. I steadied my rifle, aimed, pulled the trigger, and the bear collapsed on the trail. When I walked over to look at it, I was filled with respect and sorrow. It was a beautiful animal. I decided to honor the bear by performing an ancient European ceremony and on the hunting horn I had brought with me, blew the ancient signal, "bear dead." It must have been the first, and probably the only, time this ritual sound had been heard in Alberta.

Since it was still quite early in the morning, I left the bear where it had fallen and went back to my original spot. After a few hours wait, a faint noise behind me made me feel distinctly uneasy. I turned my head carefully, and less than five meters away I could see a bear's head and neck sticking out of a bush, sniffing to get my scent. I turned my body very slowly, aimed and shot, and a second bear rolled out of the bushes. (In those days, a hunter was allowed to take two black bears, because of the damage they did to farmland.) While I was skinning the bears, another big brown-colored black bear came along to the "funeral." It came very close—and I had left my gun in the truck. It was not a comfortable situation. Now, every time I look at the large rug made from my first bear, many memories flood my mind.

All my bear hunts have been full of surprises. On another occasion, by another oat field, a pair of ravens was busily disturbing my peace. And then at some distance, I saw the black bear—or, rather, bears, as this bear had three cubs. In the sun, her appearance was magical, and her coat almost orange in color. As the wind was blowing in my direction, the animal hadn't detected me. The cubs were running around her, tumbling over and over each other. But they came closer and closer—and who wants a mother bear with cubs at close quarters? The bears were following the edge of the forest and it wouldn't be long before they bumped into me. Although it was spectacular to be able to watch this scene close up, I stood, and began waving my arms to attract their attention. The sow stopped, raised her head, woofed, and ran off, and followed by her cubs.

I had a very different encounter with bears in Quebec. My wife Elisabet and I were staying at a hunting and fishing camp in the North Country. The fishing, for perch pike or walleye, was fantastic. But the bear hunt was the first objective. To obtain a bear, the local guide had put us in a blind up in a tree. We sat there, and nothing happened for a long time, apart from a snowshoe hare that had turned carnivorous and was nibbling on the fish laid out as bait. A raccoon came by, but didn't stay for long. A gray jay, or "whiskey jack," a symbol of the Canadian North, also put in an appearance. It made its familiar harsh sound—and flew away. Then I heard a noise behind us—and I knew that a larger animal was somewhere about. Again silence. Suddenly, out of the corner of my eye I saw movement. I nudged Elisabet in the ribs, to warn her not to move. And there was the bear.

Later, after it was all over, we dragged the bear down the hill to the shore of the lake. It was quite a haul. But fireflies were dancing all around us when darkness came, making it a magical moment. The next day, Elisabet surprised the male hunters at the camp by skinning the bear, and taking its meat. We ate the prime cut of that bear a few days later, and I still consider it one of the best game meals I have ever had.

ﬡ

Bears: a symbolic history

Bears loom large in humankind's history and prehistory, occupying an important slot in our unconscious. Bears represent fear and evil, but also have regenerative powers, sharing some of the duality of the Diana character (see Chapter 6). In popular mythology, bears occupy both the sky and the underworld. Bears can be terrifying monsters of the natural world, but also symbolic of what the wilderness is all about. Bears can take life and they can give life. They can be endearing, or menacing—like the one that knocked on my tent at five o'clock in the morning on the Alaska Peninsula. Bears attract and repel—this is what makes bear hunts such a special, even hallowed activity.

Like Faulkner, I think of bears as the arch-representation of the wilderness. They can be charming, like the glacier bears—bluish-hued bears—I watched playing and sliding down the snow in Alaska, but they also can be ferocious. When provoked, bears elicit terror and create serious havoc. Bears are both symbols of solitude and symbols of protection, no doubt because of the determined ferocity with which mother bears defend their cubs. It is probably because of this attribute that the bear or the bear claw is incorporated into so many family shields.

One reason for the persistence of bear imagery in the human imagination is its spiritual dimension. Many tribes that live in bear country view bears as spirit guides, leading people to the nether world. Findings by paleontologists indicate that the bear was one of the first animals to be revered by humans. In many ways the sacredness of the bear still occupies our unconscious. In primary process thinking (dreams), bears and humans become easily conflated. We have always had a tendency to anthropomorphize bears, perhaps because they have some resemblance to humans, particularly when they stand on their hind legs.

ﬡ

The bear constellations

Since ancient times, people from diverse cultures have known about the two bear constellations in the sky. Ursa Major, the Great Bear, is probably the most famous constellation of stars, after Orion. This constellation has a companion called Ursa Minor, or Little Bear. The body and tail of this constellation make up the Big Dipper. The Great Bear constellation is also known as the Plough, the Wain and even the Wagon.

Initially, however, not everyone thought that Ursa Major and Ursa Minor represented bears. The origin of the name seems to have been erroneous, originating from confusing approximate sounds. *Rakh* is Sanskrit for "to be bright." The Greeks corrupted the pronunciation of this word to *arktos*, which means bearish, and also describes the far northern parts of the earth, the Arctic, where the Great Bear constellation dominates the heavens. The Romans called the constellation *Ursa*, the bear. Ursa Major is highest in the sky in the spring and lowest in the Fall, when, according to Indian legends, the Bear is looking for a place to lie down for its winter hibernation.

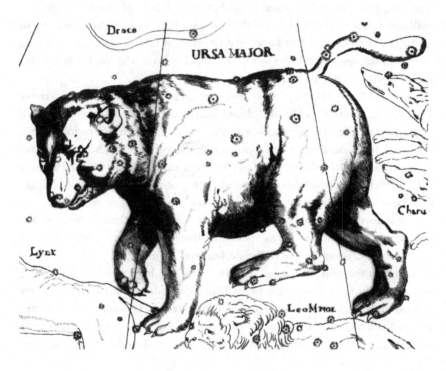

To the ancient Greeks, Ursa Major represented Callisto, one of the nymphs who accompanied Artemis (Diana). According to Greek mythology, Zeus fell in love with Callisto, who gave birth to a boy named Arcas. Hera, Zeus's wife, became intensely jealous and changed Callisto into a bear, in which form she roamed the forest. One day Arcas came upon the bear. Callisto, delighted to see her son, stood on her hind legs to greet him, but Arcas thought he was being attacked and prepared his bow and arrow to shoot. Zeus saw what was about to happen, turned Arcas into a small bear, grabbed both animals by the tail and tossed them into the sky, where they remain for eternity as Ursa Major and Ursa Minor. Another legend says Zeus seduced Callisto by assuming the form of Artemis to deceive her. As I explained in Chapter 6, Diana demanded the strictest chastity from the nymphs who accompanied her. In order to save Callisto and Arcas from the wrath of the virgin goddess, Zeus transformed Callisto into the Great Bear and set her in the stars with Arcas, their child, beside her.

The tribal people of North India saw Ursa Major in a similar way as the ancient Greeks. To explain the constellation's "tail" (bears do not have long tails in real life), they said it was made up of three bear cubs, following their mother, or three hunters following the bear. According to one version, the first hunter carries a bow and arrow to kill the bear, the second the pot in which to cook it, and the third the firewood to heat the pot.

The Arthurian legends reflect the process by which Christianity displaced the Druid tradition in Britain. Arthur (*Arcturus* in Latin) could be seen as a substitute for the pagan god Arcturus, the Bear. In ancient England, Ursa Major was called Arthur's Chariot. All in all, the Great Bear has been linked to gods and goddesses, royalty, and immortality myths throughout the ages.

Apart from its star symbolism, the bear has been many things to man over time, ranging from a powerful forest spirit that, like a shaman, mediated between our world and the next, to the teddy bear of childhood, the "transitional object" that aids our passage to individuation and takes part in our make-believe games.

In mythology and legend, the bear is a complex and contradictory creature: smart and naïve, forgiving and vicious, cuddly and threatening. The cyclical nature of bear behavior supports this personification. Bears hibernate: every winter they disappear back into the Earth, only to reappear in the spring, with cubs. This evokes associations with death and resurrection, cosmic renewal, the eternal transition of the seasons, and life-giving powers. There is also a strong feminine element associated with bears. Perhaps the bear mother, emerging from her den in the spring with her cubs, is the predecessor of Gaia—the Earth Mother. But this is simply another contradiction, because bears are also associated with masculine power and strength, and there are very good reasons why the grizzly bear is known as *Ursus horribilis*—horrible bear. We may love our teddy bears, but bears also represent unseen, dark forces in the forests of our minds. Perhaps this is why there is no consensus about a term for bear phobia: a phobia is an irrational fear—and there's nothing irrational about being afraid of bears.

⌐⊦

The bear deity

Our ancient ancestors must have feared bears, but nonetheless Paleolithic man appears to have hunted the brown bear for self-defense, food, religious purposes—or all three. Whether it derives from attraction or repulsion, the evidence shows that the interface between humans and bears is probably one of the most ancient human-animal relationships. Caches of bear bones found at ancient stone altars demonstrate the bear's symbolic significance for humankind.

The cave bear that disappeared approximately 15,000 years ago must have been a contemporary of *Homo sapiens* and its predecessors. As both species were cave dwellers, we can imagine that they must often have been in conflict. Many drawings of bears can be found in caves. I would go further and fantasize that bears may have been early man's first art teacher. Bears stand on their hind legs and make deep gashes on the trunks of coniferous trees. These marks communicate many things to other bears—in my travels through bear country, I have seen many traces of this kind of marking. Maybe the earliest humans began to imitate the bears' communicative scratches on trees and the walls of caves, and start making marks of their own.

The excavations at Drachenloch in Switzerland, suggest that Neanderthal man may have revered the cave bear (*Ursus spelaeus*) as "master of all animals" up to 70,000 years ago. In a cave near Erd, Hungary, the bones of more than 500 cave bears killed by Neanderthals have been found, dating back nearly 50,000 years. And in the Lascaux caves in France there is the headless model of a bear, dating from 17,000 BC. This model, draped in fur with a bear's head attached, was probably used ceremonially. Caves across Europe contain niches in which the bones and skulls of bears have been arranged with evident care. These "bear sanctuaries" date back to Neanderthal times. An engraving (probably of a brown bear) in the famous Trois Frères cave, in Ariège, France, shows a bear wounded by spears and vomiting blood. Bears' teeth have always been considered potent charms and bear amulets are frequently found at archeological sites.

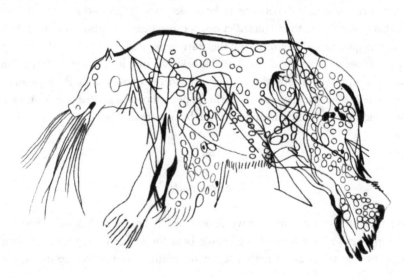

These and similar early artifacts suggest that bear worship, or arctolatry, may have been the earliest religion of the ancient hunter tribes in Eurasia and even of Neanderthal man. If so, the bear is one of mankind's oldest deities, the master of souls, bodies, and minds in transition, a guide between his world and the next. It is likely that the bear was worshipped in this way for many thousands of years, perhaps viewed as a close relative, but a relative that needed to be respected and appeased, given its potential ferocity. The bear is truly one of mankind's primal totems, if not the primal one.

The mythologist Joseph Campbell goes so far as to say that the bear cult predated the shaman. He views the Neanderthal bear sanctuaries as the "earliest evidence anywhere on earth of the veneration of a divine being."[106] For Campbell, these bear sanctuaries are the original source for the bear cults that eventually spread throughout the world. Again, the mystery of hibernation, combined with a bear's human-like appearance (standing and walking on its hind legs), would have contributed to the notion of a bear god, an entity that disappeared and then came back to life when the cold days of winter had passed. In a ritual sacrificial context, it was the ideal animal to be killed for the good of all.

Bear-cult sites, votive statues and ritual jewelry are widely distributed over ancient Celtic territory, and both the Celts and the Druids worshipped the bear goddess Artio or Andarta ("powerful bear") and the bear god Artaois, Ardehe or Arthe. An image of Artio was found in Bern ("bear city"), as was a "den of bears" that would have been used for cult practices.

An altar dedicated to the bear god Ardehe dating back to the sixth century BCE has been found in the French town of Saint Pé-d'Ardet (from Saint Père Ardehe), which lies in the Vallée de l'Ourse, "Valley of the Bear," not far from Lourdes. Bear pelts were worn as clothing, and the late Iron Age chieftain whose burial site was uncovered at Welwyn in Hertfordshire, was found lying on a bearskin. Furthermore, the characteristics of a ferocious bear were invoked before going into battle, when bearskins were often worn. Warriors went "berserk," a term from the Old Norse word for bear. There is also evidence of early bear worship as far away as China, while in Korean mythology, the bear is viewed as an ancestor.

Clearly, bears had a long history in the human imagination, from the Neanderthal "bear sanctuaries," to the ancient cave paintings in Chauvet in France, to more contemporary Ainu bear ceremonies (including ritual bear killing) on the island of Hokkaido. Of all the animals in regions where bears are present, bears have always been the object of extensive veneration. The killing of a bear had to be accompanied by elaborate ceremonies, and bearskins were used as biers and shrouds in many death-related rituals.

The Ainu and the Inuit

The Ainu originally lived in a region that included Sakhalin Island near the mouth of the Amur River, the Kurile Islands, southern Kamchatka, and Hokkaido, today the northern island of Japan. These tribal people made a living by fishing and hunting, including sea mammals. But they are especially well known for their bear ceremony, an important part of their religious rituals. The mystery of hibernation and the human-like appearance of bears meant that like many other tribal people, they viewed the bear, at some level, as the archetypal messenger to the supernatural world. The Ainu believe that when the gods visit the world of man, they take on the physical appearance of an animal.

The Ainu Iyomande Ritual on the island of Hokkaido (practiced as recently as the 1930s) was a ten-day event, usually held in midwinter when the bear meat is the best from the added fat. The ceremony was supposedly presided over by *kamui*, the Ainu god of hunting and the mountains. The rearing and sacrifice of the divine bear was a central part of the animist beliefs of the Ainu. Iyomande means sacrifice ("sending home"), and the purpose of the ritual was to send the spirit of the sacred bear—the supreme deity in disguise—back home. From the Ainu perspective, the bear spirit would report that its captors had enacted the various required rituals well and the bear god would reward them generously, food would be plentiful, and the Ainu would flourish.[107]

The Ainu captured a bear cub alive either from a den or as it emerged from a den with its mother. It was taken in triumph to the village—and if it had not been weaned, was suckled by the women. The bear was caged and raised carefully by a host family for about 18 months, always fed before the family themselves as an appeal to the spirits, in the belief that they would note the generosity of the Ainu and reward them with good hunting and harvests. Then a feast was arranged at which the bear was the guest of honor.

During the Iyomande ritual, the bear was killed, so that its spirit could be released. The animal was killed by a "sacred" arrow and strangulation between two logs. This ritual was significant both on a spiritual level and as a community event.

The bear ceremony combined deeply animist beliefs about hunting with the social merriment of eating, drinking, singing, and dancing. At the feast, everyone wore their finest clothing and jewelry. Prayers were offered to the goddess of the hearth and the deity of the house, but the major focus of the ceremony was on the deity of the mountains, who was believed to have sent the bear as a gift to humans. The Ainu believed that they were rendering a service to the bear by killing it and releasing its spirit to rejoin its divine family.

The male elders officiated at the ceremony; the women had to leave the scene while the bear was killed and skinned. The master of ceremonies was usually the political leader of the community. Male elders skinned and dressed the bear, which was placed in front of the altar hung with treasures. Its head was put in a place of honor. Every part of the bear was eaten according to specific rules. The ceremony ended when the head of the bear was presented at the altar on a pole decorated with ritual wood shavings (*inaw*). An elder spoke a farewell prayer while shooting an arrow eastward toward the sky, signifying the safe departure of the deity. The illusion was maintained that the death of the bear is not really death but the beginning of a transformative experience. [108]

The Ainu Iyomande ritual is among the better known; but many other tribal people who live in bear territory have their own rituals. The Inuit have many traditions associated with the largest carnivore on earth, the polar bear (*Ursus maritimus*, or *nanuk* in Inuktitut). *Nanuk* is a central figure in Inuit cosmology, largely because, apart from the Inuit, polar bears are the chief predators in their arctic marine environment. Both shared this environment on a virtually equal basis, until the introduction of firearms.

To the Inuit, the wily, dangerous polar bear is the animal closest to man, both quarry and kin. Their folklore is full of tales of talking bears, and otherwise magical bears. In Inuit narratives, the polar bear was a model hunter and male symbol, frequently employed as a shaman's helper. Like bears in other cultures, the polar bear has always been subjected to more ceremony before and after the hunt than any other animal. A further explanation for the bear's extensive symbolism is that neither its flesh nor its skin is used by the Inuit in everyday life.

I realized while hunting with the Inuit in the Northwest Territories that there are many taboos associated with these bears. You cannot make fun of *nanuk*, or badmouth the animal; *nanuk* remembers and retaliates. Be careful: polar bears think like people and can sense when someone dislikes them. They will come after you if you do. These mishaps can be prevented by paying due respect to nanuk.

ᕆ

The beast that walks like man

I indicated earlier that one reason for our strong identification with bears is their similarity with some human behavior—they can walk on two legs, are omnivorous and like the same food as us—honey, salmon, fruit, nuts, and meat. Also, when a bear's "coat" is removed (as I have done many times), the carcass has an eerie resemblance to a human being. No wonder that tribal people such as the Siberian Ostyaks believed that the bear was chief among all animals, and that beneath its skin is a divine being in human form. Many mythologies describe a time in the past when the boundaries between people and animals were less sharply drawn and shape-shifting, in which beings changed form freely, was common. In these cultures, bears often appear as humans wearing coats made of bearskins.

This preoccupation with bears can still be found in many polar religions, such as the Sami, Ainu, Nivkh, Gilyaks, and the pre-Christian Finns. Like the Ainu, their bear mythology takes place in three realms, the sky (the constellations), the earth's surface, and the underworld. For the Ostyaks, the bear was a delegate from the supernatural world to humankind and the Bear Mother their ancestress, a belief shared by the Nivkhs in Russia, the tribal people of Kamchatka, the Haida of North America, and many central Asian tribes. Much more recently in our history, the bear has also come to symbolize Russia. In Russian folk tales, however, bears are not just portrayed as big and powerful; they are also rather clumsy, and not always very bright. A famous Russian folktale, "Masha and the bear," tells how a young woman outwits a bear that wants to keep her a prisoner in its house.

In many folktales about bears, the distinction between human and bear becomes blurred. In these stories there is frequently a sexual dimension; bears capture girls who bear them children who are half-bear, half-human. They may decide to stay with the bear people, or take off their bear coats, and return to the humans, to become great hunters—guiding them to bear dens in the mountains, instructing humans to sing sacred songs.

In light of the awe inspired by bears, it has been given many euphemistic names, as using the real name while hunting bear could invite disaster. As I explained in Chapter 5, referring to animism, if bears would hear their name mentioned, they might take retaliatory action. I can imagine that the reasons for bears being addressed by other names would take us back to our remote past, when nature was peopled with supernatural beings on whose will the fate of human beings depended. Hunters had to pacify the spirits and observe certain prohibitions and prescriptions under the spirits' watchful eyes.

Given these beliefs that bears had a close connection with the world beyond, preparations for bear hunting were veiled in mystery. Hunters were permitted to say very little about the hunt, and were prohibited from explicitly referring to the bear. The Inuit, as we have seen, believe that polar bears know what people are thinking; when they hunt for bears, they pretend to be hunting for a different animal. I have even been told that, in the Finnish countryside, the word for "bear" is taboo to this day. This reluctance to pronounce the bear's name—just as in ancient Hebrew the name of god, or Yahweh, was never spoken—once again reflects the belief of its kinship to humans. Synonyms had to be used for the most sacred things. Hunters were always fearful of the vengeful magic of the slain beast. If the paintings in Paleolithic caves are to be believed, the bear was the first animal master among the inhabitants of the Nordic countries.

We find a dramatic illustration of the sacredness of bears in the *Kalevala*, the oldest piece of Finnish literature. This famous work is full of traces of arctolatry. Like the *Illiad*, the Bible, *Beowulf* or the *Nibelungenlied*, the *Kalevala* is a stream of tales that were gathered together in more historic times.

According to Finnish mythology, Otso, the bear, was not allowed to have teeth or claws until he had promised never to engage in acts of violence. But Otso didn't keep his promise, so Finnish hunters don't feel too guilty about hunting bears. The *Kalevala* contains a verse about a bear hunt instigated by Wainamoinen, the hero of the narrative. Wainamoinen has to face the bear that is ravaging the land and killing cattle:

> Wainamoinen, old and trusty,
> Finds the mighty bear in waiting,
> Lifts in joy the golden covers,
> Well inspects his shining fur-robes;
> Lifts his honey-paws in wonder,
> Then addresses his Creator:
> "Be thou praised, O mighty Ukko,
> As thou givest me great Otso,
> Givest me the Forest-apple,
> Thanks be paid to thee unending."
> To the bear he spoke these measures:
> "Otso, thou my well beloved,
> Honey-eater of the woodlands,
> Let not anger swell thy bosom;
> I have not the force to slay thee,
> Willingly thy life thou givest
> As a sacrifice to Northland...
>
> "Golden friend of fen and forest,
> In thy fur-robes rich and beauteous,

Pride of woodlands, famous Light-foot,
Leave thy cold and cheerless dwelling,
Leave thy home within the alders,
Leave thy couch among the willows,
Hasten in thy purple stockings,
Hasten from thy walks restricted,
Come among the haunts of heroes,
Join thy friends in Kalevala.
We shall never treat thee evil,
Thou shalt dwell in peace and plenty,
Thou shalt feed on milk and honey,
Honey is the food of strangers..."[109]

These verses from the *Kalevala* show that the dignity and respect with which the quarry was treated. Before killing a bear, the hunter would address in friendly fashion, and persuade it not to resist. These rituals were repeated among many tribes in order to ensure that bears would not return, either to seek revenge on the hunter, or to take much-needed food.

For example, when the Siberian Ostyaks lured a bear out of its den (the most common form of bear hunting before guns were invented), they would say: "Don't be angry, grandfather! Come home with us and be our guest." When they had killed the bear they would beg it not to take revenge; they even tried to blame its death on somebody else, or argue that it was an accident.

I once hunted for the Kamchatka brown bear (*Ursus arctos beringianus*) with members of the Koryak tribe, for whom bears are the most sacred animals. In olden times, they told me, hunters would perform rituals for the bears before and after the hunt. These rituals took place twice a year, in the fall and the spring, on the mountain called Kamakran (Kamak means "land spirit") before the start of the hunting season. Every hunter, with the exception of women and children, would participate in these bear rituals, even younger hunters who had never hunted bears. Each hunter would make a miniature spear, only 30 cm long, on which were tied a special sacred grass, a cloth, and a necklace. The hunters carried these small spears to Kamakran and stabbed them into the wetland behind its peak. The spear's tip had to point in the sacred direction, toward the east. The hunters would recite prayers for good luck in the hunt, and left the spears where they were. If the hunters were successful in the bear hunt, they would prepare special food to ensure good fortune on their next hunting trip. They cooked the bear's head with its jawbones and, when they had eaten, stuffed its skull with sacred grass. Once again, they took this to the east side of Kamakran, attaching it to a tree with sacred grass.

⌐╫

The "bear necessities"

From Bruintje Beer and Olivier B. Bommel to Otso, I have continued to feel a great affinity with the bear. To me, the bear is a kind of ideogram of man in the wilderness, symbolizing the harmony of society and nature, something that is rapidly disappearing in the present world. My fascination with bears was probably influenced by the many stories I heard or read about them. When I finally made it to bear country, sighting an animal on top of a mountain or on the tundra created eidetic memories for me. Although I have seen many bears in my life, each time I see one I become as excited as I was by the sight of my very first bear.

I can get equally excited, in an extremely negative way, by the exploitation of bears as entertainment, which contradicts everything that makes bears such an important symbol of the wilderness. I remember, years ago in India, seeing bears forced to dance while the owner played some kind of music. I can only imagine what treatment must have been needed to make such an animal stand on its hind legs and dance. Bear baiting has a long history; it was practiced in the Colosseum in ancient Rome, was popular in Britain until the 19th century, and can still be found today in the Punjab and Sind provinces of Pakistan, where it draws large crowds. The local warlords usually organize these events, during which the bear is tethered to a rope several meters long in the center of an arena to prevent escape. Then, their teeth and claws removed, they are put up against pit bull dogs. But perhaps the most atrocious contemporary practice is bear-bile farming in China and North Korea. Bear gall bladders are a constituent of Chinese medicine and can fetch as much as heroin on the black market. The trade in bear parts—particularly bile—is a major threat to the species' survival. I have seen for myself how valuable the gall bladder is for local hunters. For cxample, once, when I obtained a bear in Kamchatka, the first thing the guides did was to remove its gallbladder. It was the only thing on their mind and something I certainly didn't appreciate.

Most bear hunting in Europe and North America is carefully controlled, so much so that the American black bear has made an extraordinary comeback, with populations reaching levels not seen in decades—higher at the start of the 21st century than it was at the start of the 20th. Today, a species once considered in serious trouble is entering a new phase as wildlife managers shift their focus from recovery to management and, where needed, control. Predictably, the population spike has led to more bear-human contact, occasional attacks, and human fatalities.

The positions of the grizzly and polar bear are very different. Humans are not the major concern for either of these bears and the North American grizzly bear, given the wild, inhospitable country it lives in, looks set to thrive. It is not the kind of country that attracts agriculture, or building condominiums. But how viable is the future of the polar bear? Today, Inuit polar bear hunting is restricted by means of a quota-and-tag system, a regulation that has been in place since the late 1960s, and the bears are hunted at sustainable levels—although people brought up with cute stuffed polar bear toys may think differently. The naive observer may ask why the Inuit still hunt polar bear. The answer is that the Inuit don't just hunt bears for the meat and hide. Polar bear hunting is an essential part of their cultural tradition—an activity they want to pass on to their children, to prepare them to become hunters themselves, and to be familiar with the ways of the Inuit. There is also an economic incentive. Non-Inuit hunters can be given licenses to hunt a limited number of polar bears in Canada, and the hunt brings a considerable amount of money to Inuit communities.

Whether or not the current level of polar bear hunting will still be sustainable in the future remains to be seen. The bottom line, however, is that stopping people from hunting polar bears now will not protect future populations. The menace is very different and much more serious; it is climate change. Global warming poses a far greater threat than Inuit hunters. As winter comes later, and spring earlier, there is not enough time for the bears to hunt. They need the pack ice to freeze, to be able to hunt for seals, their main food supply. Taking action on climate change now is the only thing that can protect the population of polar bears in the future—and that's a much bigger challenge than quotas and licenses can cope with.

Bear witness

After so many bear hunts, I might be expected to have become rather jaded about the activity but nothing could be further from the truth. My annual spring bear hunt—mostly not "consummated"—is my way of reasserting my compact with the land, my bond with the wilderness. Every bear encounter I have had is engraved on my memory—somewhat ironically, in the case of my last major bear hunt, when I ended up with a broken spine high in the mountains of Kamchatka. I can still see the bear I was after, looking at me from the top of a snow-covered mountain. This time, the bear won, which some people see as poetic justice. Will I stop bear hunting? Or, which is much the same, stop using bear hunting as my excuse to get into wild country? I know I won't. Bears are too big a part of my inner world, although getting a bear has become much less important. Being in bear country is what really matters to me. Bears remain the symbol of immortality, the passing of the mind through two worlds. I still want new encounters with bears. I remember sitting on top of a mountain, looking at the tundra below, seeing a bear lumbering onward. It made me scribble the following:

I meet the bear inside;
It fills me with a great fear.
The tundra appears.

Clouds, hills, and valleys
Hold me back, and push at me.
Bear waiting to be.

I hear sirens call.
The cave's dark and the night's long.
My heart sings a song.

Madness draws me north
In the darkness of the night
What is starry sight?

Fearful. With what light
Will I transform the bear inside?
Draw curtains of mind.

Can the bear stay free?
Symbol of immortality
Hear and bear with me.

Without, will I be?
Hills, valleys, eternity,
Journeys to reality.

103 — Bieder, Robert E. *Bear*. London: Reaction
Books, 2005.

104 — Brunner, Bernd. *Bears: A Brief History*. New
Haven: Yale University Press, 2007.

105 — Faulkner, William. *Three Famous Short Novels,
Spotted Horses, Old Man, The Bear*. New York: Vintage,
1963, p. 245.

106 — Campbell, Joseph. *Historical Atlas of World
Mythology Volume 1: The Way of the Animal Powers, Part
1: Primitive Hunters and Gatherers*. New York: Alfred
van der Marck Editions, 1983, p. 147.

107 — Shepard, Paul and Sanders, Barry. *The Sacred
Paw: The Bear in Nature, Myth, and Literature*. New
York: Viking, 1985.

108 — Campbell, Joseph. "The Master Bear," In *The
Masks of God, Volume 1, The Way of the Animal Powers*.
New York: Viking, 1959.

109 — Crawford, John Martin. *The Kalevala: The Epic
Poem of Finland*, Rune XLVI, "Otso the Honey-Eater,"
Whitefish, Montana: Kessinger Publishing, 2004.

*Each thing is of like form from everlasting
and comes round again in its cycle.*
   —Marcus Aurelius

*You will die but the carbon will not; its
career does not end with you. It will return
to the soil, and there a plant may take it
up again in time, sending it once more
on a cycle of plant and animal life.*
   —Jacob Bronowski

*Earth teach me quiet—as the grasses are still with new light.
Earth teach me suffering—as old stones suffer with memory.
Earth teach me humility—as blossoms are humble with beginning.
Earth teach me caring—as mothers nurture their young.
Earth teach me courage—as the tree that stands alone.
Earth teach me limitation—as the ant that crawls on the ground.
Earth teach me freedom—as the eagle that soars in the sky.
Earth teach me acceptance—as the leaves that die each fall.
Earth teach me renewal—as the seed that rises in the spring.
Earth teach me to forget myself—as melted snow forgets its life.
Earth teach me to remember kindness—as dry fields weep with rain.*
   —An Ute Indian Prayer

THE CYCLE OF LIFE

Maybe hunters secretly yearn to have lived in simpler times. Certainly, hunting brings me back to basics; it's the reenactment of a historically important activity that helps me to be less alienated from my natural environment. It is a very simple way of reaffirming my role in the cycle of life. Hunting is full of symbolism, and helps me to better accept the idea of my temporary place in the world in which I live. It takes me beyond the humdrum events of daily life and enables me transcend restrictions of time and place.

In an old diary, I found a haiku that I wrote as I sat at the roof of the world, Pamir Mountains, in Central Asia:

Pamir, the roof of the world,
A haunt full of splendor and fear,
Tests of stamina.

Painting in white and blue,
Sun down, the darkness comes
Wind chills my bones.

Death, if not careful,
Debris of bones and horns,
An icy desert.

Marco Polo sheep,
Ibex, wolves, and snow leopards
Roaming in my sky.

Unforgiving landscape
Symbol of insignificance
Hail to "Pamirgrad."

I wrote these words more than fifteen years ago, sitting in front of a yurt, glassing a number of ibex that were crossing a frozen riverbed a considerable distance away. Walking to this place had been extremely difficult, because of the deep snow and particularly the lack of oxygen. I had been pleased enough to see a few Himalayan snow-cocks, large, grey, partridge-like birds that make their homes at high altitudes. But just after I spooked them I was thoroughly excited to find the fresh tracks of a snow leopard close to the camp. At the top of that mountain, I was content, my eyes drinking in the spectacular scenery. Not many people really want to go where I was now hanging out, or can get there if they do. I felt fully alive. I was in the present with all my senses.

I have always felt most alive when I am in the outdoors with a shotgun, rifle,

or for that matter a fishing rod. It's a way of finding the child inside me—the child who once loved the adventures of Karl May's heroes, Winnetou and Old Shatterhand. When I am in nature, I am attuned to each sound, wind change, movement, or shadow. All of my senses are brought to bear in an effort to become immersed in the landscape. But this super-heightened sense of being alive materializes especially when I am hunting, producing an immersion of my surroundings that is hard to imagine for people brought up in urban jungles. When I hunt, I am engaged in a wordless dialogue with nature. I am also deeply aware that I am part of the food chain, part of nature; I begin to understand how life and death spring from each other and our human insignificance in the greater scheme of things. When I hunt, it is not difficult to imagine that I have returned to my Paleolithic roots.

Apart from these "regressive" feelings, I like the physical challenge of hunting, particularly pursuing mountain game. I have never been more exhausted or more exhilarated than when attempting to approach wild sheep or goats. The climb itself is enough to make me an adrenaline junkie, even without the dangers involved—climbing slippery rocks, hanging from steep cliffs, sliding down icy shale. Mountain hunting forces me to stay somewhat in shape all year round. Hunting dangerous game brings a different kind of thrill. Anyone who hunts dangerous game has to be prepared for the unexpected, good or bad, as I have discovered many times. And there is always the haunting question: when does the predator become the prey?

Then there is the sense of purpose. Going after wild sheep or goats implies that I am not wandering aimlessly around; it means climbing a mountain with purpose. Following a Lord Derby eland track in central Africa for hours or even days can be an exhausting hike, but it will be a "hike with a purpose." Going after puma is not just a climb in the mountains. It means sitting for hours on horseback, riding a snow mobile, climbing through snow, trying to keep up with the dogs- all this for one singular purpose. I like steering a boat early in the morning, getting the cold wind in my face while I look for game or set out to fish. I even get a sense of purpose walking in the woods to find ruffed grouse, even though I have been skunked most times I've done it.

I like climbing to a mountain ridge before daylight and finding a good spot where I can overlook a valley. I enjoy waiting and watching to see a new day born. I like waiting for dusk to arrive. I like looking at the ruggedness of the land. I like the challenge of fording a stream. I like to test the degree of physical effort my body can still take. I like the exhilaration that comes from doing things that I never thought were possible.

I like glassing for elk at first light. Spotting an animal is an "eureka" moment—the expression of triumph at finding something new, or like finding

a needle in a haystack. I also like it later in the morning, when the heat waves shimmer, and I am close to a few old duggaboys—old male buffalos beyond breeding age. I enjoy planning and executing such a stalk, making a good shot, having control over my emotions, my breathing, and my heartbeat. And if successful, I like putting my hands around the horns of a buffalo, Marco Polo sheep, or elk, and admiring these incredible animals.

Making it happen is a big part of why I hunt. The spirit of adventure stimulates my fantasy life. But there is more to it than that, an essential element that is difficult to explain to non-hunters. When an animal is down, it is as if time stands still. Usually, I walk slowly over to the body, as I need time to get myself together. It feels as though I have had a spiritual epiphany. I certainly don't go over with a tape in my hands, as I know some hunters do—I'm not after records, I'm after experiences. These moments of silence in which I honor the dead animal are very important to me. I also experience what can be described as the after-effects of "flow"—the state of mind that prevails when we are fully immersed in what we are doing.

◦

Flow

Aristotle observed 2300 years ago that what men and women seek above all is happiness. In order to achieve maximum happiness, enjoyment, or even success, we need to have "flow" experiences, or "Everest feelings."[110] A state of flow has been described as an optimal experience that ensues when we are engaged in self-controlled, goal-related, meaningful activities. For me, flow happens when I am totally absorbed in what I am doing, lose self-consciousness, and feel truly alive. Flow happens in situations that are at once demanding and rewarding— some of the most enjoyable and valuable moments that a person can have.

For example, I was once hunting for urial sheep in Kazakhstan, in a steep, arid spot not far from the Caspian Sea. The sheep were very spooky due to an abundance of wolves—not to mention poachers. After some fruitless attempts, I finally managed to ambush a ram, to the great delight of Kostya (my translator), and my guide. It was very hot and I was very sweaty, and as the sea was close by, I stripped and went for a swim, floating, and feeling very happy. Certainly, at that moment, I had reached a state of flow.

Flow means achieving a state of consciousness where our feelings are in harmony with our surroundings. In flow, I experience an inner sense of peace and fulfillment that is detached from the stimuli of the external environment. I am doing something meaningful and purposeful; I am absorbed in what I am doing and have a sense of connection between my interior life and the world around me. I completely lose my sense of time.

One summer, we rented a small cottage in the north of Norway. Every day I went out with my fly rod trying to catch salmon. The first time I fished I was so preoccupied about getting at the salmon I knew were in the river that I lost track of time. Being so far north, the light was continuous, and all the normal indicators of time passing, like direction and length of shadows, were missing. It was only when I began to wobble on my feet from fatigue that I realized what time it was. In the meantime, my family had been worried sick, imagining I must have drowned. That time, I didn't get a salmon but I had been in a prolonged state of flow. Fortunately, the salmon were collaborative on other occasions.

In most instances, when I experience flow, I leave civilized life and am no longer bothered by the daily worries of existence, like job and even family, or modern living—my computer, iPad, iPhone, and traffic are left far behind. I am in a place where the only sounds I can hear are the wind, birds, and animals. In flow, I seem to step into the skin of my primitive ancestors, returning to a more natural state. The all-consuming thing is the object of the hunt, finding the animals I am after, trying to think like them, learning more about their behavior, and taking measures to protect the animals I so admire for future generations. I would like my children and grandchildren to have similar experiences. The flow forces me to think about continuity.

As I have said before, some people think it paradoxical that I like to hunt the animals I love. But it should be clear by now that my love for wildlife does not mean that I want merely to be a distant spectator of nature. There is satisfaction in accomplishing the objective of a hunt. Part of the process is taking the meat, hide, and horns of an animal I have killed back to camp and caring for them. With others, I will eat the animal's flesh. The cape, skull, and horns provide me with tangible reminders of the value of the experience. And as I have mentioned before, some people cannot understand the need for this, imagining that photographs would fulfill the same purpose. Yet each mount on the wall is imbued with a string of associations. The bear rug on the floor, the sheep head on the wall, the leopard skull on the table, are not trophies; they represent memories of special places and experiences. They are relics that may serve the same purpose as religious relics are intended to do; and this is true for all the animals I have taken. The naturalist Aldo Leopold calls these relics "certificates":

"It attests that its owner has been somewhere and done something—that he has exercised skill, persistence, or discrimination in the age-old feat of overcoming, outwitting, or reducing-to-possession. These connotations which attach to the trophy usually far exceed its physical value."[111]

Robert Ruark, the well-known novelist and nature writer, records the thoughts of Harry Selby, one of the most famous African hunting guides, on killing elephants:

> "You are not shooting an elephant," Selby told me. "You are shooting the symbol of his tusks. You are not shooting to kill. You are shooting to make immortal the thing you shoot. To kill just anything is a sin. To kill something that will be dead soon, but is so fine as to give you pleasure for years, is wonderful. Everything dies. You only hasten the process. When you shoot a lion you are actually shooting its mane, something that will make you proud. You are shooting for yourself, not shooting just to kill."[112]

Eating game I have taken is a much more satisfying experience than going to a butcher to buy chicken or steak. Game meat is healthier; the animals come to maturity in the outdoors rather than being raised and probably mistreated at an industrial factory farm. Moreover, I have not "outsourced" the killing; I have done it myself. I have not detached myself from the source of my food supply. I maintain that a game animal suffers far less than animals in modern farming units. The animals I kill and eat have not been genetically engineered, or have their mobility restricted, or fed unnatural diets. The high price of industrial farming is paid in the form of environmental degradation, human disease, and animal suffering. Compared to that, hunting contributes to a greener and more sustainable environment.

For me, hunting has become an extension of my deep appreciation of a more primitive way of life, and the animals that have sustained us. When I eat game, I remember how I hunted it, how I tested my abilities, and how I was successful.

⌐

Il momento della verità

It goes without saying that in all predator-prey relationships there is usually inequality between hunter and hunted. The belief that all creatures have an equal right to life and that all killing is immoral is a moral construction. It is not nature's way. Like it or not (and many people don't), the human animal is carnivorous, tops the food chain, and is the most accomplished hunter. (This doesn't mean that I don't respect people who want to be vegetarians—but it should be "live and let live.")

As I have reiterated, from time immemorial, hunting has been the prototypical behavior pattern of our species. During the morphological, physiological, genetic, cognitive, and emotional evolution of humankind, hunting has been the major behavior pattern that differentiated us from our nearest cousins, the apes (even though they dabble in this activity). We owe the way we have developed to our prehistoric predecessors, the first hunters. We cannot escape the importance of the hunter-gatherer way of life to the biological uniqueness of humankind. The fact of the matter is that in order for anything to live, something else must die—whether it is animals, fish, or even plants. And considering the latter, we accept that animals feel pain, but what about plants? When I prune the roses in my garden, do they suffer? When I pick something out of my herb garden for cooking, is that a hostile act toward plants? Some think so, and restrict themselves to a diet of fruit, nuts and seeds on the basis that "there is no death involved." Precious few nutrients, either.

It is impossible to be immersed in nature and not to be reminded of the predator-prey relationship. The eat-or-be-eaten interface is all around—the natural world is an exciting and dangerous place, whose subjects spend their days and nights looking for the food they need to survive while trying to avoid being food for something else. This pattern is ubiquitous, from the relatively innocuous context of the corner of a room, or a garden plant, where a spider spins a web to catch flies, to the more dramatic hunting grounds of Africa, Australia, or Asia. When I stay in Africa, I am confronted over and over again with the ruthless game of life and death. The night stalkers—lions, leopards, hyenas, jackals—silently seek out their next meal while their prey—impalas, kudus, buffalos, and other grazers—stand close together for warmth and safety. Every night a number of these animals will die. To quote the well-known wildlife artist, Ernest Thompson Seton, "For the animal there is no such thing as a gentle decline in peaceful old age. Its life is spent at the front, in line of the battle, and as soon as its powers begin to wane in the least, its enemies become too strong for it; it falls."[113]

Hunting the hunters

What is the downside of going after deadly game? Take, for example, leopards. It is not wise to mess with leopards. They may be shy, but when cornered, they are deadly—or if not deadly, will leave you with formidable scars as souvenirs. Few animals match a leopard's speed of attack, which makes hunting this hunter a special kind of endeavor and a particularly challenging assignment. But leopards can develop bad habits, like eating livestock...

Leopard hunting is usually done with bait. Essentially, to attract a leopard (or lion), you have to spend a lot of time in the meat business, checking whether a leopard has been feeding. And far too often, when you find one feeding, it turns out to be a female. But it may be your lucky day and a male has come to the bait. If that is the case, you construct a blind and hope that the leopard will come back—and not notice that people have moved into the grass-like structure that has sprung up close by. On two occasions that I well remember a leopard came to the blind, circled it, checked what was going on, discovered us, and decided to get the hell out of there. We had to start all over again, with new bait in a new place.

When you first enter the blind, there is plenty of light. I always make sure I'm as comfortable as possible as it's likely to be a long wait. I may take a nap or read a book; I usually have to kill a few irritating tsetse flies, mosquitoes, or biting ants. Then the light starts to fade. The shadows become longer and longer and I need to pay more attention to the sounds around me. Every noise can give me a jolt: insects, birds—and other less readily identifiable sounds that make me wonder what is going on. Sitting in a rickety blind made of twigs and grass listening to a cacophony of strange animal, bird, and insect noises rapidly sharpens the senses. And some of these mysterious sounds can be quite scary: elephants breaking wind nearby or spraying sand on the blind; or a hyena almost walking into it, giving both parties something to reflect on later. The barking of a bushbuck may be a sign that a predator is closing in. The birdcalls increase as the light fades. Prime time is passing fast: will the leopard come to the bait? Has it figured out that something is wrong? The hide is very close to the bait. But perhaps the leopard will make a mistake; perhaps it won't get spooked. It may be truly hungry and go for the bait. But this was a very smart leopard that had really become a pest to the local village, creating havoc among their goats.

Suddenly, having heard nothing beforehand, I hear grinding sounds. The leopard is on the bait; it is feeding. But it is dark, or almost dark. Looking through the peephole in the blind, all I can see is a shadow play. In some African countries or regions it is forbidden to use lights to see what is going on. In other countries, light is allowed until a specific hour. I am becoming a bundle of nerves. I know that, when I pull the trigger, I can't afford to blow the shot and wound the leopard. Many of the hunting guides I have been with have some impressive scars on show, made by leopards that hung from their arms or other part of their bodies while trying to disembowel them—a legacy of their clients' mistakes.

I have to shoot to kill and it is not going to be a long shot. For safety reasons, leopard blinds are usually put up close to the bait. It is a very comfortable distance for a shot. But the nerves... Leopards can do strange things to people. Maybe it is the fact that a leopard hunts in darkness, a time when human beings are at a great disadvantage. Maybe I'm intimidated by the leopard's beauty—combined with its speed and ferocity. Maybe, I am intimidated by its reputation. It is one of those animals that seem to cast a magic spell. Will the nerves get to me?

I have met many people who seemed to be jinxed as far as leopard hunting is concerned. Other people—my wife, for example—go through a Zen-like form of meditation to calm themselves down—and manage. Others are plain lucky. And yet others screw up the magic moment. Whatever the outcome, I have seen the leopard. I have pulled the trigger. I am blinded by the shot. Now comes the doubt. Was the shot accurate? Is the leopard dead? Time to find out...

Hunting leopards with dogs is another matter altogether. Instead of sitting in a blind from four in the afternoon, we rise and shine to begin the hunt at four in the morning. I have to say that the first time I went through this routine in Namibia, for ten days in a row, I didn't rise and shine very much. On the contrary, I suffered from serious sleep deprivation, as it was too hot for an afternoon nap.

The reason for such an early start is that the dogs can only get wind until around ten in the morning; after that the heat is too much. Spoor needs to be found early in the morning. Daylight arrives around seven,

making a relatively small window of opportunity as far as hunting leopard is concerned. And there is always the risk that the dogs will make a mistake, and go after a jackal or something else. On the tenth day of this hunt, I finally got lucky. Running in the direction of the furiously barking dogs, I found the pack engaged in a life and death fight with a big male leopard. Female leopards seem to tree; most males don't. This male had decided to fight it out on the ground. The animal was protecting its backside with thorn bushes, but it was obvious that it was going to lose the fight. It was not easy to get a shot with all the dogs running around. But it happened.

I went on two further hunts for leopards with dogs, both much easier; it didn't take many days to get the spoor of a leopard, both animals were male, and both were kind enough to tree, making the final act much easier. The terrain I was in must have been well populated with leopards as both were taken within a few days of each other.

As a hunter, I become yet another predator, like a lion, leopard, tiger, bear, or wolf. When I hunt, it is not difficult to see the world through their eyes. I believe very strongly that being a predator gives me a heightened sensitivity to nature, a greater understanding of what it is all about. Through hunting, I become better acquainted with the habitat of the game, I understand their patterns of behavior better, I shadow the way they live. This is a very different mindset than, say, being a photographer. As Barry Lopez observes:

No culture has yet solved the dilemma each has faced with the growth of a conscious mind: how to live a moral and compassionate existence when one is fully aware of the blood, the horror inherent in all life, when one finds darkness not only in one's own culture but within oneself. If there is a stage at which an individual life becomes truly adult, it must be when one grasps the irony in its unfolding and accepts responsibility for a life lived in the midst of such paradox. One must live in the middle of contradiction because if all contradiction were eliminated at once life would collapse. There are simply no answers to some of the great pressing questions. You continue to live them out, making your life a worthy expression of leaning into the light.[114]

To me, savvy, old wild sheep or goats represent the supreme challenge. These animals have survived many years of predation and (depending on their location) difficult summers and winters. They have been able to live for so long because their survival skills have remained fully intact. Usually, it is not easy to take such a seasoned animal. Harvesting such a "well-educated" beast in its own bailiwick—and overcoming all the hardships involved in climbing and tracking them while doing so—makes for a great sense of achievement and pride. I have succeeded where other predators have failed; I am connected to the cycle of life as it truly works in nature.

Once, in the Central African Republic, I was following the trail of a herd of buffalos, only to discover as the tracking continued that I was not alone. Other predators seemed to have had the same idea. The buffalo trail was joined by the prints of a pride of lions and, shortly afterwards, a pack of African wild dogs. These animals are not very big, but quite ferocious, and are quite capable of killing buffalo calves. I am intrigued by these wild dogs, which I find very beautiful. But they are, in fact, the ultimate killing machines. Nearly 80 percent of all wild dog hunts end in a kill. (By comparison, the success rate of lions— often regarded as the supreme predators—is only 30 percent.)

On this particular occasion, all the signs suggested that the tracking scene had become somewhat overcrowded. However, when I realized what was going on, I was intensely excited. There is no feeling in the world like that of following the tracks and signs of a predator or other dangerous animal that you know passed by just minutes earlier. It may sound strange, but coming across a pile of steaming buffalo dung, lion droppings, or bear shit, can be exhilarating. It awakens an ancient primeval feeling deep within me, a feeling that rarely comes to the fore in other situations.

When I am hunting, most of the stresses and strains of daily life simply dissipate. Although I can be quite tense, at the same time, my body seems to relax as I tune into my surroundings. Of course, my mood fluctuates as the hunt progresses. Will I be lucky and catch up with the animal I want? Will Diana be on my side? Is the weather going to favor me? Will I be calm enough to aim straight when the time comes? Am I going to be shut up in a tent for a long time (a week, once, in the Arctic)? And this sense of excitement builds up when I spot animals.

I said earlier that the best sight of all is the silhouette of a bear on the tundra, but there are other sights, sounds, and even smells, that are up there, too— wolves vanishing in the distance, the sound of a lion at last light, the honking of geese flying low over a marsh, and the scent of buffalos as you close in on them. These are the moments when I feel completely alive.

When I get closer to my quarry, my physical and mental state changes. My heart starts pumping, almost jumping out of my chest. I realize that "il momento della verità" (the moment of truth) is approaching. And when it does, my heart really starts to pound. If there is a sacred moment in the pursuit of game, it is the moment the hunter releases an arrow or touches the trigger for the fatal shot. It feels like an out-of-body experience—a sensation of floating outside your own physical body and, in some cases, watching it from a different vantage point.

Will I be able to use this short timeframe to the best of my abilities? Will I even get a chance? Some psychologists have speculated on the conflict between taking a life, especially of a male animal to which the hunter relates, and fears of inadequacy. Will I shoot myself in my foot—metaphorically speaking? Will I screw up this opportunity? At these moments, it feels like time stands still. At these moments, I need constantly to remind myself to calm down, to control my breathing, and to steady my aim, if I have decided to take the animal. But there is always anxiety about whether I will be able to do so, and not waste the opportunity. This is particularly true when hunting in the mountains where long shots are the rule rather than the exception.

I remember being in Tajikistan hunting for ibex, the mid-Asian variety. The ibex were very spooky—and I felt extremely sick. As we were so high in the mountains, I had assumed that the water was clean, and when I felt thirsty, had drunk straight from a stream. But this simple act had had disastrous effects and my gut was far from what it should be, to say the least. Several times I had to find relief behind the rocks as we climbed—not very amusing when you are in the middle of a hunting activity. Also, I couldn't ignore the fact that I was getting weaker by the hour. Sometimes, however, you get to be a lucky hunter. After hours of glassing, one ibex made a small mistake—and I managed to control my body, and was successful. Triumphantly, we made the long hike back to camp. I even managed to cross the river that separated us from the yurt without any mishap.

Hunting has given me the chance to view a huge variety of birds and animals in their natural habitat and environment—a vastly different experience than observing animals in a zoo. And as, over the years, I have had the fortune to hunt in most of the continents of the world, hunting has enriched my perspective on different cultures and helped me understand how local people live. It has broadened my knowledge about people and been a great anthropological learning experience.

I have been able to get close to the inhabitants of societies that are much closer to nature than ours. I have lived the life of the Inuit in the high Arctic, of the Kirgizians in the Pamir mountains, of the Koryaks in Kamchatka, of the Sami in Lapland, of the Altaians of the High Altai mountains, and of the Baka pygmies and the Bushmen in Africa. Over the years, I have visited many different countries, been exposed to many different landscapes, and seen an incredible parade of wildlife. I have seen all kinds of deer, antelopes, wild sheep and goats, predators, and birds (pheasants, grouse, ducks, geese, guinea fowl, birds of prey, and songbirds), in their natural habitat. These encounters would have been near impossible for me had I not been a hunter. Hunting was the only valid passport I had that brought me into these rich alternative worlds.

꒰

Beyond the kill

I have said many times throughout this book that hunting, to me, is much more than just taking possession of animals, and that as I get older it has increasingly become a spiritual act that gives great meaning to my life. Being in the hunt is like being in a slightly altered state of consciousness. Some people maintain that hunting can contribute to an oceanic feeling—a kind of "unio mystica" with nature—a sense of the sacred, the eternal, limitlessness, and wonder. Although this kind of feeling may contain a touch of fear, linked to an understanding of our insignificance in the greater scheme of things, it also may include a sense of unspeakable joy, and the conviction that all is well. It may even be compared to the primary narcissistic union between mother and child.

As I have mentioned before, those who oppose hunting find it hard to understand that hunting is not all about killing animals, that the kill is incidental. It is the context—the scenery, the natural surroundings, and the chase— that counts. They also find it difficult to accept the reality of predator-prey relationships, that killing is an undeniable part of the cycle of life, and that many of our early ancestors' characteristics—despite of the march of civilization—are hardwired within us. Plautus's fifth century aphorism—*"homo homini lupus est,"* "man is a wolf to [his fellow] man"—has been invoked through the centuries in reflections on the horrors of human treatment of their own kind. Our own recent history, as I note in Chapter 3, provides some of the most appalling examples of our capacity for violence ever recorded. It is difficult to solve the dilemma of how to live a moral and compassionate life while our capacity for violence is played out before us daily, in the images of murder and genocide that are beamed into our homes via televised news reports, and confirmed in laboratory conditions—we have only to think of Stanley Milgram's experiments in the 1960s. From this perspective, hunting can be seen as a comparatively civilized way of dealing with our aggressive disposition, compared to the violence we find in "civilized" society.

However, to me, the kill is usually somewhat of an anti-climax and after it, like hunters from time immemorial, I feel pangs of remorse, that momentary sense of pity and fear, of attraction and repulsion—regret for having killed, but also gladness for having killed well. The kill doesn't create a sense of flow—at least not for me. On the contrary, it prompts a sense of humility for having killed something that is coveted and appreciated, and guilt and remorse about the death of a beautiful animal. I relate this to an archaic feeling, the fear of retaliation by the animal, and the need to atone that I describe in Chapter 6. I firmly believe that every meritorious hunter, deep down, needs to experience this sense of unease when the moment comes to take the life of another living thing. There is an animist inside all of us.

If hunters were really the bloodthirsty killers that some anti-hunting groups think they are, they might as well go to a coop full of chickens and do what killers are supposed to do. After all, killing chickens in a henhouse is a much more efficient way to express one's bloodthirstiness than, for example, suffering hypothermia on a duck hunting trip, or calling in an elk in the snow, or sitting on a horse high in the High Altai mountains looking for wild sheep and ibex. Hunting and mass or serial murder do not go together, whatever wild associations anti-hunting groups make. Many modern hunters deliberately handicap themselves through the kind of the equipment they use, to give the hunted a fairer chance. Hunting is less about killing that about the search for greater congruity between our outer and inner selves. But don't misunderstand me; I am not saying that the kill cannot be exhilarating. It certainly can be, especially when you know you have shot well, but the kill is often merely the closing act in a long and arduous journey. My personal experience is that when the kill is too easy, it gives me very little satisfaction.

Beyond tape measures

On one bear-hunting trip, I took a plane from Paris to Moscow, where I waited a considerable time to get a connecting plane to Barnaul, in Siberia. The seating was uncomfortable, giving me little opportunity to sleep on board. In Barnaul, a helicopter was scheduled to take us to the hunting area but when we arrived, we discovered that the helicopter pilots were on strike. It was May 1st, a national holiday, and we guessed they were all drunk. Unfortunately, the only alternative to a helicopter ride was a 12-hour drive on atrocious roads to our hunting destination in a Dostoyevsky-like Siberian landscape.

By the time we arrived at our camp, I was totally out of it; I had no idea what time zone I was in. But it was late afternoon and sunny, perfect weather for bears, so I suggested it would be a good idea to go hunting. Shahin, my hunting companion, had had enough, however. He was exhausted and crawled off to bed. I decided to go for a short "stroll" in the woods with one of the guides. We had been walking for only 40 minutes—during which time it seemed to rain ticks incessantly—when the guide told me to stop moving, sit down, and be quiet. We sat and waited, listening to the sound of the forest. Close to us there suddenly came a disturbing racket of birds—rather like the noise bushbucks make when a leopard is in the area. I turned my head, trying to figure out what was going on, and out of nowhere, a bear materialized. For a couple of moments I tried to assess its size, not always easy with bears. Generally speaking, if the head looks small compared to the body, it's a big bear. On this particular occasion, however, as the bear came closer, I found out for myself that with a large bear, you stop calculating head-body ratio and grasp the fact immediately.

Many years later, during a visit to my taxidermist, I discovered that I had obtained the second largest bear ever shot in Siberia, according to the Safari Club record book. But, as I have said, I am not bothered about using tape measures. Even today, I feel that this hunt was too easy. Harvesting that bear was a bit of a let-down.

Something very different made a much stronger impression on me during that hunt. As I skinned the bear, woodcock were making their special nuptial flight calls in the forest and I was treated to their aerial mating display. The woodcock would let off a dozen or so weird, nasal, "peent" calls before bursting into flight, spiraling until they were so high that they disappeared from view into the sky.

Nearing the top of their ascent, woodcocks beat their wings into frenzy, and the whistling reaches fever pitch. When their wings can go no faster and their whistling no higher, the woodcocks burst into a cascading love song as they glide back to earth, seesawing like a falling leaf until they land back almost at the spot they started from. But as soon as it lands the woodcock starts the whole sequence again. Apparently, the woodcock engages in this performance to compete with other males. The first male to go up may finish uninterrupted, but his rivals won't wait long. Soon the displays overlap. The woodcocks' music making and their flight are still engraved in my memory.

One of my favorite books on nature is Turgenev's *A Sportsman's Notebook*. In it, he writes about the woodcock:

"Your ear grows tired of waiting, and suddenly—but only sportsmen will understand me—suddenly in the deep stillness there comes a special kind of whirr and swish, you hear the measured stroke of swift wings—and the woodcock, with its long beak drooping gracefully down, comes swimming out of a dark birch tree to meet your fire."[115]

After I had brought the bear hide and meat to the hunting lodge, I tried very hard to hunt for hazel hen, which I had never seen before, but I was unlucky. In fact, I spent most of my time at that camp preparing the meat and hide of the bear. It had all been a bit flat and not my most memorable trip—apart from the woodcocks, and the daily body search for ticks.

⌐╕

The denial of death

Hunting has made me realize the extent to which death is an essential part of life. In our post-modern society, the notion of death seems to have become increasingly taboo and as a species we seem to have become very adept at denying it. We conveniently push the fact that we are all going to die to the back of our mind. Lost in the concrete labyrinth of our cities, we tend to forget the final act in the five-act play that is our life. In our post-industrial world, suffering, dying, and death have been pushed to the periphery of our cultural experience. We have sanitized death, banishing the dying to certain wards in hospitals. Only organized religions make an effort to keep this realization in our consciousness.[116]

Hunting confronts us with the realities of the cycle of life. Knowing that death means life, and life means death helps us to see the rhythm of existence very differently. But it also raises the question of how comfortable non-hunters are with the notion of death. Perhaps seeing others hunt undermines their efforts at denial? It may take them out of their comfort zone.

And the same denial of unpleasant realities is applied to our food supply. We conveniently forget what needs to be done to provide us with the meat or fish we find on our plate. In "civilized" society we deal with food in a dissociated way. There is an almost complete disconnect between food and where it comes from. The media frequently report surveys that reveal absurdities about city children's understanding of food sources—some believe that cows lay eggs, having never seen a living chicken.[117] As we have become more estranged from the reality of life, people who actually deal with fish, fowl, or mammals are considered barbarians. But I am proud to be a barbarian, proud of the ability to deal with life's realities, proud of being a hunter and a fisherman.

In France, where I live, people tend to be more straightforward. During the hunting season, butchers' shops display game animals such as wild boar, deer, pheasants, hare, rabbits, partridges, and wild ducks—a habit that fills many foreign tourists (particularly those who have grown up in cities) with horror. Having a vague idea of the origin of their food is one thing, but seeing it hanging in a butchers' shop is quite another. In a restaurant in Paris, I recommended to an American couple, who could not read the French menu, one of the better dishes, the sea bass. Unfortunately, in this restaurant, the whole fish was served with its head attached, creating such revulsion in the couple that they couldn't eat it. They left the restaurant without touching the fish. They left me wondering what fantasy world they were living in.

Supermarket packaging is now so sophisticated that it is easier than ever to pretend not to know the origin of the food we eat. A more honest alternative would be to become a vegetarian—although from a nutritional point of view that's not a glorious solution. The hunters of the past didn't hide from the facts of life. They faced their omnivorous nature head on, and would made amends for their kills by paying respect to the dead animal and creating death rituals. This, of course, is in direct opposition to the way we eat today. We don't pay any respect to the animals we eat. We don't want to know how cows are reared and slaughtered. We close our minds to the way chickens are treated. We don't want to think about where that delicious rack of lamb comes from.

In my experience, most anti-hunters (that is, those who are not vegetarians) turn a blind eye to these issues. The idea of respecting the animals they eat is far removed from their reality, as is giving animals a dignified death. We could learn a great deal from the hunters of by-gone times. While hunters today are sometimes painted as psychologically sick social pariahs (you must be disturbed, to want to shoot animals, mustn't you?), the reality is that if you eat meat or fish, some animal is going to die, either by your hand or somebody else's. It is good to remind ourselves that a steak doesn't materialize magically in a supermarket. A lamb chop doesn't arrive miraculously packed in a plastic bag through the intervention of some unseen *deus ex machina*. A chicken leg starts out firmly attached to a warm, feathery body.

Our relationship with eating animals is well described by Jonathan Safran Foer who noted:

"Meat is bound up with the story of who we are and who we want to be, from the Book of Genesis to the latest farm bill. It raises significant philosophical questions and is a $140 billion-plus a year industry that occupies nearly a third of the land on the planet, shapes ocean ecosystems, and may well determine the future of earth's climate...[118]

Like pornography, factory farming is hard to define but easy to identify. In a narrow sense it is a system of industrialized and intensive agriculture in which animals—often housed by the tens or even hundreds of thousands—are genetically engineered, restricted in mobility, and fed unnatural diets (which almost always include various drugs, like antimicrobials)...

More than any set of practices, factory farming is a mind-set: reduce production costs to the absolute minimum and systematically ignore or 'externalize' such costs as environmental degradation, human disease, and animal farming. For thousands of years, farmers took their cues from natural processes. Factory farming considers nature an obstacle to overcome."[119]

At one point, Foer says, "someone who regularly eats factory-farmed animal products cannot call himself an environmentalist without divorcing that word from its meaning."[120] What more is there to add? Instead of going to the supermarket, I prefer to go out in the field and try to obtain my own meat, fowl or fish. If possible, I prefer not to contribute to the profitability of factory farming. At least, while hunting or fishing I am getting to know the animals, learning their habits, following their tracks, carefully tracing them through the woods. The animals gain my respect. Trying to outwit a grouse can (literally) be an uphill task. And when I eat venison, or a bird, I know where it came from. It enjoyed a life in the wild, as opposed to be fattened up for the slaughterhouse in extremely miserable circumstances.

Butchers, fishmongers, supermarkets, and restaurants are ready to encourage our knack for suppressing unpleasant facts and participate in this conspiracy of silence about the origin of their produce. I find this attitude pretty hypocritical, especially when I get an earful about what a dreadful activity hunting is from people who chew happily on a hamburger, and wear leather belts, bags, and shoes—and even fur coats. As a society, we are fairly desensitized to animal slaughter. I suspect that almost no one who has a fast-food burger or picks up a steak at the grocery will, at the point of purchase or consumption, consider how the meat was manufactured, usually the result of a brutal processes simply too horrific for most of us to contemplate.

By taking death out of our lives, so that it is no longer part of our reality, we become less human. By conveniently forgetting that an animal has to lose its life to give us life, we diminish our authenticity. We disconnect ourselves from the cycle of life. One of the reasons that I hunt is to understand what needs to be done to provide me with the food that gives me life; I hunt to help me understand that I am part of a larger ecological cycle. I hunt to remind myself that I am part of the food chain. I hunt to remind myself of my origins. I hunt to be in the wilderness, to remind myself that everything I do has a consequence. I hunt to be cognizant of death.

But of course, there is hunting and then there's hunting—and some hunting should be called something else. Hunting has its hooligans, just as soccer does. There is respectful hunting, fair chase, and hunting for sustainable development. And there is poaching. The illegal poaching of animals for their fur, skin, ivory, internal organs, and the like is a perennial problem. Countries like China continue to use many parts of animals for pseudo-medical purposes and there is inadequate law enforcement to stop such practices.

Furthermore, there are too many "slob hunters" who have given hunting a bad reputation—people who shoot at everything that moves, who don't respect the game laws, who behave unethically. For example, on one occasion my friend Jack and I had been hunting in the north of Alberta, in Canada, and were returning to Edmonton on the main north-south highway when we saw several vehicles parked at the side of the road. We slowed down to find out what was going on. It didn't take us long to work out what was happening. Next to the highway were two bull moose nibbling on some bushes. They were within 30 meters of the road, too close for legal hunting. A number of these hopeful "sports," happily knocking back beer and gin, were waiting until the moose had moved away within a legal distance so they could start their fusillade. I was not amused. These are the people who give hunters a bad name.

On the same trip, we were told about an accident caused by a group of bear hunters who wanted to play a joke on someone in their party. One of them hid in the bush, and when his friend arrived at the stand, growled like a bear. Presumably, he hoped to scare his friend half to death but the joke was on him. The terrified "hunter" shot at the sound, causing grave injuries. The first rule of a hunter is to be able to see what you aim at—something neither of these men seemed to have learned.

It is thanks to responsible hunters, however, that there are so many game animals around. In fact, the most hunted species in a country like the US—wild turkeys, elk, whitetail deer, pronghorn antelope, black bear, and wild sheep—are more abundant now than they were a hundred years ago thanks to conservation efforts of hunters. Whenever species have become endangered, through loss of habitat, poaching, or bush meat hunting, hunters have been among the first to tackle the problem.

Even though hunters may be a small minority, they are usually the ones to take action to preserve wildlife. HRH Prince Philip, Duke of Edinburgh, who has been well known for his conservation efforts, emphasizes this point:

> "I am always amazed that so many townspeople seem to be incapable of understanding that hunting and conservation are now entirely compatible so far as conservation is concerned. They simply will not, or do not wish to recognize that in most parts of the world the leadership in conservation has come from experienced hunting sportsmen."[121]

It is a pity that true hunter-conservationists are slotted together with slob hunters, commercial bush meat hunters and poachers. Hunters are often scapegoated and stereotyped as a sadistic bunch. They are blamed for the extinction of species, while the real reasons for the animals' decline is related to population explosion and the disappearance of the animals' habitat. And given the direction in which society is developing, I fear that my grandchildren will not be able to enjoy the same unique hunting experiences that I have had. It is highly questionable whether hunting can and will survive in an increasingly urbanized society.

While respecting the vegetarians' points of view, from a biological point of view, we are not designed to be that way. Research tells us that we are closer to carnivores than herbivores; our teeth are designed for meat eating, tearing, not just grinding. Our stomach acids are different from herbivores; our stomachs and intestines are different. That said, we are not built to be strictly carnivorous, either. As omnivores, however, we are not terribly good at making the conversions necessary for long-term health as vegans—unless we are in perfect health to start with.[122] There is an old Indian definition of a vegetarian—a lousy hunter. But whatever our take on hunting, there is no denying the fundamental facts of the cycle of life. It may be difficult, as complicated human beings, to take a completely logical and dispassionate perspective on the matter. Perhaps it is easier to turn to the reductionism of *Star Trek*'s Mr. Spock: "In the strict scientific sense we all feed on death—even vegetarians."

110 — Csikszentmihalyi, Mihali. *Flow: The Psychology of Optimal Experience.* New York: Harper & Row, 1990.

111 — Leopold, Aldo. *A Sand Country Almanac.* New York: Oxford University Press, 1999, p. 169.

112 — Ruark, Robert C. *Horn of the Hunter.* Huntington Beach, Cal: Safari Press, 1999, p. 81.

113 — Seton, Ernest Thompson. *Lives of the Hunted.* New York: Charles Scribner's Sons, 1901.

114 — Lopez, Barry. *Arctic Dreams: Imagination and Desire in a Northern Landscape.* New York: Bantam Books, 1989, p. 413.

115 — Turgenev, Ivan. *A Sportsman Notebook.* New York: Random House, 1992.

116 — Kets de Vries, Manfred F. R. *Sex, Money, Happiness, and Death: The Quest for Authenticity.* New York: Palgrave MacMillan, 2009.

117 — Dairy Farmers of Britain Survey, 2007.

118 — Foer, Jonathan Saffran. *Eating Animals.* New York: Penguin, 2009, p. 32.

119 — *Ibid*, p. 34.

120 — *Ibid*, p. 59.

121 — Prince Philip & Fisher, James. *Wildlife Crisis,* New York: Cowles Book, 1970.

122 — Price, Weston Andrew. *Nutrition and Physical Degeneration.* Chicago: Keats Publishing, 2003.

Let the advocate of animal food force himself
to a decisive experiment on its fitness, and
as Plutarch recommends, tear a living lamb
with his teeth, and plunging his head into
its vitals, slake his thirst with the steaming
blood; when fresh from the deed of horror let
him revert to the irresistible instincts of nature
that would rise in judgment against it, and
say, Nature formed me for such work as this.
Then, and then only, would he be consistent.
 —Percy Bysshe Shelley

I have known many meat eaters to be far
more non-violent than vegetarians.
 —Mahatma Gandhi

How, given the canine teeth and close-set
eyes that declare the human animal to be a
predator, had we come up with the notion that
oat bran is more natural to eat than chicken?
 —Valerie Martin

How can any man or woman, city born
and bred, expect to know firsthand—to
understand—that killing is a daily part of life
for all of us. They know, of course. But a lack
of thoughtful interest, even outright denial,
is easier without any personal involvement.
 —M. R. James, *My Place*

HUNTING IN POST-
INDUSTRIAL SOCIETY

On May 5, 2009, the European Parliament voted to ban the import of all seal products (mainly from Canada) into the European community, in an effort to stop that country's annual seal hunt. Greenpeace, along with the International Fund for Animal Welfare, Friends of the Earth, and the People's Trust for Endangered Animals were responsible for convincing EU bureaucrats of the importance of passing this legislation. Did they realize the devastating effect this measure would have on the indigenous Inuit population of Canada? It appears not. The people who pushed this legislation seem to have had very little understanding of Inuit culture. They didn't want to acknowledge that seal hunting is an intrinsic part of Inuit life, not only providing food and clothing, but also invested with substantial cultural and economic significance. The sale of seal pelts is a by-product of their subsistence hunting.

For the Inuit, European politics, which had so little to do with their world, took preference over their reality, adding to the major challenges they already faced, such as global warming, climate change, and the soaring costs of fuel and food. Clearly, these urbanized Europeans didn't have a clue that the new policy would spell disaster for many Inuit, who already had great difficulty surviving in their harsh Arctic land. What other foodstuffs can they raise and harvest in that climate? I wonder how much thought was given to these factors by lobbying organizations such as Greenpeace.

The Inuit saw the EU decision as both highly discriminatory and extremely ethnocentric. It was even harder to understand considering that the Inuit have always hunted sustainably and humanely. Furthermore, hunting doesn't pose any threat to the seal population, which has tripled since the 1960s. Ironically, because of the overpopulation of seals, there is an increased threat to existing fish stocks. It was not only the Inuit who were gravely affected by this decision: the seal hunt had provided a significant source of income for thousands of sealers in Canadian coastal communities (including the Inuit) for hundreds of years and more.

A propaganda war has been waged against seal hunting for decades now and many people have seen the images of the clubbing of whitecoat seal pups used in anti-hunting campaigns. Although I also think that it is a highly unattractive way of disposing of a seal, clubbing dispatches the animal quickly and humanely without damage to its pelt. But the public outrage about clubbing was so inflammatory when these images were first widely distributed that Canada banned the hunting of whitecoats in 1987. It is now more than 35 years since whitecoats could be legally hunted, yet anti-sealing groups still display these images on their websites and in their fundraising material.

The EU import ban is a good example of legislation that has more form than substance. The native people of Canada have been hunting seals for at least 4,000 years. The meat has always been an important food source, particularly for residents of small coastal communities, and the pelts prized for their warmth. As sealing has been part of these people's cultural heritage, they were truly bewildered when they learned of the ban. Seals may look cute and cuddly, but they are fish-killing "machines." What would have happened, I wonder, if the Inuit had posted a picture of a cute lamb or a calf on a European website advocating the prohibition of its slaughter? Or if the Canadian government uploaded YouTube clips of how cows are slaughtered in the EEC? What would the Brussels bureaucrats have done? Would they forbid the consumption of lamb or beef? Or what if the Inuit had the power to forbid the eating of fish in the European Community? A little reverse thinking might have put things into more perspective.

But the International Fund for Animal Welfare hailed the ending of commercial sealing in Canada as a significant victory for animal conservation and had the PR savvy to put the image of a cute-looking seal pup on their website to attract people's attention. Now, the European eel is also a critically endangered species; its numbers have fallen by 99 percent and it can only be caught under license. But no one is likely to make an eel a poster child for an anti-hunting group; eels simply don't have the same sex appeal as baby seals. More importantly for the senior management of these animal rights organizations, eels are not the kind of animal that invites financial donations.

The miscommunication between the Inuit governing body and the Brussels bureaucrats is a snapshot of our difficult relationship with the natural world in post-industrial society. The bureaucrats don't seem to understand that we are dealing with two totally different lifestyles. Most Inuit don't have the luxury of going to a local shopping center to buy their food and clothing. What this decision signifies for me is that the discussion between people favoring hunting and anti-hunting groups has, unfortunately, turned into the dialogue of the deaf.

Although, as I have shown in earlier chapters, hunting has been an intrinsic element of human activity, from a cultural-historical point of view it is interesting to note that the movement against hunting has intensified with the rise of industrialization and urbanization. This trend can be viewed as a signifier of humankind's increasing estrangement from nature. We are dealing with an urban population that is more and more alienated from the world of nature.

BE COMFORTABLE IN YOUR OWN SKIN, AND LET ANIMALS KEEP THEIRS.

When hunting transformed from a subsistence activity into a social one, the clamor of anti-hunting groups increased. Interestingly, it is not the people who have regular contact with animals and wildlife—farmers, naturalists, biologists, and zoologists—who most vehemently oppose hunting. Most people's exposure to animals is restricted to the zoo, feeding pigeons and squirrels in a park, or owning a pet. They draw their images of the natural world from the anthropomorphic stories of animals dramatized by film studios, like Disney, and like-minded people.

People who trivialize hunting as an outmoded relic of the past don't recognize its multi-faceted nature. They are completely ignorant of the important role hunting played in the evolutionary and socio-cultural development of the human species. They don't realize the social and cultural contributions hunting has made to society. They don't recognize the stability a tradition like hunting lends a society. Their behavior contrasts markedly with that of people who still have strong links with their agricultural past, in countries like France, the Scandinavian countries, Austria, Hungary, Poland, and Russia. There, people are much closer acquainted with the cycle of life and find something very comforting in following certain traditions.

I grew up in small fishing village in central Holland, where the local farmers butchered their own animals. True enough, seeing headless chickens flapping around the garden or listening to the sound of squealing pigs is not the kind of thing that gives me pleasure. But it did give me a good idea where my meat came from. Seeing the neighbors preparing (from start to finish) rabbits, chickens, pigeons, geese, and ducks for dinner was a forceful education in the cycle of life.

Urbanization has distanced us not only from our ancient heritage as hunters but also from our agricultural roots. Although it is not expressly stated, we prefer to hunt or kill "by proxy." Unless they are complete vegetarians—and even that is not possible without some form of killing, due to the use of insecticides, for example, or the effects of deforestation—people who accuse hunters of cruelty seem to forget that they outsource killing to people in slaughterhouses or do it in peripheral ways.

Unfortunately, this disconnect has created two camps that are adamantly opposed to each other. As happens in many political situations, "splitting"— having starkly opposing views—seems to be the norm. Hunting undeniably brings out strong emotions. Where there should be a middle ground, we find strife and refusal to compromise. Where there should be civilized discussion, we see degeneration into simplistic sound bites. In some instances, the defense of ideological vegetarianism assumes almost religious proportions, allowing very little or no place for dialogue. Although hunter and anti-hunter relationships have been particularly conflictual since the beginning of this century, this does not mean that there was any lack of discussion about the topic in pre-industrial times. On the contrary, a long list of philosophers had been preoccupied with the question of humankind's relationship with animals.

⌐

Philosophers and beyond

Philosophical concern for animal welfare is as ancient as the philosophers themselves, who in some instances seem to have anticipated contemporary discussions about the hunting conundrum. Many of the best-known philosophers and theologians—including Plato, Aristotle, Aquinas, Descartes, Hobbes, Locke, Hume, Berkeley, Kant, Leibniz, Rousseau, Herder, Schopenhauer, Bentham, Mill, and Nietzsche—on various occasions (and sometimes at great length) explored fundamental questions about the nature of animals, including their capacity for reasoning, language, self-consciousness, whether or not they have souls, and whether our power over them is acceptable. They also pondered whether it is right to kill animals for food and for "recreational" purposes. Throughout the centuries, there have always been voices reflecting on the morality of hunting.

Pythagoras, who lived toward the end of the sixth century BCE, was the first prominent philosopher to oppose hunting. And it seems he practiced what he preached by being a vegetarian. The Pythagorean diet meant a total avoidance of the meat of slaughtered animals. Pythagoras advocated a universal and absolute law that would include injunctions against killing any living creature, abstaining from animal sacrifice, and never eating meat. He even dreamt of changing the diets of pure carnivores. Ovid described the Pythagorean philosophy in *Metamorphoses*:

"Human beings, stop desecrating your bodies with impious foodstuffs. There are crops; there are apples weighing down the branches; and ripening grapes on the vines; there are flavorsome herbs; and those that can be rendered mild and gentle over the flames; and you do not lack flowing milk; or honey fragrant from the flowering thyme. The earth, prodigal of its wealth, supplies you with gentle sustenance, and offers you food without killing or shedding blood.

Flesh satisfies the wild beast's hunger, though not all of them, since horses, sheep and cattle live on grasses, but those that are wild and savage: Armenian tigers, raging lions, and wolves and bears, enjoy food wet with blood. Oh, how wrong it is for flesh to be made from flesh; for a greedy body to fatten, by swallowing another body; for one creature to live by the death of another creature! So amongst such riches, that earth, the greatest of mothers, yields, you are not happy unless you tear, with cruel teeth, at pitiful wounds, recalling Cyclops's practice, and you cannot satisfy your voracious appetite, and your restless hunger, unless you destroy other life!"[123]

The historian Xenophon (circa 430–354 BCE) disagreed, and wrote a treatise on hunting called *Cynegeticus*: "My advice to the young is, do not despise hunting or the other training of your boyhood, if you desire to grow up to be good men, good not only in war but in all else of which the issue is perfection in thought, word, and deed." Xenophon believed hunting was good for the health of young men, improving their sight, hearing, and longevity, and was the best training for war: "For men who are sound in body and mind may always stand on the threshold of success." Hunting also "makes men sober and upright ... because they are trained in the school of truth."[124] He added, "Therefore I charge the young not to despise hunting or any other schooling. For these are the means by which men become good in war and in all things out of which must come excellence in thought and word and deed."[125]

Aristotle (384–322 BCE) also praised the many benefits of hunting. He noted that "after the birth of animals, plants exist for their sake, and that the other animals exist for the sake of man, the tame for use and food, the wild, if not all at least the greater part of them, for food, and for the provision of clothing and various instruments. Now if nature makes nothing incomplete, and nothing in vain, the inference must be that she has made all animals for the sake of man."[126] He concluded, "If some animals are good at hunting and others are suitable for hunting, then the Gods must clearly smile on hunting."[127]

Many years later, the philosopher and theologian Saint Augustine (354–430) put another, more religious spin on the hunting controversy. His view was that the non-human world was created by God for our benefit and put under our dominion and at our disposal. And he definitely did not advocate vegetarianism:

"Some people have tried to extend [you shall not kill] to wild and domestic animals to make it mean that even these may never be killed. But then why not apply it to plants and to anything rooted in the earth and nourished by the earth? For although this part of creation is without feeling, it is called 'living,' and is hence capable of dying and being killed, when violence is done to it...We reject such fantasies, and when we read 'You shall not kill' we assume that this does not refer to bushes, which have no feelings, nor to irrational creatures, flying, swimming, walking, or crawling, since they have no rational association with us, not having being endowed with reason..."[128]

One thousand years later, the Dutch humanist and theologian Desiderius Erasmus (1466–1536) expressed himself very differently about hunting. Erasmus did not care for outdoor life and noted sarcastically: "They [hunters] take unbelievable pleasure in the hideous blast of the hunting horn and baying of the hounds. Dogs' dung smells sweet as cinnamon to them."[129] The Renaissance scholar, Michel de Montaigne (1533–92) concurred. In his essay *Of Cruelty*, he wrote: "As for me, I could never so much as endure, without remorse and griefe, to see a poore, sillie, and innocent beast pursued and killed, which is harmelesse and voide of defence, and of whom we receive no offence at all."[130] The lexicographer Samuel Johnson (1709–84) also joined the anti-hunting chorus, observing, "It is very strange, and very melancholy, that the paucity of human pleasures should persuade us ever to call hunting one of them."[131]

The German philosopher Immanuel Kant (1724–1804) maintained that cruelty to animals was wrong solely on the grounds that it was bad for humankind. He argued that humans have duties only toward other humans, and that "cruelty to animals is contrary to man's duty to *himself*, because it deadens in him the feeling of sympathy for their sufferings, and thus a natural tendency that is very useful to morality in relation to other humans is weakened."[132]

The philosopher, Jeremy Bentham (1748–1832), was also adamantly opposed to hunting. Indeed, he famously wrote of animals that, "The question is not, Can they *reason*? Nor, Can they *talk*? But Can they *suffer*?"[133] and maintained that we have a duty not to cause suffering to animals. He also stated that right and wrong are determined by "the greatest good for the greatest number." We don't know if Bentham practiced what he preached, to the extent of being a vegetarian. But perhaps he considered eating meat to be the greater good.

The philosopher and naturalist Henry David Thoreau (1817–62) had a serious crisis of conscience about the rights and wrongs of hunting. As a young man, he loved to hunt and had a keen curiosity about wildlife. But later in his life became ambivalent about hunting, pondering at length whether it was right to hunt wild animals and eat meat. He concluded that the primitive, animal side of humans drives them to do so, but that a person who transcends this propensity is superior to those who don't. He did not deny the influence of his early years, however: "These modern ingenious sciences and arts do not affect me as those more venerable arts of hunting and fishing, and even of husbandry in its primitive and simple form; as ancient and honorable trades as the sun and moon and winds pursue, coeval with the faculties of man, and invented when these were invented."[134] In the same way, he acknowledged the lasting benefits of the woodcraft he had learned: "I like sometimes to take rank hold on life and spend my day more as the animals do. Perhaps I have owed to this employment and to hunting, when quite young, my closest acquaintance with Nature. They early introduce us to and detain us in scenery with which otherwise, at that age, we should have little acquaintance."[135]

One of the world's greatest novelists, Leo Tolstoy, also had philosophical struggles about hunting. On the estate where he grew up, hunting took up a considerable amount of his time. In the winter of 1858, Tolstoy went on a bear hunting expedition with a companion, during which he was nearly killed by a wounded bear. He used his adventure in the short story, "The Bear Hunt":

"Something was coming towards me like a whirlwind, snorting as it came; and I saw the snow flying up quite near me. I glanced straight before me, and there was the bear, rushing along the path through the thicket right at me, evidently beside himself with fear. He was hardly half a dozen paces off, and I could see the whole of him—his black chest and enormous head with a reddish patch. There he was, blundering straight at me, and scattering the snow about as he came. I could see by his eyes that he did not see me, but, mad with fear, was rushing blindly along; and his path led him straight at the tree under which I was standing. I raised my gun and fired. He was almost upon me now, and I saw that I had missed. My bullet had gone past him, and he did not even hear me fire, but still came headlong towards me. I lowered my gun, and fired again, almost touching his head. Crack! I had hit, but not killed him!

...I tried to rise, but something pressed me down, and prevented my getting up. The bear's rush had carried him past me, but he had turned back, and had fallen on me with the whole weight of his body. I felt something heavy weighing me down, and something warm above my face, and I realized that he was drawing my whole face into his mouth. My nose was already in it, and I felt the heat of it, and smelt his blood. He was pressing my shoulders down with his paws so that I could not move: all I could do was to draw my head down toward my chest away from his mouth, trying to free my nose and eyes, while he tried to get his teeth into them. Then I felt that he had seized my forehead just under the hair with the teeth of his lower jaw, and the flesh below my eyes with his upper jaw, and was closing his teeth. It was as if my face were being cut with knives. I struggled to get away, while he made haste to close his jaws like a dog gnawing. I managed to twist my face away, but he began drawing it again into his mouth."[136]

A doctor had some impressive stitching to do after Tolstoy's unfortunate incident. Soon after, the bear was found and killed by his friend, who gave Tolstoy the bear hide. Tolstoy had the beast stuffed and placed in one of his rooms in his estate. Later in life, however, he converted to vegetarianism and stopped hunting. In his essay, *On Civil Disobedience*, he wrote: "A man can live and be healthy without killing animals for food; therefore, if he eats meat, he participates in taking animal life merely for the sake of his appetite. And to act so is immoral."[137]

Not all philosophers or literary figures agree. The Spanish philosopher José Ortega y Gasset (1883–1955) wrote an essay on the importance of hunting for human development. Some consider his *Meditations on Hunting*, originally meant as an introduction to a friend's now long-forgotten hunting memoirs, the finest work on the essence and ethics of hunting ever written. Ortega's essay is still topical today, when people who enjoy hunting and fishing are often roundly condemned.

Ortega points out that life is a dynamic interchange between our surroundings and us. He explains that hunting is part of our basic nature, "a universal and impassioned sport," and "the purest form of human happiness."[138] He adds: "In order to subsist, this early man had to dedicate himself wholly to hunting. Hunting was, then, the first occupation, man's first work and craft. ... Hunting was, then, the first *form of life* that man adopted, and this means—it should be fundamentally understood—that *man's being consisted first in being a hunter.*"[139] Ortega also touches on the spiritual element of hunting: "[It] submerges man deliberately in that formidable mystery and therefore contains something of a religious rite and emotion in which homage is paid to what is divine, transcendent, in the laws of nature."[140]

The philosopher and Nobel laureate Bertrand Russell (1872–1970) took a rather different angle in his Nobel Prize acceptance speech, raising questions about humans' "love of excitement," and how it contributes to destruction and violence:

"I incline to think that our mental make-up is adapted to the stage when men lived by hunting. When a man spent a long day with very primitive weapons in stalking a deer with the hope of dinner, and when, at the end of the day, he dragged the carcass triumphantly to his cave, he sank down in contented weariness, while his wife dressed and cooked the meat. He was sleepy, and his bones ached, and the smell of cooking filled every nook and cranny of his consciousness. At last, after eating, he sank into deep sleep. In such a life there was neither time nor energy for boredom. But when he took to agriculture, and made his wife do all the heavy work in the fields, he had time to reflect upon the vanity of human life, to invent mythologies and systems of philosophy, and to dream of the life hereafter in which he would perpetually hunt the wild boar of Valhalla. Our mental make-up is suited to a life of very severe physical labor... This cure for bellicosity is, however, impracticable, and if the human race is to survive—a thing which is, perhaps, undesirable—other means must be found for securing an innocent outlet for the unused physical energy that produces love of excitement. This is a matter which has been too little considered, both by moralists and by social reformers..."[141]

In his philosophical book about hunting, *The Old Man and the Boy* (1957), the novelist Robert Ruark is clear about his position on hunting:

"Hunting... is the noblest sport yet devised by the hand of man. There were mighty hunters in the Bible, and all the caves where the cave men lived are full of carvings of assorted game the head of the house dragged home. If you hunt to eat, or hunt for sport for something fine, something that will make you proud, and make you remember every single detail of the day you found him and shot him, that is good too. But if there's one thing I despise it's a killer, some blood-crazy idiot that just goes around bam-bamming at everything he sees. A man who takes pleasure in death just for death's sake is rotten somewhere inside, and you'll find him doing things later in life that'll prove it." [142]

Ruark touches upon the unacceptable behavior of some hunters. In every human pursuit, we will always find spoilers, people whose motivation is destructive or disruptive. And among hunters, there are those who are not interested in ethical hunting.

A common and important theme for some of these philosophers is that of cruelty, and its anti-social implications. It was the awareness of cruelty that drove the humanitarian movement of the 19th and 20th centuries to oppose bull baiting, bear baiting, cock-throwing (throwing sticks at a cock) and cockfighting, and why bull-fighting and rodeos were made illegal in many places. If we review the early debates concerning animal protection, two rationales are frequently prevalent: Cruelty is not only unjust to other creatures, but it also harms the perpetrator by diminishing his or her humanity.

It's clear from this cursory look at the writing of philosophers over several centuries that most are not advocates of hunting. The world has changed; it has become increasingly urbanized; and the voices raised against hunting have increased in volume, as they become associated with many other concerns:

overpopulation, food shortages, lack of water, disease, war, and ecological changes due to global warming.

rᴴ

To eat meat or not to eat meat

The fundamental question posed by people against hunting may well be whether to eat meat or not to eat meat. Or, to put it differently (and to be somewhat more flexible) should we only eat meat from farmed animals?

Of course, meat eating may never have been a real choice for a number of vegetarians. Some people may have come to a vegetarian diet because of a shortage of first-class protein in the first place, after which, the diet may have become institutionalized. Today, however, there are some people who seek out vegetarianism not from nutritional logic, but because of their political or ideological convictions. That would be fine of course, as long they let others have their own food habits, and refrain from proselytizing.

In democratic societies all of us should be able to make choices and be tolerant and refrain from interfering in other people's lives. I am troubled by the self-righteousness of people who are driven by the kind of ideological zeal that compels others to support their point of view and carries an undertone of violence. Few are open to a discussion of other points of view. They close their minds to conflicting views and pronounce their truths with unyielding, and arrogant certainty.[143] In spite of the observations by nutritionists that it is difficult for omnivores like us to be vegetarian and remain healthy without arming ourselves with a whole battery of dietary supplements and vitamins, they find a multitude of reasons to deny such data. Fortunately, I have encountered people who are willing to listen to the facts about nature and wildlife conservation, and prepared to accept that their beliefs, assumptions, and expectations may not be correct.

What I am trying to emphasize is that any form of living implies some form of killing. In fact, we could see life as a cycle of endless, murderous activity. Like it or not, we survive as human beings by eating other living things. There is no such thing as vegan perfection; given our biological make-up, such a state is as unattainable as it is impractical.

Some animal rights groups maintain that although hunting (and eating meat and fish) might once have been a crucial element of human survival, nowadays it represents a complete anachronism, an irrelevant remnant of the behavior of prehistoric man. Today, it should be viewed as nothing more than a violent form of recreation, especially since the vast majority of hunters do not hunt for reasons of economic survival. They see the term "blood sport" as symptomatic of the hunters' state of mind. The general public should no longer tolerate this kind of "amusement," as it is based on the maltreatment of animals. There is no way to rationalize hunting. And when it is done for pleasure, it is even more morally abhorrent.

Their argument continues: hunting has contributed to the extinction of animal species all over the world, including the Tasmanian tiger, the passenger pigeon, the great auk, and the dodo. (In fact, when humans first arrived on Mauritius, they brought with them animals that had not existed on the island before, including dogs, pigs, cats, and rats, which plundered the dodo nests.) Many antis believe that the delicate balance of ecosystems would ensure their own survival, if left unaltered. But I wish that were the case. Unfortunately, humankind has put its footprint everywhere, with the implication that the environment needs to be managed, one way or another.

Although these anti-hunters note that starvation and disease are often the tragic consequences of overpopulation, they maintain that these are nature's way of ensuring that strong, healthy animals survive, and that shooting animals because they may starve or become sick is arbitrary and destructive. Natural predators will keep the balance by killing only the sickest and weakest individuals. Hunting is not needed to maintain this equilibrium. (This argument ignores the fact that many of these natural predators are themselves extinct, or seriously threatened.) In addition, they claim that hunting brutalizes human beings, and is a breeding ground for violence—even though there is no scientific proof that this is the case. As I have said earlier, some even compare hunters to serial killers. We may dismiss this kind of statement, and joke about the naivety of anti-hunting groups and their ignorance of both wildlife and the natural world. The fact is, however, that many anti-hunters belong to well-funded and well-represented pressure groups.

So what motivates people who sign up with anti-hunting groups? Ignorance of the fundamentals of the natural world has a lot to do with it. People swallow the line that hunting is an act of cruelty against wildlife; that hunters are a bunch of criminals, sadists out to destroy the natural state of things. They blame hunters for the elimination of many species, ignoring the consequences of an ever-increasing human population on the biosphere. But there may be other factors that linger in their subconscious. Hunting used to be the privilege of the aristocracy and is still associated in the popular imagination with money, status, feudalism, and landownership. Do the antis romanticize their role, aligning themselves with the Robin Hoods of fiction—outlaws and poachers who were seen as noble or tragic heroes, rebelling against the oppressive upper classes? Is this really all about the class struggle?

The most frequent objection all non-hunters (not just anti-hunters) have to hunting is that it causes animals unnecessary suffering. One can sympathize with this, as it does happen, at times. Hunters don't always make a clean kill; they make mistakes and wound animals. But why single out the hunter? Animals die naturally and painfully every day. Hyenas and African wild dogs eat their prey while it is still alive. An antelope that is shot suffers less than one maimed but not dispatched by an adult cheetah, which uses it to teach its young how to hunt and kill. It would be enlightening for some antis to take a look at what drought can do to animals in Africa. Seeing kudu lying in ditches in Namibia, dying from lack of food is not a very attractive sight. It is a bonanza for the hyenas, however. I have seen starving elephants, lying down because they are too weak to stand, being eaten alive by warthogs and other creatures. These sights hardly conform to a rose-tinted view of nature.

I sometimes wonder how good the reality testing is of some of these anti-hunting groups. Perhaps, they should take a reality check on some of their options. For example, farming a wheat field wreaks more carnage—killing and maiming small animals and birds, destroying shelter and nesting areas—than the average hunter does in a lifetime. Soybeans are a common source of protein for vegetarians and Brazilian soy is a common ingredient in tofu and soymilk. Much of Brazilian deforestation is connected to soybean cultivation. As much as 70 percent of areas newly cleared for agriculture in the Mato Grosso state of Brazil is used for growing soybeans. In fact, industrial-scale soybean cultivation is destroying the Amazon rain forest, and with it the habitat for endangered or even unknown species of wildlife. Soybean cultivation increases greenhouse gases, which are believed to contribute to global warming. It also disrupts the life of indigenous tribes who depend on the forest for food and shelter. Current agricultural practices—especially the use of combine harvesters—leave the land a biological desert. So not only does vegetarianism not exempt vegetarians from the killing system, it is also a highly unrealistic option for the future of the planet. In the context of global warming, it is better to find more sustainable ways to use the land and *do the least harm*—and hunting is just one of the ways to go about this. Animal rights and anti-hunting campaigners would do better to use their resources for advocating population control. But this kind of reality doesn't necessarily fit their *Weltanschauung*. Many anti-hunting organizations want to renounce *Homo sapiens'* origins, negate our biological make-up, and refuse to accept that hunting can meet our spiritual, physical, and social needs. They consider the needs of present-day humans as being very different from the needs of our Paleolithic ancestors. Such an assumption is highly questionable, however. In the march of evolution we occupy only a small segment of time. And given the ease in which we regress, can we really be sure how different we are?

Worryingly, we only hear of these campaigners being *against* things. What about taking a more positive stand vis-à-vis wildlife? What about being *for* some things? We never hear much about what they are investing in to protect wildlife. Most of their resources are being used to be anti whatever they are anti about. A more constructive approach would be to take part in activities like restoring wetlands, protecting elk habitat, saving animals from natural catastrophes, helping bottom breeders breed, or helping to arrest poachers—as many hunters do.

ꭇ

"Bambi Syndrome"

People like simple messages. "Thou shall not kill" has always resonated, as do blanket statements like "Hunters are responsible for wiping out wildlife." People also need scapegoats. However, nobody wants to hear "Death is a way of life." The more complicated arguments of pro-hunters about the interconnectedness of wildlife and the growth of the human population are a tough sell in a world where the urban population is increasingly estranged from the natural world, and where, due to an ever-increasing population, the question of sustainability of resources has become a very serious issue.

To complicate a hunter's life even more, the popular media do not present a realistic picture of wildlife management. Instead of taking a more informed position, they prefer to operate at the glib sound-bite level. Much of this is due to expedient imagery. For example, it's very easy to impress your friends by identifying the villain in a TV crime thriller or legal drama at an early stage in the proceedings. Just watch and listen for the cues that there's hunter among the suspects, or someone who mounts trophies on a wall.

Elsewhere, hunters are depicted as stupid rednecks and gun-toting hillbillies. As a rule, popular entertainment condemns hunting for recreational purposes. Film and TV viewers are subjected to a steady diet of hunters as evil, plotting sociopaths who enjoy killing the animals and people they encounter. Perhaps this tendency to stereotype is due to the fact that most TV scriptwriters, producers, and directors live in Hollywood, New York, or other large urbanized areas, and don't know anyone who could counterbalance their world view. In which case, it shouldn't surprise us that hunters come across as a cruel, unpleasant, and even mentally unstable in TV programs or movies where hunting is a major theme.

In contemporary Western societies, the conflict over the moral meanings associated with non-subsistence hunting (and even subsistence hunting, as we saw in the case of the Inuit) has made it the focal point of intense and protracted political debate. Most people consider hunting for recreational purposes to be politically incorrect. This point of view is exacerbated by our tendency to anthropomorphize animals. Ascribing human traits to animals has a long history, starting with the stories in the Hindu *Panchatantra*, and the stories of Aesop. Among the more famous recent contributions are the extremely popular stories of Beatrix Potter, who published 23 books featuring rabbits, squirrels, mice, frogs, and pigs as protagonists. Many other books followed, such as *The Wind in the Willows*, and *Watership Down*.

Hunters are portrayed almost universally negatively in animated films, in which hunters come across as bumbling idiots who are outsmarted by the animals they are hunting—think of Bugs Bunny fighting off Elmer Fudd, Yogi Bear, and *Bambi*. More realistically, most filmed depictions of hunting by aboriginal cultures, like the Native Americans or the Inuit, treat the subject with much more respect, acknowledging the implication that they are hunting for what they need to survive and no more.

But perhaps we should blame Walt Disney, and more specifically *Bambi*, in which an evil hunter shoots and kills the fawn's mother. His father then saves Bambi, a crazy idea thrust upon a naive public, completely unaware of the bitter truth of life in the wild, where bucks are totally uninterested in protecting the young. The Disney Corporation has pushed this romanticized pseudo-reality to generations of children in a way that is insulting to the logic of the human mind.

The chief contributing factor to "Bambi Syndrome" is misinformation. From what I have observed, this "disorder" usually begins in early childhood and is reinforced into adolescence, and beyond. It is passed down from an "infected," misinformed parent to the child, then from that child to the next generation, and on and on. Children growing up on a farm, or in the countryside, are less likely to contract "Bambi Syndrome," as they actually do get some exposure to the reality of the natural world.

It is important to remember that children often have difficulty distinguishing what they see in movies and on television, or read in books, from what happens in real life. At an early age, fantasy and reality are intertwined. Unfortunately, early exposure to a bizarre, fairy-like view of the natural world may linger on into adulthood. In other words, people afflicted with "Bambi Syndrome" are less likely to accept the reality of animal behavior. They are unable to cope with the facts of life, and the intrinsic amorality and indifference of the natural world. They resist the truth that, beyond the cinema screen, the lion doesn't lie down with the lamb—nor, indeed, with baboons, warthogs, meerkats, and hyenas, as Disney's *Lion King* would have us believe. Animals don't smile, laugh, frown, talk, sing, or tap dance, either. Very few of them ever die of old age. Basically, what animals do is try to avoid each other. They may spend time together, but not as a harmonious, loving community. If they get the chance, they will stalk, maim, kill, and eat each other. The cycle of life is ruthless, and only the ablest killers survive. The only drama is Darwinian.

"Bambi Syndrome" feeds into phenomenon I have already mentioned—our dissociation from the source of our food, ignorance of the process of industrial killing that brings butchered meat to the table. It is reflected in the way people anthropomorphize their pets, castrating, declawing, and caging them, and attributing all kinds of human emotions and motivations to them, without ever considering their natural state.

A good example of what "Bambi Syndrome" can do to people is the documentary *Grizzly Man* (2005), made by Werner Herzog. The film is a chronicle of the life and death of the bear enthusiast Timothy Treadwell. It contains Treadwell's footage of his interactions with grizzly bears before he and his girlfriend were killed and partially eaten by a bear in 2003. The documentary also includes interviews with people who knew or were involved with Treadwell.

The protagonist of this sad tale is a somewhat misinformed individual who obsessively idealized the bears that would ultimately eat him (along with his poor girlfriend). Treadwell had the delusory idea that he had developed a special relationship with the bears and was their trusted friend. It didn't help that some of the bears allowed him to approach them, and sometimes even touch them. Although park officials repeatedly warned Treadwell that his interaction with the bears was unsafe to both parties, he didn't listen. The grizzly (pun intended) outcome was inevitable. This film demonstrates how dangerous a Disney-like view of animal behavior can be. Bears are not like Baloo, the lovable bear depicted in Walt Disney's film, *Jungle Book*. Bears don't save the Mowglis of this world. They eat them.

╓┐

Denial of ecological reality

Unfortunately, "Bambi Syndrome" has other consequences that are acted out on a mega-scale. When game populations become imbalanced, the cruelest thing is to forbid hunting. It is not pleasant to see a herd of animals slowly starve to death because of lack of food due to overpopulation.

Humankind has had such a massive effect on the environment that there is no alternative but to manage the world's biosphere in a responsible manner. Anti-hunting campaigners may not want to hear it, but the greatest threat to wildlife is not hunting but human encroachment. The biotype of many animals has been wiped out, making it almost impossible for them to survive. In other situations, animal populations have gotten out of hand.

For example, Holland, the country where I was born, has seen a dramatic increase in its population, and increasing urbanization. As in many other countries, foxes moved into built-up areas for the easy pickings there, and the urbanized Dutch thought these animals were so cute to have around that they were protected by legislation. This decision had disastrous consequences. Not only did foxes become regular visitors to everyone's garbage can, they also managed to wipe out all the surface breeders in the country. Eventually, the government and general public realized the idiocy of the prohibition on fox hunting and the laws were changed.

Similarly, without hunters keeping the deer population in check, the overall health of many herds would deteriorate rapidly. Disease, starvation, and death by predators would become commonplace. In France, the exploding population of wild boar has always been a cause for worry. If these animals were not strictly controlled and hunted intensively, there would be outcry from the farming community. Farmers would march on Paris to demonstrate against the government.

Bio-systems are exceedingly fragile and complex. To truly understand how they operate, we need to have a systemic outlook. To take an extreme example I could even argue that to conserve lions, we may, at times, have to kill elephants. Their complex interrelationship is a good example of what ecological systems

are all about. When we find a situation when there are too many elephants for the existing biotope, the result is habitat destruction—an elephant eats for about 16 hours a day, during which time it can get through up to 600 lbs. of food and 50 gallons of water. As a consequence, elephants destroy the basic food supply of the various antelope and buffalo. This in turn affects the breeding patterns and fertility of predators; prides of lion produce fewer young, and their population decreases rapidly. Although it sounds bizarre, elephants may have to be culled to maintain the lion population. This example demonstrates how, ecologically, death can contribute to life. (And of course, given the dire straight elephants are in at the moment due to almost industrialized poaching fostered by the increasingly wealthy populations in Asia, such a recommendation is to be taken tongue-in-cheek.) However, it is very difficult to explain these systemic ecological interrelationships to people with a "Bambi Syndrome."

It would be instructive for people not familiar with the reality of wildlife conservation to visit Africa and see at first-hand the likely effects of some of their well-intentioned efforts. Take, for example, the idea of capturing and sterilizing elephants, including giving roaming bulls vasectomies. It sounds great —at a distance from the locations where these animals live. Selling this idea to local wild life officials will be another matter. Once they've stopped falling about laughing, they will give these well-meaning people an earful. Fantasy that isn't grounded in reality is hallucination.

⛩

The end of the game

In the 1970s the Kenya Game Department and its successor, the Wildlife Conservation and Management Department (WCMD) banned all hunting. Few people realize that this ban was not imposed to put an end to "recreational" hunting, but resulted from a corrupt process of animal control hunting and commercial cropping. The WCMD ran a massive illegal trade through these two activities.

Since the ban came into force in 1977, the country has seen a disastrous decline in wildlife due to poaching and illegal human encroachment on land reserved for wildlife. Those who implemented the ban didn't take into consideration that when a demand exists for something that cannot be obtained legally, it will be supplied illegally. Since 1977, industrial size poaching in Kenya has killed almost all the elephants, white and black rhinoceros, lions, leopards, and cheetahs, as well as various antelope species. This illegal activity has been encouraged by politically well-connected Kenyans who recognize an opportunity to make a considerable amount of money out of ivory and "bush meat" sales. In less than 20 years, Kenya's elephant population fell from 150,000 to fewer than 6,000.

But astonishingly, in spite of this dramatic decline in wildlife, anti-hunting organizations still welcome the ban. Kenya has been the showcase of the anti-hunting lobby. Ironically, to keep the ban in place, the anti-hunting lobby operating in Kenya supports the ineffective efforts of the corrupt WCMD. It is simpler to manipulate and control this organization than to take a more proactive stand on the management of wildlife—which would include management through hunting. The consequence of this policy is that wildlife in Kenya has little purpose, and no official, legal value. No wonder that politicians who represent wildlife districts see very little or no benefit in preserving game in these areas. Some have even come to the conclusion that it is best for everyone to get rid of game completely.

The disastrous decline in wildlife in Kenya has been exacerbated by accelerated population growth. It is very difficult to convince a farmer with many hungry mouths to feed of the benefits of conserving wild animals without offering some kind of financial incentive. In many developing countries, the attitude toward game is "if it pays, it stays." Thanks to the support of the anti-hunting lobby, bills to mandate the reinstitution of legal hunting in Kenya, make landowners responsible for wildlife, and liable for damage caused by wild animals—legislation that is active in countries neighboring Kenya—have consistently been defeated. The local communities that live with the wildlife are not amused. Wildlife becomes considered as a hindrance or a threat (in case of dangerous game). But if wildlife were to have value (through the collection of trophy fees for animals at the end of their breeding cycle), the situation would be quite different.[144]

For the anti-hunting organizations that have contributed to this miserable outcome, ideology has triumphed over the best interests of wildlife conservation. With no money coming in through legal hunting to fight poaching, the inevitable result (with the exception of a few parks) will be the end of the game. In comparison, countries like Botswana, Namibia, and South Africa, where their wildlife resource has been carefully managed, the game population has been kept at a sustainable, or even increasing, level. One result of this careful management is that the number of elephants in these countries has increased. But even in these countries, in spite of effective anti-poaching measures, the situation for the rhinoceros has become desperate. The temptation due to ignorance, making for a phenomenal value of the horns, seems to be their downfall.

What fascinates me about the situation in Kenya is the serious disconnect between the worldview of the anti-hunting lobby and reality. I assume that these people must have a modicum of intelligence; they can see; they can count. They must have observed the tragic decline of wildlife in the country. They must be aware of the effects of organized wildlife poaching rings. They must also have some idea of the economic realities of life. They must understand that if wildlife has no economic value, livestock will replace it. They must have noticed the different levels of game populations in neighboring countries—yet they continue to stick to their dogmatic point of view. In that context, Kenyan President Daniel arap Moi's gesture, in July 1989, of setting fire to 12 tons of elephant tusks to demonstrate his government's support of wildlife conservation can be viewed as a totally empty, futile, and wasteful gesture. It makes you wonder how well informed Moi was about wildlife management. It was a sad example of form over substance; his act did nothing to address the underlying problems. But all evidence inconsistent with these antis' prevailing ideology is viewed as irrelevant. Thus organizations that are supposedly put into place to protect wildlife, end up creating an implicit, unholy alliance with the kinds of people that exploit and even destroy wildlife.

I was recently on the island of Mauritius, where the population of Rusa deer threatens to reach pest proportions. There are so many, that if these deer were

not hunted they would totally destroy the island's rather fragile eco-system. Fortunately, the people responsible for wildlife on the island recognize this dynamic. Closed eco-systems like Mauritius force us to rethink practically every aspect of life on our planet. It makes the romanticization and idealization of "Mother Nature" difficult to maintain, and demonstrates that our perception of the need to keep any meaningful distance from nature is shockingly illusory.

᚛

Pleasure and its vicissitudes

So, thanks to the "Bambi Syndrome," there is denial of the realities of the natural world and denial about the source of our food. Most city dwellers (and many antis) don't want to acknowledge that an entire international industry has been developed to raise domestic animals to satisfy our carnivorous needs; nor that enormous fishing fleets sieve the oceans daily for their benefit. Of course, there are anti-hunting advocates who accept the notion of hunting for subsistence; but avocational hunting, or hunting for pleasure, is unacceptable. But, again, how realistic is such a view of things? Even for the most primitive hunters, pleasure is an intrinsic part of the hunting experience—a pleasure that is connected to many other factors.

In earlier chapters, I have tried to demonstrate that the motivations for hunting are multifarious and highly complex—and include a range of social, economic, cultural, and personal dimensions. Bringing meat to the table is an important part of it. In earlier times, when a hunter killed an animal, there would be celebration because he provided food for his family or tribe. And, in spite of the "progress" of civilization over the march of time, this response hasn't changed very much. My family always welcomed me excitedly when I brought home game. And I experienced a sense of pleasure, personal achievement, and fulfillment of a tradition in doing so. Hunting that is done in a social context brings the pleasure of bonding with others; it is a way to momentarily forget the obligations of work and home. All these aspects of hunting are important from a mental health perspective.

᚛

Sin

The anti-hunting groups are the Saint Augustines of the modern world, with their notion that a basic human activity like hunting may be OK, as long as it's done for expedience sake and you get no pleasure from it. This is reminiscent of the early church fathers' take on sex. Saint Augustine (354–430) said that sex motivated by pleasure was sinful and only morally right if performed for procreation. Erections should be functional but lust-less; the necessity of the act was regrettable; and the participants should certainly not enjoy themselves. The preferred state of humankind was chastity—but Saint Augustine was enough of realist, having fathered a child of his own, to acknowledge that the male body could mock the will in the form of spontaneous erections, wet dreams, premature ejaculations, or other forms of loss of control during orgasm. Unfortunately, he was not enough of a realist to realize that of all the sexual aberrations, chastity may be the strangest. I suspect that even those who are entirely focused on a reproductive goal may have at least a twinge of enjoyment, let alone emotional and psychological gratification, from the sex act. Hunting, the quest for food, is another biological function that involves numerous other motivations, including pleasure, which cannot reasonably be separated from one another.

But there is a significant element to the antis' behavior that makes me wonder whether they can ever present a compelling argument that hunting, even for recreational purposes, is wrong in some objective sense—and that is their own violence. What makes many of them, given their non-violent philosophy, so violent themselves? Animal rights campaigners have been jailed for offenses like sending hoax bombs to the homes of people involved with animal experimentation, daubing their houses and cars with graffiti, making physical threats, posting leaflets accusing company directors of being pedophiles, and making abusive phone calls.[145] In the UK, hunt sabotage became so prevalent and violent at one point that it was made a criminal act in the 1990s.

Clinical psychologists and psychoanalysts may wonder whether some of these antis are not acting out a very different agenda, connected to their own personal background? As we all know, difficult early experiences often become externalized and may be acted out on a public stage. I wonder how these dogmatic, violent antis cope with their internal aggression.

I can't help but contrast my own efforts to understand the deeper motivations of the anti-hunting groups with their superficial assumptions about the enigma of hunting. They are not prepared to consider its symbolic role and the important part it plays in our social heritage. They pay little or no attention to the systemic issues about wildlife management. They don't acknowledge the significant role played by hunters in wildlife conservation. They dismiss these activities as self-interested, geared only to the continued killing of game.

In whatever I am saying, I am not denying, however, that hunting has had its part in bringing some animals to extinction through market hunting—the great auk and passenger pigeon are notorious examples. But the greatest threat

to wildlife comes from various forms of human encroachment into their habitat, including industrialized poaching.

⊨

"If we lose the animals, we will lose our souls"

The 64 million dollar question is whether hunters really are the great destroyers the anti-hunting movement makes them out to be. I maintain that the opposite is true. Hunters go out of their way to establish organizations to support the preservation of the species they hunt and it is not merely selfish reasons or guilt that drive them. Most hunters are motivated by their love of wildlife and nature. We hunt to reaffirm our identity, and earn our human legacy. At a time of societal alienation, hunters who affirm a deep, abiding love for nature, and are willing to commit time, money, and energy to conservation, are among those who are making a difference. We want to leave behind a better world for our children.

There is the risk of sounding defensive when claiming that hunting is a necessary element of contemporary wildlife management. Hunters are essential to helping to maintain a population of healthy animals within an environment's ecological carrying capacity (when natural checks such as predators are absent). Hunting controls the annual crop of new animals and birds, allowing the animals that remain sufficient food and shelter to survive.

Obviously, predators give hunters a helping hand, but with increasing human encroachment on their territory the days are long gone when predators alone can achieve this balance. And let's be realistic: how many of us would like to have lions, leopards, elephants, crocodiles, grizzlies, and cougars hanging around our backyard?

It is easy to make a case for predators while sitting in a city café, philosophizing about the meaning of life; but try putting the point to farmers in Africa when their crop is being devastated by elephants, or when their children and neighbors are taken by crocodiles. Put the same point to sheep farmers while cheetahs, leopards or lions are eradicating their livestock—as I have seen in Namibia. They will disagree—or at least counter with questions about where the money is to come from to set aside protected territory for these predators.

An often-repeated claim of anti-hunting groups is that hunters destroy ecosystems, whereas the reality is quite different. Ethical hunters—even if it is for mainly selfish reasons—have made major contributions to improving the biotope for wildlife, and have brought many threatened species back from extinction. They have supported the introduction of laws to protect animals and play an important role in protecting animals from poachers. They advocate the sustainable use of wildlife. Throughout most of the world, the level of predation from hunting has had little or no effect on animal populations. Hunters are not over-killers.

I was once in Cameroon, hunting bongo. On one part of the terrain, as a result of the efforts of he anti-hunting lobby, hunting was forbidden and the area was to be turned into a nature reserve. Although this idea had a lot of merit, exactly the opposite was happening. The area where hunting was permitted was well patrolled, preventing the setting of snares for bush meat. Game was plentiful. Only a small, sustainable percentage of the animals was taken out. The nature reservation—from which the economic incentive had been removed—had turned into poaching central. While I was there, I observed the continual coming and going of poachers, carrying baskets of "bush meat" on their back. I imagined that it would not take very long before the nature reservation was transformed into a total wasteland, devoid of game. Walking through the rain forest there, I found snares all over the place. Driving along the forest roads, everywhere I went, there were signs indicating the sale of "bush meat," a seemingly indiscriminate selection of everything that fell into the local hunters' snares. Vendors openly displayed smoked monkeys, gorillas, snakes, wild cats, antelopes, crocodiles and more bounty from the country's receding forests. At one point in time, I was struck by a very bad smell. Helped by my pygmy trackers, I found out what caused the stink—a large, beautiful bongo caught in one of the snares in this particular "nature reservation." It was an exceedingly depressing experience. And as the population continues to increase in Cameroon's cities, as well as forest logging concessions and mining camps, the demand for wild meat will increase with it.

The anti-hunting movement may not like to hear it, but without a financial incentive system, game populations would be rapidly replaced by cattle, goats, and sheep. Ideology aside, basic business principles also apply to wildlife management. In many regions of the world there are simply insufficient economic alternatives for land use, other than agriculture, forestry, or fisheries. In such instances, hunting tourism becomes a highly effective way to promote rural development, a practical tool for the sustainable use of a natural resource, while preserving the environment. Hunting creates the economic incentive to protect game populations.

Notwithstanding all the rhetoric of the anti-hunting organizations, it is hunters who provide the bulk of the resources to finance and establish programs for game management, habitat protection, and restoration, and conservation education. Many pro-hunting organizations go out of their way to restore and protect the habitat of the wildlife in which they are interested. In the US, for example, there are many organizations whose main role is the protection of special game species—Ducks Unlimited, the Foundation for Wild Sheep, the Rocky Mountain Elk Foundation, the National Wildlife Turkey Federation, the Mule Deer Foundation, the Audubon Society, the National Wildlife Federation, the Nature Conservancy, the Sierra Club, the National Wildlife Federation, the North American Wildlife Foundation, the Wilderness Society... I could go on. These organizations have made extraordinary efforts to preserve America's wildlife heritage. The same can be said of many European, Australian, and New Zealand wildlife organizations. Modern, sustainable wildlife management could not exist without their efforts. On a global scale, the International Council for Game and Wildlife Conservation (CIC), a non-profit, politically independent advisory body, advocates sustainable hunting and is internationally active.

Thanks to the efforts of hunters associated with these organizations, wildlife populations have been maintained or increased. And excellent proof of the essential role that hunters play in the sustainable development of game is the fact that wildlife populations in North America (deer, elk, antelope, black bears, wild turkeys, pheasants, many grouse species, doves, etc.) are at their highest levels in modern history. Game populations in most European countries have also been successfully maintained. The problem persists in countries where such organizations don't exist or are marginalized.

But of course, the reassuring thought that I am making a major financial contribution to maintaining the wildlife population is not the principal reason why I hunt. I hunt because I enjoy it. Hunting is not just putting food on the table or a head on the wall. To me (as I have said numerous times), it is a social, emotional, and spiritual activity that brings me closer to nature and gives my life more meaning. But I recognize that these very personal reasons are never going to convince anti-hunters.

rᴁ

Trophy hunting

To an extent, I have also become a trophy hunter. Of course, for animal rights advocates, trophy hunters are beyond the pale. When people hear the term "trophy hunter," they tend to think of a wealthy individual, who wants to obtain big trophy heads at any cost, while leaving the meat of the animal in the field to rot. I am pretty sure that such people exist but they are not hunters—killers, perhaps, or collectors may be a better description.

I don't think I fit this description, and neither do other fair chase hunters. However, I do enjoy going to different places in the world to hunt animals that are not available where I live. I like to see different places, cultures, and people.

In hunting—wherever I go and helped by local guides—I try to get animals that are close to the end of their life cycle, animals that have fulfilled their breeding purpose. I realize that some people may interpret this as a rationalization.

With buffalo, this means the older males who have been replaced by younger bulls in the herd. With red deer, stronger competitors will have taken over the animal's harem. Although these animals may be superannuated in strictly biological terms, they are far from easy game. The fact that they have lived so long is testament to their skill and wiliness. The hunter's chances are also reduced by the fact that there will be far fewer of them in a game population. Testing my skill as a hunter by restricting myself to the pursuit of these uncommon, individual animals raises my personal standard. In this context, seeking a trophy is consistent with a sensitive hunting ethic. Elgin Gates, one of the world's most famous hunters, once said:

"The true trophy hunter is a self-disciplined perfectionist seeking a single animal, the ancient patriarch well past his prime that is often an outcast from his own kind. This hunter is a mixture of sportsman and conservationist, testing his skills and resources against the crafty instincts and wariness of a wise old ram, hunting with the intent to kill the very animal he admires and respects. If successful, he will enshrine the trophy in a place of honor. This is a more noble and fitting end than dying on some lost and lonely ledge where the scavengers will pick his bones, and his magnificent horns will weather away and be lost forever."[146]

Some people will sympathize with this point of view; others will find it repugnant. But to me, trophy animals can represent the supreme challenge. These animals have survived many years of predation and brutal winters with their survival skills fully intact. Taking such an animal under fair chase conditions is a real challenge. To go into the wilds, often alone, to find such an animal, and obtain it, is very difficult. Eating such an animal and using its horns or skin to decorate my house is not something I will apologize for. The trophy becomes a lifelong reminder—almost a religious icon—reviving a totemistic feeling of kinship with the animal hunted, a phenomenon I have described in Chapter 6. The trophy on the wall represents the hunter's effort to retain the memory of a precious experience.

In addition to hunting these animals in foreign lands, I am prepared to make a financial contribution to whoever is responsible for game management in the areas where these animals live, a contribution that can be used for sustainable development. This is a way to compensate for potential damage caused by the game. The alternative, in which the animal starves to death—as happens with elephants once they lose their three sets of teeth —is not a very attractive proposition. The money can be used to incentivize the local population to counter poaching, manage their wildlife in a more sustainable way, and have their children enjoy it. But whatever arguments I make, sadly, I doubt the anti-hunting groups will hear me. I wish they would, however. It would be so much better for wildlife management if it would not be a dialogue of the deaf. To have a dialogue based on the reality of what hunting represents, not an ideological standstill would be in the interest of both parties.

123 — Ovid, *Metamorphoses*, Book 15, 60-142, http://etext.virginia.edu/latin/ovid/trans/Ovhome.htm.

124 — Arrian. *Arrian on Coursing: The Cynegeticus of the Younger Xenophon*. New York: Bastian Books, 2008.

125 — Phillips, A. A. and Willcock, M. M. *Xenophon & Arrian On Hunting With Hounds*, contains Cynegeticus original texts, translations & commentary. Warminster: Aris & Phillips Ltd., p. 18., 1999.

126 — Aristotle. (Trans. Benjamin Jowett) *Politics*, Book 1, Chapter 8, http://jim.com/arispol.htm

127 — Jolma, Dena Jones. *Hunting Quotations: Two Hundred Years of Writings on the Philosophy, Culture and Experience*. New York, Mcfarland & Co, 1992.

128 — Saint Augustine, *The City of God*, I.20.

129 — Desiderius Erasmus, *In Praise of Folly*, chapter 38.

130 — Jolma, Dena Jones. *Hunting Quotations: Two Hundred Years of Writings on the Philosophy, Culture and Experience*. New York, Mcfarland & Co, 1992.

131 — *Ibid.*

132 — Kant, Immanuel. "Groundwork of the Metaphysic of Morals," part II (*The Metaphysical Principles of the Doctrine of Virtue*), paras 16 and 17, 1785.

133 — Bentham, Jeremy. "An Introduction to the Principles of Morals and Legislation," inWilfred Harrison (Ed.), *A Fragment on Government and An Introduction to the Principles of Morals and Legislation*, 1823 edn. Oxford: Blackwell, 1823/1948, pp. 411-41.

134 — Thoreau, Henry David. "A Week on the Concord and Merrimack Rivers,", 1849, in *The Writings of Henry David Thoreau*, Vol. 1. Boston, Houghton Mifflin, 1906, p. 57.

135 — Thoreau, Henry David. "Walden," 1854, in *The Writings of Henry David Thoreau*, Vol. 2. Boston, Houghton Mifflin, 1906, p. 232.

136 — Tolstoy, Leo. *The Bear-Hunt, and Other Stories*. New York: Little Leather Library Corporation, 1918.

137 — Tolstoy, Leo. *Writings on Civil Disobedience and Nonviolence*. 1886. London: Peter Owen Ltd, 1968.

138 — Ortega y Gasset, José. *Meditations on Hunting*, H. B. Wescott (trans.), Belgrade, MT: Wilderness Adventures Press, 1985, p. 57.

139 — *Ibid*, p. 112.

140 — *Ibid*, p. 106.

141 — Russell, Bertrand. *Nobel Lectures—Literature 1901–1967*, in Horst Frenz, (ed.), Amsterdam, Elsevier, 1969.

142 — Ruark, Robert. *The Old Man and the Boy*. New York, Henry Holt and Co, 1953, p. 56.

143 — Rokeach, Milton. *The Open and Closed Mind*. New York: Basic Books, 1960.

144 — *Ibid.*

145 — *Daily Mail*, "Animal activists who launched smear campaign branding lab suppliers paedophiles and murderers are jailed," October 25, 2010.

146 — Gates, Elgin. *Trophy Hunter in Asia*. Winchester, Ontario: Winchester Press, 1971.

When the Earth is sick, the animals
will begin to disappear, when that
happens, The Warriors of the
Rainbow will come to save them.
  —Chief Seattle

Who loves nature? Who does not? Is
it only poets, and men of leisure and
cultivation, who live with her? No; but
also hunters, farmers, and butchers,
though they express their affection in
their choice of life, and not in their choice
of words. The writer wonders what
the ...hunter values in riding, in horses,
and dogs. It is not superficial qualities.
When you talk with him, he holds these
at as slight a rate as you. His worship is
sympathetic; he has no definitions, but
he is commanded by nature, by the living
power which he feels to be there present.
No imitation, or playing of these things,
would content him; he loves the earnest
of the north wind, of rain, of stone, and
wood, and iron. A beauty not explicable,
is dearer than a beauty which he can
see to the end of. It is nature the symbol,
nature certifying the supernatural,
body overflowed by life, which he
worships, with coarse but sincere rites.
  —Ralph Waldo Emerson,
    Self-Reliance and other Essays,
  New York, Dover, 1993

[T]here are no words that can tell
the hidden spirit of the wilderness,
that can reveal its mystery, its
melancholy, and its charm.
  —Theodore Roosevelt,
    African Game Trails

When you come home empty-handed,
you sleep and you say to yourself, "Oh,
what have I done? What's the matter
that I haven't killed?" Then the next
morning you get up and without a
word you go out and hunt again.
  —!Kung San hunter

ECCE HOMO

It is difficult to be objective about hunting when you are as biased as I am. For me, as it is for most people who hunt, hunting is an intensely personal experience that comes with ambiguous choices. Hunting has given me pride in my woodcraft skills; it has helped me know and understand the behavior of the animals I encounter in the outdoors; hunting has motivated me to learn how to read the land and harvest the hunt. As a father and a grandfather, I have tried to pass this affinity for nature and wildlife on to my children and grandchildren. I would like them to experience the mystery and beauty of wild country, and the deep emotional experiences that come with hunting.

I am very aware that people who hunt now are regarded very differently than they were when I was growing up. Once, at the beginning of my hunting career, I remember how I took a bus dressed in my green hunting kit, with a shotgun (cased) on my shoulder, and a dead pheasant and hare sticking out of my hunting bag. I assume (as I have not lived in the country for a long time) you can't walk around like that in Holland nowadays. It would, at the very least, arouse great consternation. The world has clearly changed.

Despite these obstacles, I will continue to advocate the important role hunters play in creating a better, and more sustainable world for our children. I will continue to transmit to others—paradoxical as it may seem to some—my love for the natural world and its creatures. I will continue to explain nature's systemic complexity, and the interconnectedness of nature's inhabitants. I will retain my love of living systems; I will continue to stress the deep affiliation human beings have with nature, rooted in our biological makeup; and I will continue to describe this profound need to interact with and relate to nature and the living world around us.

⌐

Biophilia

The psychoanalyst Erich Fromm first used the term biophilia to describe a mindset that attracts us to everything that is alive and vital.[147] Literally, "biophilia" means a passionate love for everything that is alive. Biophiles don't merely love the natural world because it is beautiful or stirs us emotionally; we love it because we may be hardwired to do so. The human attraction to the natural world—refined through socialization and cultural influences—is the product of our biological evolution. We are human exactly because of the particular way we are affiliated with other organisms. To put it most simplistically, biophilia is bonding with the earth, and being in touch with what nature offers.

The opposite of phobias—or irrational fears—philias grow from positive feelings. If we really look, we can find signs of biophilia everywhere: people walking their dogs, stroking their cats, tending their gardens, buying flowers, taking a stroll in the woods, picking wild strawberries. Unfortunately, with the seemingly unstoppable march of civilization, urbanization, and industrialization, there are also many people who have acquired a biophobic attitude toward nature and become distinctly anxious when removed from their urban comfort zone.

The Harvard biologist Edward Wilson popularized the term biophilia in his book *Biophilia: The Human Bond with Other Species*.[148] Like Fromm, Wilson suggests that biophilia describes "the connections that human beings subconsciously seek with the rest of life."[149] To Wilson, it seems incontrovertible that human beings need and have an innate sensitivity to other living things, because we have co-existed in the closest relationship with the natural world for many tens of thousands of years.

Wilson (and others) adopt a rather anthropocentric perspective on biodiversity: to be fully human, we need the multiple other species that exist with us. As humanity is part of an interconnected web of life, the implication is that the survival of our own species is ultimately dependent on the survival of the natural world. Thus human relationships with the flora and fauna that surround us are necessary not just for our physical wellbeing—food, shelter, medicine, and clothing—but also (as I have said repeatedly) for our mental, emotional, and spiritual health. The restorative value of the natural world helps us recover from sickness and prevents psychological burnout. The extinction of vast numbers of species and its habitat will diminish and ultimately threaten the human condition.

Advocates of the biophilia hypothesis (and I am one of them) suggest taking a systemic evolutionary point of view, regarding all other species as our kin.[150] Humanity did not arrive on earth as an alien entity from another planet. On the contrary, we evolved from other organisms that were already present. In nature's gigantic laboratory—conducting experiment upon experiment trying out new life forms—one of the outcomes was the human species.

Some biologists suggest that our yearning to relate to other elements in the natural world may be one of the reasons why we care for animals. Our evolutionary genetic links may explain why humans are attracted to animal babies as well as baby humans. It would be unwise to kill our young or the young of our lower-level cousins as (from a systemic point of view) that would have a negative effect on the natural population as a whole, and endanger human survival. We do care for our planet, even though so many of our actions seem to indicate otherwise.

Biophilia is not merely a genetically based, evolutionary pattern; it comprises complex internalized rules and emotional responses as a result of socialization patterns. Our love of nature has both a genetic and a developmental/cultural connection that is constantly being expanded and revised. Multiple emotional responses are woven into symbols composing a large part of our culture. Our need to conserve derives from more than merely altruistic sympathy or compassionate concerns: it is driven by a profound sense of self-interest and a biological imperative. Just as a baby cannot exist without a mother, as individuals we cannot exist without a context, the most obvious one being our natural environment. Caring for nature has always been a key to our own survival.

Biophilia is a corollary to basic ecological interconnectedness. The more species that inhabit an ecosystem (forest, mountain range, marsh, lake, river, or ocean), the more productive and stable that ecosystem will be. The naturalist's love for nature, and the drive to conserve it, are expressions of this genetically determined human drive. This is why nature makes us feel good, reduces stress, and helps our mental health. Our mental and physical wellbeing are compelling arguments for nature conservation. Cultivating the wilderness should not be considered a luxury in developed societies. We must recognize our basic human need to affiliate deeply and positively with life's diversity.

If biophilia is the expression of our in-built love for nature, biophobia—the fear of the natural world, or the sense of danger it awakens in us—is also an integral part of our repertoire of responses to the natural world. The Greeks associated the irrational, bowel-loosening fear that can come over you in the woods with the presence or influence of the god Pan (from which we derive the word "panic"). Diana imagery, with its duality of attraction and fear of nature, is present in all of us, and profoundly affects our response to wild places. The realistic tension derived from the threat and danger posed by nature is part of the challenge of survival. I would go as far as to say that as well as our capacity to appreciate nature's magnificence and sublimity, some measure of fear of the natural world is essential for our survival. The power of the wilderness to inspire and challenge our physical and mental development requires the recognition of fear and danger.

Clearly, nature's diversity and healthy functioning are worth maintaining because they represent the best chance for us to experience a satisfying and meaningful existence. A degraded relationship with nature increases the likelihood of a diminished material, social, and psychological existence—slum areas in cities, without any green spaces, are a good example.

🛋

Biophilic development

Some people seem to be more sensitive to biophilia than others, and have a more intense relationship with the natural world—I am one of them. But why, if we are all the same under the skin, do these differences occur? To answer this question, we have to look at culture and socialization patterns. For example, a sheep farmer may not have the same emotional response to young lambs larking about in a field as the visiting city dweller who goes gaga over their cuteness. For the farmer, lambs represent future food or wool yield.

City people who talk about "getting out in the country" (visiting a farm, taking a walk in the woods, going to the seashore, walking in the mountains, or even relaxing in a park) have a very different notion of exploiting nature than, say, a pygmy living in central Congo. Our biophilic roots and socialization patterns explain why some people seem to thrive in the outdoors, while others are frightened at finding themselves in a wood. People who are highly biophilically sensitized can be stimulated just by being in an office with lots of plants, or keeping a caged bird or aquarium at home.

When human beings remove themselves from their natural environment, biophilic learning can become distorted, contributing to feelings of anomy, alienation, isolation, and loneliness, and can even lead to mental disorders. Our agricultural, industrial, and information technologies may have contributed to this state of estrangement. Many of these technologies have caused nature to become unbalanced, facilitating outbreaks of disease and the loss of species. As our evolutionary past has made us particularly susceptible to biophilia, this might explain why we only really thrive through work or hobbies that help us stay connected at all times to some non-human elements of the natural world.

These hypotheses are all well and good, but the fact is that our relationship to nature is one of the most unexamined areas of human psychology. Very few psychologists have addressed this issue seriously, and explored how this relationship influences and affects our personal growth and development. We are only just beginning to develop a more systemic outlook and starting to explore the deeper layers of our unconscious mind that relate to the natural world. Far too many questions about our interconnectedness with nature remain unanswered. For example, how does urbanization affect the human mind? How does crowding relate to outbreaks of violent behavior? How does it affect our propensity to wage war? How can violence be kept within boundaries? How has the distortion of our biophilic heritage affected our mental health? Why do some people inflict damage on the natural world, while others fight to prevent it? What are the causes of such estrangement?

Urbanization means that some of us are totally alienated from the natural world. Others maintain a very close connection. Perhaps, from a developmental point of view (nature versus nurture), there may be a specific periods in childhood when we develop appreciation and respect for the natural world most readily. Do we need to create childhood experiences that enable biophilia to take root? We may have to facilitate experiences through which children can learn about the interconnectedness of nature, to help them understand the cycle of life. As a child, I acquired what felt like a magical capacity to look at nature, to see the land as an animal does, to experience the sky from the perspective of a bird, to smell the earth deeply, and listen to the sounds of the rain. When we have these kinds of experiences, we find reserves of strength when times are difficult that will stay with us all our life.

The artist and writer Gwen Raverat was Charles Darwin's granddaughter. In her memoir, *Period Piece* (1952), she recounts a childhood experience of biophilia—the profound attraction of some black pebbles that her grandfather had brought back from his travels and set into a path at his house:

"I adored those pebbles. I mean literally, adored; worshipped. This passion made me feel quite sick sometimes. And it was adoration I felt for the foxgloves at Down, and for the stiff red clay out of the Sandwalk clay pit; and for the beautiful white paint on the nursery floor. This kind of feeling hits you in the stomach and in the ends of your fingers, and it is probably the most important thing in life. Long after I have forgotten all my human loves, I shall still remember the smell of a gooseberry leaf or the feel of the wet grass on my bare feet; or the pebbles in the path. In the long run it is this feeling that makes life worth living, this which is the driving force behind the artist's urge to create."[151]

I don't want my children's and grandchildren's concept of nature to be dominated by fake, Disney-ish imagery. I don't want them to acquire a distorted perception of nature's realities. I don't want them to be separated from the experience of the natural world, which is highly likely in an urbanized environment. Children growing up in large towns and cities no longer learn how to read the great book of nature. They have no chance to realize that one of our tasks in life is to live in agreement with nature. Without continuous hands-on experience, it is impossible for them to internalize the kind of deep intuitive understanding of the natural world that is the foundation of sustainable development.

As adults, we have the responsibility of creating a learning environment that reaffirms a more realistic view of the cycle of life, where there is acceptance that life has a beginning, an end, and a new beginning. Observing my own children, I have seen that not much is required to help them develop a special affinity for the environment—it comes naturally to them. A good illustration of this is how very young children, whatever culture they come from, quickly understand the elementary rules of predatory behavior, rapidly assessing who is the prey and who is the predator, an important skill from an evolutionary survival point of view. According to the anthropologist Clark Barrett:

"Children in industrialized countries are very unlikely to encounter wild lions, jaguars, crocodiles, or sharks, and they are unlikely indeed ever to encounter a *Tyrannosaurus rex*. Why, then, are children's cognitive resources so devoted to an understanding of animals and their behavior?[152] ...

From an evolutionary perspective, it is not implausible to assume that the basic set of intentional schemas that are part of children's and adults' capacity to reason about animal and human behavior have been shaped by natural selection, albeit perhaps in skeletal forms that are then fleshed out by experience.[153] ...

A study in which children were asked to play out an imaginary predator-prey interaction using animal models found that by age four, children reliably attribute the goals of prey capture and predator evasion to predator and prey respectively, and use these goals to accurately predict the responses of predator and prey to each others' behavior, as proposed by the predator-prey schema hypothesis. Identical results were found both for city-dwelling children in Berlin, Germany, and rural children among the hunter-horticulturalist Shuar of Ecuador. Furthermore, children understood that encounters with a predator can lead to death, and were able to make realistic judgments about the behavioral consequences of death, i.e., that the ability to act ceases at death, and that this is irreversible."[154]

Barrett suggests that children have an instinctive understanding of the workings of the natural world. This may very well be an evolutionary legacy of archaic prey-predator experiences, explaining the fascination of small children for the natural world—and dangerous creatures in particular. However, to further children's natural inclination for biophilia, from a developmental point of view, they must be given appropriately timed opportunities to learn about the natural world. Their learning needs to include developmentally appropriate contact with nature in their formative years so they can bond with the natural world, learn to love it, and feel comfortable being part of it. Because we tend to bond with what we know well, it is critical that young children be given many opportunities to learn how to do so.

My youngest daughter Alicia first went out bird hunting at the age of seven. Her desire to do so must have had something to do with imitating and identifying with her parents. She had seen me hunt, many times. Child development studies tell us that copying adult actions is a universal human activity. The willingness to assume that an action has some unknown purpose, and to copy it, may be part of how humans develop and share culture. Clearly, my daughter wanted to follow my example. And perhaps, on my part, one of the reasons for giving in and allowing her to come with me was to help her understand death better. I have never felt that making death a taboo is the best way of dealing with this difficult subject. Perhaps by giving her a chance to pursue this bird, she would have a better idea of the meaning of mortality and vulnerability. She would grasp one of the realities of life—that death is not reversible.

However, I also suspected that given my path as a hunter, it was more than likely that she had already become quite aware of the fact of death. She had seen me bringing dead animals home. She had seen dead birds, insects, and animals at the side of the road. She saw death portrayed every day on the television. What's more, she is an avid reader of fairy tales and it is hard to miss death in those stories. So, after some initial reluctance, I said she could join me.

The bird was a Swainson's francolin, a kind of partridge that is plentiful in the specific area of Zimbabwe where we were hunting. I remember very clearly

her efforts to sneak up to the francolin and get in range. She missed the bird with her first shot; it jumped up, but didn't go very far. Nobody was bird hunting in the area, which made the birds relatively easy to approach. Her second shot was a hit. Seeing her come to me, proudly holding the bird, is a sight I will not easily forget. But much more importantly, it will be a memory that will stay with her for the rest of her life. The older I get, the more I prefer to see other people hunt. Having reached the stage of generativity, I like to pass on some of my knowledge to the next generation. I like to contribute to the continuation of hunting.

My orientation toward becoming a psychoanalyst and organizational anthropologist must have originated with my observations of insects, birds, and other creatures when I was very young. Many of my recollections reflect an early awareness of some primary relatedness to the earth and the universe. These early experiences with the natural world must have been positively linked with the development of play, imagination, and creativity. I know that I could sit for hours watching insect behavior. As a child, I was particularly intrigued by the ant lion, and its habit of digging shallow cone-shaped pits and waiting at the bottom for an ant or other insect to slip on the loose sand and fall in—the suspense of it all. What this says about me, and the way I dealt with the aggression within, is another matter. To me, these observations of nature were imaginative opportunities for adventure, construction, and re-invention. And it taught me about death.

Childhood is the time during which the most active creative learning takes place. Early exposure to the natural world creates a special sense of wonder that may serve as a life-long source of joy and enrichment, as well as being an impetus, or motivation, for further learning. We must find ways to let our children roam beyond the pavement, to go to places where they can tunnel, climb, swing, and fall. Human beings have basic exploratory need systems; it is easy for children to find excitement and beauty in outdoor physical activities, without direct instruction. A solid interaction between the child and the natural environment makes for authentic childhood experiences. By reinforcing the child's ways of knowing, we will foster a life-long love of the natural world.

Conversely, if children's natural attraction to nature is not given the opportunity to flourish during their early years, biophobia, or aversion to nature, may result. Biophobia can range from discomfort at being in outdoor places to active scorn for anything that is not man-made or constructed. Biophobia is also expressed in the tendency to look exploitatively at nature, which can play havoc with both the natural environment and the human spirit. Just a few examples of the physical manifestations of biophobia include strip mines, clear-cuts, blighted cities, polluted rivers, and toxic air. Much of the scenery I have encountered when traveling in places like Siberia or Africa blight the eyes.

The biophilic hypothesis helps negate the anti-hunting lobby's arguments about humankind's moral duty to abstain from killing out of respect for nature. Anti-hunters who deny this connectivity are being biologically naïve. We have an evolutionarily determined niche as omnivores. We may not like it, but it is a fact of life. Many natural practices are biologically determined. Such systemic certainties cut through many sophistical arguments about animal rights. For example, when a human being kills an animal, does he or she violate the animal's right to life? If the answer to this question is "yes," where does that leave the fox that kills a rabbit? Has the fox violated the rabbit's right to life? Or was it just performing a natural, inevitable act? Could we use the word immoral (overused in the antis' lexicon) about the fox's action?

Fair chase

Given our biophilic heritage, the evidence that humans depend on other living organisms for their survival, and the dramatic intrusion into the natural world of agricultural, industrial, and information technologies, it is essential to have a "conservation ethic" that respects wildlife and the habitats of other animals. Hunters make particularly good stewards of the natural world through the "rules" of fair chase. It goes without saying that hunters have technological advantages that game cannot appreciate or share; and these advantages increase all the time with our technological expertise. In the interest of fairness, specific rules need to be followed in the hunt, many of which are culture specific, vary greatly, and can be defined in many different ways. Generally speaking, these rules regulate the actions of the hunter so that wildlife has a fair chance to escape.

These rules make a lot of sense. As I have said repeatedly, hunting should never be easy. If animals don't have a reasonable chance of getting away, the hunt becomes meaningless. When I engage in the natural struggle of predator and prey, nature has to be treated with respect. There should be no short cuts. This is one of the reasons why mountain hunting has such a special cachet. As I know myself, getting a trophy too easily diminishes its value. The best way to measure whether hunting behavior is ethical or unethical is to assess the chances of game to escape unharmed; any practice that gives the hunter an unfair advantage over his prey is deemed unethical. In real hunting, we can never be sure we will be successful.

I have to confess to having once hunted on a game farm in Texas. It was fascinating to see the great variety and density of animals, especially some of the more exotic ones. I also gained some insight into the importance of "breeding" these exotic animals, which are often endangered or extinct in their original habitat. But I have never felt very good about that hunt; it was too easy. Even though the animals had a large territory in which to roam—and a good chance of avoiding the hunter—I didn't feel that it was truly fair chase and I don't ever want to do it again. However, I have hunted many times on very large territories in South Africa and Namibia that are rather like game farms, in that the public or private landowners run hunting safaris within them. Hunting here is a very different story. I have been "skunked" while hunting in these places more often than I have been successful.

From a fair chase point of view, I may even be quite pleased when I don't get what I want (more in retrospect, perhaps, than at the time). Failing to get my quarry keeps me interested. This is sometimes called the Zeigarnik effect—named after the Russian psychologist Bluma Zeigarnik[155]—which maintains that people remember uncompleted or interrupted tasks better than completed ones. For example, many years ago I was fishing for trout in a river in Vermont. It had been a long drive to get there from Montreal, where I was living at the time, and I carried on busily casting until it was almost dark. I was just telling myself, a few more casts in this very attractive pool and then I'll head home, when, at that specific moment as my fly landed, a gigantic trout rose—larger than any I had ever seen in that river—and hit the fly. In my excitement, I was too quick in setting the hook. I pulled the fly right out of the trout's jaw. After that mishap, I kept on casting for a very long time. I couldn't forget the image of that particular trout. It lingered with me. A week later, I drove the three hours from Montreal to the same spot, and cast incessantly for many, many hours. And I went back the week after—and the week after that. But to no avail. I never saw that trout again, but it has never left me. It is still eidetically etched in my memory.

I had a similar experience fishing for salmon with my daughter Oriane at the Moisie river in Quebec. Oriane caught a very big salmon on a dry fly. Because she was standing high on the rocks, the guide who was with us had to go down to the water level to net the fish and I ran to help him. I saw the fish—at least a 30-pounder—come up from the water, almost spent. My daughter saw it too and I saw her smile. The guide swung the net, but missed, and cut the line. My daughter and I still talk about that fish. Do we talk about other fish we've caught? Not really.

The Zeigarnik effect has been at work on numerous occasions away from the riverbank, as well. I can still see that large Marco Polo sheep disappearing high in the snowy mountains. I remember the "pink" bear that disappeared into the brush and the gray ghost of a glacier bear that simply vanished after looking at me motionless for a very long time. I still dream of the big ibex that I missed lying flat-out on the rocks in the Pamir. I remember the wolves that were gnawing at a moose carcass, but saw me coming. Then there is that yellow-backed duiker that vanished in a bako of the Central African Republic, and the nice roebuck that got away in a cornfield in Estonia...

Real hunters believe in fair chase, and never take unfair advantage of the game being hunted. In Holland, where I was born, we talk about the need for a hunter to be *"weidelijk"*—to hunt in a correct, ethical way. *"Weidelijk"* hunters are familiar with the ins-and-outs of hunting, respect nature, and hunt responsibly. They obey the laws of the country in which they hunt. They do everything in their power to prevent the animals they hunt suffering. If animals are wounded, they follow and recuperate them. But the Zeigarnik effect is also something to be cherished.

Trophy hunting is an important element of fair chase hunting. Trophy hunters predetermine the criteria for the game they want to obtain. For example, in Europe, much attention is paid to whether an animal is taken at an appropriate time in its life cycle. If not, the person responsible for the territory who takes the decision to harvest the animal may get a red mark on his or her record. Picking the right animals is what makes their reputation. Non-Europeans find it strange that many of the animals taken are those with miserable or "unusual" trophies—not the kind many US hunters look for. In most cases, there's no need to get the measuring tape out. I get irritable with people who run about with tape measures. That is not what hunting is all about. Although I appreciate obtaining a good trophy, is size the only thing that matters? But for the European gamekeeper it is important that "miserable" and very old animals are taken out of the herd. This contrasts sharply with deer hunting in North America, for example, where too often the first animal encountered is shot, without considering whether it is too young, and far from its prime.

When I hunted chamois in Austria, Willie, my guide, spent an enormous amount of time studying the animals before allowing me to shoot (very different from hunting chamois in New Zealand.) And I lost count of the number of red stags Willie decided we couldn't go after. If I was successful, and obtained the animal, it would be at least a year before I received the trophy. The horns of any animal taken (with teeth—to determine the animal's exact age) are sent to the annual exhibition of animals harvested in the region. A jury decides on examination whether the animal has been taken at the right time. A certain amount of shame falls on gamekeepers who have not assessed the animal properly—but additionally, sanctions can be imposed, for example, limiting the following year's quota.

Once, when I was bear hunting in Kamchatka (where I have been many times), we saw a bear way off in the distance. We crept up to it but when we were close I realized—despite the local guide's urging—that the bear was far too young to take. He deserved to live for many more years. In the end, I waved at it until it went away. The numbers of excursions I have made for roebuck without taking one are impossible to recall. Maybe their time would come a few years later, but not yet. It was the same when hunting cape or savanna buffalo. There have been many occasions when I have let magnificent specimens go because they were still in their breeding prime, not the kind of old duggaboy I was looking for. In those instances, I quietly withdrew.

The older I get, the more important the aesthetics of hunting become to me. Obtaining what I am after, has become less and less important. Nowadays, more often than not, I let the animal go. The aesthetic aspect of being in nature— being in a beautiful place—is what really counts. For example, I remember hunting for capercaillie and black grouse in the middle of Sweden with a dog that had been specially trained for the purpose. The Finnish Spitz—which looks a bit like a fox with a curved tail—is an expert at birds, especially black grouse and capercaillie. It makes a great noise when the birds are treeing and is superb at flushing them. There is nothing more exciting than following the sound of a barking dog and sneaking up, unnoticed, on a capercaillie nestled in a tree. On that occasion, I was lucky enough to shoot a few birds but getting them was a minor part of the whole experience, which remains intensely vivid to me. What I remember most is sitting on a stump, eating a sandwich, keeping warm by the fire the gamekeeper had made, looking at the snowy landscape, and feeling extremely content.

I have a similar memory of hunting for capercaillie in Russia in the spring— although we went about it in a very different way. The yellow-billed capercaillie is similar to its Eastern, black-billed or rock capercaillie cousin, except that it is somewhat larger, and has a larger bill. Because it was spring, getting closer to the bird necessitated starting out very early in the morning, and a kind of dance. The first time I went on this kind of hunt, the Russian game warden took my hand, and pulled me along every time the bird stopped singing. In the last phase of its mating song, the capercaillie swallows its tongue and becomes temporarily deaf, the ideal time to make an approach. Onlookers might well have wondered what the two of us were doing, performing our forest ballet, hand in hand. Eventually, the guide stopped the dance and began making desperate silent gestures. It took me some time to understand what he was trying to tell me. The bird was in the tree right above us.

Because game animals are well equipped and highly effective at survival, it takes an extraordinary degree of skill for most hunters to hunt them successfully, if we are prepared to follow fair chase rules and do so on their terms. Hunting according to self-imposed limitations that result in a relatively low success rate may be an indicator that these rules are being applied. The hunting threat I represent should be close to the normal dangers the animal faces every day—I should act like one of their natural predators. (As I said earlier, lions, for example, have only a 30 percent success rate.) And if I am hunting in the animal's natural environment, giving it a sporting chance, the smart ones still usually get away.

Fair chase implies involvement and commitment to issues relating to wildlife, habitat and environmental concerns, and the development of the skills and knowledge necessary to become a safe, responsible and effective hunter. Many of these build on ancient survival skills developed by our ancestors— identification, shot placement and shot selection, precision shooting, and the ability to track and recover wounded wildlife. The most successful hunter is not necessarily the best shot; it is usually the person who is really familiar with their quarry, and has a deep and intimate knowledge of its habitat and behavior.

But with fair chase, rules will never replace ethics, and as I have indicated, the rules vary between different cultures. For example, in Holland a hunter can only shoot at a flying bird or a running rabbit or hare. In the Scandinavian countries, Northern Canada, or Siberia, a light caliber rifle is the weapon of choice for capercaillie or snowshoe hare and you wouldn't usually shoot at these animals when they are flying or running—particularly when hunting in the snow on skies. There are also cultural differences concerning distance. What is the right distance to shoot? How far is too far? Again, it is possible to be a law-abiding hunter but not a fair chase hunter. For example, it is not illegal to shoot at a running sheep 500 meters away, or at geese or ducks flying 80 meters overhead. But is it really ethical? At those distances, there is a high probability that we will only wound the animal. I am always astonished when I hear stories of people shooting at animals at these distances. It is simply not done in most European countries but it certainly happens elsewhere. I once visited the famous gun maker Kenny Jarrett (from whom I have bought a number of guns), in Jackson, South Carolina, who told me about his thousand-yard shooting range. Obviously, some people have the kinds of rifles, ammunition, trajectory knowledge, and skills capable of accuracy at such ranges.

Clearly, if you can hit a target at such a long distance, stalking the animal becomes less of an issue. But can this really be called fair chase? To me, it looks more like long-distance target practice. You need to be a specialist in ballistics to get it right and there's an increased likelihood of wounding the animal. I view these activities as borderline unethical.

I must confess that once, hunting in Iran, I aimed at a bezoar goat (a kind of ibex) from a very long distance. It was my second visit to the country. My first attempt to hunt for this kind of ibex—*Capra aegagrus,* the wild goat of Iran and adjacent regions—had come to a bad end. There were too many people trying to "help" me, disturbing the game, making my hunt very difficult, and I ended up missing a very nice ibex. On that trip, despite some strenuous climbing, I didn't get a second chance. Now I was back; it was the last day of the hunt and after a long hike up the mountains, I had only seen one very spooked bezoar goat at a great distance. It was getting late, time to turn back and get down the mountain before it got dark. Suddenly, one of the guides became extremely agitated. Down below, he had seen a group of nannies with one male. As the guide was some way in front of me, I only saw the ibex running up the next mountain. The male was traversing the cliff opposite the mountain on which we were positioned. Against my better judgment—particularly because I had no stable rest—I shot at the running ibex. As I have said repeatedly, I am not

really a good shot, but this time Diana was looking favorably on me. Not only had I killed a running ibex, but also the only tree growing on the side of the cliff opposite had caught the animal in its branches. If it hadn't, the ibex would have fallen down into the ravine, the body mauled, and the horns probably smashed to smithereens. I measured the distance with my laser binoculars. I had shot the animal at precisely 376 meters. It was a never to be repeated feat. I was elated but also totally exhausted and unable to go down the mountain, and climb up again to get at the ibex. But the young man who was with me, climbed down, put the ibex on his back (without gutting it), and climbed all the way up again. Given the fact that males can weigh up to 90 kilos, he must have been in prime shape to have been able to do so.

As much as we aim for fair chase, and however much we may regret it, there will always be times when an animal is wounded. If you hunt and shoot a lot, such events are inevitable. A branch may deflect the bullet; the bullet may be poor quality; the wind may be too strong; you're out of breath and trembling too much. Shit happens. Most hunters have been in these situations. The wounding and losing of game are some of the greatest concerns of the anti-hunting community. As a hunter who has signed up for fair chase, I do everything in my power to recover game. I avoid shooting beyond reasonable range (beyond my personal limits or that of my equipment). But again, in the excitement of the chase, these things happen. All big game hunters may occasionally be tempted to take a shot beyond their skill level. Water fowlers may shoot at ducks and geese far beyond the power of their shotgun. Avoiding high-risk and selecting high probability shots is the mark of an accomplished and fair chase hunter.

There are many contingencies associated with the ethics of hunting. For example, is the use of electronic game calls ethical? Or the use of all-terrain vehicles? Obviously, running antelopes down in the desert with motor vehicles or aircraft, or hunting bear from helicopters, or spotlighting deer, are not examples of fair chase. For example, in Kazakhstan the locals (including the local police) used motorbikes to go after saiga antelopes on poaching expeditions. The people were driven by poverty and other everyday challenges and the saiga were taken for their meat and horns, which are used in traditional Chinese medicine. Unsurprisingly, the population of saiga crashed, and they are now totally protected. In this case, the saiga's fate was closely tied to economic changes in the former Soviet Union, whose breakup in 1991 was accompanied by the collapse of rural economies, causing widespread unemployment and poverty. The local people needed to totally change their attitude toward this game species to help it recover, as it has now done.

There are also many borderline situations, very much dependent on the socio-cultural environment where the hunt takes place, and the time it happens. For example, is baiting deer or bears unethical? In some areas the use of bait is prohibited, in others not, as baiting is often the only way to entice these animals out into the open and have a chance at them. In the Northern part of Alberta where I have hunted many times, and where the boreal forests are impenetrable, it is extremely difficult to hunt bears without baiting. Earlier in this book I described getting bears by sitting out at the edge of an oat field. Bears are crazy about oats— was this baiting? Was it unethical? I wouldn't have stalked a bear on ground strewn with dead leaves. It would sound like walking on potato chips. The only way to have a chance of a bear was to get it to come to me. On the other hand, it would not be ethical to bait bears in the mountains, where you can see far and wide.

The same argument can be made for leopard hunting in Africa. Hunting leopards is almost impossible without the use of bait. Although I have visited Africa many, many times, I have only once had a glimpse of a leopard in daylight. Leopards are night hunters, and tracking them, given the faint prints they leave, is in most cases almost impossible.

I have been very successful in hunting leopard and bongo with dogs. Again, is this fair chase? Is it ethical to have a dog yapping at the bongo, to stop its flight? But very few hunters have been successful at sneaking up on a bongo in the thick rainforest without the use of dogs. In most cases, the bongo hears the hunters before the hunters see it, and disappears. A dog makes quite a difference, as the yelping distracts the bongo, giving the hunter a chance to get closer.

Many hunters make a distinction between eating what they kill and not killing what they don't eat. If the game is not eaten, some people view the hunt as unethical. This implies that few predators are taken. I try to be consistent in following the rule "eat what you kill," and in my time I have eaten leopard, cougar, lynx, and bobcat, but not hyena or lion. This leaves open the question whether hunting is permissible if an animal is only killed for the challenge it represents. Of course, other reasons can be given—the most common is excessive predation, of which wolves are a good example. Wolves first crossed the Alps and re-entered France from Italy, without any human assistance, in the early 1990s, having been exterminated in France in 1939. Although the European wolf population is protected by the Bern Convention (1979), the French government now allows shepherds to defend their sheep against wolves. This has put environmental groups and sheep farmers at loggerheads. I do hunt predators for the challenge—but I have a good friend who will not hunt cats. There is no straightforward answer to what constitutes ethics in hunting.

rᆏ

Existentialism

So, why do I hunt? Most people put this question to me sooner or later. Why do I need to spend time in the woods, mountains, savannas, rain forests, tundra or steppes, learning about and pursuing animals? Why is this so important to me? One reason was summed up by the philosopher Bertrand Russell in his Nobel Prize lecture: "Civilized life has altogether grown too tame, and, if it is to be stable, it must provide a harmless outlet for the impulses which our remote ancestors satisfied in hunting."[156] Ortega y Gasset, in *Meditations on Hunting*, points out that life is a dynamic interchange between man and his surroundings. He explains "the most appreciated, enjoyable occupation for the normal man has always been hunting."[157] Ortega views hunting as the purest form of human happiness, and emphasizes that he uses the word happiness, not pleasure, deliberately. Although there is pleasure in all happiness, pleasure is passive, while happiness necessitates energetic effort. The microbiologist René Dubos extrapolated on this aspect of happiness, when he said:

"Even though he lived by hunting, primitive man worshipped animals. In modern man also, the desire to hunt is paradoxically compatible with love of wild life. Hunting is a highly satisfying occupation for many persons because it calls into play a multiplicity of physical and mental attributes that appear to be woven into the human fabric... Certain aspects of a hunter's life are probably more in keeping with man's basic temperament and biological nature than urban life as presently practiced."[158]

I began this chapter by presenting one of the overriding arguments for hunting: the biophilic one. We can assume that our appreciation of nature, wildlife, and our disposition to hunt is partially hardwired. In evolutionary terms, we are a product of nature's mutative force. The passion to hunt is in our blood. How it manifests itself, however, very much depends on prevailing socio-cultural influences: I assume that this feeling expresses itself very differently for people brought up in a city state like Singapore compared to people growing up in the Swedish countryside. Having reflected deeply on these issues (and having discussed my interests in hunting and fishing with people who have nothing to do with them), I realize that my motivation to hunt is very complex, and has developed from a number of economic, social, and very personal influences.

What has hunting done to and for me? Why is it so important? Here, in brief, are the results of some of my reflections, summaries of my thoughts about this lifelong passion. Some of them inevitably overlap.

⌐

Reflection 1 Managing the aggression within

From an evolutionary perspective, I strongly believe that the desire to hunt, the biophilic part of me, is wired into my DNA. I see the hunting imperative as one of the most fundamental elements of my (and *Homo sapiens'*) nature. The intensity of this desire, and the way it manifests itself, differs from individual to individual, depending on differing cultural and socialization practices. Each of us tries to find appropriate ways to express our evolutionary heritage.

To me, hunting is one of the most natural ways of expressing what is essential about me. It is my way of actualizing *Homo sapiens'* ancient lineage. Being in the wilderness makes it easier to accept the wildness within me. Although admittedly it is not necessarily a conscious process, I hunt in an effort to maintain these primordial connections. I hunt to prevent modern living removing me spiritually from the natural cycle of life. And as inter-species aggression is to be recommended above intra-species aggression, hunting can also be viewed as a less subtle form of sublimation. The asphalt jungle of the city is not for me. After a while, being surrounded by all these high rises (like in cities like Singapore or New York), I need to be in the country to feel at ease.

A fox pursues a pheasant instinctually, and many hunters seem to experience the same impulses when they pursue game. The hunt brings these feelings out into the open. And although others may be frightened by these intra-personal experiences—this evidence of the aggression within—I like the wildness of it all. When I hunt I am immersed mentally, physically, and even spiritually in an age-old predatory-prey relationship that is the prevailing model in nature. While hunting, I relate to very basic instincts and memories that I have inherited from my archaic ancestors. Through participation in the hunt, I become an active participant in nature. Hunting gratifies some of my basic psychological and physiological needs in a way that will never happen by going to McDonald's and ordering a burger.

I think it is this connection to something very primitive, to the natural rhythms of life, attuning myself to the seasons and (at times) being placed in extreme situations that explains the hunt's special attractiveness for me. I acknowledge that many of my associations with hunting are outside conscious awareness, and are derived (as Carl Jung would say) from humankind's collective unconscious.[159]

⌐ᴎ

Reflection 2 Playing the game

This admission may be abhorrent to many anti-hunting groups but, to me, hunting is also a type of pleasurable play. Maybe this is another form of "regression in the service of the ego," a therapeutic-like regression that fosters my creativity. It is a way of adapting to changing internal and external conditions—of getting unstuck, and moving forward in life. By this I mean the capacity to relax my hold on reality, to experience aspects of myself that are ordinarily inaccessible, and to emerge with increased adaptive capacity as a result of these creative integrations.

Positive regressive processes are linked to early days of make-believe—childhood games, in particular peek-a-boo, the earliest game we play as babies. This game should not be seen as merely innocuous. There is much more to it than that. For example, the father of psychoanalysis, Sigmund Freud, observing his young grandson Ernst, learned firsthand about this capacity to play, and interpreted it as representing the child's inner concerns. He recorded how his grandson would toss a spool of string over the side of his cot and retrieve it, a game like "peek-a-boo" that he called "*fort-da*" ("here-there").[160] Extrapolating on Freud's insights, developmental psychologists believe the peek-a-boo game demonstrates an infant's initial inability to understand the permanence of things. This game can be interpreted as a critical marker in the development of our self-awareness and identity. Bear in mind that for the infant "out of sight, is out of mind."

While peek-a-boo differentiates between looking and being looked at, another childhood game, hide-and-seek, is a game of detection. In hide-and-seek, one player gives the others time to hide and then attempts to find them. In this game, the pleasure and excitement come from knowing that you are being sought. There is also an element of real fear involved—the danger that the person who is "lost" may not be "found." The game teaches endurance and develops courage, self-confidence, and alertness.

Hide-and-seek is one of the most important games that children play among themselves because it takes place in that intermediate area between play and reality described so well by the psychiatrist Donald Winnicott.[161] According to Winnicott, it also fosters the creative process. In hide-and-seek, we can be the center of attention, and tease others into mild frustration as they fail to discover where we are.

From an evolutionary perspective, games like peek-a-boo and hide-and-seek relate to a large component of animal behavior, hiding from predators and searching for food. These games are also about the development of a greater awareness of our own position in relation to others and external events. They enable us to be on guard for the unexpected and sharpen perceptions. Think back to playing hide-and-seek when you were a child, hiding alone in a safe place, how much more you noticed—the different textures of clothes in a cupboard, the smell of dust under a bed. Or, if you played outdoors, what grass looked like close up, insects buzzing, the feel of a breeze, the sounds of birds. Hunting is a logical continuation of these games, but with different stakes. The hunt provides us with a new opportunity to hone our observational skills. When I hunt, I play hide-and-seek with the game and, to continue the developmental process, after playing the game myself, I have continued playing it with my children and grandchildren.

The hide-and-seek element of hunting also has an element of surprise. Like children wondering what is in their Christmas stocking, I enjoy anticipating what the game has to offer. What am I going to find, when I am busily glassing from the top of a mountain? What will I find at the next bend in the river? I like this kind of tension. It is similar to the feeling of having a fish on the hook. What kind of fish is it? If it really pulls—how big is it? I enjoy hoping, searching, and finding. It all makes for an enormous amount of suspense.

Recently, I was fishing in Brazil's Pantanal (Portuguese for "large swamp"), the world's largest wetland, which aesthetically was a truly special experience. The birdlife was incredible but the birds that particularly caught my imagination were the large macaws that flew over our little boat. Their loud calls, squawks, and screams echoed through the forest canopy. Kingfishers colored like jewels flew everywhere. Everywhere, I saw capybaras, the largest rodents in the world, and jacarés or alligators, and in the middle of this spectacle, I was casting for fish. Given the diversity of fish life in the Pantanal, every time I had a bite, I was excited. Would I see what was on the other end of the line or would the fish break off first? The tension I experienced was a clear reminder of the hide-and-seek games of my youth that retained their important developmental influence.

Reflection 3 A greater scheme of things

Being in the wilderness gives me the opportunity to be part of something bigger than myself, part of the mystery of nature. I am convinced that the opportunity to appreciate natural beauty has made a positive contribution to my mental health. The vision of a snow-capped mountain, the path of a meandering stream, or a sweep of windswept tundra, has always been a kind of special spiritual experience for me. There are endless opportunities for meditation while sitting in a blind, waiting for wild boar, roebuck, red deer, or chamois, or at the forest edge, hoping for deer or bear. Climbing onto a mountain ledge, glassing the world below, creates a great pause in my usual, hectic life style. Hunting is an authentic and irreplaceable means of communion, not only with the animal world but also with the greater, non-human world. Hunting—the ultimate life-and death activity—awakens the spiritual side in me. It reconciles me to the often-violent nature of the human condition.

Hunting (or fishing) is the easiest way for me to get in a state of flow.[162] When I think about the occasions when I have felt truly alive, most were in the outdoors, when I could forget all my daily concerns and troubles, and time and space seemed to become unimportant. Through nature, I acquire a sensation of immortality—of being part of a greater scheme of things.

Reflection 4 Transcending death

Hunting is a magnificent way of overcoming the fear of death—death anxiety being our most fundamental driver. For example, I get feelings of joy, renewal, regeneration, and continuity from blue skies, a mushroom springing up in a meadow, fiddleheads at the edge of a stream, or a whitetail deer crossing a river.

We all find ways of repressing the knowledge of our mortality. There are numerous cultural mechanisms for doing so, including ideas about personal transcendence, such as resurrection, reincarnation, or continuing in some form of disembodied spiritual existence. The natural mode of symbolic immortality involves the continuation of the natural world beyond my own lifetime, as well the feeling of being part of an eternal universe. Our perceptions of nature and our associations with immortality are symbolically closely connected. A communion with nature is one way of assuring continuity.

Hunting gives me this sense of continuity and being surrounded by mountains, valleys, forests, streams, and oceans is a form of communion. To me, hunting is much more than a mere recreational activity. Ultimately it is participating in a sacred act that has as much or more meaning than participation in organized religion. Hunting forces us to deal with questions of life and death and becomes a way of transcending death. In that respect, I am a naturalistic pantheist—I feel part of nature and the wider universe.

Reflection 5 What makes a man?

Whatever the make-up of an individual's inner world, nature contains imagery that simultaneously frightens and attracts, seduces and repels. The wilderness can be a mysterious, secretive, and terrifying place—an arena where I can challenge myself—and thus a testing ground of the self. Being in wild places destroys whatever pretensions I have, and shows me the truth about myself. Nature, a place where tranquility and terror live harmoniously together, is a great place to test my hardiness and resilience. In the wilderness you go through rites of passage that foster self-discovery, community, and connection with the natural world. Forests and the fields, lakes and the rivers, mountains and the sea, are excellent teachers.

The dangers of the wilderness are very different from the dangers of the city, both literally and symbolically. The wilderness is a metaphor for an inner journey in which I come face-to-face with my inner demons. It is also a place where I can find solitude. In the wilderness I have to deal with two worlds that are superimposed onto each other: the real and the unreal. In the wilderness I can face and conquer my darkest fears and doubts.

But apart from this psychological journey, hunting is above all a physical testing ground. Living in primitive circumstances, surviving on woodcraft skills, helps me understand what really matters. Like everyone else, I am dependent on modern conveniences like microwave ovens, cell phones, PCs, iPads, cable television, hot and cold running water, electricity, pre-packaged food, and gas-powered vehicles. Without my experiences in the wilderness, I wouldn't survive a fortnight in the wild. It makes me wonder, at times, if too many of us have become aliens on our own planet—incapable of surviving, much less thriving, in a harmonious relationship with the wilderness around us. Wilderness experiences can be extremely informative. The wilderness is a living classroom in which knowledge about our world and of ourselves are waiting to be learned.

In wild country, I have learned about complex ecological processes, primitive cultures, and small group dynamics. The wilderness has also provided me with many lessons on leadership. I have learned to accept—and not always willingly—many responsibilities. Being in the wilderness taught me the power of self reliance, self-knowledge, and self-awareness. Finding myself in difficult settings tested my tenacity and courage and allowed me to transcend what I thought were my limits, to push myself beyond many comfort zones.

The wilderness has frequently tested my physical fitness and I have been able to endure things I never thought possible—a hunt for Marco Polo sheep in Tajikistan at 5000 meters with no oxygen; a horseback hunt in the High Altai mountains, during which I lost almost a kilo a day. It is profoundly satisfying to be able to pursue game under such extreme conditions. Hunting for wild goats and sheep may be the ultimate metaphor for struggling with the forces of nature, or striving for the unattainable.

Though my tutelage in the wild, I have learned how to identify edible and medicinal plants and mushrooms, how to collect drinking water, and how to creep silently through the underbrush and slide unseen over open ground. I know how to make fire in difficult circumstances. I have learned how to build a shelter with very few or no tools. I have developed the mental alertness and intuition to track animals. I have learned how to blend in to the jungle, the savannas, the tundra, or the mountains. Nowadays, very little disturbs me when I am in nature. This knowledge has been internalized. It is part of me.

Reflection 6 A healthy mind

I would argue that hunting forms the fourth basic human activity, along with eating, sleeping, and having sex. Looking at the world in which we live, with all its rampant violence and destruction, I am tempted to deduce that whenever we deny our instinctual needs, we create problems for ourselves, for those around us, and for the world.

The wilderness is a refuge from the many responsibilities society places on me. Hunting represents freedom from society's demands and restrictions. When I am hunting, I relax; I feel more at peace with myself; it reinvigorates me. I go to nature to be soothed and healed, and to have my senses put in order. It's better than a trip to the doctor; and it certainly tops the list of tranquilizers and stress reducers. I go to the wilderness to hear the wind and feel the rain, to see the clouds and the stars, to smell the pine trees, to drink the cold water of the streams, to listen to loons call, to eat wild strawberries, to pick wild mushrooms, to walk along the seashore collecting clams, and to realize why it is good to get away from urbanization.

Anyone who has climbed a mountain, walked in a forest, paddled down a river, or swum in an ocean will recall a wide range of emotions associated with such experiences. It might be exhilaration, fear, excitement, exhaustion, achievement, connection, frustration, awe, or wonder, along with all the other associated benefits of physical activity. These collective responses to outdoor experiences add up to a greater awareness of self, feelings of wellbeing, and a sense of connection with others and the world—all opportunities to facilitate significant growth.

The impact of going from "civilization" to the wilderness should not be underestimated; it's a dramatic changeover. Being placed in unfamiliar circumstances requires adaptation. As awesome as it is to be in mountains, forests, lakes, and moorlands, it can also be quite disturbing. It necessitates stepping outside my comfort zone, and doing some rapid sense-making. The novelty provides me with an opportunity to re-examine my beliefs about myself, and to have transformational experiences.

From my activities in the outdoors, I derive empowerment, confidence, self-esteem, hardiness, resilience, and problem-solving skills. My adventures have strengthened my ability to work as a member of a team. It is a therapeutic, curative experience—in short, being in the wilderness helps heal my soul. I attain a renewed sense of the earth as a home, of belonging to the land, of being connected to all other living things. As Ortega y Gasset once said, "When you are fed up with the troublesome present, take your gun, whistle for your dogs, and go out to the mountain."[163]

Reflection 7 Food for the table

There is an undeniable sense of triumph attached to coming home with an animal I have obtained while hunting—whether it is a buffalo, eland, or caribou. Being recognized as a provider—bringing home something I have gathered, rather than something I have bought in a supermarket—gives me the kind of sense of pride and fulfillment that you just don't get from receiving a salary statement in the mail. Being an effective food provider is part of our evolutionary and psychological make-up. But this very basic role—a defining human activity that originated in primeval times—seems to have lost its place in contemporary society.

I get a huge amount of satisfaction from being this kind of provider. It is easy to imagine a cave man coming back with whatever game he managed to kill, and the excitement of the hungry people who have been waiting for him. His arrival meant that they would not starve—at least, not yet. Such scenes probably still have a lot of meaning for Inuit or pygmy hunters returning to camp. Plucking a pheasant or duck in the garden with your children, or cleaning trout and salmon, is a very different kind of activity than going to the supermarket and buying a chicken wrapped in plastic. Making a meal from start to finish—I mean the *real* start—gives a whole new meaning to this activity. A pheasant or duck I have shot has had a very different life than a chicken raised on an intensive farm and killed in a slaughterhouse. And game is far healthier and more nutritious than domestic meat.

Reflection 8 Showing off

Reluctant as I am to admit it (and I don't think I am alone in this), there is a certain amount of showing off associated with hunting. At times it brings out a competitive spirit. We should never forget that in the Darwinian wilderness only the strong survive. It is always attractive to succeed where others have failed, as I have witnessed when climbing mountains, trekking in the rain forest, or tracking buffalo.

I like to collect feathers, hides, teeth, skulls, and horns to demonstrate how successful I am at hunting. Although I have said repeatedly in this book that I don't need to kill anything when I hunt, I don't mind if I'm successful. I may pretend not to care, but do I really like it when everyone else in a hunting camp is successful and I am not? Frankly, no.

Envy is a shameful sin most hunters are well acquainted with but don't like to admit. However, when I am in a hunting camp, there have been times when I was envious seeing a trophy much bigger than mine. And there have also been times when I felt quite self-satisfied when I was the one with the biggest trophy. At the same time, I know that there is a huge element of luck attached to hunting—some people just happen to be at the right place at the right time—but still, why not me? Perhaps, deep in our unconscious, there lingers the feeling that the people who count in your life will admire you more for obtaining an impressive animal.

Reflection 9 Fellowship of the hunt

I enjoy hunting in solitude but there are occasions when I like to hunt with others. I enjoy the common bond, and the companionship. I like being with a few people I really care for—people with whom I can share experiences, discuss strategies and tactics, and exchange advice in an effort to make the hunt more memorable. In an overcrowded world, there is something to be said for sharing experiences with like-minded people. I have learned a lot from listening to the stories in the various hunting camps where I have stayed. I cherish the moments I have spent both with people who are very close to me, and with strangers.

In my father's hunting cabin, where I was the youngest, I used to listen enthralled to the stories of the older hunters, the things they had done, the places they had visited. It was the stuff dreams were made of. I wanted to do the same; I also wanted to visit these wild places. I would have loved to be able to join my father and uncle on their bear-hunting expedition in the old Yugoslavia—even though that trip ended unsuccessfully. These stories had a great bonding effect at the time, although now they give me a great sense of melancholy; most of those people I listened to have gone off to the happy hunting grounds—but they are still very much alive within me.

Sharing hunting stories also has a mellowing effect. It is fun to have stories to tell, and fun to exchange experiences with others. Being with like-minded people makes for easy bonds. I have made many new acquaintances, and created bonds that have lasted for a long time, in several hunting and fishing camps. For some hunters, the camaraderie is a major reason why they hunt. I believe this has been a pattern throughout the ages. Thousands of years ago, a hunter would have recounted his adventures to his clan brothers by the fire—as contemporary traditional hunters still do today. The women and children would listen in awe, while the old men—now beyond hunting—nodded in approval. Much of this behavior is still with us. I will continue telling stories about my exploits by the fire, and so will many other hunters.

⌐╀

Reflection 10 The unbearable lightness of sex

It would be wrong to exclude hunting and sex from this list of reflections. For anyone so inclined, everything is associated with sex. Many anti-hunters seemed to have come to that conclusion; some go so far as to equate hunting with sublimated sexual sadism, another statement to be filed under the category of "wild analysis." However, among most hunting cultures around the world, an abundance of animals has always been associated with sexuality. Indigenous peoples' concerns with fertility were inextricably linked with the fecundity of the earth, plants, and animals. As I emphasized in Chapter 1, although hunting yielded highly valued protein in the form of meat, it also provided males with currency that they could exchange for sexual favors.

A derivative of this "trade" still exists. Hunting can be an excuse for escaping the humdrum concerns of day-to-day life—but it can also be an excuse to get away from one's partner, a search for sexual freedom, engaging in another kind of "hunting." I have heard and read of (but so far never seen) hunting camps in Africa, Europe, and North America where women are part of the package. For example, in Ernest Hemingway's posthumously published *True at First Light*, a fictionalized account of a safari he made with his fourth wife, the splendor of daily life in Kenya is described as well as a fling with a young African girl, who lived in a nearby *shamba* (a small cultivated area, like a farm).[164] The photographer, explorer, and hunter, Peter Beard is famed not only for his photographs of endangered African elephants, crocodiles, and other animals, but also for his adventures with local African women.

An early predecessor of these two adventurers (and no stranger to the interface of sex and hunting) was Richard Burton (1821–90), the English explorer and polymath. Burton was famed for his travels and exploration within Asia and Africa, as well as his extraordinary knowledge of languages and cultures. But in a society where sexual repression was the norm, Burton's writing was unusually open and frank about his interest in sex and sexuality. His travel writings described in great detail the sexual techniques common in the regions he visited, and hinted at his own participation. Burton's sexual frankness probably explains why his widow, in an effort to "preserve his reputation," burned his memoirs after his death.[165]

Another signifier connecting the hunt and sexual imagery is weaponry.

The gun is an obvious phallic symbol, conferring on its owner a feeling of potency and masculinity. Gun barrels and penises stick out; vaginas don't. From a symbolic point of view, hunters (the male) enter nature or Gaia, the earth mother (the female) in a continuous play between masculine and feminine.

Then there is the language of hunting. We talk about "buck fever," the anxiety about shooting an animal, which evokes associations with male potency. The death of an animal is sometimes called the "climax." While hunting, we have "hot and heavy action." In the Southeast Asia many animal products (tiger bones, rhinoceros horn, deer antlers) have sexual associations, their use supposed to increase male potency.

Some people against hunting argue that hunting attracts people who suffer from a sense of sexual inadequacy or an inferiority complex. The gun becomes a compensatory accessory, like a big car in another context. Hunters are perceived to have a desperate need to demonstrate their masculinity. Hunting becomes a way of dealing with a crisis in masculinity, an anxiety over the loss of virility. Ritualistic, coming-of-age activities, such as smearing blood on a person's face, drinking blood, or eating the testicles of the animal killed are not very subtle indications of concerns about potency.

Personally, I have not consciously experienced this kind of urge to prove my masculinity, but the macho behavior of some hunters I have met at conventions, or hunting camps, at times does puzzle me. No question about it, the language of hunting contains a lot of sexual imagery (as does the language of organizations). It can also be a language of domination, which denigrates women. What is the purpose of some of the "jokes" told? Can't these hunters resort to another kind of language? Why do they have this desperate need to show off?

Reflection 11 Exploration

Exploration is an essential part of *Homo sapiens'* psychology, starting with the curiosity of children to explore new things. This pattern is more developed in some people than others, depending on the encouragement they receive from their parents.[166] I certainly have a strong dose of it. I am always looking for adventure; I seek excitement; I like discovering new ideas, meeting new people, and putting strange theories into practice. I don't like routine and don't tolerate boredom very well. I like taking risks. My curiosity draws me to different situations where I can play with new ideas, test them out, and generate new thoughts. Hunting facilitates my life-long pursuit of new things, a search that is never complete. Hunting leads me to travel, to meet new people, to visit new places, to penetrate new cultures. It is a good excuse to step off the trodden path and not be subjected to anyone else's rules.

Hunting can be compared to fly fishing in a river. There is always another bend in the river, just a little bit further on, where a pool with monster trout or salmon is waiting for me. It has never been easy for me to turn back when exploring a river. I always want to see what is waiting around the next bend—rock ledges, rapids, cliffs, and waterfalls. There might be a hidden lake in the hills where they have ouananiche, landlocked salmon that grow to monster sizes. Although I have tried, I have rarely found this kind of Shangri-la, but I still hope that there will be such finds. In hunting, just by travelling a little bit further, we may to our delight come across a saltlick where bongo, forest buffalo, giant forest hogs, and forest sitatunga roam.

Reflection 12 Collecting memories

As I mentioned earlier, I collect trophies to collect memories. Every trophy I have reminds me of the time I shared the terrain with the animal now in my possession. When I look at the tahr, I think once again of the ridge on which I found the animal, high in the mountains of New Zealand's South Island. When I see my big savanna buffalo, I remember the hot, seemingly endless stalk through the bamboo forest of Central Africa—and running away from killer bees, roused through the stupidity of one of the trackers who had started a fire. When I see capercaillie, I think of my early morning hunt in Siberia and the capercaillie singing their mating songs. I could go on...

Collecting has been described as a human superstructure raised upon the foundation of an instinct. This indicates that the desire to collect has archaic origins. As a species, we have a deeply ingrained need to hoard—to survive the next winter, or the next siege; in one way or another to safeguard the future. Having "collected" gives a feeling of security. Some of us may have a packrat mentality that drives us to accumulate anything that looks useful. The processes of collecting and acquisition are rife with psychological, cultural, and political meaning.

Generally, however, in collecting, we find elements of compulsion and competition. The motivation that determines the mindset of the collector may run the gamut from a quest for scientific knowledge or class status, to obsession, compulsion, or greed. Collecting can be viewed as a blend of acquisitiveness, intellectual curiosity, the desire to possess and organize tangible objects, and a certain amount of showing off. Showing the collection to others is a subtle means of self-expression, self-emphasis, and self-extension. Collecting reflects an urge to preserve and memorialize. Collections may be seen as a means to immortality or fame, inevitably tinged with mortality and decay. Collecting can also be motivated by psychological security, with possession used as a way to fill a void in a sense of self. In this way, showing a collection is an implicit demonstration of what the collector stands for.

Collecting can also become obsessive. For example, the Safari Club International (SCI), the largest hunting organization in the world, has dozens of award categories, including "Slams" and "Inner Circles", for collecting a prescribed list of animals. This quite literally buys into members' competitiveness and obsession for record-keeping, as it is a highly pragmatic moneymaking activity for the club. The flip side to an award program like this is that it also feeds self-destructive, anal-compulsive, escapist obsessions. People obsessed by numbers may lose the essence of what hunting is all about. For them, collecting, taping, and measuring trophies is all that counts.

A small walk in Afghanistan

The trip had started ominously. Not far from the Afghanistan border, our four-wheeled, sub-Volkswagen bus gave up on life. It was many hours before Yuri and his team were able to lay their hands on the parts and get the car moving again. I was dressed in the uniform of a Russian soldier. Private hunting excursions were regarded as frivolous, and rightly so, because there was a war going on—the last phase of the Russian invasion of Afghanistan, as the coming and going of planes at Dushanbe airport testified. Before we reached the border we could see the shells of heavy Russian artillery blasting the mountains not far from us. It was quite dark by the time our little group of hunters crossed the border. Along the dirt road were villages, primitive constructions of mud and clay. The road turned, and turned, and turned some more. At one point a wolf ran in front of the bus. Just past a darkened village, more mujahedeen types joined us in the car, all armed with the usual Kalashnikovs. We were following a meandering river—and finally stopped to make a camp for the night. The weather was relatively mild, in sharp contrast to the cold in the Pamir Mountains where I had just been hunting ibex. I could even wash in the river. And, mercifully, the mountains were not as high. My lungs didn't have to work overtime. They were, however, extremely steep in comparison to the mountains in Tajikistan; they went up almost vertically. I picked some pistachios from a wild pistachio tree.

Climbing these mountains—according to Yuri, my long-term friend and outfitter—was *"сумасшедший"* (crazy). And he was right. Our local mujahedeen guide, despite his pitiable footwear, seemed to have glue on his soles, and had no trouble clinging to the mountains. I had a sudden insight into how the various would-be invaders of Afghanistan must have felt over the centuries. I was also reminded of Eric Newby's *A Small Walk in the Hindu Kush*, which describes the hazards and foibles of Newby and companions who managed to do everything wrong in order to climb a remote mountain in Afghanistan. It is one of the greatest travel books I have ever read and a good example of Newby's habitual self-effacement, since his journey (which included a near-ascent of the 19,800-foot Mir Samir) not only turned out to be extremely dangerous, but was also anything but short.[167]

I was hunting for Bukharan markhor (*Capra falconeri*), the unusual goat antelope found in the Western Himalayas. Its name is derived from the Persian word *mar*, meaning snake, and *khor*, meaning eater, which is said to signify either the species' ability to kill snakes or its corkscrewing horns, which are somewhat suggestive of coiling snakes. We had arrived in a terrain made up of an arid cliff-side habitat with sparsely wooded covering. The climbing was exceptionally dangerous, following the direction of the markhor's call (it was the rutting season), at times holding on with my nails to keep from falling. The shot, when I made it, was almost vertical, Yuri holding on to my feet. When I see this trophy hanging in my study, it brings back memories of hunting in that miraculous country—the smell of the pistachio trees, the call of the markhor, the sight of soaring eagles. I felt alive.

147 — Fromm, Erich. *The Anatomy of Human Destructiveness*. New York: Holt, Rinehart and Winston, 1973.

148 — Wilson, Edward O. *Biophilia*. Cambridge: Harvard University Press, 1984.

149 — Wilson, Edward O. *The Diversity of Life*. Cambridge: Harvard University Press, 1992, p. 350.

150 — Kellert, Stepher R. and Wilson, Edward O. (eds.), *The Biophilia Hypothesis*. Washington, D.C.: Island Press, 1993.

151 — Raverat, G. *Period Piece: A Cambridge Childhood*. London: Faber & Faber, 1952.

152 — Barrett, H. Clark. "Cognitive Development and the Understanding of Animal Behavior," In *Origins of the Social Mind*, B. Ellis and D. Bjorklund (eds.). New York: Guilford Press, 2004, p. 239.

153 — Barrett, Clark. op. cit., p. 450.

154 — Barrett, Clark. op. cit., p. 451.

155 — Zeigarnik, Bluma V. "On finished and unfinished tasks," in W. D. Ellis (Ed.), *A Sourcebook of Gestalt Psychology*, New York: Humanities Press, 1967.

156 — Russell, Bertrand. *Nobel Lectures—Literature 1901–1967*, in Horst Frenz, (ed.), Amsterdam, Elsevier, 1969.

157 — Ortega y Gasset, José. *Meditations on Hunting*. H. B. Wescott (transl.).Belgrade, MT: Wilderness Adventures Press, 1995, pp. 39-42.

158 — Dubos, René. *So Human an Animal: How we are Shaped by Surroundings and Events*. New York: Scribners & Sons, 1968, p. 209.

159 — Jung, C. G. "Archetypes and the Collective Unconscious," *The Collected Works*. Translated by R. C. F. Hull. Bollingen Series XX, vol. 9. Princeton: Princeton University Press, 1959.

160 — Freud, Sigmund. "Beyond the Pleasure Principle," in J. Strachey, (ed.), 1953, *The Standard Edition of the Complete Psychological Works of Sigmund Freud*, Volume 18. London: Hogarth Press, 1920.

161 — Winnicott, D. W. *Playing and Reality*. New York: Basic Books, 1982.

162 — Csíkszentmihályi, Mihály. *Flow: The Psychology of Optimal Experience*. New York: Harper and Row, 1990.

163 — *Ibid*.

164 — Hemingway, Ernest. *True at First Light: A Fictional Memoir*. New York: Scribner, 1999.

165 — Brody, Fawn M. *The Devil Drives: A Life of Sir Richard Burton*. New York: Norton, 1984.

166 — Lichtenberg, Joseph D., Lachmann, Frank and Fosshage, James L. *A Spirit of Inquiry: Communications in Psychoanalysis*. Hillsdale, NJ: Analytic Press, 2003.

167 — Newby, Eric. *A Short Walk in the Hindu Kush*. New York: Lonely Planet, 1998.

When elephants fight it is
the grass that suffers.
    —African saying

However much you knock at
nature's door, she will never answer
you in comprehensible words.
    —Ivan Turgenev

The conservation of natural resources
is the fundamental problem. Unless
we solve that problem it will avail
us little to solve all others.
    —Theodore Roosevelt

Voluntary adherence to an ethical
code elevates the self-respect of the
sportsman, but it should not be forgotten
that voluntary disregard of the code
degenerates and depraves them.
    —Aldo Leopold,
      A Sand County Almanac

There is a patience of the wild—dogged,
tireless, persistent as life itself—that
holds motionless for endless hours
the spider in its web, the snake in its
coils, the panther in its ambuscade;
this patience belongs particularly to
life when it hunts its living food.
    —Jack London,
      The Call of the Wild and
      other Stories, p. 69

What is religious about hunting is that
it leads us to remember and accept the
violent nature of our condition, that
every animal that eats will in turn one
day be eaten. The hunt keeps us honest.
    —Dudley Young,
      Origins of the Sacred: the Ecstasies
      of Love and War, p. 129.

FINAL REFLECTIONS

While driving in Germany, I saw a bumper sticker that read *"Ohne Jäger, keines Wild"* (without hunters, there will be no game). Although hunting is no longer a survival issue for *Homo sapiens*, it remains a survival issue for wildlife. While humankind is multiplying at an accelerated pace, in many areas of the world, wildlife is dwindling. This state of affairs is unacceptable. As I have said repeatedly, although it may seem paradoxical to many people, hunters' emotional attachment to nature means that they are these wild creatures' closest allies. They are familiar with the symbiotic relationship between humans and animals. Unfortunately, with the ever-increasing urbanization of our society, the people most concerned about wildlife—the hunters—are becoming the next endangered species.

In this book, I have discussed the symbolic role of hunting, and the important role hunters play in wildlife conservation. I have argued that hunting should not be viewed as a simplistic retro activity; it is not just an outdated relic from our prehistoric past. It should be seen as the oldest expression of our biogenetic and socio-cultural history. And as hunting goes to the heart of our existence as human beings (the activity being *the* signifier of the natural dance of life and death), it has very much colored humankind's economic and socio-cultural history. Most hunters hunt to search for meaning, create connectivity, and to find ways to discover their innermost self. These are significant statements, but my concern is that they will not have the slightest effect on most anti-hunting groups, which argue that all hunting is wrong. Many of them believe that taking hunting out of the human equation will be a significant marker of societal progress.

As I have said repeatedly, whatever arguments I bring to the table, I wonder whether they will change the minds of those vehemently opposed to hunting. The anti-hunter's position remains at the easily understood "thou shall not kill" level. Many fail to see hunting as an effective wildlife management tool, and a signifier for so many other things.

I am not saying that some of the antis' arguments are invalid—my comments about fair chase, slob hunters, and poaching speak for themselves. From my perspective, the behavior of these people poses one of the greatest threats to hunting. But at the same time, I question the easy righteousness and naivety of people who have little first hand experience of the interconnectedness of our bio-systems and are themselves not very knowledgeable about nature and the role of wildlife.

⌐

Rara avis: Paying the bill for wildlife

Contrary to the negative propaganda distributed by many anti-hunting groups (and as I have said throughout this book), hunters have always been at the forefront of the conservation movement. Throughout history, true hunters have been the catalysts to ensure the long-term sustainability of natural resources and wildlife habitats. And as I have repeatedly argued, hunters are often at the forefront of efforts to set aside land for wildlife conservation, and are passionate spokesmen for conservation in the media and in government. They have also been among the most vocal advocates of legislation to prevent climate change. They are among the most passionate supporters of a plethora of game management programs. Significantly, they are *the* critical element of the economic equation, in that they pay a large proportion of the costs of supporting wildlife. The hunting community has made and continues to make an enormous contribution toward ensuring the future of many species and habitats.

But notwithstanding the evidence of these efforts, much of the media seem to ignore the connection between hunting and conservation. Negativity prevails; news reports generalize from the behavior of a few slob hunters or poachers; hunters are blamed for the loss of biodiversity; the simplistic theme that hunting endangers wildlife is reiterated; all the things hunters do for the good are ignored. In the words of the well-known outdoors writer, Gene Hill (1928–97):

356

"It seems that more and more people today find it hard to be for the environment and all that it stands for without being against those of us who like to hunt and fish. I don't really know why it has to be that way, and I'm hurt that these well-meaning people won't take the time to think the problem out; won't see or understand my side of it.

We sportsmen have done a magnificent job of educating each other. We work together and talk our problems out. We write articles about the fine job we've done in bringing back the wild turkey. We show films about the reclamation of wetlands. We count ducks and regulate ourselves on seasons and bag limits. Our good works are legion—but in a way we've kept them all to ourselves. I think we should do something a little different; we're not asking for love necessarily, but for understanding."[168]

As Gene Hill emphasizes, whatever hunters do, their activities (at least to an increasingly urban population) will always be controversial. Dealing with questions of life and death is never value- or emotion-free. Hunting is a polarizing issue; there seems to be no middle ground where opposing viewpoints can meet, or even have room to agree to disagree.

But if some effort were made to work out the differences, the bickering parties might very well find out that they may have more in common than they expect. Arriving at such a stage of mutual understanding, however, will require more education about the role of hunters, nature, and wildlife, starting with our children. New generations should be sensitized to the intricate connectedness of all human life on our planet, and the role that *Homo sapiens* plays in the food chain. This means less Disney.

The real challenge for hunters is to make an increasingly urban population aware that there is another reality beyond slick TV documentaries and fantastical cartoon views of nature, and that parents have the responsibility of developing their children's "nature" intelligence. Children (and adults) have to realize that death and killing will always be part of our daily life; that humans cannot exist without hurting animals in one way or another.

Our challenge is to have non-hunters (especially those who oppose hunting) acquire a less sentimental, more realistic view of nature. If all of us could realize that the biology of our biosphere demands that all forms of life feed on others, hunting would have a place in the general scheme of things. The only way to save hunting is to bridge the gap between naturalists and hunters. It is critical for both parties to work together.

The hunting naturalist

Given the state of most ecosystems, hunting remains an essential tool for controlling the populations of species that might otherwise exceed the carrying capacity of their habitat and threaten the well-being of other wildlife species, occasionally even human health and safety. Hunting reduces the annual crop of new animals and birds to allow the remaining animals sufficient feed and shelter to survive. Hunting can take out sick wildlife to sustain the survival of the healthy.

Some of these arguments about "controlling the herd," "maintaining the balance," or the need for "harvesting" to keep the animal population under control, may sound hollow to an increasingly urbanized population. It is a sad fact that a lot of eco-hunting talk is unconvincing and has the same sound bite quality as the anti-hunting propaganda. Frankly, the real reason for being a hunter is to become an active participant, not a distant observer, in nature's play of life and death. The question is whether taking on such an active role is still viable in the kind of society in which we live. Will hunting survive in the future?

For the vast majority of people, hunting is no longer a necessity. Although it has its usefulness as a wildlife management tool, it arouses controversy among an increasingly urbanized population, and politicians who take their cue from the polls go with the flow. Hunting no longer serves its original purpose of taking care of our basic food needs. Furthermore, guns are dangerous if placed in the wrong hands. From a political point of view, it is much easier to ban hunting altogether, as a number of countries have done. But frankly, if we follow these ideas to their ultimate conclusion, and stop hunting altogether, the result would be a catastrophe for many species, including humankind. Taking one very specific example, the number of fatal incidents involving moose in the Scandinavian countries is already alarming. If the moose population of Northern Europe were no longer controlled by hunting, many more people would be killed in road accidents. There would be outbreaks of disease in many species (geese, ducks, rabbits, deer, foxes, and others) due to overcrowding, and starvation due to lack of available food. Farmers, whose crops would be devastated by wildlife and livestock threatened, would not be very happy either.

A recent example of the disconnect between theory and reality is the wolf issue in the Alpes Maritimes in France, close to where I have a house. For wolves, it is much less effort to kill sheep than roebuck or mouflon. Following highly vocal protests from the farming community, shepherds in that area are now allowed to defend their flocks and kill the predators, which had previously been protected under the Bern Convention of 1979. This doesn't mean that I am not pleased to see that wolves have returned to France, half a century after their extermination. I like to be in wolf country; to me, wolves, like bears, are a great symbol of the wilderness. Hearing them howl hits me in the pit of my stomach. But I am also aware of the complex interrelationship between wolves and man, of the need to find a middle ground.

Some countries (like the Scandinavian countries, France, Austria, and many East European countries) are realistic about the people-environment interface. Other, more urbanized societies, or societies with a political elite that may have a totally different agenda, are not. They do not know how to take care of the land. But as Aldo Leopold (1887–1948) pointed out, we need to assume this responsibility, if only for selfish reasons. In his words, "a land ethic changes the role of *Homo sapiens* from conqueror of the land-community to plain member and citizen of it. It implies respect for his fellow-members, and also respect for the community as such."[169]

If hunting were outlawed, and condemned as morally repugnant, generations of people who actually live on the land would be deprived of a vital means of knowing themselves, their immediate world, and the lives and habits of their fellow creatures. They would be removed from their basic connections to nature, with all the psychological and sociological ramifications that implies.

How not to do it

Let's take a closer look at the dangers of banning hunting by examining the position of the African elephant. One logical fallacy is to assume that if no one is allowed to kill an animal, its population will grow. If only it were that simple. Unfortunately, this is not the case. In spite of a hunting bans, some species are still endangered. In fact, some have become even more so since prohibitions were put in place. *Homo sapiens* expansion can be costly on the environment. In Chapter 9, I have explained how the number of elephants killed by poachers in Kenya soared as a result of legal hunting bans. Unfortunately, in far too many societies, if animals have no economic value, they are likely to be killed and replaced by cattle or crops.

People living in developed countries who have gathered what they know about elephants through striking photographs or television documentaries are unlikely to be aware of the general unpopularity of these animals with the local population. Elephants damage crops and threaten people's lives. It is easy to be high-minded about elephants, crocodiles, hippos, leopards, and lions while sitting in a café in Paris. It is another matter altogether if a member of your family is trampled to death or eaten by one of these animals.

The only viable philosophy as far as wildlife management is concerned is sustainable use. And although the slogan "follow the money" may seem inappropriate, it's a very simple formula for facilitating a high degree of sustainability. Like it or not, hunting brings in substantial money through hunting fees, safari costs, and the sale of legal ivory that can be reinvested in conservation programs. Ironically, legal hunting can be the elephant's salvation, instead of its death warrant, if the profits from the *strictly controlled* legal sale of licenses go to local governments, and to people prepared to manage the herds for sustainability.

Paradoxically, the current ban on the trade in ivory (or the prohibition of the collection of license fees for elephants at the end of their breeding cycle) means that African countries with elephant populations have little incentive to maintain them. It's a desperate measure given the present slaughter by poaching rings. But what need to be kept in mind is the equation, no value, no elephants.

No local community involvement, no game. Giving the decision power of managing wildlife to a centralized authority in places far removed from the action (usually urban centers) is utter lunacy. So it makes good sense to give the resource a value and give local communities a financial incentive to ensure that one of their major sources of income does not disappear. Selective harvesting of animals that are beyond the breeding cycle, or whose survival is not viable in the ecosphere in which they live, is the way to go. (Of course, the best way to save the elephant—and the rhinoceros--is to create greater ecological awareness among people in China, Vietnam, the Philippines, and Yemen to stop buying trinkets made of ivory and rhinoceros horn.)

Saving the elephant (and for that matter the rhinoceros) through community involvement is well worth the effort. Operation Campfire, Zimbabwe's Communal Areas Management Program For Indigenous Resources, is probably the best-known African example of co-management of wildlife resources; under the scheme, wildlife management and the profits from it are shared with local people. Operation Campfire allows villages to cull a percentage of certain animals for meat. As the scheme developed, it became clear that game licenses could be sold to hunters, increasing profitability. The money was then re-invested into local projects selected by the villagers.

Selling hunting licenses reduced illegal hunting and helped local villagers who had to live with the wildlife in their area. It didn't take long for the villages participating in Operation Campfire to realize the benefits of such management programs. The income from regulated hunting on their territory was used to improve schools and health facilities. When everyone has an economic stake in the matter, wildlife becomes valuable, and is more likely to be preserved—as opposed to what has happened in Kenya.

Reflecting on the transience of things

People are complex beings; they can make deserts bloom and rivers die. As the saying goes, "It takes one tree to make 10,000 matches, but one match to burn 10,000 trees." With this in mind, I sometimes wonder whether my children and grandchildren will ever have the hunting opportunities that I have had. I have done what I can, in a small way, to enrich their experiences. I have taken my children along on some of my hunting expeditions. For example, after perestroika came to the Soviet Union, I was one of the first hunters who went hunting in Russia and its satellite states. In hindsight, some of these hunts had surrealistic qualities. I went to the Kamchatka peninsula for the first time with my teenage daughter Oriane, who still talks about this specific "bonding" experience. We were together twenty-four hours a day, sleeping in leaky tents, riding badly behaved horses, dealing with drunken guides, and getting stuck on cliffs.

Most non-hunters who hear the story of this "exploratory" hunt assume that it was quite a miserable experience. When we arrived at the airport of Ust Kamchat nobody showed up to welcome us; a drunken cook made everyone sick by serving geriatric salmon roe; the tent leaked; the guides couldn't climb, thanks to their heavy smoking habit; we got stuck on icy ridges with no idea how to get down. I could go on. But then there were humorous memories, like our rides on horseback, using streams as trails, while the horses did their utmost to get rid of us. Once the helicopter that had taken us to our hunting camp stopped without warning and dumped us in the middle of nowhere in the tundra, as we couldn't go with the crew to pick up gasoline at a high security military camp. Then there was the communal swimming in steaming hot geyser water in the snow at a Russian military R&R camp. Many of these people meant well, but obviously had a very different idea of what "fair chase" was all about. I still remember the climbing to reach the heights where the Kamchatka snow sheep were hanging out. It was a real challenge to both of us.

Once, my father gave me a book about fishing in Outer Mongolia for hucho taimen, a species of fish in the salmon family, which inspired another kind of pioneering expedition. The mighty taimen or Mongolian "terror trout" is the largest salmonid on earth. They are capable of reaching lengths of over two meters and a weight of 100 kilograms. They are as powerful as large salt-water fish. Their large mouths, two rows of sharp teeth, lightning-fast speed, acute senses and enormous size make them one of the world's greatest river assassins. Not only are they cannibalistic, eating other fish like the abundant grayling, but they also have been accused of killing birds, squirrels, lemmings, and even rabbits.

I wrote to the tourist office in Ulan Bator to find out how I could attempt to organize a fishing trip and received a telegram telling me to contact "the embassy in Europe." "Europe" turned out to be Boulogne, just outside Paris, where I studied various Mongolian maps with a number of apparatchiks (this was still the communist period) to find out where the fishing might be good. The embassy staff didn't know much about fishing, as the Outer Mongolians are primarily hunters, but we decided on a few hot spots. With my wife and two of our children we flew to Outer Mongolia's capital, where we admired the statue of Josef Stalin (then still standing). Going to Outer Mongolia, at that time at least, was like going back in time. Going to the "Land of the Eternal Blue Sky," the homeland of Genghis Khan, makes you realize its spectacular natural beauty. The emptiness of a land with no fences and no privately owned land is awe-inspiring. First, we travelled to the Gobi desert region to admire Gobi argali and ibex, then carried on to the region where we hoped to find the fish. We ended up in a number of tents at the edge of a river, including one tent for a dead sheep that became riper and riper. In the morning my waders would be frozen, but by the afternoon it would be about 30° Celsius. But I did finally catch the infamous hutcho taimen, as well as grayling. The others also fished, at times, but mainly visited the locals and rode, especially after our Communist Party "minder" began to relax.

Thinking about flow, I remember one instance of seeing a hucho taimen jump, roll, and take my lure, only to disappear into the sunset, lure and all. I can still see my broken line... But was it exciting. I vividly remember fishing that river another time in the evening and catching a 20-pounder. I brought the fish to the shore, and admired it. Suddenly, I heard a noise behind me and saw two Mongolians on horseback descending the steep river slope and approaching me. They looked at the fish and admired the flies I was using to catch them. Unfortunately, we had a hard time communicating with each other, and it was getting dark. To help me up the slope, they tied the fish to a horse, and we made the climb. When we reached the top, I heard the sound of the jeep that was coming to pick me up. I tried to use sign language to tell the two horsemen that they could keep the fish, if they wanted it. But they left it, jumped on their horses, and rode into the sunset.

One morning, fishing in the same river, I had positioned myself at an attractive looking pool. I threw a mouse fly in the water, as the fish seemed to like them—I had learned that the Mongolians use live lemmings to catch big fish. As the fly hit the water, I saw a "monster of the deep" rising slowly. I tried to control my nerves while I prayed that the fish would take my fly—and it did. I ended up in a shallow pool almost sitting on that fish, to keep it from disappearing. It made me the world champion (temporarily) for catching the mighty hutcho on the fly. The children also became "champions" in different line categories. They still talk about this adventure.

I sometimes wonder how long I will have the physical strength to do these things. Will I still be able to hunt for Marco Polo sheep? Will I be able to handle the strange things that the height, the cold, and the snow do to my body in the Pamir Mountains or the High Altai? The conditions in the latter are the toughest I have ever encountered. It is not a terrain for the weak in heart or spirit. I still remember leaving my tent to pee and getting back just in time to prevent the tent being blown down the mountain. Many hours later, while hunting for ibex in a snowstorm, I saw something colorful sticking out of the snow, way down the mountain. I discovered it was my tent.

There was also the experience when the whole family went to hunt in British Columbia. The Steffey family was our guides. The circumstances were very primitive, and as we expected, it rained a lot, but we had fantastic time together. I climbed the mountains close to the camp looking for wild goats with my children. It was there that I learned that in goat country everything rolls— and I almost rolled with it, after shooting one of these animals. But being on top of the mountain with Eva, Fredrik, and Oriane, looking at the Rocky Mountain goats, was a great experience of togetherness.

On that trip, I decided to stay an extra ten days to try to get a grizzly, and I remember how lonely I felt when I saw the family leave in the small bush plane. The next ten days were very wet and cold, or it may be more accurate to say, even wetter and colder. One day, after a seven-hour stalk, I harvested a mountain grizzly that I had spotted several mountains away while we were looking for mountain caribou. When I remember these experiences, an observation made by José Ortega y Gasset resonates:

> "Man is a fugitive from Nature. He escapes from it and began to make history, which is trying to realize the imaginary, the improbable, perhaps the impossible. History is always made against the grain of Nature. The human being tries to rest from the enormous discomfort and the all-embracing disquiet of history by 'returning' transitorily, artificially, to Nature in the sport of hunting. We are such paradoxical creatures that each day will require greater artifice to give us the pleasure of sometimes being 'natural beings'."[170]

In this book I have tried to explain why I need to hunt but beyond the reasons I have given, it has to be accepted that like so many things in life, the need to hunt cannot be explained on purely rational grounds. Sometimes we need to go beyond rationality to live life to the fullest. It will be a sad world if all our strange, eccentric passions are forbidden; it will be a sad day if we can no longer be "natural beings"—if the chance to hunt is taken away from us and we become strangers in the wilderness. Teddy Roosevelt once noted, "To protest against all hunting of game is a sign of softness of head, not of soundness of heart."[171]

But perhaps such a response is too simple. As I have tried to show, the desire to hunt is a very complex phenomenon that touches the core of *Homo sapiens*. The hunt can be a source of happiness, energy, and spiritual elevation, and contribute to self-awareness. As Russian novelist and playwright Ivan Turgenev (1818–1883) said, "Nature cares nothing for logic, our human logic: she has her own, which we do not recognize and do not acknowledge until we are crushed under its wheel."[172] He dramatizes these inner contradictions in his poem "Nature":

> "I dreamed I had come into an immense underground temple with lofty arched roof. It was filled with a sort of underground uniform light.
> In the very middle of the temple sat a majestic woman in a flowing robe of green color. Her head propped on her hand, she seemed buried in deep thought.

At once I was aware that this woman was Nature herself; and a thrill of reverent awe sent an instantaneous shiver through my inmost soul.

I approached the sitting figure, and making a respectful bow, 'O common Mother of us all!' I cried, 'Of what is thy meditation? Is it of the future destinies of man thou ponderest? Or how he may attain the highest possible perfection and happiness?'

The woman slowly turned upon me her dark menacing eyes. Her lips moved, and I heard a ringing voice like the clang of iron.

'I am thinking how to give greater power to the leg-muscles of the flea, that he may more easily escape from his enemies. The balance of attack and defense is broken.... It must be restored.'

'What,' I faltered in reply, 'What is it thou art thinking upon? But are not we, men, thy favorite children?'

The woman frowned slightly. 'All creatures are my children,' she pronounced, 'and I care for them alike, and all alike I destroy.'

'But right ... reason ... justice ...' I faltered again.

'Those are men's words,' I heard the iron voice saying. 'I know not right nor wrong.... Reason is no law for me—and what is justice?—I have given thee life, I shall take it away and give to others, worms or men ... I care not.... Do thou meanwhile look out for thyself, and hinder me not!'

I would have retorted ... but the earth uttered a hollow groan and shuddered, and I awoke."[173]

Turgenev's descriptions of nature bring back to me the innocence of my boyhood, clothed in the magic of recollection. These memories include picking berries with my grandmother, climbing (and falling out of) trees under the anxious eyes of my grandfather, finding mushrooms with my mother, or playing in a fast-moving little stream while instructed by my father. And always doing these things together with my brother, Florian.

As I grow older, I realize that my sense of tragic pensiveness is increasing. Death is no longer a mere abstraction. The shadow of death is coming nearer. It is sobering to look down the road and sense that it has to end; death has become a growing presence. When loved ones die, the fragility of life becomes more real. It makes the "kill" fraught with deepened ambivalence. Although life is possible only because of the death of others, elation at having successfully killed the prey is increasingly mixed with a sense of bittersweet remorse. It makes me more aware of life's finality.

Finding the happy hunting grounds

Thinking about the end of things brings me to the journey to the happy hunting grounds, a name given to the concept of the afterlife by many Native American people. According to their belief system, the souls of warriors and hunters go to the happy hunting grounds after death, to hunt and feast. The happy hunting grounds are portrayed as a place where every need is fulfilled, and where every activity can be pursued without restrictions. It is an afterlife conceived of as a paradise in which hunting is plentiful and game unlimited.

The Algonquin Indians had a story about the Mischief Maker, a person similar to Till Eulenspiegel (the German peasant trickster whose pranks feature in numerous folk and literary tales). The Mischief Maker played so many tricks, that the tribes sent out runners to catch him and punish him for his mischief. Although they looked for him everywhere, the Mischief Maker was an expert at hiding. According to one of the stories, to escape from his pursuers, he hid in a tree. The people searching for him camped and built a fire under the tree.

As the smoke drifted up among the branches, it rose in a straight column to the sky and took the Mischief Maker with it. He rose higher and higher with the smoke, past beautiful lakes stocked with fish, and valleys and mountains full of game. He floated by great gatherings of Indians, whose wigwams were hung with dried venison, bear's meat, and salmon. He floated on and up to the wigwam of the Great Chief.

The Great Chief told him that he had to return to his own people. But the Mischief Maker was very happy where he was and didn't want to leave. The Great Chief said, "You are at the happy hunting grounds. We let you in so that you could go back and tell your people about this place and teach them what they have to do to get here. If you do as I ask, you may live here forever. You shall hunt and fish with us, and have whatever you want."

A cloud of smoke appeared and promptly changed into the form of an eagle. The Mischief Maker sat on its back and was flown down to the top of the tree where his adventure had started. His pursuers were long gone. Awed by what he had seen, the Mischief Maker decided that he would stop playing tricks on people and tell them about his experience at the happy hunting grounds.

He went straight to the nearest village, where he told the villagers that he had changed his name—he was no longer the Mischief Maker, he was to be called the Peace Maker. He told them what had happened to him, and everything he had seen and heard. He described how the Great Spirit had taken him to the happy hunting grounds to show him what the place was like, so that he could tell others how to get there and the rules they needed to obey to be able to do so. He explained how the Great Spirit controlled the changes in the seasons and sent the sun, clouds, and rain. The Great Spirit made sure game and fish were plentiful, and that the crops grew in the fields. The Peace Maker said nature had to be thanked for its bounty. If humankind obeyed these rules, the Great Spirit would protect and take care of them.

When he finished speaking, the villagers threw tobacco on the fire, as he had instructed, and the Peace Maker was carried away once more to the happy hunting grounds on the column of smoke, while the people danced and sang around the dying embers of the fire.

I hope that all of us, not only in death—a journey we know very little about—but also in life, will be able to make these happy hunting grounds part of our inner journey. The imagery of nature and the self has sustained me during difficult times, and I wish the same to others. Our memories of encounters in nature can guide and protect us as we navigate the depths of our unconscious minds, helping us to transform consciousness, and enable our own personal journey toward insight and renewal. Most importantly, nature will remind us of our "oneness" with all that was, is and will be.

168 — Hill, Gene. *A Listening Walk and Other Stories.*
Clinton, NJ: New Winchester Publishing, 1985, p. 7.

169 — Ibid.

170 — Ortega y Gasset, José. *Meditations on Hunting.*
H. B. Wescott (transl.). Belgrade, MT: Wilderness
Adventures Press, 1995, p. 129.

171 — Roosevelt, Theodore. *On Hunting.* Guilford,
CT.: Lyons Press, 2003, p. 275.

172 — Turgenev, Ivan. *Smoke.* New York: Turtle Point
Press, 1995, p. 41.

173 — Turgenev, Ivan. "Nature," In *Dream Tales and
Prose Poems,* Trans. Constance Garnett, New York:
The Macmillan Company, 1920.

ACKNOWLEDGEMENTS

We are grateful to the following for permission to reproduce copyright material:

Illustrations
Design and Artists Copyright Society (DACS) for an illustration of 'The Scream' by Edvard Munch, © The Munch Museum/The Munch – Ellingsen Group, BONO, Oslo/DACS, London 2013; Mosfilm Cinema Concern for an illustration of a scene from the feature film 'Dersu Uzala', director Akira Kurosawa © Mosfilm Cinema Concern, 1975 year; Natraj Publishers for an illustration of the cover of *The Man-Eaters of Tsavo* by Colonel J. H. Patterson (1999), pub. Natraj Publishers, India; Oliver B. Bumble cartoon © Stichting het Toonder Auteursrecht.

Text
The Aldo Leopold Foundation and Oxford University Press for an extract from *Round River* by Leopold, edited by Leopold (1993) 20 words from pp.145-46 for use as an epigraph © 1972 by Oxford University Press, Inc. By permission of Oxford University Press, USA; Dover Publications, Inc. for an extract from *Self-Reliance and other Essays* by Ralph Waldo Emerson (1993); The Hebrew University of Jerusalem for two quotations, Albert Einstein to Margot Einstein and Albert Einstein to Norman Salit, © The Hebrew University of Jerusalem; Houghton Mifflin Harcourt and Scovil Galen Ghosh Literary Agency, Inc. for an excerpt from *Merle's Door* by Ted Kerasote. Copyright © 2007 by Ted Kerasote. Reprinted by permission of

BIBLIOGRAPHY

1. Lévi-Strauss, Claude. *Structural Anthropology*. New York: Basic Books, 1962, p. 199.
2. Fromm, Erich.*The Anatomy of Human Destructiveness*. New York: Holt, Rinehart and Winston,1973, p. 132.
3. Fromm, Erich. "Man would as soon Flee as Fight." *Psychology Today*, August, 1973, p. 42.,
4. Kerasote, Ted. *Bloodties: Nature, Culture, and the Hunt*. New York: Kodanska International, 1993, p. xvii.
5. Ortega y Gasset, José. *Meditations on Hunting*, H. B. Wescott (trans.). Belgrade, MT: Wilderness Adventures Press, 1995, p. 42.
6. *Ibid*, p. 105.
7. Kerasote, Ted. *Bloodties: Nature, Culture, and the Hunt*. New York: Kodansha International, 1993, pp. 245-246.
8. Mathiessen, Peter. *The Tree where Man was Born*. London: Harville Press, 1998, pp. 79-80.
9. McPhee, John. *Coming into the Country*. New York: Bantam Books, 1977, p. 397.
10. Arseniev, Vladimir Klavdiyevich. *Dersu the Trapper*. (transl. Malcolm Burr). Kingston, NY: McPherson & Co., 1996.
11. Armory, Cleveland. *U.S. News & World Report*, February 5, 1990.

12. Roosevelt, Theodore. *The Wilderness Hunter.* New York: Elibron Classics, 2004, p. xiv.

13. Ardrey, Robert. *African Genesis.* London: Collins, 1961, p. 9.

14. Atkinson, Quentin D. "Origin of language," *Science,* Vol. 332 (6027), 2011,, pp. 281–28.

15. Johanson, Donald C. and Wong, Kate. *Lucy's Legacy.* New York: Crown Publishing, 2009.

16. Dart, R. "Australopithecus africanus. The man-ape of South Africa," *Nature,* Vol. 115, 1925, pp. 195–199; Dart, R. *Adventures with the Missing Link.* Philadelphia: The Institutes Press, 1967.

17. Wilford, John Nobel. "A New Ancestor Redraws the Human Family Tree," *International Herald Tribune,* Friday, October 2, 2009, pp.1, 4; Jamie Shreeve, Jamie. "The Evolutionary Road," *National Geographic,* 218 (1), 2010, pp. 34–67.

18. Tirrell, M. "Wandering 9-Year-Old Stumbles Upon Unknown Human Ancestor in South Africa," *Bloomberg,* April 8, 2010.

19. "Butchering dinner 3.4 million years ago," *Nature News,* August 11, 2010.

20. McGrew, W.C., Baldwin, P.J., Marchant, L.F., Pruetz, J.D., Scott, S.E. and Tutin, C.E.G. "Ethoarchaeology and elementary technology of unhabituated wild chimpanzees at Assirik, Senegal," *Paleoanthropology* 1, 2003, 1–20.

21. Baumeister, Roy F. and Vohs, Kathleen D. "Sexual Economics: Sex as Female Resource for Social Exchange in Heterosexual Interactions," *Personality and Social Psychology Review,* Vol. 8, (4), 2004, 339–363; Hawkes, Kristen, O'Connell, J.F. and Coxworth, J.E. "Family Provisioning is not the only Reason Men Hunt," *Current Anthropology,* 51 (2), 2010, 259–264.

22. Vaillant, John. *The Tiger: A True Story of Vengeance and Survival.* London: Sceptre, 2010, p. 114.

23. Pfeiffer, John E. *The Emergence of Man.* New York: Harper & Row, 1978.

24. Goodall, Jane. *The Chimpanzees of Gombe: Patterns of Behavior.* Cambridge, Massachusetts: Harvard University Press, 1986.

25. Goodall, Jane. *The Chimpanzees of Gombe: Patterns of Behavior.* Cambridge, Massachusetts: Harvard University Press, 1986; Pruetz, Jill D. and Bertolani, Paco. "Savannah Chimpanzees, Pan troglodytes verus, Hunt with Tools," *Current Biology,* Vol. 17, 2007, 412–417.

26. Smith, David Livingston. *The Most Dangerous Animal: Human Nature and the Origins of War.* New York: St Martin's Griffin, 2007, p. 24.

27. Bednarik, Robert G. "The First Stirrings of Creation," *UNESCO Courier,* April, 51(4), 1998, p. 4; Bower, B. "French Cave yields Stone Age Art Gallery," *Science News,* 147(4), 1995, p. 52.

28. Brise, Gabriel. "Medieval hunting scenes: Illuminated manuscripts," in *The Hunting Book* by Gaston Phoebus, Paris: Miller Graphics, 1978.

29. Kellert, Stephen. "Attitudes and Characteristics of Hunters and Antihunters," *Transactions of the Forty-third North American Wildlife and Natural Resources Conference*, 1978, pp. 412–423.

30. Emerson, Ralph Waldo. *Nature and Selected Essays*. New York: Penguin Classics, 1982, pp. 38–39.

31. Ruark, Robert. *Use Enough Gun*. London: Gorki Books, 1972, p. 41.

32. Winnicott, Donald. "Transitional Objects and Transitional Phenomena," *International Journal of Psychoanalysis*, 34, 1952, pp. 89-97.

33. Turgenev, Ivan. *Sketches from a Hunter's Album*. London: Penguin Books, 1990, p. 385.

34. Roosevelt, Theodore (1893). *The Wilderness Hunter*. New York: Irvington Publishers, 1993 ed.

35. Arseniev, Valdimir K. *Dersu the Trapper*, (Trans. Malcolm Burr). Kingston, NY: McPherson & Company, 1996, p. 213.

36. Krakauer, Jon. *Into the Wild*. London: Pan Books, 2007.

37. Leopold, Aldo. *A Sand Country Almanac*. New York: Oxford University Press, 1949, pp. 63-64.

38. Martin, Glen. *Game Changer: Animal Rights and the Fate of Africa's Wildlife*. Berkeley: University of California Press, 2012, p. 89.

39. Ortega y Gasset, José. *Meditations on Hunting*. H. B. Wescott (transl.).Belgrade, MT: Wilderness Adventures Press, 1995, pp. 96-97.

40. Thoreau, Henry David. "Walden," 1854, in *The Writings of Henry David Thoreau*, Vol. 2. Boston: Houghton Mifflin, 1906.

41. Leopold, Aldo. *A Sand Country Almanac*. New York: Oxford University Press, 1949, p. 121.

42. Ruark, Robert. C. *Horn of the Hunter*. Huntington Beach, Cal: Safari Press, 1999, p. 285.

43. de Waal, Frans. *Our Inner Ape*. New York: Riverhead, 2005.

44. Ardrey, Robert. *African Genesis: A Personal Investigation into the Animal Origins and Nature of Man*. London: Collins, 1961, pp. 18-19.

45. *Ibid*, p. 6.

46. *Ibid*, p. 81.

47. Sigmund, Freud. *Civilization and Its Discontents*. New York: W. W. Norton & Company, 1989, p. 58.

48. Lorenz, Konrad. *On Aggression*. New York: Harcourt, Brace & World, Inc., 1966, p. ix.

49. Fromm, Eric. *The Anatomy of Human Destructiveness*. Greenwich, CT: Fawcett Crest, 1973, p.17.

50. Bandura, Albert. "The Social Learning Theory of Aggression." In R. A. Falk

and S. S. Kim (Eds.), *The War System: An Interdisciplinary Approach*. Boulder, CO: Westview Press, 1980.

51. Kets de Vries, Manfred F.R. *Lessons on Leadership by Terror: Finding Shaka Zulu in the Attic*. Chelteham: Edward Elgar, 2004.

52. *Ibid*, p. 348.

53. Lichtenberg, Joseph. *Psychoanalysis and Motivation*. Hillsdale, NJ: Analytic Press, 1989.

54. Hayes, Nicky. *Foundations of Psychology*. 3rd ed., Andover, Hampshire: Cengage Learning Business Press, 2000.

55. Milgram, Stanley. *Obedience to Authority: An Experimental View*. New York: Harper and Row, 1974.

56. Ancient Warfare Fighting for the Greater Good http://www.newscientist.com/article/dn17255-ancient-warfare-fighting-for-the-greater-good.html

57. Dickey, James. *Deliverance*, New York: Dell Publishing, 1970.

58. Kets de Vries, Manfred F.R. *Lessons on Leadership by Terror: Finding Shaka Zulu in the Attic*. Cheltenham: Edward Edgar, 2004.

59. Jung, Carl G. "Psychology and Religion". In *Psychology and Religion: West and East. Collected Works* (Vol. 11). Princeton: Princeton University Press, Bollinger series, 1938, p.131.

60. Pfeiffer, John E. *The Emergence of Man*. New York: Harper & Row, 1978.

61. Swan, James A. "Hunting and Mental Health," *IWMC World Conservation Trust*, 2005 http://www.iwmc.org/IWMC-Forum/JamesSwan/041024-01.htm

62. Fromm, Eric. *The Anatomy of Human Destructiveness*. New York: Fawcett Crest, 1975, p. 160.

63. Turnbull, Colin. M. *Wayward Servants, or the Two World of the African Pygmies*. London: Eyre & Spottiswood, 1965, p. 72.

64. Konner, Melvin. *The Tangled Wing: Biological Constraints on the Human Spirit*, 2nd ed. (original 1982). New York: Times Books, 2002.

65. Flynn, Clifton P. "Hunting and Illegal Violence Against Humans and Other Animals: Exploring the Relationship," *Society and Animals*, 10, (2), 2002, pp. 137-

66. Shelley, Percy Bysshe. "Vindication of a Natural Diet," 1813. http://www.animal-rights-library.com/texts-c/shelley01.htm

67. Ardrey, Robert. *The Hunting Hypothesis: A Personal Conclusion Concerning the Evolutionary Nature of Man*. New York: Antheum, 1976, p. 187.

68. Laughlin, William S. "Hunting: An Integrated Biobehavior System and its Evolutionary Importance," In *Man the Hunter*, Irvin DeVore and Richard Lee (eds). Illinois: Aldine, 1968, p. 304.

69. Ricciuti, Edward R. *Killer Animals: The Menace of Animals in the World of Man.* Guilford, Delaware: The Lyons Press, 2003.
70. Hemingway, Ernest. *Green Hills of Africa.* New York: Scribner, 1996.
71. Lopez, Barry. *Arctic Dreams: Imagination and Desire in a Northern Landscape.* New York: Bantam Books, 1989, pp. 199-200.
72. Swan, James A. *In Defense of Hunting.* San Francisco: Harper Collins, 1994, p. 42.
73. Leopold, Aldo. "A Plea for Wilderness Hunting Grounds," *Outdoor Life,* November, 1925. Reproduced in David E. Brown & Neil B. Carmony, (eds), *Aldo Leopold's Southwest.* Albuquerque: University of New Mexico Press, 1990, pp. 160-161.
74. Leopold, Aldo. *A Sand County Almanac, and Sketches Here and There (1948).* New York: Oxford University Press (1987).
75. *Ibid,* p. 145.
76. *Ibid,* p. 140.
77. Darwin, Charles. *The Origin of the Species.* Philadelphia: University of Pennsylvania Press, pp.120-121, 2006.
78. Huxley, Thomas Henry. *Conditions of Existence as Affecting the Perpetuation of Living Beings.* Project Gutenberg, 2001.
79. Corbett, Jim. *Man-Eaters of Kumaon.* Long Beach: Safari Press, 1991, p. 54.
80. *Ibid.*
81. Annabell, Robert. "Now you Take a Bear," *Field & Stream,* 1943.
82. Neihardt, John. *Black Elk Speaks. The Life Story of a Holy Man of the Oglala Sioux as Told to John G. Neihardt,* http://www.lesekost.de/biograf/hhlb13.htm
83. Patterson, J. H. *The Man Eaters Of Tsavo And Other East African Adventures.* London: Kessinger Publishing, 2004.
84. Corbett, Jim. *Man-Eaters of Kumaon.* Long Beach: Safari Press, 1991.
85. *Ibid.*
86. Vaillant, John. *The Tiger: A True Story of Vengeance and Survival.* London: Sceptre, 2010, p. 191.
87. Golding, William. *Lord of the Flies.* New York: Penguin, 1999.
88. Freud, Sigmund "Totem and Taboo," *The Standard Edition of the Complete Psychological Works of Sigmund Freud,* Vol. XIII, Transl. James Strachey, London: Hogarth Press and Institute for Psychoanalysis, 1913.
89. Ruark, Robert. *Use Enough Gun: On Hunting Big Game.* London: Corgi Books, 1972.
90. Tylor, Edward B. *Primitive Culture.* 2 vols., 7th ed. New York: Brentano's [orig. 1871], 1924.

91. Willerslev, Rane. *Soul Hunters: Hunting, Animism, and Personhood among the Siberian Yukaghirs*. Los Angeles: University of California Press, 2007, p. 1.

92. Lévy-Bruhl, L. *How Natives Think*, Translated by Lilian A. Clare, London, 1926.

93. Ogden, Thomas H. *Projective Identification and Psychotherapeutic Technique*. London: Karnac, 1992.

94. Douglas, Claire. *Visions: Notes of the Seminar given in 1930-1934 by C.G. Jung*, Volume 1. Princeton: Princeton University Press, 1997, p. 988.

95. James, William. *The Varieties of Religious Experience* (1902). New York: Touchstone, 1997.

96. Anonymous. "The White Monkey," In *Dragon King's Daughter: Ten Tang Dynasty Stories*, Honolulu: University Press of the Pacific, 2001.

97. Ch'eng-en, Wu. *Monkey: Folk Novel of China*. New York: Grove Press, 1994.

98. Kets de Vries, Manfred F.R. "Abominable Snowman or Bigfoot: A Psychoanalytic Search for the Origin of Yeti and Sasquatch Tales, *Fabula: Journal of Folktale Studies*, 23 (3/4), 1982, pp. 246-261.

99. Houston, Pam. *Women on Hunting*. New York: Norton & Co, 1996.

100. *Ibid*, p. x.

101. G. Jung, Carl G. *The Archetypes and the Collective Unconscious*. London: Routledge, 1996.

102. Yolen, Jane. *The Wild Hunt*. New York: Harcourt Brace, 1995.

103. Bieder, Robert E. *Bear*. London: Reaction Books, 2005.

104. Brunner, Bernd. *Bears: A Brief History*. New Haven: Yale University Press, 2007.

105. Faulkner, William. *Three Famous Short Novels, Spotted Horses, Old Man, The Bear*. New York: Vintage, 1963, p. 245.

106. Campbell, Joseph. *Historical Atlas of World Mythology Volume 1: The Way of the Animal Powers, Part 1: Primitive Hunters and Gatherers*. New York: Alfred van der Marck Editions, 1983, p. 147.

107. Shepard, Paul and Sanders, Barry. *The Sacred Paw: The Bear in Nature, Myth, and Literature*. New York: Viking, 1985.

108. Campbell, Joseph. "The Master Bear," In *The Masks of God, Volume 1, The Way of the Animal Powers*. New York: Viking, 1959.

109. Crawford, John Martin. *The Kalevala: The Epic Poem of Finland*, Rune XLVI, "Otso the Honey-Eater," Whitefish, Montana: Kessinger Publishing, 2004.

110. Csikszentmihalyi, Mihali. *Flow: The Psychology of Optimal Experience*. New York: Harper & Row, 1990.

111. Leopold, Aldo. *A Sand Country Almanac*. New York: Oxford University Press, 1999, p. 169.

112. Ruark, Robert C. *Horn of the Hunter.* Huntington Beach, Cal: Safari Press, 1999, p. 81.

113. Seton, Ernest Thompson. *Lives of the Hunted.* New York: Charles Scribner's Sons, 1901.

114. Lopez, Barry. *Arctic Dreams: Imagination and Desire in a Northern Landscape.* New York: Bantam Books, 1989, p. 413.

115. Turgenev, Ivan. *A Sportsman Notebook.* New York: Random House, 1992.

116. Kets de Vries, Manfred F. R. *Sex, Money, Happiness, and Death: The Quest for Authenticity.* New York: Palgrave MacMillan, 2009.

117. Dairy Farmers of Britain Survey, 2007.

118. Foer, Jonathan Saffran. *Eating Animals.* New York: Penguin, 2009, p. 32.

119. *Ibid*, p. 34.

120. *Ibid*, p. 59.

121. Prince Philip and Fisher, James. *Wildlife Crisis,* New York: Cowles Book, 1970.

122. Price, Weston Andrew. *Nutrition and Physical Degeneration.* Chicago: Keats Publishing, 2003.

123. Ovid, *Metamorphoses*, Book 15, 60-142, http://etext.virginia.edu/latin/ovid/trans/Ovhome.htm

124. Arrian. *Arrian on Coursing: The Cynegeticus of the Younger Xenophon.* New York: Bastian Books, 2008.

125. Phillips, A. A. and Willcock, M. M. *Xenophon & Arrian On Hunting With Hounds*, contains Cynegeticus original texts, translations & commentary. Warminster: Aris & Phillips Ltd., p. 18., 1999.

126. Aristotle. (Trans. Benjamin Jowett) *Politics,* Book 1, Chapter 8, http://jim.com/arispol.htm

127. Jolma, Dena Jones. *Hunting Quotations: Two Hundred Years of Writings on the Philosophy, Culture and Experience.* New York, Mcfarland & Co, 1992.

128. Saint Augustine, *The City of God,* I.20.

129. Desiderius Erasmus, *In Praise of Folly,* chapter 38.

130. Jolma, Dena Jones. *Hunting Quotations: Two Hundred Years of Writings on the Philosophy, Culture and Experience.* New York, Mcfarland & Co, 1992.

131. *Ibid.*

132. 140 Kant, Immanuel. "Groundwork of the Metaphysic of Morals," part II (*The Metaphysical Principles of the Doctrine of Virtue*), paras 16 and 17, 1785.

133. Bentham, Jeremy. "An Introduction to the Principles of Morals and Legislation," inWilfred Harrison (Ed.), *A Fragment on Government and An Introduction to the Principles of Morals and Legislation,* 1823 edn. Oxford: Blackwell, 1823/1948, pp. 411-41.

134. Thoreau, Henry David. "A Week on the Concord and Merrimack Rivers,"

, 1849, in *The Writings of Henry David Thoreau*, Vol. 1. Boston, Houghton Mifflin, 1906, p. 57.

135. Thoreau, Henry David. "Walden," 1854, in *The Writings of Henry David Thoreau*, Vol. 2. Boston, Houghton Mifflin, 1906, p. 232.

136. Tolstoy, Leo. *The Bear-Hunt, and Other Stories*. New York: Little Leather Library Corporation, 1918.

137. Tolstoy, Leo. *Writings on Civil Disobedience and Nonviolence*. 1886. London: Peter Owen Ltd, 1968.

138. Ortega y Gasset, José. *Meditations on Hunting*, H. B. Wescott (trans.), Belgrade, MT: Wilderness Adventures Press, 1985, p. 57.

139. *Ibid*, p. 112.

140. *Ibid*, p. 106.

141. Russell, Bertrand. *Nobel Lectures—Literature 1901–1967*, in Horst Frenz, (ed.), Amsterdam, Elsevier, 1969.

142. Ruark, Robert. *The Old Man and the Boy*. New York, Henry Holt and Co, 1953, p. 56.

143. Rokeach, Milton. *The Open and Closed Mind*. New York: Basic Books, 1960.

144. *Ibid*.

145. *Daily Mail*, October 25, 2010.

146. Gates, Elgin. *Trophy Hunter in Asia*. Winchester, Ontario: Winchester Press, 1971.

147. Fromm, Erich. *The Anatomy of Human Destructiveness*. New York: Holt, Rinehart and Winston, 1973.

148. Wilson, Edward O. *Biophilia*. Cambridge: Harvard University Press, 1984.

149. Wilson, Edward O. *The Diversity of Life*. Cambridge: Harvard University Press, p. 350, 1992.

150. Kellert, Stepher R. and Wilson, Edward O. (eds.), *The Biophilia Hypothesis*. Washington, D.C.: Island Press, 1993.

151. Raverat, G. *Period Piece: A Cambridge Childhood*. London: Faber & Faber, 1952.

152. Barrett, H. Clark. "Cognitive Development and the Understanding of Animal Behavior," In *Origins of the Social Mind*, B. Ellis and D. Bjorklund (eds.). New York: Guilford Press, 2004, p. 239.

153. Barrett, Clark. op. cit., p. 450.

154. Barrett, Clark. op. cit., p. 451.

155. Zeigarnik, Bluma V. "On finished and unfinished tasks," in W. D. Ellis (Ed.), *A Sourcebook of Gestalt Psychology*, New York: Humanities Press, 1967.

156. Russell, Bertrand. *Nobel Lectures—Literature 1901–1967*, in Horst Frenz, (ed.), Amsterdam, Elsevier, 1969.

157. Ortega y Gasset, José. *Meditations on Hunting*. H. B. Wescott (transl.).Belgrade, MT: Wilderness Adventures Press, 1995, pp. 39-42.

158. Dubos, René. *So Human an Animal: How we are Shaped by Surroundings and Events*. New York: Scribners & Sons, 1968, p. 209.

159. Jung, C. G. "Archetypes and the Collective Unconscious," *The Collected Works*. Translated by R. C. F. Hull. Bollingen Series XX, vol. 9. Princeton: Princeton University Press, 1959.

160. Freud, Sigmund. "Beyond the Pleasure Principle," in J. Strachey, (ed.), 1953, *The Standard Edition of the Complete Psychological Works of Sigmund Freud*, Volume 18. London: Hogarth Press, 1920.

161. Winnicott, D. W. *Playing and Reality*. New York: Basic Books, 1982.

162. Csíkszentmihályi, Mihály. *Flow: The Psychology of Optimal Experience*. New York: Harper and Row, 1990.

163. *Ibid*.

164. Hemingway, Ernest. *True at First Light: A Fictional Memoir*. New York: Scribner, 1999.

165. Brody, Fawn M. *The Devil Drives: A Life of Sir Richard Burton*. New York: Norton, 1984.

166. Lichtenberg, Joseph D., Lachmann, Frank and Fosshage, James L. *A Spirit of Inquiry: Communications in Psychoanalysis*. Hillsdale, NJ: Analytic Press, 2003.

167. Newby, Eric. *A Short Walk in the Hindu Kush*. New York: Lonely Planet, 1998.

168. Hill, Gene. *A Listening Walk and Other Stories*. Clinton, NJ: New Winchester Publishing, 1985, p. 7.

169. *Ibid*, p. 204.

170. Ortega y Gasset, José. *Meditations on Hunting*. H. B. Wescott (transl.). Belgrade, MT: Wilderness Adventures Press, 1995, p. 129

171. Roosevelt, Theodore. *On Hunting*. Guilford, CT.: Lyons Press, 2003, p. 275.

172. Turgenev, Ivan. *Smoke*. New York: Turtle Point Press, 1995, p. 41.

173. Turgenev, Ivan. "Nature," In *Dream Tales and Prose Poems*, Trans. Constance Garnett, New York: The Macmillan Company, 1920.

INDEX

ABOUT THE AUTHOR

Manfred F. R. Kets de Vries has been a pioneer at the interface between personality theory, organizational studies, and psychoanalysis. His specific areas of interest are leadership development, career dynamics, stress, leadership coaching, high performance teams, entrepreneurship, family business, cross-cultural management, and the dynamics of corporate transformation and change—this book being an exploration in a very different territory.

Kets de Vries is the Distinguished Clinical Professor of Leadership Development and Organizational Change at INSEAD, France, Singapore & Abu Dhabi. He has been the Founder of INSEAD's Global Leadership Center, one of the foremost leadership development centers in the world. He is a Visiting Distinguished Professor in Leadership Development Research at the European School of Management and Technology in Berlin. He has also held professorships at McGill University, the Ecole des Hautes Etudes Commerciales, Montreal and the Harvard Business School. He is also a trained psychoanalyst, a member of the Canadian Psychoanalytic Society, corresponding member of Paris Psychoanalytic Society, and the International Psychoanalytic Association.

The Financial Times, Le Capital, Wirtschaftswoche, and *The Economist* have rated Kets de Vries one of world's leading leadership thinkers. They have named him among the world's top 50 leading management thinkers and among the most influential contributors to human resource management. To honor his contributions to leadership studies, he has been given the Lifetime Achievement Award by the International Leadership Association, being considered as one of the world's founding professionals in the development of leadership as a field and discipline. He is also a founding member of the International Society for the Psychoanalytic Study of Organizations (ISPSO) of which he became (in 2009) a Lifetime Distinguished Member. He has received the Distinguished Teacher Award at INSEAD five times. The American Psychological Association

(Organizational Consultation Division) has honored him for his contributions to the field of consultation (The Harry and Miriam Levinson Award for Exceptional Contributions to Consulting Organizational Psychology). Furthermore, he has received the Dutch "Freud Award" for his contributions to the interface of psychoanalysis and organizations. He has also received two honorary doctorates. The Dutch government has knighted him and made him an Officer in the Order of Oranje Nassau.

Kets de Vries is the author, co-author, or editor of more than 40 books, and has published over 360 scientific papers as chapters in books and articles. He has also written approximately a hundred case studies, including seven that received the "Best Case of the Year" award. He is a regular writer for a number of magazines. His work has been featured in such publications as *The New York Times*, *The Wall Street Journal*, *The Los Angeles Times*, *Fortune*, *Business Week*, *The Economist*, *The Financial Times*, and *The International Herald Tribune*. His books and articles have been translated into thirty-one languages. He is a member of 17 editorial boards and has been elected a Fellow of the Academy of Management.

Kets de Vries is a consultant on leadership issues, organizational design/ transformation, strategic human resource management, and family business to leading U.S., Canadian, European, African, Australian and Asian companies. He is the chairman of the Kets de Vries Institute (KDVI), a boutique top management consulting firm. As an educator and consultant he has worked in more than forty countries.

Kets de Vries was the first fly fisherman in Outer Mongolia and is a member of New York's Explorers Club. In his spare time he can be found in the rainforests or savannas of Central Africa, the Siberian taiga, the Pamir and Altai Mountains, Arnhemland, or within the Arctic Circle.